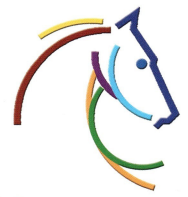

FEI World Equestrian Games
Aachen 2006

Der Aachen-Laurensberger Rennverein
und die Aachener Reitturnier GmbH
danken Ihnen sehr herzlich für Ihre Unterstützung
anlässlich der
Pferdesport-Weltmeisterschaften Aachen 2006.

*The Aachen-Laurensberger Rennverein
and the Aachener Reitturnier GmbH
thank you very much for your support
on the occasion of the
FEI World Equestrian Games Aachen 2006.*

IMPRESSUM | *IMPRINT*

Bibliografische Information der deutschen Bibliothek
Die Deutsche Bibliothek verzeichnet diese Publikation in der Deutschen Nationalbibliografie;
detaillierte bibliografische Daten sind im Internet über http://dnb.ddb.de abrufbar.

© 2006 **FN**verlag der Deutschen Reiterlichen Vereinigung GmbH, Warendorf/ *of the German Equestrian Federation*

Alle Rechte vorbehalten.
Das Werk ist urheberrechtlich geschützt. Die dadurch begründeten Rechte, insbesondere die der Übersetzung, des Nachdrucks, der Entnahme von Abbildungen, der Funksendung, der Wiedergabe auf fotomechanischem oder ähnlichem Wege und der Speicherung in Datenverarbeitungsanlagen bleiben, auch bei nur auszugsweiser Verwertung, vorbehalten. Die Vergütungsansprüche des § 54, Abs. 2, UrhG, werden durch die Verwertungsgesellschaft Wort wahrgenommen.
All rights reserved.
No part of this publicatiobn may be reproduced in whole or in part or stored in a retrieval system, or transmitted in any form or by any means, electronic, mechanical, photocopying, recording, or otherwise, without written permission of the publisher.

HERAUSGEBER/ *PUBLISHER*
Aachen-Laurensberger Rennverein e.V. (ALRV), Aachen
Deutsche Reiterliche Vereinigung e.V. (FN), Warendorf

AUTOREN/ *AUTHORS*
Ramona Billing, Adelheid Borchardt, Dr. Teresa Dohms, Renate Faßbender, Dr. Hanfried Haring, Uta Helkenberg, Niels Knippertz, Kim Kreling, Ralf Mader, Dr. Klaus Miesner, Dennis Peiler, Donata von Preußen, Rudolf Temporini, Patricia Tietje

ÜBERSETZUNG/ *TRANSLATION*
Victoria Schorn, Schleiden-Gemünd

KORREKTORAT/ *CORRECTION*
Dr. Carla Mattis, FNverlag Warendorf

BILDNACHWEIS/ *PICTURE CREDITS*
TITELFOTOS/ *COVER PHOTOS*
www.arnd.nl
Arnd Bronkhorst (6), Frédéric Chéhu (1), Charles Mann (2)
Joachim Kropp, Zweibrücken (1)
Walburga Schmidt, Wolfenbüttel (1)

FOTOS INHALT/ *PICTURES*
www.arnd.nl
Arnd Bronkhorst: Seiten: 8 li., 10 (3), 11 o., 12, 13 o., 15, 16 (2), 18 (2), 19 u., 21 (2), 22 (2), 23 (2), 24 (2), 26 (2), 28. u., 29 (2), 32 (4), 33 o. (2), 34, 35 (2), 36, 37, 39 o., 41 (2), 42 o., 43, 44 (2), 45 o.re., 46 u., 47, 48 (2), 49 u. (2), 50 (2), 51 (2), 52, 53 (2), 58 o., 60 m., 64 u., 65, 66, 68 (5), 69, 70 u., 72, 73 (2), 74 (3), 75 (2), 76, 79, 80 (2), 81 o., 82 o., 84 u. (2), 86, 87 (2), 88 u., 93, 101 o., 105 re., 112 u., 113 o., 117 m., 118 o. (2), 119 (2), 121 o.li., 122 li., 123 o., 128 u. (2), 130/131 (4), 133
Frédéric Chéhu: Seiten 19 o., 24, 25 u., 39 u., 49 o.
Charles Mann: Seiten 25 o., 33 u., 45 o.li., 46 o., 68 o.li., 71 li., 77 u., 90 u., 107 (2), 110, 111, 112 u., 113 o., 115 u. (2)
Jacques Toffi: Seiten 42, 64 m.

Archiv Bundeskanzleramt: Seite 3
Archiv ALRV: Seiten 5, 62/63 (36), 130 m.li.
Archiv FN: Seite 6
Fotostudio Brückner: 108 m.
Werner & Tammo Ernst, Ganderkesee: Seiten 13 u., 17, 20, 27, 28 o., 51 m., 117 li., 118 (3), 119 (6), 120 (3), 121 o.m.
Wolfgang Filser, Arzbach: Seiten 102 u.li.+o.re. (2), 105 li.
K.-H. Frieler, Gelsenkirchen: Seiten 132, 133 (5)
Ronald Hogrebe, Prisdorf: Seiten 55, 56, 57, 58 u., 59, 60 u., 61, 67, 70 o., 71 o.
www.horsEmotion.de: Seiten 108 li., 109, 114, 115 m.
Joachim Kropp, Zweibrücken: Seiten 96, 97 (3), 98 li.+u., 99 (3), 100 (3), 101 u.re., 102 o.li.+ u.re. (3), 103 (3), 122 re.
Andreas Mamerow, Heiligenhaus: 106
Persburo Melissen, NED: Seite 131 m.
Doris Melzer, Lautertal: 31, 88 o., 89 (3), 90 o., 91 (3), 92 m.
Julia Rau, Mainz-Hechtsheim: Seiten 54, 96 o., 104
Walburga Schmidt, Wolfenbüttel: Seite 117 re., 123 u. (2)
Barbara Schnell, Krefeld: Seiten 8 u., 38, 40, 128 u.re., 129 (7), 130, 131, 132 u.m.
Franz Steindl, Aachen: Seiten: 78 o. (2), 81 u., 83, 84 re., 85 u., 121 u. (3), 124 o.
Foto Studio Strauch, Eschweiler: Seiten 9 (2), 11 u. (2), 45 u., 92 o. (2), 124 u. (3), 125 (3), 128 o.li., 129 (3), 130 u. (4), 131 (5), 132 (7), 133 m (2)
Judith Temporini, Lindenfels-Seidenbuch: Seiten 77 li., 78 u., 82 u., 84 o., 85 (2)

HERSTELLUNGSKOORDINATION/ *PRODUCTION COORDINATION*
Siegmund Friedrich, Beate Kreienbaum, **FN**verlag, Warendorf

GESAMTGESTALTUNG/ *CONCEPTION/DESIGN*
mf-graphics, Marianne Fietzeck, Gütersloh

DRUCK UND VERARBEITUNG/ *PRINTED BY*
Media-Print Informationstechnologie, Paderborn

ISBN-10 3-88542-484-3
ISBN-13 978-3-88542-484-0

VORWORT | FOREWORD

Ich freue mich, dass die Weltreiterspiele 2006 in Deutschland stattfinden konnten und ich als Schirmherrin alle Teilnehmerinnen und Teilnehmer sowie die Zuschauerinnen und Zuschauer auf das Herzlichste willkommen heißen durfte.

Die Vergabe der Weltreiterspiele 2006 an Deutschland war ein deutliches Zeichen für das Vertrauen in die Verantwortlichen des Aachen-Laurensberger Rennvereins und der Deutschen Reiterlichen Vereinigung. Aktive und Zuschauer haben optimale Bedingungen vorgefunden, um pferdesportliche Wettbewerbe auf höchstem Niveau zu bestreiten und zu erleben.

Mein Dank geht an die Veranstalter und Sponsoren sowie an die zahlreichen Helferinnen und Helfer. Sie alle sorgten für eine ausgezeichnete Organisation und eine gastfreundliche Atmosphäre.

Ich glaube, dass sich der Wunsch nach einem spannenden und reibungslosen Verlauf der Weltreiterspiele 2006 und einem erfolgreichen und glücklichen Verlauf für die Reiterinnen und Reiter sowie den Mannschaften voll und ganz erfüllt hat.

I am delighted that the FEI World Equestrian Games 2006 were able to be held in Germany and that in my function as patron of the event, I was able to welcome all of the participants and spectators.

The fact that the FEI World Equestrian Games 2006 were awarded to Germany is a clear sign of the trust placed in the Aachen-Laurensberger Rennverein, as the organisers of the event. Both the competitors and the spectators were presented with excellent conditions to contest and experience equestrian competitions at the highest level.

My thanks go to the organisers and sponsors as well as to the many volunteers, who all contributed towards the excellent organisation and an hospitable atmosphere.

I believe, the desire to guarantee the smooth running of the FEI World Equestrian Games 2006 and exciting sport as well as a successful and fortunate course of events for the riders and teams was fully achieved.

Dr. Angela Merkel
KANZLERIN DER BUNDESREPUBLIK DEUTSCHLAND
CHANCLLOR OF THE FEDERAL REPUBLIC OF GERMANY
SCHIRMHERRIN DER/ *PATRONESS OF THE*
FEI WORLD EQUESTRIAN GAMES AACHEN 2006

Vorwort | Foreword

Es war mir eine große Freude, alle Pferdesportlerinnen und Pferdesportler sowie die tausenden enthusiastischen Zuschauer im Namen der Fédération Equestre Internationale (FEI) auf das Herzlichste zu den fünften FEI World Equestrian Games in Aachen begrüßen zu dürfen. Ich selbst war 12 Jahre alt, als ich zum ersten Mal nach Aachen gekommen bin: Seitdem weiß ich, wie viele andere Pferdefreunde auch, dass dies ein ganz besonderer Ort ist, ein Ort, der herzliche Sympathie und Ehrfurcht gleichermaßen weckt.

Für jeden Pferdesportler ist es ein Traum, in der Aachener Soers antreten zu dürfen. Für mehr als 900 Aktive aus mehr als 60 Nationen wurde dieser Traum in den sieben FEI-Disziplinen Springen, Dressur, Vielseitigkeit, Fahren, Distanzreiten, Voltigieren und Reining jetzt Wirklichkeit.

Aus meiner Sicht boten die FEI World Equestrian Games der ganzen Welt des Pferdesports eine hervorragende Möglichkeit der gemeinsamen Begegnung an einem zentralen Ort. Ich hoffe, dass die Sportler, die Offiziellen, die Pferdebesitzer, Medienvertreter und Zuschauer während der zwei Veranstaltungswochen diese strahlende Inszenierung des Pferdesports rundum genießen konnten.

Meine besondere Anerkennung gilt dem Organisationskomitee der FEI World Equestrian Games. Seiner Erfahrung, seiner Professionalität sowie seiner harten und hingebungsvollen Arbeit ist ein Ereignis zu verdanken, das mit Sicherheit in die Geschichte des Pferdesports eingehen wird.

Ein herzliches Dankeschön gilt allen Sponsoren, ohne deren großzügige Unterstützung dieses Projekt ein Traum geblieben wäre. Ebenfalls danken möchte ich allen ehrenamtlichen Helfern, deren Bereitschaft und Enthusiasmus Grundvoraussetzungen für jede erfolgreiche Sportveranstaltung sind.

Die fünften FEI World Equestrian Games waren getragen von einer Atmosphäre gegenseitigen Respekts und aufrichtigen Fair Plays.

It was a great pleasure for me to be able to heartily welcome all of the equestrian sportsmen and women and the enthusiastic spectators in the name of the Fédération Equestre Internationale (FEI) to the fifth FEI World Equestrian Games in Aachen. I was 12 years old the first time I came to Aachen myself: Since then I know, together with many other horse friends, that this is a very special place, a place which arouses heart-felt sympathy and at the same time reverence.

It is the dream of every equestrian athlete to be able to compete at the Soers. This dream came true for more than 900 participants from over 60 nations in the FEI disciplines dressage, driving, endurance, eventing, show-jumping, reining and vaulting.

In my opinion the FEI World Equestrian Games offered the entire world of equestrian sport an excellent opportunity to gather together at one centralised location. I hope that the competitors, officials, horse owners, media representatives and spectators were able to enjoy this wonderful equestrian event during the two weeks of the tournament.

My particular gratitude goes to the Organising Committee of the FEI World Equestrian Games. Thanks to their experience, professionalism and their hard work and dedicated efforts, this event will without doubt go down in the history of equestrian sport.

I address a sincere thank you to all of the sponsors; this project would have remained only a dream without their generous support. I would also like to thank the many volunteers, their readiness and enthusiasm is a prerequisite for every successful sporting event.

The fifth FEI World Equestrian Games were hallmarked by an atmosphere of mutual respect and honest fair play.

HRH Princess Haya Bint al Hussein of Jordan
Präsidentin der/ President of the
Fédération Equestre Internationale (FEI)

VORWORT | FOREWORD

Liebe Freunde des Pferdesports in aller Welt,

was wird von den zwei WM-Wochen in Erinnerung bleiben? Welche Momente haben die Menschen in der Aachener Soers und weltweit an den Bildschirmen bewegt? Die Geschichte mag ihr Urteil in den kommenden Jahren fällen. Wir als Veranstalter aber sind schon heute überzeugt, dass diese WM neue Maßstäbe im Pferdesport gesetzt hat. Mehr noch: Sie hat unserem Sport den Weg in eine glanzvolle Zukunft bereitet. Bei uns in Deutschland und international. Mehr Menschen als je zuvor haben sich von den sieben Disziplinen begeistern lassen. 576.000 Zuschauer aus aller Welt waren in Aachen zu Gast. Nie zuvor haben die Medien für eine solch weltweite Beachtung und Euphorie gesorgt: In 157 Ländern hat es Fernsehübertragungen gegeben. Allein in Deutschland fast 70 Stunden in ARD, ZDF und WDR. Dazu Live-Übertragungen zur Prime Time am Abend. Nie zuvor ist es gelungen, alle sieben Disziplinen zentral durchzuführen. Und nie zuvor sind Weltmeisterschaften mit einer schwarzen Null abgeschlossen worden. Mein aufrichtiger Dank gilt daher allen, die dazu beigetragen haben, diese WM zu einem Erfolg werden zu lassen. Den über 800 Sportlern und ihren Pferden, den Funktionären, den Medien, den Sponsoren, der Stadt und dem Kreis Aachen, den Besuchern aus aller Welt und dem gesamten Team des Aachen-Laurensberger Rennvereins und der Aachener Reitturnier GmbH sowie den vielen, vielen Helfern. Ein besonderer Dank gilt jedoch der FEI, die uns vor vier Jahren ihr Vertrauen geschenkt hat, und der Deutschen Reiterlichen Vereinigung für ihre vielfältige Unterstützung.

Uns als Ausrichter ging es dabei aber nicht in erster Linie um Rekorde, sondern um Spitzensport und Völkerverständigung. Zusammen haben die Menschen ein friedliches und harmonisches Fest gefeiert – woher auch immer sie zu uns in die Soers gereist sind. In Aachen haben wir gezeigt, dass das Pferd – wie Ihre Königliche Hoheit Prinzessin Haya es als Präsidentin der FEI formuliert hat – ein Botschafter des guten Willens ist und die Menschen vereint. In Aachen haben wir Maßstäbe für ein friedliches Miteinander der Nationen gesetzt. Wohl wissend, dass wir Weltpolitik damit wohl kaum beeinflussen können. Aber wir können Orientierung geben und Beispiel sein für gegenseitige Achtung und Toleranz.

Für zwei Wochen schienen die Konflikte dieser Welt vergessen, hat der Sport viele Nationen und Kulturen zusammengeführt. Ein kleiner Beitrag dieser Weltmeisterschaft zur Völkerverständigung auf dem Globus. Möge dies das Vermächtnis für die WM 2010 in Kentucky sein.

Dear equestrian sport friends all over the world,

What memories will remain from the two weeks of the World Championships? Which moments moved the people at the Soers and the TV viewers worldwide? History may make its judgement over the coming years, but we, the organisers, are already convinced that the FEI World Equestrian Games have set new benchmarks in the equestrian sport. What's more they have paved the way into a glamorous future, both here in Germany and internationally. More people than ever before enjoyed the seven equestrian disciplines. 576,000 spectators from all over the world were our guests in Aachen. The media has never assigned as much attention and euphoria to the equestrian sport before: TV broadcasts were transmitted to 157 countries. Almost 70 hours by ARD, ZDR and WDR alone in Germany, including live broadcasts during prime-time viewing hours. No one has managed to execute all seven disciplines at one venue before. And the World Equestrian Games have never broken even before. My sincere gratitude is addressed to all of those people, who have contributed towards making these World Championships such a success. To the 800 sportsmen and women as well as their horses, to the officials, the media, the sponsors, the City and District of Aachen, the visitors from all over the world and the entire team of the Aachen-Laurensberger Rennverein and the Aachener Reitturnier GmbH as well as the many, many volunteers. My particular thanks also go to the FEI, who placed their confidence in us four years ago and to the German Equestrian Federation, the FN, for their manifold support.

However, for us the organisers, the event wasn't about setting records, it was about top sport and uniting the nations. The people celebrated a peaceful and harmonious festival together – wherever they travelled from to be with us here at the Soers. Here in Aachen we have underlined the fact that the horse is – as Her Royal Highness Princess Haya, the President of the FEI, put it – a messenger of good will, which unites people. Here in Aachen we have set benchmarks for the peaceful interchange among the nations. Of course we know that we will hardly be able to influence world politics, but we can provide an orientation and act as an example of mutual respect and tolerance.

The conflicts of the world seemed to have been forgotten in these two weeks, the sport brought together many nations and cultures. A small contribution of these FEI World Equestrian Games towards a better understanding between the nations around the globe. Let this be our legacy for the FEI World Equestrian Games 2010 in Kentucky.

Klaus Pavel
PRÄSIDENT DES AACHEN-LAURENSBERGER RENNVEREINS E.V. (ALRV)
PRESIDENT OF THE AACHEN-LAURENSBERGER RENNVEREIN E.V. (ALRV)

VORWORT | *FOREWORD*

Die positive Resonanz des In- wie Auslandes auf die Weltmeisterschaften in den sieben FEI-Disziplinen hat alle Erwartungen weit übertroffen. 576.000 Menschen erlebten in den Aachener Stadien Sternstunden des Pferdesports, ein Millionenpublikum in 157 Nationen verfolgte die Wettkämpfe vor dem Fernsehschirm. Eine derart überwältigende Präsenz in der Öffentlichkeit war dem Pferdesport niemals zuvor vergönnt.

Dieselbe Euphorie, mit der die Fußballfans wenige Wochen zuvor ihre Weltmeisterschaft gefeiert hatten, prägte auch die Aachener Championatstage. Das ohnehin für seine Begeisterungsfähigkeit und Fairness berühmte Publikum in der Soers wuchs einmal mehr über sich hinaus. Nirgends werden selbst schwächere Leistungen mit so herzlichem Applaus bedacht wie hier. Eine Goldmedaille für dieses Publikum!

Wir haben viel gelernt. Mancher betrachtete im Vorfeld den neuen Austragungsmodus der Dressur, der nunmehr zwei Goldmedaillen in der Einzelwertung vorsieht, mit Skepsis. Jetzt wissen wir, dass der Grand Prix Special mit Medaillenvergabe die Weltmeisterschaft bereichert hat. Diese Prüfung war einer der sportlichen Höhepunkte der Veranstaltung. Wir haben auch gelernt, dass wir uns intensiver mit den noch nicht so populären Disziplinen auseinander setzen müssen. Das Distanzreiten verlief nicht ganz zu unserer Zufriedenheit. Hier gilt es, gemeinsame Anstrengungen zu unternehmen, um auch dieser Sportart den Stellenwert zu geben, den sie verdient.

Mit elf Einzel- und Mannschaftsmedaillen, darunter sechs Goldmedaillen, ist die Pferdesportnation Deutschland ihrer Favoritenrolle gerecht geworden. Mehrfacher Weltmeister ist zugleich die deutsche Pferdezucht. Rund die Hälfte aller Dressur- und Springpferde trug ein deutsches Brandzeichen. Insgesamt errangen deutsche Pferde 40 Medaillen in Dressur, Springen, Vielseitigkeit, Fahren und Voltigieren. Allein in den Disziplinen Reining und Distanzreiten sind deutsche Pferde noch deutlich unterrepräsentiert. Nicht nur die deutsche Kompetenz in der Pferdezucht wurde bei diesen Weltmeisterschaften eindrucksvoll bestätigt. Auch unser Ausbildungssystem gilt als wegweisend. Dies wird durch die Tatsache unterstrichen, dass über 30 deutsche Dressurtrainer ausländische Reiter betreuen. Dies ist einer der Gründe dafür, dass die großen Pferdesportnationen in ihrem Leistungsniveau enger zusammen rücken.

Das vorliegende Werk aus dem FN*verlag* hält mit spektakulären Bildern die „schönsten Weltreiterspiele aller Zeiten" fest. Mit diesen Worten lobte FEI-Präsidentin Prinzessin Haya von Jordanien, die mit ihrem Auftreten die Anerkennung der Sportler und Funktionäre gewonnen und die Herzen des Publikums erobert hat, die Championatstage. Wir stimmen ihr gerne zu, und wir sind sicher, dass diese Weltmeisterschaften den Pferdesport national wie international beflügeln werden.

The positive reaction to the FEI World Equestrian Games in seven disciplines received from home and abroad exceeded all expectations. 570,000 people experienced equestrian highlights in the stadiums in Aachen, millions of viewers followed the competitions on TV in 157 countries. The equestrian sport has never enjoyed such an overwhelming presence in the public eye before.

The Championship days in Aachen were characterised by the same euphoria that the football fans celebrated their World Championships with a few weeks previously. The crowds at the Soers, who are known for their enthusiasm and fairness, surpassed themselves. Nowhere else in the world are weaker performances rewarded with such heart-felt applause as here. The spectators definitely earned a gold medal!

We learnt a great deal. In the run-up to the event many people were sceptic about the new rulings in the dressage, which now foresee the awarding of two individual gold medals. Now, we know that the exciting Grand Prix Spéciale allocated with medals enriched the World Championships. This competition was without doubt one of the sporting highlights of the event.

We also learnt that we must occupy ourselves more intensively with the disciplines that were not so popular in the past. We were not totally satisfied with the organisation of the endurance competition, which was staged right at the opening of the Championships. Joint efforts must be undertaken here to make sure this discipline receives the significance it deserves.

Claiming overall eleven individual and team medals, six of which were gold, the equestrian nation Germany lived up to its role as favourite. The German horse breeders also took several World Championship titles. Around half of all of the dressage and show-jumping horses carry a German brand. In total German horses won 40 medals in the dressage, show-jumping, eventing, driving and vaulting competitions. The German horses are, nevertheless, still clearly underrepresented in the reining and endurance disciplines.

Not only the German competence in the field of horse breeding was impressively confirmed at these World Championships, but our training system is also considered to be pioneering. This was particularly underlined by the fact that over 30 German dressage trainers coach foreign riders and also some individual eventers, and in some cases have been doing so for years. This is one of the perhaps most important reasons why the level of the performances of the important equestrian nations is becoming more uniform, giving the sport a wider foundation on an international basis.

The present publication by the FNverlag has captured the best moments of the World Championships with spectacular photos. The expert coverage by the authors, enhanced by comprehensive background information, is a documentation of the "best World Equestrian Games of all times" that is definitely worth reading. These were the words used by the FEI President, Princess Haya of Jordan, who won the recognition of the equestrian athletes and the officials as well as conquering the hearts of the crowd during her appearances, to describe the Championships in Aachen. We are pleased to agree with her and are convinced that these World Equestrian Games will stimulate the equestrian sport, both nationally and internationally.

Breido Graf zu Rantzau
PRÄSIDENT DER / *PRESIDENT OF THE*
DEUTSCHEN REITERLICHEN VEREINIGUNG E.V. (FN)

Inhalt | Contents

Vorworte/ Forewords
- Dr. Angela Merkel 3
- HRH Princess Haya Bint al Hussein of Jordan 4
- Klaus Pavel 5
- Breido Graf zu Rantzau 6

Phantastische Show zur Eröffnung/ Fantastic Opening Show 8

Springen/ Jumping — 12
- Wenn WM-Würfel fallen ... / When the WEG dice fall 13
- Das Zeitspringen/ The speed competition 14
- Nationenpreis – der 1. Umlauf/ Nations' Cup – the first round 21
- Nationenpreis – der 2. Umlauf/ Nations' Cup – the second round 23
- Runde der 25 Besten/ The 25 best 26
- Das Finale/ The final 32

Dressur/ Dressage — 36
- Dressur Grand Prix/ Grand Prix Dressage 37
- Dressur Grand Prix Special/ Dressage Grand Prix Spéciale 48
- Dressur Grand Prix Kür/ Dressage Grand Prix Freestyle 51

Vielseitigkeit/ Eventing — 54
- Die sportliche Antwort auf Athen / The sporting reply to Athens 55
- Dressur: Gelungener Start auf dem Viereck/
  Dressage: Succesful start in the dressage arena 56
- Die Querfeldeinstrecke/ The Cross-country Course 60
- Springen: Go for Gold/ Show-jumping: Go for gold 69

Fahren/ Driving — 76
- Mannschaftsgold, Einzelbronze und ein wehmütiger Abschied/
  Team gold, individual bronze and a sad farewell 77
- Die Dressurprüfung/ Dressage 77
- Die Marathonfahrt/ The Marathon 78/79
- Hindernisfahren/ Obstacles Driving 82

Distanzreiten/ Endurance — 86
- Gold, Silber, Bronze: Französische Trikolore in neuen Farben/
  Gold, silver, Bronze: French tricolour with new colours 87

Voltigieren/ Vaulting — 96
- Deutsche Voltigierer in Aachen weltmeisterlich/
  Champion performance by German vaulters in Aachen 97

Reining/ Reining — 106
- Reining – zweit höchstdotierte Mannschaftswertung der WM/ Reining –
  Team competition with second highest prize-money at World Championships 107
- Packendes Einzelfinale/ Exciting individual final 111/112

Die Dominanz gezielter Zuchtprogramme 116
The dominance of targeted breeding programms

Modernste Wettkampfstätten – WM der kurzen Wege
Top modern competition sites – WEG with the shortest routes 124

Kultur/ Culture 126

Good Bye – Aachen 2006! 128

Ergebnisse/ Results 134

AUTOR/AUTHOR
RALF MADER

Phantastische zur Eröffnung
Fantastic Opening Show

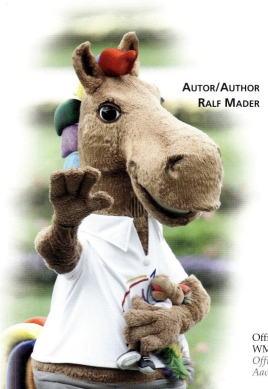

Offizielles Maskottchen der WM Aachen 2006: Karli
Official mascot of the WEG Aachen 2006: Karli

„Große Dinge werden zuerst in der Soers verwirklicht", sagt niemand anderes als Hans Günter Winkler, der erfolgreichste deutsche Springreiter aller Zeiten. „Es war immer klar: Wenn es die Pferdesport-Weltmeisterschaften erstmals in Deutschland geben sollte, dann nur in Aachen." Und mit großen Emotionen wurde die Welt auch bei den fünften Weltreiterspielen, den FEI World Equestrian Games Aachen 2006, bei der offiziellen Eröffnungsfeier im Hauptstadion des Aachen-Laurensberger Rennvereins (ALRV) am Sonntag, 20. August, begrüßt. Mit Olympiasiegern, Welt- und Europameistern, hunderten Jugendlichen aus der Region, spektakulären Schaubildern und natürlich vielen Pferden. „Wir wollten mit der rasanten Eröffnungsfeier Begeisterung für die zwei Wochen wecken. Die WM lebt vom Sport, vor allem aber von Emotionen," sagt Frank Kemperman, ALRV-Geschäftsführer und WM-Turnierdirektor.

Und so wird auf den Tribünen harmonisch im Takt der Musik mitgeklatscht – der niederländische Komponist Cees Slings hat eigens eine stimmungsvolle Ouvertüre geschrieben –, es werden eifrig Fahnen geschwenkt und Fotos geschossen. Und es gibt eine echte Weltpremiere zu sehen: Die große Quadrille der deutschen Landgestüte mit 64 Hengsten. Als sie ihre Kreise und Sterne auf dem Rasen formieren, geht so manches Raunen durchs weite Rund. Knapp 38.000 Zuschauer – darunter Prominenz aus Politik, Sport, Wirtschaft und Showbusiness – sitzen gebannt auf den Tribünen, 1,83 Millionen erleben die Übertragung des ZDF in ihren Wohnzimmern. Als zum Start der Zeremonie um 15 Uhr Rauchkometen über dem Stadion emporschießen und 50 Islandpferde auf den Platz galoppieren, als 450 Aachener Schulkinder mit Schirmen hereinströmen, ist auch der Wettergott an diesem Nachmittag gnädig gestimmt. Die Schirme sind auch nicht zum Schutz vor Regen bestimmt, sondern um eines der aufwändigsten Bilder des Tages zu kreieren: Schnell ist jedes Kind an seinem Platz – und zusammen bilden sie alle das WM-Logo in den Farben der sieben Disziplinen nach. Auf den Tribünen klicken die Kameras, die Menschen erheben sich spontan zum Applaus von ihren Sitzen. Vier Jahre hatten sie der WM in Aachen entgegengefiebert, nun wollen sie feiern. Dazu gehört jetzt auch eine vom Stadionmoderator initiierten La-Ola-Welle und lauter Jubel. Menschen aus über 60 Nationen sind in Aachen zu Gast – und so

"Important things are always realised at the Soers first," says none other than Hans Günter Winkler, the most successful German show-jumper of all time. "It was always quite clear: If the World Equestrian Games were ever to be held in Germany, then only in Aachen." And the world was greeted emotionally at the fifth FEI World Equestrian Games Aachen 2006, at the official Opening Ceremony in the main stadium of the Aachen-Laurensberger Rennverein (ALRV) on Sunday, August 20th. By Olympic gold medallists, World and European Champions, hundreds of youths from the region, spectacular show performances and of course by plenty of horses. "The fast-paced Opening Ceremony was intended to increase the enthusiasm for the coming two weeks. The World Championships live from the sport, but also from emotions," explained Frank Kemperman, ALRV General Director and WEG Tournament Director.

So the spectators on the stands clapped harmoniously to the rhythm of the music – the Dutch composer Cees Slings had written an impressive overture especially for the occasion – flags were waved eagerly and photos were

Nadine Capellmann führt die Deutschen WM-Teilnehmer ins Stadion.
Nadine Capellmann leads the German WEG participants into the stadium.

Show

bunt wie das Programm auf dem Rasen sind die mit Flaggen geschminkten Gesichter. „Wir sind dankbar, dass Deutschland uns alle mit offenen Armen empfängt", sagt Prinzessin Haya von Jordanien (Foto rechts), Präsidentin des internationalen Reitsportverbandes FEI, freudestrahlend auf der Ehrentribüne. „Aachen und Deutschland nehmen einen besonderen Platz im Pferdesport ein."
Zahlreiche Welt- und Europameisterschaften in der Dressur und im Springen, dazu das alljährliche Weltfest des Pferdesports, CHIO Aachen, hat das in den Jahren zuvor modernisierte Turniergelände in der Aachener Soers schließlich schon erlebt. Und so wird die 100-minütige Eröffnungsfeier unter der Regie des Hamburger Dramaturgen Jürgen Nees auch zur nostalgischen Rückschau. Die Geschichte des Pferdesports in Aachen – der Legende

taken. And there was even a world premiere display: The big quadrille of the German state-run studs comprising of 64 stallions. There were gasps from the crowd as they formed their circles and stars in the arena. Almost 38,000 spectators – including celebrities from the world of politics, sport, the economy and show-business – sat mesmerised on the stands, the show also broadcast on television by ZDF was also enjoyed by 1.83 million at home in their living-rooms. As smoke rockets shot up into the sky over the stadium when the ceremony began at 3 p.m. and 50 Island horses galloped around the arena, as 450 school children from Aachen poured into the stadium holding umbrellas. But luckily the weather gods were merciful on the opening afternoon. The umbrellas were not to protect the children from the rain, but in fact to create one of the most elaborate images of the day: Each child took up his position quickly and together they formed the WEG logo in the colours of the seven disciplines. The cameras on the stands started clicking wildly, spontaneously everyone on the stands stood up to applaud. Everyone had been waiting impatiently for four years for the World Championships to commence in Aachen, and now they wanted to celebrate. A La-Ola wave was initiated by the stadium commentator and accompanied by loud cheering. People from over 60 nations were guests in Aachen – and they were as colourful as the programme

FEI World Equestrian Games Aachen 2006

64 Hengste der deutschen Landgestüte präsentieren die große Quadrille.
64 stallions from the German state-run studs performing the big quadrille.

on the grass with their faces decorated with flags. "We are grateful that Germany has welcomed us with open arms," said Princess Haya of Jordan, President of the FEI, radiantly from the Honorary Stand. "Aachen and Germany has a significant standing in the equestrian sport."

Numerous World and European Championships in dressage and show-jumping, plus the annual World Equestrian Festival, CHIO Aachen, had already been celebrated in previous years at the extremely modern show grounds of the Soers in Aachen. So, the 100 minute Opening Ceremony directed by the dramatist Jürgen Nees from Hamburg presented a nostalgic review. The history of equestrian sport in Aachen – according to the legend it was Charles the Great's horse that discovered the famous Aachen thermal springs – the history of the World Championships, the history of Aachen: There is plenty to recount and thus plenty of colourful images. Of course Charles the Great was present in

nach war es das Pferd Karls des Großen, das die berühmten Aachener Thermalquellen entdeckte –, die Geschichte der WM, die Geschichte Aachens: Es gibt viel zu erzählen und damit zu sehen.

Deshalb ist Karl der Große auch leibhaftig im Stadion. Majestätisch reitet er mit seinem Gefolge zu folkloristischen Klängen ein. Gefühlvoll hebt er die Lanze (Foto oben), schleudert sie ins Wasserbassin und löst damit eine 15 Meter hohe Fontaine aus. Wieder klicken die Kameras, wieder bricht der Applaus von den Tribünen. Stars wie der Springreiter Christian Ahlmann oder die zweifache Dressur-Weltmeisterin und Lokalmatadorin Nadine Capellmann repräsentieren die sieben Disziplinen, Showacts erinnern an die bisherigen Weltreiterspiele in Stockholm (1990), Den Haag (1994), Rom (1998) und Jerez (2002). Dann wird es beim Einzug der Nationen eng auf dem Rasenplatz. Tosender Applaus empfängt die WM-Teilnehmer – egal, ob sie aus Saudi-Arabien, den USA, Mexiko, Malaysia, der Ukraine oder Namibia angereist sind. „Zusammen werden wir ein sportliches Großereignis erleben, das zur Völkerverständigung beiträgt", sagt ALRV-Präsident Klaus Pavel. Bunte Luftballons steigen in den Aachener Himmel, „Magic in the air", klingt die Musik aus den Lautsprechern. Magisch und unvergesslich – so sind sich alle einig – werden auch diese zwei WM-Wochen.

person. He rode in majestically followed by his entourage accompanied by folklore music. He raised his lance gently, threw it into the water basin and triggered off a 15 metre high fountain. The cameras started clicking again, the crowd applauded from the stands. Stars such as the show-jumper Christian Ahlmann or the double World Dressage Champion and local rider Nadine Capellmann presented the seven disciplines, show acts reminded the spectators of the previously staged World Equestrian Games in Stockholm (1990), The Hague (1994), Rome (1998) and Jerez (2002). Finally, things started getting a little crowded in the arena when the "Parade of the Nations" rode in. The competitors of the World Championships were greeted with deafening applause – whether they came from Saudi Arabia, the USA, Mexico, Malaysia, the Ukraine or Namibia. "Together we will experience a huge sporting event, which will contribute towards a better understanding among the nations," said ALRV President Klaus Pavel. Bright balloons floated up to the sky over Aachen, the song "Magic in the air" sounded from the loudspeakers. Everyone was unanimous – the two coming weeks of the World Championships would also be magical and unforgettable.

Kutschen bringen Luftballons in den Farben der sieben Disziplinen ins Hauptstadion.
Carriages bring in the balloons in the colours of the seven disciplines in the main stadium.

Doppel-Europameister Marco Kutscher saß auf der Ersatzbank.
Double European Champion was sitting on the reserve bench.

AUTORIN/*AUTHOR*
KIM KRELING

Die Disziplin Springen

1953 pilgern 200.000 Menschen zur Premiere der Weltmeisterschaft der Springreiter in das Pariser Prinzenpark-Stadion. Elf Nationen schicken ihre Teams zur ersten WM nach Paris. Viele Springreitnationen wie Großbritannien und Schweden fehlen, weil sie ihre Skepsis gegenüber dem Finale mit Pferdewechsel nicht überwinden können. Dieser Modus wird bei der WM 1953 eingeführt und besteht noch heute. Fast alle Springen werden unter Flutlicht ausgetragen. Fritz Thiedemann erspringt sich mit dem erst siebenjährigen Diamant die Silbermedaille. Der Spanier Francisco Goyoaga wird der erste Weltmeister. Nach damaliger Sitte trifft sich die Weltelite ein Jahr später zur nächsten WM im Land des amtierenden Weltmeisters. Im Madrider Reitstadion Club de Campo springt erstmals Hans Günter Winkler zu Weltruhm und wird mit Halla Weltmeister. 1955 steht Winkler mit Orient in Aachen auf dem Siegerpodest. Die nächsten beiden Titel gewinnt der italienische Ausnahmereiter Raimondo d'Inzeo. Anfangs jährlich und nur als Einzelwettbewerb ausgetragen, findet die Weltmeisterschaft der Springreiter seit 1956 in Vierjahres-Rhythmus statt, zunächst noch nach Reiterinnen und Reitern getrennt. Diese Unterteilung fällt 1978 mit der WM in Aachen weg. Vier Jahre später, 1982 in Dublin, wird die Einzelentscheidung um einen Mannschaftswettbewerb erweitert. Es ist das Jahr von Norbert Koof, der nach Hans Günter Winkler, Hartwig Steenken (1974) und Gerd Wiltfang (1978) als vierter Deutscher Weltmeister der Springreiter wird. Zwölf Jahre später werden die in die Weltreiterspiele von Den Haag integrierten Weltmeisterschaften zu einem deutschen Doppel-Erfolg. Franke Sloothaak siegt nach dem Pferdewechsel mit Weihaiwej in der Einzelwertung, das Team reitet zu Mannschafts-Gold. Den Mannschaftssieg können die Deutschen vier Jahre später bei dem Weltreiterspielen in Rom wiederholen. 2002 im spanischen Jerez werden die deutschen Springreiter vom WM-Pech verfolgt. Knapp schliddern sie mit Platz vier an einer Mannschaftsmedaille vorbei. Zwar qualifizieren sich alle vier Teammitglieder für die Runde der besten 25, aber keiner schafft es bis ins Finale der letzten Vier. Die Weltmeisterschaften der Springreiter werden über drei Prüfungen und ein Finale mit Pferdewechsel entschieden. Die erste Wertungsprüfung ist ein Zeitspringen. Die Ergebnisse (umgerechnet in Strafpunkte) nehmen die Teilnehmer mit in die zweite Prüfung, den Nationenpreis. Er entscheidet sowohl über die Vergabe der Mannschaftsmedaillen als auch über den Einzug der besten Reiter in die dritte Wertungsprüfung. Im Nationenpreis gilt es, zwei Umläufe zu absolvieren. Für das Mannschaftsergebnis werden die drei besten Ritte je Umlauf gewertet. Erstmals erstreckt sich bei den Weltmeisterschaften in Aachen der Nationenpreis über zwei Tage. Dem ersten Umlauf (bei Tageslicht) folgt am nächsten Tag der zweite Umlauf als Flutlichtspringen. Der Wassergraben wird in Aachen bei dem Flutlichtspringen aus dem Parcours gestrichen, damit die Pferde keine Angst vor den Lichtreflektionen im Wasser bekommen. Somit sind zum ersten Mal die beiden Parcours der Nationenpreis-Umläufe nicht 100-prozentig identisch. Über zwei verschiedene Umläufe führt die dritte Wertungsprüfung, zu der die punktbesten 25 Reiter nach erster und zweiter Qualifikation zugelassen sind. Das Ergebnis rangiert alle Teilnehmer von Platz 5 bis 25, die an erster bis vierter Stelle platzierten Reiter ermitteln die Medaillengewinner im Finale mit Pferdewechsel. Dieser Modus gilt lediglich bei Weltmeisterschaften und nicht bei Europameisterschaften bzw. Olympischen Spielen. Jeder Reiter reitet im Finale sein eigenes Pferd und das seiner drei Konkurrenten. Gewertet wird nur die Zahl der Fehler, die benötigte Zeit im Parcours spielt keine Rolle, sofern nicht die erlaubte Zeit überschritten wird. Haben nach vier Runden zwei (oder mehrere) Reiter dieselbe Fehlerzahl, entscheidet ein Stechen, dann wieder mit den eigenen Pferden, über Gold, Silber bzw. Bronze.

The Show-jumping Discipline

200,000 people visited the first World Show-jumping Championships in the Paris Prince Park Stadium in 1953. Eleven nations sent their teams to Paris for the first World Championships. Many show-jumping nations were missing, such as Great Britain and Sweden, because they were not able to overcome their scepticism about the Finals with a rotation of horses. This mode was introduced at the World Championships in1953 and still exists today. Almost all of the show-jumping competitions were carried out under floodlit conditions. Fritz Thiedemann took the silver medal with his seven-year-old horse, Diamant. The Spanish rider Francisco Goyoaga became the first World Champion. In line with the customs of the time, the world elite met again the following year for the next World Championships in the country of the reigning World Champion. In the Club de Campo Equestrian Stadium in Madrid, Hans Günter Winkler jumped to fame after taking the World Championship title with Halla. In 1955 Winkler claimed the title in Aachen with Orient. The next two gold medals went to the outstanding Italian show-jumper, Raimondo d'Inzeo. Originally held as an annual event and only for individuals, the Show-jumping World Championships have been staged in the four-year rhythm since 1956, initially with separate titles for the ladies and the men. At the World Championships in Aachen, the separate titles were done away with. Four years later in Dublin in 1982, the World Championships were expanded with an extra team classification. It was the year that Norbert Koof became the fourth German rider to take the title, after Hans Günter Winkler, Hartwig Steenken (1974) and Gerd Wiltfang (1978). Twelve years later the World Championships were integrated into the World Equestrian Games in The Hague, the Germans experienced a double victory. Franke Sloothaak won the individual classification with Weihaiwej after the rotation of horses and the German squad took team gold. The Germans were able to repeat their team victory four years later at the World Equestrian Games in Rome. In 2002 in Jerez, Spain the German show-jumpers were very unlucky. They just missed out on the bronze medal. Indeed all four team members qualified for the round of the 25 best riders, but none of them managed to make it into the Final among the last four.

The World Show-jumping Championships are determined in three competitions and a Final with rotation of horses. The first rating competition is a speed competition. The results (converted into penalty points) are carried over into the second competition, the Nations' Cup. This competition determines the allocation of the team medals, and is also the qualifier for the next round. In the Nations' Cup two rounds have to be completed. The three best rides per round count towards the team result. In Aachen for the first time ever at the World Championships, the Nations' Cup was staged over two days. The first round (in daylight) was followed by the second round on the following day as a floodlight competition. The water jump was taken out of the course in Aachen for the floodlight competition, so that none of the horses were frightened by the reflection of light in the water. As a result it was the first time that the course was not 100 percent identical in both Nations' Cup rounds. The 25 riders with the best scores after the first two qualifying competitions go into the third rating competition. The result of this third rating competition is the final ranking of all participants in the individual classification from fifth to 25th place and then the top four riders compete for the medals in the Final with rotation of horses. This mode is unique to the World Championships and does not apply for either the European Championships or the Olympic Games. In each Final each competitor rides his own horse and that of his three fellow-competitors. Only the faults count, the time taken for the course doesn't play a role, as long as the allowed time is not exceed. If two (or more) riders have the same number of faults after the four rounds, there is a jump-off for the gold, silver or bronze medal. The show-jumpers rider their own horses in the jump-off.

Die deutsche Mannschaft / *The German Team*

Reiter *Rider*	Alter *Age*	Pferd / *Horse* Pfleger / *Groom*	Alter *Age*	Zuchtgebiet *Breeding Area*	Züchter / *Breeder* Besitzer / *Horse Owner*
Christian Ahlmann (Marl)	32	Cöster Melanie Mayering	13	Holstein	Werner Lattreuter (Hannover) Marion Jauß
Ludger Beerbaum (Riesenbeck)	43	L' Espoir 7 Marie Johnson	10	Zangersheide	Catherine Duez (Belgien) Madeleine Winter-Schulze (Wede)
Marcus Ehning (Borken)	32	Noltes Küchengirl Florian Darcourt	9	Bayern	Eva-Maria Schmid (Utting) Echo Büromöbel Vertriebs GmbH
Meredith Michaels-Beerbaum (Thedinghausen)	36	Shutterfly Anu Harrila	13	Hannover	Uwe Dreesmann (Hesel) Octavia Farms LLC (USA) Meredeth Michaels-Beerbaum
Equipechef / *Chef d'Equipe* Peter Hofmann		Bundestrainer / *National Trainer* Kurt Gravemeier		Tierarzt / *Veterinarian* Dr. Björn Nolting	Hufschmied / *Farrier* Dieter Kröhnert

SPRINGEN | JUMPING

Wenn WM-Würfel fallen ...

„Klasse statt Masse wäre besser, als zu zeigen, wie viele Nationen überhaupt eine Mannschaft haben, von denen viele der Aufgabe nicht gewachsen sind." Mit diesem Appell hatte sich WM-Sportdirektor Frank Kemperman im Vorfeld an die FEI gerichtet. Letztendlich gingen bei der WM 2006 25 Teams und 22 Einzelreiter an den Start, macht insgesamt 116 Teilnehmer. Und alle Befürchtungen zerplatzten wie Seifenblasen: Die Weltmeisterschaft der Springreiter war durchweg ein sportlicher Höchstgenuss.

Springprofis im Gespräch: WM-Sportdirektor Frank Kemperman (Mitte) mit Parcourschef Frank Rothenberger und dem FEI-Manager Springen John P. Roche (links).
Show-jumping officials in discussion: WEG Tournament Director, Frank Kemperman (centre) with course builder, Frank Rothenberger, and the FEI Show-jumping Manager, John P. Roche (left).

Das deutsche Team war früher denn je nominiert worden – schon vor der Deutschen Meisterschaft in Münster. So herausragend waren die Leistungen der fünf Spitzenreiter Meredith Michaels-Beerbaum, Marcus Ehning, Christian Ahlmann, Ludger Beerbaum und Marco Kutscher. Drei Teamplätze standen schnell fest, aber um Platz vier wurde lange diskutiert: Marco Kutscher oder Ludger Beerbaum? Am Ende aller Überlegungen saß Doppel-Europameister Marco Kutscher auf der Ersatzbank.

Die Titelverteidiger, die Franzosen, reisten mit einer komplett ausgetauschten Equipe im Vergleich zu ihrer Siegermannschaft in Jerez an. Der Trainer der schwedischen Silbersieger von 2002, Henk Nooren, gestand: „Ich bin froh, wenn ich vier Paare zusammenkriege." Und bei den Belgiern, die in Spanien Bronze gewonnen hatten, rutschte in letzter Sekunde die jüngste Reiterin des Springfeldes ins Team, die 19-jährige Judy-Ann Melchior.

Das Team Brasilien musste kurzfristig mit drei Reitern auskommen. Baloubet du Rouet von dem amtierenden Olympiasieger Rodrigo Pessoa hatte sich verletzt. Ersatzreiter Vitor Teixeira zog sein Pferd O de Pommes nach dem Vet-Check zurück. Die USA, Sechste von Jerez, hatte mit Beezie Madden und McLain Ward zwei Reiter vom erfolgreichen Olympiateam aus Athen in der Equipe. Für Gesprächsstoff hatte bereits im WM-Vorfeld das Team aus der Ukraine gesorgt. Der ukrainische Öl- und Gasmillionär Alexandre Onischenko hatte sich ein Team ‚zusammengekauft': Die Deutsche Meisterin von 2003, Katharina Offel, die Ex-Belgier Jean-Claude Vangeenberghe und Gregory Wathelet und erst vier Wochen vor der WM kam noch der deutsche B2-Kaderreiter Björn Nagel hinzu.

When the WEG dice fall ...

"Class instead of the masses is better than showing how many nations have got a team, who are overtaxed with the task at hand." This is the appeal that the WEG Sports Director, Frank Kempermann, made to the FEI in the run-up to the event. Ultimately 25 teams and 22 individual riders competed in the FEI World Equestrian Games, in total 116 competitors. And all of the fears burst like a bubble: The World Show-jumping Championships were a sporting climax from start to finish.

The German team had been nominated earlier than ever – even before the German Championships in Munster, as a result of the excellent performance of the five top riders Meredith Michaels-Beerbaum, Marcus Ehning, Christian Ahlmann, Ludger Beerbaum and Marco Kutscher. Three of the team members had already been determined, but who was going to occupy the fourth place prove to be a long debate: Marco Kutscher or Ludger Beerbaum? In the end all considerations saw double European Champion, Marco Kutscher, sitting on the reserve bench.

The defending champions, the French, travelled to Aachen with a completely new equipe compared to their victorious team in Jerez. The trainer of the Swedish silver medallists of 2002, Henk Nooren, admitted: "I am happy, if I get four pairs together." And the Belgians, who had won the bronze medal in Spain, had to swap their youngest rider, the 19-year-old Judy-Ann Melchior, into the team at the very last minute.

Brazil had to make do with a team of three riders at short notice, after the reigning Olympic gold medallist Rodrigo Pessoa's horse, Baloubet du Rouet, sustained an injury. The reserve, Vitor Teixeira withdrew his horse O de Pommes after the vet check. The USA, sixth in Jerez, had two members of their successful Athens Olympic team on board: Beezie Madden and McLain Ward. The team from the Ukraine had been a popular topic of conversation prior to the Games. The Ukraine oil and gas millionaire Alexandre Onischenko had "bought" himself a team: The German Champion of 2003, Katharina Offel, the ex-Belgians Jean-Claude Vangeenberghe and Gregory Wathelet and the German B2 cadre rider, Björn Nagel, who joined the team just four weeks before the World Championships.

Neu-Ukrainer Björn Nagel mit Pilgrim – Überraschung im WM-Parcours.
The now-Ukraine rider, Björn Nagel, with Pilgrim – surprised at the World Championships.

Ergebnisse/ Results Seite/ page 134/135

FEI World Equestrian Games Aachen 2006

WM der Superlative

Vom Gipfel des Mount Everest in die Schlucht des Grand Canyon. Im Senkrechtstart gen Himmel, im Sturzflug in die Hölle. Platzen vor Freude und Verkriechen im Frust. Und 48.000 fliegen, stürzen, leiden und freuen sich mit.

Die Springwettbewerbe der Aachener Weltmeisterschaft sind nur mit Superlativen zu beschreiben: am besten, tragischsten, emotionalsten, fraulichsten, fantastischsten…

Die tragischste Figur des deutschen Teams ist Marcus Ehning, die Nummer eins der Welt. Als Topfavorit angereist muss er in der zweiten Runde des Nationenpreises aufgeben. Tragisch auch die letzte Runde von Ludger Beerbaum. Nach sensationellen Diensten für sein Team scheidet er kurz vor dem Finalziel aus. Tragisch muss man auch das Abschneiden der Titelverteidiger bezeichnen: Die Franzosen erreichen mit ihrem Team noch nicht einmal die zweite Runde des Nationenpreises – ebenso die Silbermedaillengewinner von Jerez, die Schweden. Im unerwarteten Goldrausch badet dagegen das niederländische Team mit WM-Gold. Die Ukrainer schwanken zwischen Euphorie über ihre erreichte Olympiaqualifikation und Frust: Team-Bronze haben sie um eine hundertstel Sekunde verpasst und den Deutschen überlassen müssen. Und: Drei Frauen im Finale der Springweltmeisterschaft – das hat es noch nie gegeben. Eine davon ist Meredith Michaels-Beerbaum. Die Runde der letzten Vier toppt alle Erwartungen. Drei Reiter stechen nach fantastischem Pferdewechsel um Gold.

WEG the superlative

From the tip of Mount Everest to the gorge of the Grand Canyon. A vertical take-off up to heaven, a nose dive down to hell. Bursting for joy and hiding away in frustration. And 48,000 riding high, diving deep, suffering and celebrating with them.

The show-jumping competitions of the World Championships in Aachen can only be described using superlatives: the best, the most tragic, most emotional, most feminine, most fantastic…

The most tragic character of the German team is Marcus Ehning, the number one rider in the world. Hailed as top favourite on arrival, he had to retire in the second round of the Nations' Cup. Ludger Beerbaum's final round was also tragic. After doing a sensational job for his team, he didn't quite make it into the Final. The performance of the titleholders must also be described as tragic: The French team didn't even make it to the second round of the Nations' Cup – nor did Sweden, the silver medallists in Jerez. In contrast the Dutch team bathed unexpectedly in gold fever. The Ukraines are ranging between euphoria at having qualified for the Olympics and frustration: They missed team bronze by one hundredths of a second and had to relinquish the medal to the German team. And: Three ladies in the World Show-jumping Championships Final – this has never happened before either. One of them was Meredith Michaels-Beerbaum. The round of the last four topped all expectations. Three riders in the jump-off for gold after the rotation of horses.

Das Zeitspringen
Parcoursbegehung – mit Hans Günter Winkler

The speed competition
Course inspection – with Hans Günter Winkler

Das Zeitspringen, die erste Wertungsprüfung für die Team- und Einzelwettbewerbe, geht über 13 Hindernisse mit 16 Sprüngen. Eine besondere Herausforderung für Parcoursbauer Frank Rothenberger bedeutet das Dressurviereck, das für die WM mitten auf dem Springplatz angelegt worden war. So muss Rothenberger auf dem 17.000 Quadratmeter WM-Rasen 1.200 Quadrat-

The speed competition, the first rating competition for the team and individual classifications, comprised of 13 obstacles with 16 fences. One of the particular challenges for course builder, Frank Rothenberger, was the dressage arena, which had been integrated into the jumping ring for the World Championships. This meant that Rothenberger had to do without 1,200 m² of the

1. Qualifikation – Zeitspringen
1st Qualification – Speed Competition

Parcoursdaten/ Course Data:

Länge/ Length:	600 m
Hindernisse/ Obstacles:	13
Sprünge/ Efforts:	16

Hindernis Nr./ Obstacle-No.	Höhe/ height	Breite/ width
1	144	150
2	148	160
3	150L/ 155R	
4		420
5a	149	160
5b	150	
6	148	170
7	150	
8	150	200
9a	148/ 150R	160R
9b	150/ 150R	150
10a	149	
10b	150	180
11	150	
12	158L/ 149/ 148R	
13	150	180

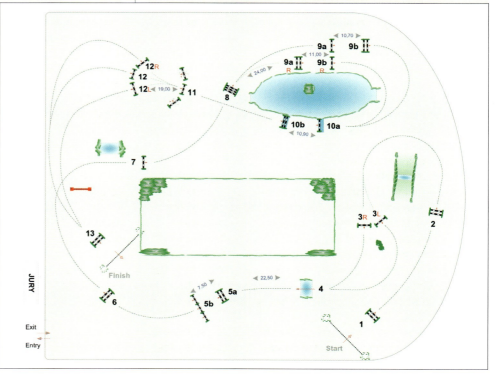

meter Sandviereck aussparen. Das hat es auf einer WM noch nicht gegeben.

Die ersten beiden Sprünge sind Oxer mit „reellen Abmessungen", so Springsport-Legende Hans Günter Winkler, „aber ohne besondere Schwierigkeit." Hindernis drei bietet die erste Alternative. „Wer hier mit einem echten Championatspferd an den Start geht, wählt nicht die Alternative". Nach dem Wasser wartet auf gebrochener Distanz die erste Kombination Oxer-Steilsprung. „Hier haben wir die erste Schwierigkeit", erklärt Winkler. „Nach dem Wasser sind die Pferde im Vorwärts, dann müssen sie zurückkommen und für die Kombination wieder voll beim Reiter sein." Nach der Kombination geht es wiederum auf gebrochener Distanz zum Sprung Nummer sechs, einem Oxer. „Den Oxer müssen die Pferde auf die große Tribüne zu springen. Das kann irritieren." Zum Steilsprung sieben kann man einen langen oder den direkten Weg nehmen. Fast alle wählen die Direktissima. „Selbst auf diesem kurzen Weg hat man noch genug Zeit, eine Postkarte nach Hause zu schreiben", witzelt Winkler. Es folgt die Tripplebarre Nummer acht und die zweite Alternative: entweder Oxer-Steil-Kombination auf direktem Weg oder Steil-Oxer auf dem ‚chicken-way'. Nun kommt die größte Herausforderung: eine Steil-Oxer-Kombination, unter beiden Sprüngen schillert ein Wassergraben. „Das ist die schwerste Kombination", betont Winkler. „Da gucken die Pferde erst ins Wasser und dann kommt da noch die ‚Klamotte' von einem Oxer." Die Hindernisse elf und zwölf bieten die nächste Alternative. Beide Hindernisse bestehen aus je drei Elementen. Der kürzeste Weg führt bei elf über die Mitte und bei zwölf über das linke Element. Erst der 45. Starter traut sich an diesen Weg. Der letzte Sprung ist noch einmal ein gewaltiger Oxer.

Favoriten durch Himmel und Hölle

In der ersten WM-Woche hat es ungewöhnlich viel geregnet: 52,8 Liter pro Quadratmeter. Und das Springstadion hatte bereits die Eröffnungsfeier, Schaunummern, den Einritt der Distanzreiter und Siegerehrungen überstanden. An einigen Stellen lugte aus dem edlen Grün matschiges Braun, aber der Untergrund war immer noch griffig und fest. „Der Boden ist nach all dem Regen immer noch unglaublich gut", loben Ludger Beerbaum und Kollegen.

29. August 2005, 11.00 Uhr. 40.000 Zuschauer warten auf den ersten Starter der Springwettbewerbe: Ludger Beerbaum. Bundestrainer und „Glücksfee" Kurt Gravemeier hat für das deutsche Team die Startnummer eins gezogen. „Das war schon ein anderes Gefühl, als Erster in den Parcours zu gehen", erklärt Beerbaum. „Aber ich habe mich irgendwie auch befreit gefühlt auf dieser Position. Ich habe versucht, eine flüssige Runde hinzulegen, nicht verrückt schnell." Für L'Espoir sei das Zeitspringen vielleicht die schwerste Aufgabe gewesen, betont Beerbaum. Er habe noch nicht so viel Erfahrung in Zeitspringen gesammelt. „Ich habe im Vorfeld ein paar Mal an meine „Priamos-Runde" bei der WM in Rom gedacht. Da habe ich auch richtig losgelegt und hatte dann zwei um. Vielleicht bin ich auch deswegen so vorsichtig geritten." Die Vorsicht hat sich gelohnt: fehlerfrei in 83,01 Sekunden.

Der zweite Reiter liefert gleich die zweite Nullrunde, der Italiener Emilio Bicocchi. In einer ‚Kamikaze-Runde' unterbietet er Beerbaums Zeit um sechs hundertstel Sekunden und hält 33 Starter

17,000 m² sized World Championships arena. A situation that has never happened at World Championships before.

The first two fences are oxers with "decent dimensions", noted the show-jumping sport legend, Hans Günter Winkler, "but without any special degree of difficulty." Obstacle three offered the first alternative. "Anyone who is competing with a real Championship horse, won't choose the alternative," judged Winkler. The water was followed by the first combination comprising of an oxer and an upright. "This is where the first challenge lies," explained Winkler. "After the water the horses are cantering forwards and have to let themselves be checked and brought back under the full control of the rider for the combination." After the combination the course led on a curved line to jump number six, an oxer. "To take the oxer the horses have to jump towards the big stand. This can be irritating." It was possible to take a longer route or the direct route to number seven, an upright. Almost all of the riders chose the directissima. "Even taking the short route, you've still got enough time to write a postcard home," joked Winkler. Number eight, the triple barre, followed and with it the second alternative: Either an oxer/upright combination on a direct line or an upright/oxer combination as the "chicken's-way". The course then led to the biggest challenge: An upright/oxer combination with a water ditch under both jumps. "This is the most difficult combination," stressed Winkler. "The horses are first of all occupied with staring at the water and then all of a sudden the huge oxer appears." Obstacles 11 and 12 offered the next alternative. Both obstacles comprised of three elements. The shortest route ran over the middle of 11 and over the left element of jump 12. The crowd had to wait for the 45th competitor to see this plucky alternative. The last fence was another mighty oxer.

Favourites went through heaven and hell

An incredible amount of rain fell in the first week of the World Championships: 52.8 litre/m². And the jumping stadium had already survived the Opening Ceremony, show programmes, the finish of the endurance riders and prize-giving ceremonies. In some places one could see the brown mud emerging between the green grass, but the subsurface was still firm and offered a good grip. "In spite of the heavy rainfall the footing is still unbelievably good," praised Ludger Beerbaum and his colleagues.

August 29th, 2005, 11.00 a.m. 40,000 spectators were waiting to see the first riders of the show-jumping competitions: Ludger Beerbaum. The National Coach Kurt Gravemeier had drawn first place in the starting order for the German team. "It was an unusual feeling, being the first to enter the course," explained Beerbaum. But somehow I also felt liberated in this position. I tried to accomplish a rhythmic round, not amazingly fast." The speed competition had perhaps been the most difficult task for L'Espoir, Beerbaum had stressed, since he hadn't collected much experience in speed competitions yet. "Beforehand I had been thinking about my Priamos round at the World Championships in Rome, where I had really put my foot down and collected eight faults. Perhaps that is why I rode so carefully." The caution paid off: Clear in 83.01 seconds.

The second rider also delivered a clear round, the Italian Emilio Bicocchi. In a 'kamikaze round' he beat Beerbaum's time by six hundredths of a second and held the lead for the next 33 rides. The former top pair Malin Baryard-Johnsson and Butterfly Flip

FEI World Equestrian Games Aachen 2006

Ludger Beerbaum mit L'Espoir sicher übers Wasser – von zu wenig Erfahrung keine Spur.
Ludger Beerbaum with L'Espoir safely over the water – no trace of a lack of experience.

lang die Führung. Fast tragisch ist der Auftritt des einstigen Superpaares Malin Baryard-Johnsson und Butterfly Flip. Das Schweden-Duo scheidet nach zweifachem Verweigern aus. Als zehnter Starter tritt der britische Altmeister John Whitaker auf dem neunjährigen Peppermill in Szene. Der 51-Jährige beginnt seine fünfte Weltmeisterschaft mit einer stilvollen Nullrunde. Die Teamkollegen von John Whitaker sind sein fünf Jahre jüngerer Bruder Michael, der 48-jährigen Nick Skelton und Teamküken Tim Gredley (20). Zusammen bringt es diese Mannschaft inklusive der WM 2006 auf 56 Championats-Teilnahmen.

made an almost tragic entrance. The Swiss duo was eliminated after two refusals. The British veteran John Whitaker entered the ring on the nine-year-old Peppermill as tenth rider. The 51-year-old opened his fifth World Championships with a stylish clear round. His team colleagues comprised of his younger brother Michael (46), the 48-year-old Nick Skelton and the team youngster Tim Gredley (20). Including the WEG 2006, in total the team had taken part at 56 Championships.

Cöster, pretty good, but ...

25th on the starting list: Christian Ahlmann and Cöster. At the FEI World Equestrian Games four years earlier in Jerez, the pair had turned down the opportunity of competing. Cöster was only nine at the time and his owner Marion Jauß felt that it had been too early for him to compete at World Championships. In the meantime the pair won double gold at the European Championships 2003, were part of the Olympic team in 2004 and part of the gold-winning team at the European Championships in 2005. They started their ride in Aachen fluently and harmoniously until jump seven when the rail fell. "It wasn't exactly the most difficult jump in the course," commented a disappointed Ahlmann. "I actually had a good approach to the jump, but on taking off Cöster pulled to the right and hit the rail with his right leg." An expensive mistake. Christian Ahlmann landed in 23rd place after the speed jumping: "World Championships are measured in centimetres. One mistake can catapult you right to the back."

Der britische Altmeister John Whitaker – die WM in Aachen war sein 19. Championat.
The British veteran John Whitaker – the World Equestrian Games in Aachen were his 19th Championships.

SPRINGEN | JUMPING

Cöster, eigentlich gut, aber ...

Startplatz 25: Christian Ahlmann und Cöster. Bei den Weltreiterspielen vier Jahre zuvor in Jerez hatten die beiden einen Start noch abgelehnt. Cöster war damals neun und Besitzerin Marion Jauß hielt einen WM-Einsatz für verfrüht. In der Zwischenzeit haben die beiden bei der EM 2003 Doppelgold gewonnen, gehörten 2004 zum Olympia-Team und 2005 zur goldenen EM-Mannschaft. Das Paar beginnt in Aachen flüssig und harmonisch bis bei Sprung sieben die Stange fällt. „Das war sicher nicht der schwerste Sprung im Parcours", kommentiert Ahlmann enttäuscht. „Eigentlich kam ich mit guter Distanz zu dem Sprung, aber Cöster hat im Absprung nach rechts weggezogen und mit dem rechten Bein die Stange getroffen." Ein teurer Fehler. Christian Ahlmann landet nach dem Zeitspringen auf dem 32. Platz: „Bei einer WM geht es um Zentimeter. Da wird man mit einem Fehler schon nach hinten durchgereicht."

Der norwegische Einzelreiter Geir Gulliksen übernimmt zwischenzeitlich die Führung bis der Franzose Laurent Goffinet mit dem französischen Hengst Flipper d'Elle als Erster die Abkürzung in der Hindernisfolge elf-zwölf wagt. Für eine Überraschung sorgt der Olympiasieger von Sydney, Jeroen Dubbeldam. Eigentlich sollte er sein Team auf Nassau, mit dem er 2005 bei der EM Doppel-Bronze gewonnen hat, unterstützen, aber der war nach einer Verletzung noch nicht wieder in Top-Form. So sattelt er kurzfristig auf den neunjährigen Belgier Up and Down um. Eine gute Wahl: Die beiden drehen eine sichere Nullrunde.

The Norwegian individual rider Geir Gulliksen had taken over the lead until the French show-jumper Laurent Goffinet was the first rider who dared to take the short cut in the obstacle sequence 11/12 with his French stallion Flipper d'Elle. The Olympic gold medallist from Sydney, Jeroen Dubbeldam, surprised everyone. He was supposed to support his team on Nassau, who he won double bronze with at the European Championships in 2005, but he still wasn't in top form after sustaining an injury, so at the last minute the Dutchman had decided to saddle the nine-year-old Belgian-bred Up and Down. A good choice: The two of them accomplished a solid clear round.

The wrong way to the water

Shortly afterwards the third German team member was ready to start, Meredith Michaels-Beerbaum and Shutterfly: "I wanted to take one less canter stride to the water ditch than the others, but I didn't get an ideal approach. Shutterfly did a huge jump alright, but unfortunately it was too high and not far enough." She was the first female rider to be nominated for a German World Showjumping Championships team and was considered to be one of the favourites. "Of course I am disappointed, but I am totally happy with my horse. The mistake at the water was my fault." It was in fact the only mistake the two of them were to make.

At 2.40 p.m. the second half of the field of 116 competitors was in the starting box. The Hungarian rider Mariann Hugyecz shocked the crowd for a moment. Her horse Superville took off too soon at an oxer, and both the horse and rider landed in the middle of the jump. The rider was not injured, but the horse

Christian Ahlmann und Cöster – fit, aber nicht top.
Christian Ahlmann and Cöster – fit, but not top.

FEI World Equestrian Games Aachen 2006

Shutterfly und Meredith Michaels-Beerbaum –
im perfekten WM-Stil.
*Shutterfly and Meredith Michaels-Beerbaum –
in perfect World Championship style.*

Der falsche Weg zum Wasser

Kurz darauf kommt das dritte deutsche Teammitglied an den Start, Meredith Michaels-Beerbaum und Shutterfly: „Ich wollte zum Wassergraben einen Galoppsprung weniger machen als die anderen, deswegen kam ich nicht optimal da an. Shutterfly hat zwar einen riesigen Sprung gemacht, aber leider zu hoch und nicht weit genug." Sie war die erste Frau in einem deutschen WM-Springteam und galt als eine der Favoriten. „Natürlich bin ich enttäuscht, aber mit dem Pferd bin ich super zufrieden. Das am Wasser war mein Fehler." Es bleibt der einzige Fehler, den sich die beiden leisten.

Um 14.40 Uhr geht es mit der zweiten Hälfte der 116 Starter weiter. Die Ungarin Mariann Hugyecz sorgt für einen Moment des Schreckens. Ihr Pferd Superville springt zu früh vor einem Oxer ab, Pferd und Reiter stürzen in das Hindernis. Die Reiterin bleibt unverletzt, das Pferd prellt sich die Schulter. Der US-Amerikaner McLain Ward hat zwischenzeitlich mit der belgischen Stute Sapphire die Führung übernommen. Aber als 84. Starter ist der Kanadier Eric Lamaze noch schneller. Lamaze ist so schnell unterwegs, dass sein zehnjähriger Holländer Hickstead fast am letzten Hindernis vorbeirast. Lamaze ist ein bekannter Name. Zweimal war er wegen Kokain-Missbrauchs gesperrt und musste auf einen Start bei den Olympischen Spielen 2000 verzichten.

Der Kanadier Eric Lamaze und Hickstead – von der anderen Seite der Welt auf Platz zwei im Aachener Zeitspringen.
The Canadian rider Eric Lamaze and Hickstead – from the other side of the world to second place in the speed competition in Aachen.

bruised its shoulder. In the meantime the rider from the US, McLain Ward, was heading the field with the Belgian mare, Sapphire. But the 84th rider, the Canadian Eric Lamaze was even faster. Lamaze was going at such a speed that his 10-year-old Dutch-bred Hickstead almost ran past the last fence. Lamaze is a well-known name. He has been banned twice for taking cocaine and had to miss out on competing at the Olympic Games in 2000 as a result.

„Ich habe es übertrieben."

Endlich: Als 90ster Reiter kommt Marcus Ehning in das Stadion. Lange hat Ehning geschwankt, welche seiner Topstuten er für die WM satteln soll: Gitania oder Noltes Küchengirl. Er entscheidet sich für die neunjährige Bayernstute Noltes Küchengirl. „Das war eine Bauchentscheidung." Das Paar beginnt den Parcours in überragender Manier, aber die Hindernisfolge elf-zwölf wird ihnen zum Verhängnis: „Die Stute ist so überragend gesprungen, dass da einfach etwas mit mir durchgegangen ist. Ich habe es übertrieben. Der Fehler geht zu 100-Prozent auf meine Kappe", ist Ehning erschüttert. Eigentlich hat der Führende der Weltrangliste geplant, von Sprung elf auf zwölf den geraden Weg zu nehmen. Urplötzlich hat er sich zwischen den Hindernissen umentschieden und wollte scharf nach links. Küchengirl landet mehr oder weniger im Hindernis. „Danach hatte sie am letzten Oxer ein bisschen Angst", erklärt Ehning. Und so stockt die Stute vor dem letzten Sprung und trifft die Stangen. Um der Sensiblen wieder Vertrauen zu geben, macht Ehning danach noch ein paar

"I overdid it."

At last: 90th on the starting list, Marcus Ehning entered the stadium in. Ehning had deliberated for a long time as to which of his top mares he should saddle for the WEG: Gitania or Noltes Küchengirl. He finally opted for the nine-year-old Bavarian mare Noltes Küchengirl. "It was an intuitive decision." The pair started off the course majestically, but the obstacle sequence 11/12 proved to be their doom: "The mare was jumping so superbly that I simply got carried away. I overdid it. It was 100 percent my mistake," Ehning was devastated. The number one rider in the world rankings had actually planned to take the direct route from obstacle 11 to 12. He suddenly changed his mind in between the obstacles and wanted to pull sharply to the left. Küchengirl landed more or less in the jump. "After that she was a bit frightened

Springen | Jumping

Sprünge auf dem Abreiteplatz. „Ich hoffe, dass ich ihr das Vertrauen für den Nationenpreis wiedergeben kann."

Während Ludger Beerbaum fast unerwartet nach WM-Runde eins im Himmel schwebt, ist die erste WM-Erfahrung 2006 für Topstar Ehning die Hölle. Trotz seiner Fehler rangiert Ehning nach dem Zeitspringen noch auf dem 24. Platz und liefert das zweitbeste Ergebnis für sein Team. Mit seiner Zeit von 76,7 Sekunden hätte er ohne Abwurf fast eine Sekunde vor Prüfungssiegerin Beezie Madden aus den USA gelegen.

Mit vier fehlerfreien Runden steht das niederländische Quartett nach dem Zeitspringen an der Spitze, gefolgt von den USA und Brasilien. Das deutsche Team liegt auf Platz sechs. Noch drängen alle Teams auf den vorderen Plätzen dicht aneinander. Zwischen Platz eins und fünf liegen weniger als vier Fehlerpunkte – noch ist alles möglich.

„Die Stute ist bis dahin so überragend gesprungen, dass da einfach was mit mir durchgegangen ist."
(Marcus Ehning)

"The mare was jumping so superbly up until then, that I simply got carried away."
(Marcus Ehning)

Top-Favorit Marcus Ehning auf Noltes Küchengirl – im Zeitspringen gingen die Nerven durch.
Top favourite Marcus Ehning with Noltes Küchengirl – lost his nerves in the speed competition.

at the last oxer," explained Ehning. Which is why the mare hesitated in front of the last jump and knocked the pole. In order to regain the sensitive horse's confidence, Ehning returned to the warm-up arena to jump a couple more fences. "I hope I can regain her trust for the Nations' Cup."

Whereas almost unexpectedly Ludger Beerbaum is in seventh heaven after the first WEG round, the first 2006 World Championships experience was hell for top star Ehning.

In spite of his mistake Ehning was still in 24th place after the speed competition and had delivered the second best team result. With his time of 76.7 seconds he would have knocked almost one second off Beezie Madden's time, the US American rider who won the first rating competition, if he hadn't have collected any faults.

After completing four clear rounds the Dutch quartet was in the lead after the speed competition, followed by the USA and Brazil. The German team was in sixth place. All of the top teams were lying close together. Less than four faults separated the first five teams – everything was still wide open.

„Bei einer WM geht es um Zentimeter. Da wird man mit einem Fehler schon nach hinten durchgereicht."
(Christian Ahlmann)

"World Championships are measured in centimetres. One mistake can catapult you right to the back."
(Christian Ahlmann)

Flink wie ein Wiesel – Authentic unter Beezie Madden, Sieger im Zeitspringen.
As swift as the wind – Authentic under Beezie Madden, winners of the speed competition

FEI World Equestrian Games Aachen 2006

Der Nationenpreis
Parcoursbegehung mit Hans Günter Winkler

The Nations' Cup
Course inspection with Hans Günter Winkler

Nationenpreis Runde A / Nations Cup Round A

Parcoursdaten/ *Course Data:*

Länge/ *Length:*	650 m
Geschwindigkeit/ *Speed:*	400 m/min
Erlaubte Zeit/ *Time limit:*	98 Sec
Hindernisse/ *Obstacles:*	14
Sprünge/ *Efforts:*	17

Hindernis Nr./ Obstacle-No.	Höhe/ height	Breite/ width
1	148	
2	150	160
3	160	210
4a	156	
4b	149	170
5	153	170
6	162	
7	410	
8	160	100
9a	151	170
9b	154	
9c	153	170
10	152	180
11	159	
12	160	
13	148	190
14	162	

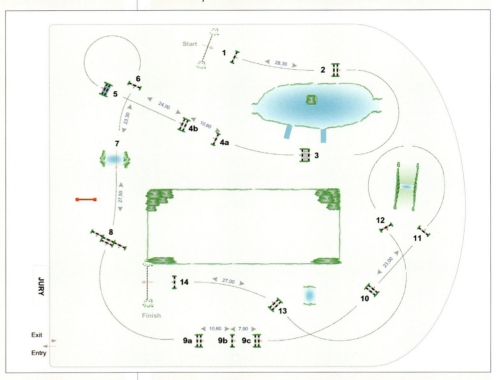

Der Startsprung zur ersten Nationenpreisrunde ist mit 1,48 m nicht zu gewaltig, der folgende Oxer „reell, aber nicht übertrieben hoch", so Experte Hans Günter Winkler. „Nach dem Oxer geht es etwas bergab, da muss man aufpassen, dass die Pferde nicht auf die Vorhand kommen. „Die Tripplebarre, Sprung drei, ist ungewöhnlich mit den gekreuzten weißen Stangen in der Mitte. Routiniers sollte das nicht irritieren." Die Tripplebarre ist mit 2,10 m sehr weit und liegt im leichten Bergauf. Die Kombination 4a/b und der Oxer 5 liegen auf gerader Linie. Von fünf auf sechs kommt die erste scharfe Wendung. „An dieser Stelle wird es das erste Mal etwas technischer." Mit fünf oder sechs Galoppsprüngen geht es zum Wassergraben, danach in gebrochener Linie mit sechs oder sieben Sprüngen zum Karree-Oxer Nummer acht. „Das ist schwierig – einerseits die Linienführung und andererseits, weil die Pferde von dem Oxer nur die erste Stange sehen." Zudem sind die Stangen des Oxers nicht rund, sondern eckig und etwas dünner und leichter als die anderen. Ein leichtes Touchieren genügt, um sie aus der Auflage zu schubsen. Die Kombination 9a/b/c, Oxer-Steil-Oxer, ist mit 10,60 m zunächst für zwei kurze Galoppsprünge gebaut, dann folgt mit 7,90 m ein Galoppsprung nach vorne. „Es geht hier ein bisschen bergab, das hilft bei dem größeren Galoppsprung zu 9c." Die Hindernisse 10 bis 12 sind normale Einzelsprünge im WM-Maß, der Oxer 13 ist gewaltig, vor allem im Bergauf. Tückisch ist der letzte Sprung in Richtung Ausgang, ein Steilsprung von nur drei Metern Breite mit weißen Planken, die mit schwarzen Strichen durchzogen sind. „Dieser Sprung wirkt filligran. Zudem liegen die Planken nur leicht auf. Hier kann schnell ein Fehler passieren."
Im Normalfall führen die beiden Umläufe im Nationenpreis über identische Parcours. Anders in Aachen 2006, weil der zweite Umlauf erstmals einen Tag später unter Flutlicht ausgetragen wurde.

The first jump in the first round of the Nations' Cup was not too mighty measuring 1.48 m in height, the following oxer was "stately" but not exaggeratedly high," the expert Hans Günter Winkler commented. "After the oxer it goes downhill a bit, so you have to be careful that the horses don't carry too much weight on the forehand. The pattern in the middle of the white poles of the triple barre, fence three, is unusual. But it shouldn't irritate experienced horses." With a width of 2.1 metres the triple barre was very broad and was slightly uphill. The combination 4a/b and the oxer 5 were on a straight line. The first sharp turn came between 5 and 6. „The course starts getting more technical here." Five or six canter strides took the rider to the water ditch, and then the course followed a curved line of six or seven strides to the parallel oxer number eight. "This is difficult – on the one hand due to the complicated line of the course, and also because the horses only see the front rail of the oxer." In addition to which the poles of the oxer were not round, but square and a little thinner and lighter than the others. They only had to be knocked gently and they would fall. The combination 9a/b/c, oxer/upright/oxer, was built at 10.6 m for two short canter strides followed by a distance of 7,9 m which meant a one stride with forwards impulsion. "It runs a little downhill here, so that will help the riders achieve the larger stride to 9c." Obstacles 10 to 12 were normal individual jumps with WEG dimensions, the oxer, jump number 13, was mighty and furthermore uphill. The last jump towards the exit was tricky, a narrow upright only three metres wide with white planks that were decorated with black strokes. "This jump looks fragile. What's more the planks aren't very stable. Faults will happen quickly here."
Normally both rounds of the Nations' Cup are identical. However, this was not the case in Aachen 2006, because for the first

Springen | Jumping

"Wir haben Testspringen im Stadion unter Flutlicht gemacht", erklärt Parcoursbauer Frank Rothenberger. "Das Flutlicht hat sich unheimlich in dem Wasser gespiegelt, von der anderen Seite waren es die Spotlights von der Tribüne. Aus Fair Play-Gründen den Pferden und Reitern gegenüber haben wir uns entschieden, das Wasser beim Flutlichtspringen rauszunehmen."

Nationenpreis – der 1. Umlauf

Die Schwalbe ohne Sommer

"Ja, das war für uns ein schöner Auftakt – aber eine Schwalbe macht noch keinen Sommer!" Ludger Beerbaum und L'Espoir gehen wie gehabt als Erster für das deutsche Team in den Parcours. Und wieder bleiben sie fehlerfrei. "Das ist ja eigentlich der gleiche Auftakt wie gestern und da haben wir am Ende doch noch lange Gesichter gemacht", warnt Beerbaum vor frühzeitiger Euphorie. "Aber ich bin sicher, dass wir heute noch aufholen können." Verblüfft hatte bereits als vierter Starter der 28-jährige Björn Nagel für die Ukraine: ohne Hindernisfehler, ein Zeitfehler. Der erste Reiter der führenden Niederländer, Piet Raymakers hatte fünf Fehlerpunkte vorgelegt.

Die Nummer zwei für Deutschland: Christian Ahlmann. Zweimal stößt das Paar an die Stangen, an Sprung fünf und 14, dem Schlusssprung. Mit schüttelndem Kopf verlässt der Doppel-Europameister von 2003 den Parcours. "Cöster ist im Grunde gut gesprungen, wirklich erklären kann ich die beiden Fehler nicht. Vielleicht hat die allerletzte Konzentration gefehlt", ist Ahlmann ratlos. Das Oranje-Team verteidigt auch mit seinem zweiten Reiter die Führungsposition: Ein Zeitfehler für Jeroen Dubbeldam. Die Ukraine holt weiter auf – fehlerfrei bleibt Jean-Claude Vangeenberghe. Die Brasilianer fallen nach hinten. Mit ihren ersten beiden Runden haben sie neun (Alvaro Miranda) und vier (Cassio Rivetti) Fehlerpunkte gesammelt. Die USA liefern zwei Runden mit je einem Abwurf und stabilisieren sich auf ihrer Position.

Meredith Michaels-Beerbaum ist die dritte Reiterin für Deutschland. Shutterfly springt fantastisch, aber: "Ich bin etwas zu langsam geritten. Ich habe zwar die Pfiffe vom anderen Ende des Stadions von meinem Mann und Ludger gehört, aber da konnte ich nur noch machen, was möglich war, ohne zu viel zu riskieren."

Nations' Cup – the first round

Swallow without the summer

"Yes, we had a great start – but one swallow doesn't mean its summer yet!" Ludger Beerbaum and L'Espoir are once again the first pair to enter the course for the German team. And they rode

Schwache Schweden – Rolf-Göran Bengtsson konnte sein Team nicht retten: Aus für Runde zwei des Nationenpreises.
A weak Sweden – Rolf-Göran Bengtsson wasn't able to save his team: They didn't make it to the second round of the Nations' Cup.

clear once again. "That is exactly how everything started off yesterday, but we still all had long faces at the end of the day," warned Beerbaum against premature euphoria. "But I am sure that we will be able to catch up today." The fourth competitor, the 28-year-old Björn Nagel riding for the Ukraine was amazed: No jumping faults but one time fault. The first rider of the leading Dutch team, Piet Raymakers, had clocked up five faults.

Number two for Germany: Christian Ahlmann. The pair knocked the rail twice at jump 5 and at the final fence. The double European Champion of 2003 left the ring shaking his head. "In fact Cöster jumped well, I really can't explain the two jumping faults. Perhaps the last touch of concentration was missing," Ahlmann said at a loss. The second member of the Oranje team also defended their lead: Jeroen Dubbeldam rode home with just one time fault. The Ukraine caught up again – after Jean-Claude Vangeenberghe put in a clear round. The Brazilians fell right back. In their first two rounds they collected nine (Alvaro Miranda) and four (Cassio Rivetti) faults. The USA had one fence down in each of their two rounds, which meant their position remained stable.

Der Beste seines dreiköpfigen Teams –
der Brasilianer Bernardo Alves.
*The best of a three-man team –
the Brazilian rider, Bernardo Alves.*

FEI WORLD EQUESTRIAN GAMES AACHEN 2006

Ein Zeitfehler geht auf ihr Konto. Dennoch: eine Runde, die Mut macht und die Gastgeber-Nation nach dem dritten Reiter im Nationenpreis auf den zweiten, hoffnungsvollen Teamplatz setzt.
Mit Spannung warten alle auf den Schlussreiter, Marcus Ehning. Für Fans, für Insider und Fachleute, für Trainer und Equipechefs, sogar für den Reiter ist nicht absehbar, wie die sensible Stute das Erlebnis aus dem Zeitspringen ‚verdaut' hat. Es ist verblüffend wie ruhig 48.000 Zuschauer in gespannter Erwartung sein können. Wie sehr 48.000 mitleiden können, wenn eine Stange kullert. So geschehen bei Marcus Ehning am vorletzten Sprung. „Ich bin erst einmal total happy, dass mein Pferd wieder so gesprungen ist", ist der Weltranglisten-Erste nicht enttäuscht über diesen Fehler. „Und ich bin froh, dass ich heute unserer Mannschaft helfen konnte und nicht das Streichergebnis geliefert habe. Ich konnte wirklich vorher nicht sagen, wie die Stute das Erlebnis von gestern im Zeitspringen wegstecken würde. Dieser eine Fehler heute war eher ein Flüchtigkeitsfehler."
Gerco Schröder liefert für das bisherige Spitzenteam noch eine Nullrunde – die Führung bleibt unangetastet. Katharina Offel gönnt sich und ihrem Team eine Runde ohne Hindernis-, mit nur einem Zeitfehler. Beezie Madden bleibt fehlerfrei für die USA.
Nach der ersten Nationenpreisrunde liegen die Niederländer gesichert an der Spitze. Etwas mehr als ein Abwurf trennt sie vom dichtesten Verfolger, dem Team aus der Ukraine. Die Teams zwei bis fünf liegen weniger als vier Fehlerpunkte auseinander: Ukraine, USA, Deutschland. Der Abend vor dem Flutlichtspringen lässt noch allen Spekulationen freien Raum. Ein herrliches Kribbeln für alle Fans, aber auch eine sportliche Herausforderung für die Nerven aller Beteiligten.

Fehlerfreie Runde für den Jordanier Ibrahim Hani Kamal Bisharat –
zur Belohnung gab's eine Umarmung von „Landsmännin" Prinzessin Haya.
Clear round for the rider from Jordan, Ibrahim Hani Kamal Bisharat – he was rewarded with an embrace from "fellow-countrywomen", Princess Haya.

Meredith Michaels-Beerbaum was the third rider for Germany. Shutterfly jumped fantastically, but: "I was too slow. I heard Ludger and my husband's whistles from the other end of the stadium, but I could only do what was possible, without risking too much." She added one time fault to her score. Still it was a motivating round and it put the host nation back in a hopeful second place in the team classification of the Nations' Cup after the third rider.
Everyone was waiting tensely for the final rider, Marcus Ehning. Neither the fans, insiders and experts, trainers and Chef d'Equipes, nor the rider himself could be sure whether the sensitive mare had "got over" her experience in the speed competition. It is amazing how quiet 48,000 spectators can be when they are waiting in suspense. How regretful 48,000 people can be when a pole falls. As it did when Marcus Ehning took the last jump. "I am just totally happy that my horse jumped like she did again," the number one rider in the world was not disappointed about this jumping fault. "And I am pleased I was able to help the team today, not delivering the scratch result. I really couldn't say beforehand how the mare would react after her experience in the speed competition yesterday. The four faults today were merely a routine mistake."
Gerco Schröder achieved a further clear round for the interim leaders – no one could catch them. Katharina Offel treated herself and her team to a round without jumping faults, but did incur one time fault. Beezie Madden jumped clear for the USA.
After the first Nations' Cup round the Dutch team had secured the top ranking. Just over one jumping fault separated them from their closest pursuers, the team from the Ukraine. Less than four faults separated the teams in 2nd to 5th place: the Ukraine, the USA, and Germany. All sorts of speculations were articulated on the eve before the floodlight competition. Wonderfully exciting for the fans, but a sporting challenge for the nerves of all parties involved.

Obelix unter Hervé Godignon – der einzige Franzose,
der es unter die letzten 25 geschafft hat.
Obelix under Hervé Godignon – the only French rider who managed to qualify under the best 25.

Springen | Jumping

Die Zwischenbilanz...
...von Bundestrainer Kurt Gravemeier:

„Ludger hat bisher hier eine unglaubliche Leistung abgeliefert, Cöster präsentierte sich etwas enttäuschend. Er ist etwas nachlässig im Parcours. Shutterfly springt genial. Und bei Küchengirl sind wir sehr froh, dass sie heute wieder so gut gesprungen ist. Beide Teams, die in der Zwischenwertung vorne liegen, sind überraschend gut: Was die Holländer hier bringen ist toll und die Ukraine hat sehr gute Reiter und Pferde."

The interim balance...
...by National Coach Kurt Gravemeier:

"Up until now Ludger has given an unbelievable performance, Cöster was slightly disappointing. He is a little careless in the ring. Shutterfly is jumping masterfully. And we are very happy that Küchengirl jumped so well again today. Both teams that are lying ahead in the interim results are surprisingly good: The Dutch are performing very well and the Ukraine has got very good horses and riders."

Nationenpreis – der 2. Umlauf
Aachen ist Oranje-Boden

Nation's Cup – the second round
Aachen is Oranje ground

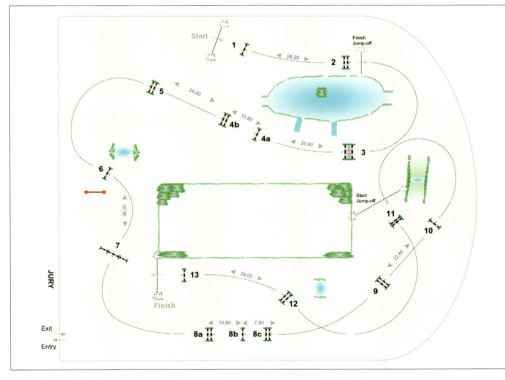

Nationenpreis Runde B / Nations Cup Round B

Parcoursdaten/ Course Data:	
Länge/ Length:	610 m
Geschwindigkeit/ Speed:	400 m/min
Erlaubte Zeit/ Time limit:	92 Sec
Hindernisse/ Obstacles:	13
Sprünge/ Efforts:	16

Hindernis Nr./ Obstacle-No.	Höhe/ height	Breite/ width
1	148	
2	150	160
3	160	220
4a	148	
4b	156	170
5	153	190
6	161	
7	165	
8a	151	170
8b	156	
8c	153	180
9	152	180
10	165	
11	160	110
12	153	190
13	164	

Im Goldrausch – das Team Niederlande mit Teamchef Rob Ehrens.
In gold fever – the Dutch equipe with team boss, Rob Ehrens.

Nobody thought the small neighbouring country with a big heart for equestrian sport would manage it: The Dutch riders overtrumped themselves in Aachen. In 1991 they became the European Champions in La Baule, in 1992 Olympic gold medallists in Barcelona. But that's where the Oranje team's gold series came to an end. 28 years ago Holland claimed the silver medal at the World Championships. That had been the Oranje riders' best World Championships result todate and was also celebrated on Aachen's ground too.

They already took up their position ahead of the other 24 teams after the first rating competition and kept continually increasing their lead. Piet Raymakers the first rider for Holland added a terrible score to the list: 16 jumping faults and two time faults. The 49-year-old veteran of the team took it calmly: "I had a lot of faults, but I have certainly made the sport more interesting." The next rider, Jeroen Dubbeldam displayed nerves of steel and jumped clear, Albert Zoer and Okidoki brought further excite-

FEI World Equestrian Games Aachen 2006

Das hat dem kleinen Nachbarland mit dem großen Herz für Pferdesport niemand zugetraut: die Niederländer wachsen in Aachen über sich hinaus. 1991 sind sie Europameister in La Baule geworden, 1992 Olympiasieger in Barcelona. Seitdem musste das Oranje-Team auf Golderfolge verzichten. Vor 28 Jahren gab es WM-Silber für die Niederlande. Das war der größte WM-Erfolg für die Oranje-Reiter bisher und auch den feierten sie auf Aachener Boden. Sie haben sich schon nach der ersten Prüfung an die Spitze der 25 Teams gesetzt und bauen ihren Vorsprung immer weiter aus. Piet Raymakers stockt als erster Reiter für das führende Holland-Team das Fehlerkonto mächtig auf: vier Abwürfe und zwei Zeitfehler. Der 49-jährige ‚Altmeister' des Teams nahm es gelassen: „Ich hatte viele Fehler, aber ich habe den Sport interessant gemacht." Jeoren Dubbeldam behält als Folgereiter die Nerven und dreht eine Nullrunde, Albert Zoer und Okidoki sorgen für einen spannenden Moment. Zoer verliert den Steigbügel, prompt kassiert er einen Abwurf, findet den Bügel wieder und bleibt für den Rest des Kurses fehlerfrei. Schlussreiter Gerco Schröder und der zwölfjährige Holsteiner Hengst Berlin tragen eine von nur drei Doppel-Nullrunden zur Nationenwertung bei. Mit 11,01 Fehlerpunkten nach drei Runden bringen die Niederländer ihren Weltmeistertitel sicher ins Ziel.

Mehr als zwei Abwürfe trennen sie vom Verfolger USA. Auch die Amerikaner müssen auf ihr Konto nach dem zweiten Umlauf nur vier Fehlerpunkte hinzurechnen. McLain Ward und Beezie Madden bleiben fehlerfrei, Margie Engle trifft eine Stange, Laura Kraut liefert mit zwei Fehlern das Streichergebnis.

So knapp wie noch nie geht das Rennen um die Bronzemedaille aus. Eine hundertstel Sekunde trennen am Ende das deutsche und das ukrainische Team. Die Schicksalsreiterin heißt Katharina Offel. Sie geht als Schlussreiterin der Ukraine an den Start. Bleibt sie fehlerfrei, bekommt ihr Team die Bronzemedaille. So viel steht schon bei ihrem Einritt fest. Die Neu-Ukrainerin reitet konzentriert, berührt keine Stange, aber lässt sich zu viel Zeit: ein Zeitfehler. Ein Zeitfehler, der die Ukraine von den Medaillenplätzen drängt. „Meine Teamkollegen haben mir beim Einreiten zugerufen: Egal, was Du machst, wir haben unsere Olympiaqualifikation. Das war für uns das Wichtigste", freut sich Offel trotzdem. Die ersten fünf Teams der WM haben ihr Ticket für Hongkong sicher in der Tasche. Nach der Ukraine hat das noch die Schweiz mit dem fünften Platz geschafft.

Jeroan Dubbeldam und Gerco Schröder – springen und jubeln WM-Gold entgegen.
Jeroen Dubbeldam and Gerco Schröder – jump with joy at winning gold.

McLain Ward – wertvoller Punktesammler für die USA auf dem Weg zu Teamsilber.
McLain Ward – collected valuable points for the USA on the way to team silver.

ment, when Zoer lost his stirrup and promptly had a fence down, then after finding his stirrup again, he finished the course without a further fault. The final rider Gerco Schröder with his 12-year-old Holstein stallion Berlin contributed to the team result with a double clear round (one of three overall). After three rounds the Dutch team took a secure hold of the World Championships title with an overall score of 11.01 faults. More than eight faults separated them from the Vice-World Champions, the USA. The Americans only added four faults to their score in the second round of the Nation's Cup. McLain Ward and Beezie Madden rode clear, Margie Engle had once fence down, and Laura Kraut was the scratch result with eight faults.

The battle for bronze was closer than ever. One hundredths of a second separated the Germans and the Ukraines in the end. It was all down to Katharina Offel. She was the last member of the Ukraine team. If she had ridden clear, her team would have taken bronze. She concentrated hard, didn't touch a pole, but took far too much time: one time fault. A time fault that cost the Ukraines the medal. "My team colleagues called to me as I rode in: It doesn't matter what happens, we have already qualified for the Olympic Games. That was our main goal," Offel said happily. The first five teams in the World Championships already have their tickets for Hong Kong. Together with the Ukraine this also applies for Switzerland who came fifth overall.

Springen | Jumping

Die totale Tragik oder die Rettung der Ehre

Das deutsche Team ist als Favorit nach Aachen gereist. Fast schon erschreckend dominant waren sie in der Saison 2006 – sowohl mit Einzelerfolgen als auch mit dem Team, wie den drei Siegen bei Superliga-Nationenpreisen. Am Ende bleibt ihnen in Aachen die Bronzemedaille.

Dabei ist auch noch am Anfang der zweiten Nationenpreisrunde alles möglich. Ludger Beerbaum und L'Espoir vollbringen, was keiner im Vorfeld erwartet hat: Doppel-Null im Nationenpreis. Der Superprofi spielt seine ganze Routine aus und zaubert zwei stilistische Runden aus dem Lehrbuch aufs WM-Parkett. Christian Ahlmann und Cöster kassieren einen Abwurf, Meredith Michaels-Beerbaum und Shutterfly bleiben souverän ohne Fehler. Alles kommt jetzt auf Marcus Ehning und Noltes Küchengirl an. Auf die beiden, die wenige Wochen zuvor im selben Aachener Stadion ihren fantastischen Sieg im Großen Preis gefeiert haben. Bleiben die beiden fehlerfrei, ist immer noch die Silbermedaille drin. Schon bei den ersten Sprüngen fehlt der Stute die sonstige Überlegenheit am Sprung, an der Mauer in Gestalt der Aachener Sonderbriefmarke ist Schluss. Küchengirl springt einfach nicht mehr ab und fällt in die Mauer. 48.000 Zuschauer im Stadion halten den Atem an. Fassungslosigkeit macht sich breit. Marcus Ehning, seit Monaten die Nummer eins der Welt, der Topfavorit für die WM, gibt auf. Er macht deutlich, was alle wissen und oft vergessen: Auch Topstars haben Nerven. „Mit meinem Fehler im Zeitspringen am ersten Tag habe ich alles verhauen. Davon hat sich Küchengirl nicht wieder erholt." Sein Jahr habe fantastisch begonnen, er habe eine tolle Saison gehabt, aber immer schon versucht, die Euphorie, die seiner Person entgegenschlug, flach zu halten. Und nun war tatsächlich alles anders gekommen als erwartet. Tapfer und echt Sportsmann fügt er hinzu: „Morgen geht mein Leben weiter, ich habe noch was zu essen im Kühlschrank und tolle Pferde im Stall. Ich werde mich jetzt nicht in einer Ecke verkriechen."

Total tragedy or saving one's face

The German team arrived in Aachen as the top favourites. They had been frighteningly dominant throughout the entire 2006 season – individually and as a team, as the three victories in the Super League – Nations' Cups had shown. In the end they claimed bronze in Aachen.

Even though everything had been still wide open when the second round of the Nations' Cup kicked off. Ludger Beerbaum and L'Espoir managed a double clear in the Nations' Cup, which nobody had reckoned with beforehand. The top professional put his entire experience to use and conjured up two stylish exemplary rounds on the WEG platform. Christian Ahlmann and Cöster collected four faults, Meredith Michaels-Beerbaum and Shutterfly didn't pick up any jumping faults. Everything was down to Marcus Ehning and Nolte's Küchengirl. Down to the pair, who had celebrated their fantastic victory in the Grand Prix of Aachen in the same stadium only weeks previously. If they had jumped clear, Germany could have still claimed the silver medal. Even at the first jump, the mare's immense jumping potential was missing, then suddenly it was all over at the wall designed in the format of a stamp. Küchengirl simply didn't take off and literally fell into the wall. 48,000 spectators in the stadium held their breath. The world was speechless. Marcus Ehning, who had ranked number one in the world for months, who had been the top favourite for the World Championship title, retired. He pointed out something that everyone is aware of, but often forgets: Even top stars get nervous. "I ruined everything with my mistake in the speed competition. Küchengirl didn't get over it." He explained that the year had got off to a fantastic start, he had had a great season, but had always tried to dampen the euphoria that surrounded him. And now things had really taken a different turn. Bravely the real sportsman added: "Tomorrow my life goes on, I have got food in my fridge and brilliant horses in my stables. So I won't be crawling into a corner yet."

Wenn Favoriten stürzen – das Aus an der Mauer für Marcus Ehning und Noltes Küchengirl.
When favourites fall – everything came to an end at the wall for Marcus Ehning and Noltes Küchengirl.

FEI World Equestrian Games Aachen 2006

Die Silbersträuße fest in der Hand – das Team USA.
The flowers for the silver medallists still firmly in their hands – the US team.

Im gebremsten Jubel – das deutsche Team auf dem Bronzerang.
Reserved joy – the German team in third place to take bronze.

Runde der 25 Besten

Die Selektion
Parcoursbegehung – mit Hans Günter Winkler

The 25 best

The selection
Course inspection – with Hans Günter Winkler

Runde der 25 Besten, Runde A
Round of the best 25, Round A

Parcoursdaten/ Course Data:	
Länge/ Length:	540 m
Geschwindigkeit/ Speed:	400 m/min
Erlaubte Zeit/ Time limit:	81 Sec
Hindernisse/ Obstacles:	12
Sprünge/ Efforts:	15

Hindernis Nr./ Obstacle-No.	Höhe/ height	Breite/ width
1	148	150
2	159	
3	150	180
4	450	
5	163	
6	152	180
7	160	120
8a	157	
8b	153	170
8c	153	180
9	166	
10a	153	185
10b	155	
11	160	
12	153	200

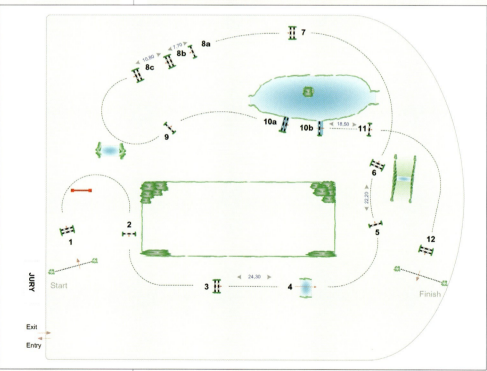

Die erste Runde der besten 25 beginnt mit einem großen Oxer vom Ausgang weg. In enger Rechtswendung geht es auf einen Steilsprung zu, es folgt eine längere Galoppstrecke auf einen naturfarbenen Karree-Oxer, darunter ein Graben mit hellem Sand. „Hier muss man aufpassen. Auf dem Weg zu dem Oxer dürfen die Pferde nicht auseinander fallen. Weil es sich hier um einen Karree-Oxer handelt, sehen die Pferde beim Absprung die hintere Stange noch nicht. Man muss sie also in der Luft mit Schenkel und Körper animieren, damit sie genug Fliegkraft entwickeln und nicht die hintere Stange mitnehmen." Mit fünf bis sechs Galoppsprüngen geht es zum Wassergraben. Mit 4,50 m ist er 30 Zenti-

The first round of the best 25 began with a big oxer away from the exit. The track continued on a tight right bend to an upright followed by a longer canter stretch approaching a natural-coloured parallel oxer, with a sand-filled ditch underneath. "You have to be careful here. You mustn't let the horses get too long on the way to the oxer. Because it is a parallel oxer, the horses don't see the pole at the back when they take off. So you have to animate them on the way up with your leg and body, so that they develop enough flight and don't knock the back pole." The water jump is reached in five or six strides. 4.5 m wide – 30 cm more than in the competitions so far. "You mustn't make the

meter breiter als in den Springen bisher. „Man darf nicht den Fehler machen, dass man schon über dem Oxer an das Wasser denkt. Man muss unbedingt erst den Sprung zu Ende machen." Im Bogen geht es zu Sprung Nummer fünf, ein Steilsprung in Bogenform. „Mit gehorsamen Pferden wird man versuchen, etwas rechts oder links von der Mitte zu springen, weil der Sprung da nicht so hoch ist." Es folgen zwei weitere Karree-Oxer. „Das sind sehr respektable Einzelsprünge." Jetzt geht es in die dreifache Kombination. Der Einsprung ist ein Steilsprung mit einer Naturplanke in flachen Auflagen. „Das ist schwierig, eine echte Weltmeisterschafts-Herausforderung." Es folgen zwei weitere Karree-Oxer, 8b und 8c. „Man darf nur an den Einsprung denken, dann hat man automatisch die richtige Distanz für die anderen. Sobald das Pferd landet, muss man sofort wieder das Gewicht auf die Hinterhand bekommen. Das ist wie ein Schaukelsystem." Sprung 9 ist ein schmaler Steilsprung, mit 1,66 m der höchste Sprung des Parcours. Die Kombination 10 a/b führt über die überbauten Wassergräben, dieses Mal in Bergabrichtung. „Diese Sprünge gibt es hier seit 30 Jahren – die haben immer ihre Opfer gefordert", betont Winkler. Nach drei Galoppsprüngen erwartet die Reiter ein weiterer Steilsprung. „Das ist eine Herausforderung an die Rittigkeit der Pferde. Da müssen Gas und Bremse funktionieren." Schlusssprung der ersten Runde: wieder ein Karree-Oxer mit der sagenhaften Breite von zwei Metern. „Das ist ein Kurs vom ersten bis zum letzten Sprung mit Höchstmaß-Anforderungen. Hier wird noch einmal richtig selektiert."

Runde zwei ist mit neun Hindernissen und elf Sprüngen etwas kürzer, aber die Abmessungen bleiben im Höchstmaßbereich. Auf gebogener Linie geht es von Steilsprung 1 zu Oxer 2. Der Oxer ist schmal, die Stangen kürzer. „Da muss man aufpassen. Diese Stangen fallen schneller." Es folgen nach einer Rechtskurve die Sprünge 3 und 4, Oxer, Steil, und auf gebogener Linie noch einmal Steil und Oxer. „Alle Sprünge sind einzelne Jokersprünge. Jeder Reiter muss selbst entscheiden, wie weit er die gebogenen Linien anlegt, aber er muss immer im Rhythmus bleiben und immer die Zeit im Kopf haben." Für die Schlusslinie des fünften WM-Parcours hat sich Parcoursbauer Frank Rothenberger etwas Besonderes einfallen lassen. Die dreifache Kombination Tripplebarre-Oxer-Steilsprung schimmert in goldfarbenem Glanz-Outfit. „Auf die Tripplebarre mit zwei Metern Breite muss man vorwärts reiten – aber ohne dass die Pferde flach werden. Es geht außerdem etwas bergauf. Für diese Kombination muss man die Pferde zusammenschieben wie einen Flitzebogen." Auf gerader Linie geht es nach der Dreifachen über einen weiteren Oxer und einen Steilsprung zum Ziel. „Achtung – wenn man bis hier null war, ist die Versuchung groß, nachlässig zu werden. Und dann auch noch in Richtung Ausgang."

Das WM-Kompliment

„Der Parcoursbauer Frank Rothenberger hat hier ein Meisterstück abgeliefert", lobt Hans Günter Winkler den Chef der Aachener WM-Parcours – und er spricht im Namen aller Reiter. „Rothenberger hat es geschafft, Reiter aus den unterschiedlichsten Zeitzonen und Ländern erstklassig zu präsentieren." Tatsächlich hat es bei den 116 Startern nur sehr wenige unschöne Bilder gegeben. Frank Rothenberger hat den

mistake of thinking about the water while you are jumping the oxer. It is essential that you finish each jump first." A curved line took the riders to jump 5, an arched upright. "Riders with obedient horses will try to jump to the left or the right where it is not so high." This was followed by two further parallel oxers. "These are respectable individual fences." Then it was on to the triple combination. The first upright had a natural coloured plank with flat safety cups. "This is difficult, a worthy World Championships challenge." 8b and 8c were two further parallel oxers. "You are only allowed to think about the first fence, then you will automatically have the right approach for the other two. As soon as the horse lands you have to get the weight back on the hindlegs. It is like the swing principle.2 Jump 9 was a narrow upright measuring 1,66 m, the highest jump in the course. The combination 10 a/b led over the water ditches, this time downhill. „These jumps have been here for 30 years – and they have always found their victims," underlined Winkler. A further upright was waiting for the riders three canter strides later. "This challenges the rideability of the horses. The gas and the brakes have to work." The final jump in the first round: Another parallel oxer with a two metre spread. "This is a course of maximum demands from the first to the last fence. This is a true selection process."

Round two *was slightly shorter with nine obstacles and eleven jumps, but they still displayed maximum dimensions. A curved line took the riders from upright 1 to oxer jump no. 2. The oxer was narrower, the poles shorter. "You have to be careful here. The rails fall quickly." After a right-hand bend, 3 and 4, oxer, upright and on a curved line another upright and an oxer. "All of the jumps are individual joker jumps. Each rider has to make his own decision, how flat or who wide his curved line must be, and he always has to retain his rhythm and keep an eye on the clock." Course builder Frank Rothenberger had come up with something special for the final line of the fifth WEG course. The triple combination triple barre/oxer/upright had a shiny gold-coloured outfit. "You have to have enough forward impulsion for the 2 m wide triple barre – but you mustn't let the horses jump too flat. And not to forget it is slightly uphill. For this combination you really have to shorten your horse to attain that arched bow effect." After the triple combination it was a straight line to a further oxer and an upright to the finish. "Careful if you are clear up until now, you often get careless. Particularly when you are heading towards the exit."*

The World Championships compliment

"The course builder Frank Rothenberger accomplished a master piece here," Hans Günter Winkler praised the course designer of the Aachen World Championships – also in the name of all of the riders. "Rothenberger has succeeded in presenting the riders from the different time zones and countries in an excellent light." It is true that there were very few ugly scenes among the 116 competitors. Frank Rothenberger had managed to do the balancing act between all of the demands that World Championships courses have to fulfil: Appropriate for all and nevertheless selective. Challenging to horse and rider, but not over demanding. Doing justice to the sponsors and media as well

Frank Rothenberger

FEI World Equestrian Games Aachen 2006

Mit Top-Leistungen knapp am Finale vorbei –
Ludger Beerbaum und L'Espoir.
*Showed top performances, but just missed the Final –
Ludger Beerbaum and L'Espoir.*

as to the spectators in the stadium. The 48-year-old course builder received nothing but praise for his World Championships premiere – from all over the nations.

A tragic end to history

Dreams burst and the unexpected becomes true. Hans Günter Winkler was right with his appraisal: the two last rounds before the final really shook the field up. The first three were separated by less than four faults, Ludger Beerbaum was in third place, followed by twelve pairs that were separated by even less than four faults, including Meredith Michaels-Beerbaum in sixth place.

The Spanish rider Ricardo Jurado opened up the round of the best 25 and finished on eight faults. Samantha McIntosh who rides for New Zealand picked up three jumping faults and a time fault. The only French rider under the best 25, Hervé Godignon, retired after two jumping faults. It soon became clear that this course was a championship challenge. The big surprise came after Edwina Alexander's (AUS) round. At first the unimaginable value of her clear round wasn't given the due credit. The 48,000 spectators had to wait another 14 rides to see the next clear round – from the Belgian rider Jos Lansink on his 13-year-old Holstein stallion Cumano. The team Olympic gold medallist Otto Becker was also on the press stand, recruited for Aachen by ZDF as co-presented: "I think a lot of rider mistakes are being made here out of respect for the dimensions."

Die Stangen verachtend – Cumano unter Jos Lansink.
Scoffed at the rails – Cumano ridden by Jos Lansink.

SPRINGEN | JUMPING

Spagat geschafft zwischen all den Anforderungen, die WM-Kurse erfüllen müssen: Passend für alle und trotzdem selektierend. Pferde und Reiter fordernd, aber nicht überfordernd. Sponsoren und Medien ebenso wie den Zuschauern im Stadion gerecht werdend. Bei seiner WM-Premiere als Parcoursbauer erntet der 48-Jährige nur Lob – quer durch alle Nationen.

Der Sport hat der Geschichte ein tragisches Ende gegeben

Träume platzen und Ungeahntes wird wahr. Hans Günter Winkler behält mit seiner Einschätzung Recht: die beiden letzten Runden vor dem Finale würfeln das Feld noch einmal durcheinander. Die ersten Drei liegen bisher weniger als einen Fehler auseinander, darunter Ludger Beerbaum auf Platz drei. Dann kommen zwölf Paare von Platz vier bis 15, die ebenfalls weniger als ein Abwurf trennt, darunter Meredith Michaels-Beerbaum auf Platz sechs.

Der Spanier Ricardo Jurado eröffnet die Runde der besten 25 und beendet seinen Parcours mit acht Fehlerpunkten. Die für Neuseeland reitende Samantha McIntosh kassiert drei Abwürfe und einen Zeitfehler. Und der einzige Franzose in der 25er Runde, Hervé Godignon, gibt nach zwei Abwürfen auf. Schon wird deutlich, dass dieser Kurs noch einmal eine weltmeisterliche Herausforderung ist. Die Überraschung folgt mit der fünften Starterin, der Australierin Edwina Alexander. Noch weiß man den unvorstellbaren Wert ihrer Nullrunde nicht zu schätzen. Erst 14 Reiter später erleben die 48.000 Zuschauer den nächsten fehlerfreien Ritt – von dem Belgier Jos Lansink auf seinem 13-jährigen Holsteiner Hengst Cumano. Auf der Pressetribüne sitzt auch Mannschafts-Olympiasieger Otto Becker, in Aachen als Co-Moderator vom ZDF engagiert: „Ich glaube, hier werden viele Reiterfehler aus Respekt vor den Abmessungen gemacht."

14.50 Uhr: Nach Lansinks Nullrunde reitet Meredith Michaels-Beerbaum in den Parcours. Shutterfly springt erstklassig. Dann kommt der Wassergraben. Zwischen Oxer und Wassergraben haben die meisten Reiter fünf Galoppsprünge gemacht, einige auch sechs. Aber Meredith Michaels-Beerbaum nimmt so sehr das Tempo raus, dass sie mit sieben Galoppsprüngen und zu wenig Schwung an den 4,50 m breiten Graben kommt: Fehler! Wie schon im Nationenpreis kassiert sie noch einen Zeitfehler dazu. Enttäuschung macht sich breit und trotzdem jubeln die Fans. Noch ist der Sprung ins Finale möglich. Es folgt der US-Amerikaner McLain Ward, der einst für das CHIO Aachen gesperrt war, weil man bei ihm kleine Plastikteilchen unter den Gamaschen seines Pferdes entdeckt hatte. Ward galt mit seiner Stute Sapphire als einer der Favoriten. Zwei Abwürfe entfernen ihn von allen Hoffnungen. Ebenso ergeht es dem Olympiasieger von 2000, Jeroen Dubbeldam. Der drittletzte Starter, Ludger Beerbaum, reitet ein. Souve-

2.50 p.m.: After Lansink's faultless round, Meredith Michaels-Beerbaum entered the ring. Shutterfly jumped first rate. Then came the water ditch, where most riders had taken five strides between the oxer and the water, some even six. But Meredith Michaels-Beerbaum collected her horse so much that she did seven strides and didn't have enough impulse for the 4,50 m wide ditch: Four faults! As in the Nations' Cup she also picked up an additional time fault. The disappointment spread and still the fans cheered. It was still possible for her to reach the finale. She was followed by the American rider, McLain Ward, who had once been banned from the CHIO in Aachen, because small plastic pieces had been discovered inside his brushing boots. Ward was considered one of the favourites with his mare Sapphire. Two jumping faults divided him from all his dreams. The same applied for the Olympic gold medallist of 2000, Jeroen Dubbeldam. The third last competitor, Ludger Beerbaum, rode in. The 43-year-old mastered the first seven jumps souvereignly, then the triple combination loomed. The 1.7 m wide oxer in the middle of the combination sealed Beerbaum and L'Espoir's fate – the pole fell. They mastered the rest of the course without further faults. Gerco Schröder didn't leave the course clear either: eight faults. Beezie Madden, with a clean sheet up until then got wet feet at the water ditch.

German chances

After the first round of the 25 best things were looking pretty different: With her clear round, one of just two, Edwina Alexander had worked her way up to sixth place. Meredith Michaels-Beerbaum had moved up to fifth place, Jos Lansink with the second clear round from seventh to second place. Beezie Madden was still in the lead and Ludger Beerbaum had managed to stay in third position. He still had the chance of taking the one title that was missing from his list of victories: individual World Cham-

Die Überraschung – Australierin Edwina Alexander auf dem Weg von Platz 22 ins Finale.
The big surprise – the Australian rider Edwina Alexander made her way from 22nd place into the Final.

Ergebnisse/Results Seite/page 134/135

rän meistert der 43-Jährige die ersten sieben Sprünge, dann kommt die dreifache Kombination. Der 1,70 m breite Oxer in der Mitte der Kombination wird dem Paar Beerbaum/L'Espoir zum Verhängnis – ein Abwurf. Den Rest bewältigen sie fehlerfrei. Auch Gerco Schröder verlässt den Parcours nicht ohne Fehler: zwei Abwürfe. Beezie Madden, bisher ohne jeden Fehlerpunkt auf ihrem Konto, bekommt nasse Füße am Wassergraben.

Deutsche Chancen bleiben

Nach dem ersten Umlauf der 25-Besten-Runde sieht einiges anders aus: Edwina Alexander hat sich mit einer von nur zwei Nullrunden in diesem Umlauf von Platz 21 auf sechs katapultiert, Meredith Michaels-Beerbaum ist von sechs auf fünf gerutscht, Jos Lansink mit der zweiten Nullrunde von sieben auf zwei. Beezie Madden bleibt in Führung und Ludger Beerbaum hat seinen dritten Platz behauptet. Noch hält er die Chance in den Händen, endlich den einzigen Titel, der ihm noch fehlt, zu ergattern: Den Einzeltitel bei einer Weltmeisterschaft. Gerco Schröder hat sich von Platz zwei auf vier gesprungen und der zweite Topreiter der Niederländer, Dubbeldam, ist aus den vier Finalplätzen auf den achten Platz abgerutscht. Dennoch: Die ersten Drei sind noch immer weniger als einen Springfehler auseinander, die nächsten Fünf ebenso. Es ist eine Hommage an Parcoursbauer Frank Rothenberger.

Die Entscheidung

Endlich – nach fünf spannenden und an den Nerven zehrenden Tagen in der Soers steht die entscheidende Runde bevor: Wer kommt ins Finale?
Der zweite Umlauf des Finalspringens beginnt. Edwina Alexander gelingt eine weitere Nullrunde. Meredith Michaels-Beerbaum kommt nach der Australierin in den Parcours und auch sie bleibt fehlerfrei. Gerco Schröder leistet sich einen Abwurf und damit ist

pion. Gerco Schröder had jumped from second into fourth place and the second Dutch top rider, Dubbeldam, had slipped from under the first four down to eighth place. And yet the first three riders were still only four faults apart as were the next five too. Homage to the course builder Frank Rothenberger.

The deciding round

Finally – after five exciting rounds and nerve-racking days at the Soers it was time for the deciding round: Who would reach the Final?
The second round of the decider began. Edwina Alexander rode clear again. Meredith Michaels-Beerbaum followed her into ring and she too rode clear. Gerco Schröder had four faults, which meant one lady was definitely going to be in the Final – Meredith Michaels-Beerbaum.
Ludger Beerbaum rode into the stadium just as the commentator announced this joyous piece of news. The stadium cheered ecstatically and then fell silent in suspense. Beerbaum's dreams were shattered at the third jump. Jos Lansink and Beezie Madden both jumped clear. Which meant Edwina Alexander was in the Final. From 22nd place to under the best four – the 32-year-old was shocked: "I had already packed my cases, because I was planning on going home this evening. I never imagined I'd make it. This is a wonderful shock for me!" Ludger Beerbaum only managed to take fifth place – exactly the same as in Rome in 1998. "Better fifth than fourth in the Final," the rider from Riesenbeck had once judged. And he knows what he is talking about. He was namely fourth at The Hague in 1994. But his disappointment was enormous. "It is terribly shit that I am not in the Final," and everyone had understanding for his choice of wording. The way up to and in Aachen had been so long and hard for the head of the German team. He had wiped away so much doubt and criticism with his two superb clear rounds. He had steered his 10-year-old sports colleague L'Espoir so master-

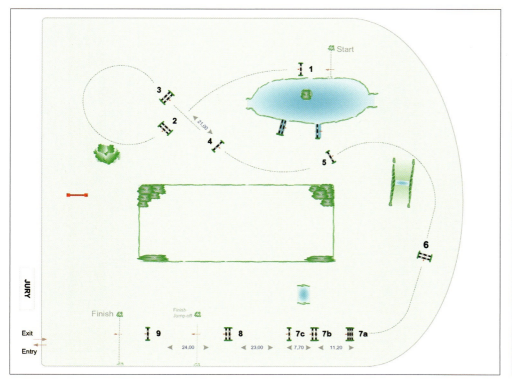

Runde der 25 Besten, Runde B
Round of the best 25, Round B

Parcoursdaten/ Course Data:	
Länge/ Length:	430 m
Geschwindigkeit/ Speed:	400 m/min
Erlaubte Zeit/ Time limit:	65 Sec
Hindernisse/ Obstacles:	9
Sprünge/ Efforts:	11

Hindernis Nr./ Obstacle-No.	Höhe/ height	Breite/ width
1	155	
2	153	180
3	150	180
4	165	
5	160	
6	155	190
7a	155	190
7b	155	100
7c	160	
8	152	180
9	165	

SPRINGEN | JUMPING

klar: Im Finale wird eine Frau dabei sein – Meredith Michaels-Beerbaum.

Ludger Beerbaum reitet just in dem Moment in das Stadion, in dem der Stadionsprecher diese frohe Botschaft verkündet. Das Stadion tobt, um dann in gespannte Ruhe zu verfallen. Schon am dritten Sprung ist Beerbaums Traum vorbei – ein Abwurf. Jos Lansink und Beezie Madden bleiben wieder fehlerfrei. Danach steht fest: Edwina Alexander ist im Finale. Von Platz 22 unter die besten Vier – die 32-Jährige ist geschockt: „Ich hatte die Koffer schon gepackt, weil ich heute Abend nach Hause fahren wollte. Ich hätte nie damit gerechnet. Für mich ist das ein herrlicher Schock!" Aber für Ludger Beerbaum bleibt nur der fünfte Platz – wie schon 1998 in Rom. „Lieber Fünfter als Vierter im Finale", so hatte der Riesenbecker schon einmal geurteilt. Und er weiß, wovon er spricht. 1994 in Den Haag war er Vierter. Aber die Enttäuschung ist enorm. „Das ist eine riesengroße Scheiße, dass ich nicht im Finale dabei bin", und jeder hat Verständnis für die Härte seiner Wortwahl. So lang und stolprig war für den Kopf des deutschen Teams der Weg bis und in Aachen. So viel Zweifel und Kritik hatte er mit seinen herrlichen Nullrunden für das deutsche Team weggefegt. So erstklassig hatte er seinen zehnjährigen Sportkollegen L'Espoir durch die WM-Parcours geführt. Das Finale wäre ein herrlicher Lohn gewesen, aber der Sport hat die Geschichte mit anderem Ausgang, mit fast tragischem Ende für Ludger Beerbaum geschrieben.

fully around the course. The Final would have been a handsome reward, but the history of sport had written a different final chapter and almost tragic one for Ludger Beerbaum.

„Die nächste WM ist in vier Jahren. L'Espoir ist dann im besten Alter, aber ich bin dann schon ein Grenzfall." (grinsend LUDGER BEERBAUM, er wäre dann 47)

"The next World Championships will be in four years. L'Espoir will be in his best years then, but I will already be a border case by then." (LUDGER BEERBAUM said with a grin, in 4 years he will be 47)

„Das ist schon eine Riesenenttäuschung. Wenn einem so kurz vor dem Loch der Ball liegen bleibt." (LUDGER BEERBAUM)

"It is such a huge disappointment. When the ball stops just short of the hole." (LUDGER BEERBAUM)

Ohne einen einzigen Fehler an der Stange bis zum Final-Stechen – Meredith Michaels-Beerbaum und Shutterfly im WM-Parcours.
Not one jumping fault until the final jump-off – Meredith Michaels-Beerbaum and Shutterfly in the World Championships course.

FEI World Equestrian Games Aachen 2006

Das Finale / The Final
Allein unter Frauen / Alone with the ladies

Finale Einzelwertung – Springen
Final Individual – Jumping

Parcoursdaten / Course Data:

Länge / Length:	380 m
Geschwindigkeit / Speed:	400 m/min
Erlaubte Zeit / Time limit:	57 Sec
Hindernisse / Obstacles:	8
Sprünge / Efforts:	10

Hindernis Nr. / Obstacle-No.	Höhe / height	Breite / width
1	145	150
2	156	
3	150	160
4a	154	
4b	150	160
4b	157	
5	150	170
6	160	
7	156	
8	152	170

So ein WM-Finale hat es noch nicht gegeben. Es ist eine herrliche Mischung der Geschlechter und Nationen am Start: Der Belgier Jos Lansink allein unter drei Frauen, Meredith Michaels-Beerbaum, der Amerikanerin Beezie Madden und der Australierin Edwina Alexander. Am Vorabend des Finals sind sich alle einige: Die Pferde der drei Frauen sind alle ähnlich zu reiten – flink, handlich, wendig. Dagegen steht der Riese Cumano, wuchtig und massiv.

Mit acht Hindernissen und zehn Sprüngen, darunter eine dreifache Kombination, hat Parcoursbauer Frank Rothenberger wieder einen WM-würdigen Kurs aufgebaut, wenn auch etwas niedriger als an den Vortagen. Es ist verblüffend: Obwohl Pferden und Reitern schon fünf schwere Runden in den Knochen stecken und die Reiter nur drei Minuten Zeit haben, sich auf die Fremdpferde einzustellen, passiert in allen 16 Runden nur ein einziger Fehler. Edwina Alexander erwischt mit Shutterfly eine Stange in der dreifachen Kombination. „Einer musste ja Vierter werden. Unglücklicherweise war ich das. Aber ich bin sowieso schon wahnsinnig glücklich, dass ich unter die letzten Vier gekommen bin." Alle anderen Ritte bleiben fehlerfrei. Das ist einzigartig in der Geschichte des Springsports.

Such a World Championships Final had never been experienced before. A wonderful mixture of sexes and nations: The Belgian Jos Lansink alone against three ladies, Meredith Michaels-Beerbaum, the American Beezie Madden and the Australian Edwina Alexander. On the eve of the Final everyone is in agreement: The horses of the ladies are all similar to ride – nimble, compact, and agile. In contract the huge Cumano, who is well-built and solid.

The course designed, Frank Rothenberger, had built another worthy course comprising of eight obstacles and ten fences, including a triple combination, even if it was a little lower than on the previous days. It was astonishing: Although the horses and riders had already completed five difficult rounds and the riders only had three minutes to get used to the new horses, there was only one jumping fault in all 16 rounds. Edwina Alexander knocked one of the rails in the triple combination with Shutterfly. "One of us had to come fourth. Unfortunately it was me. But I am incredibly happy to have made it under the final four." All other rounds were clear. That is unique in the history of show-jumping. Meredith Michaels-Beerbaum swarmed that she had felt comfortable on all of the other horses, but had enjoyed riding, Authentic, Beezie Madden's horse best. Jos Lansink admitted: "Authentic wasn't really my type." And Beezie Madden was impressed by Shutterfly: "I felt really at home on him."

Eine Dame, vier Final-Partner: Meredith Michaels-Beerbaum auf Shutterfly, Cumano, Pialotta und Authentic (v. li.).
One lady, four partners in the Final: Meredith Michaels-Beerbaum on Shutterfly, Cumano, Pialotta and Authentic (f.t.l.).

SPRINGEN | JUMPING

Meredith Michaels-Beerbaum schwärmt, sie habe sich auf allen drei Fremdpferden wohl gefühlt, am meisten habe ihr das Pferd von Beezie Madden gelegen, Authentic. Jos Lansink gesteht: „Authentic war nicht so mein Typ." Und Beezie Madden ist von Shutterfly begeistert: „Auf ihm habe ich mich unheimlich gut gefühlt."

Der einen hilft die Wasserflasche, der anderen der Zeigefinger – Meredith Michaels-Beerbaum und Beezie Madden beim Pferdewechsel.
One needed a water bottle, the other an index finger – Meredith Michaels-Beerbaum and Beezie Madden during the rotation of horses.

Mit der reinen Bilanz von null Fehlern müssen also drei Reiter ins Stechen. Gestochen wird über denselben Parcours mit den eigenen Pferden. Jos Lansink muss als Erster an den Start. Zügig, aber nicht übertrieben dreht er eine sichere Nullrunde. „Ich weiß, Cumano ist nicht der Schnellste, also habe ich versucht, eine fehlerfreie Runde zu drehen, um den anderen etwas Druck zu machen." Der Plan geht auf: Beide Damen leisten sich einen Abwurf. Zu schnell und flach kommt Meredith Michaels-Beerbaum an Sprung 3, einen Oxer, und nimmt die vordere Stange mit. „Ich wusste schon vor dem Stechen, dass das schwierig wird mit Shutterfly. Er war von dem Reiterwechsel so aufgeregt und nervös. Das waren nicht die besten Voraussetzungen, um ein gutes Stechen zu reiten." Sie habe ihn vor dem Oxer nur ein bisschen an der Hand losgelassen ... „und er wollte so schnell wie möglich nach Hause." Shutterfly wird nach dem Finale schweißnass vom Platz geführt. Er ist durch das ständige Umsatteln in dem Stadion und den Reiterwechsel total verunsichert und kaum noch zu halten. Nur mit Mühe haben Kurt Gravemeier und Markus Beerbaum überhaupt noch den Sattel auf den Hannoveraner bekommen.

Beezie Madden macht es noch einmal spannend. Sie dreht eine phänomenale Runde mit Authentic, sprintet dem letzten Oxer entgegen und die Stangen fallen. Sie ist fast eineinhalb Sekunden schneller als Lansink, aber der letzte Sprung kostet sie die Goldmedaille. Jos Lansink wird mit dem einzigen Null-Fehlerritt im Stechen Weltmeister – es ist der erste Spring-Weltmeister für Belgien. Beezie Madden bekommt Silber und Meredith Michaels-Beerbaum ihre zweite Bronzemedaille bei den Weltmeisterschaften 2006.

Schnell im Stechen bis zum Schlusssprung – dann kullert Gold dahin: Beezie Madden auf Authentic.
Fast in the jump-off up until the last fence – then all hopes of a gold medal were shattered: Beezie Madden on Authentic.

Since all three riders had still not picked up a single fault there was a jump-off over the same course, this time on their own horses again. Jos Lansink had to go first. He accomplished a fast, clear round, without taking too many risks. "I know that Cumano is not the fastest, so I tried to ride clear to put the others under pressure." His plan worked: Both ladies had one fence down. Meredith Michaels-Beerbaum approached jump three, an oxer, too fast and too flat and took the first pole down. "Even before the jump-off I knew it was going to be difficult with Shutterfly. He was so worked up and nervous as a result of the change of riders. Not the best circumstances for riding a good jump-off." She explained that she had slackened the reins a bit in front of the oxer... "And he wanted to get home as quickly as possible." After the Final Shutterfly was lead from the arena covered in sweat. He was totally confused after being resaddled so often in the stadium and he was difficult to hold. Kurt Gravemeier and Markus Beerbaum had real difficulties even getting his saddle off. Beezie Madden made it exciting up to the very end. She rode a phenomenal round with Authentic, raced to the last oxer and the poles fell. She was almost one and a half seconds faster than Lansink, but the last jump had cost her the gold medal. Jos Lansink became World Champion with the only clear round in the jump-off – he is the first Belgian World Show-jumping Champion. Beezie Madden took silver and Meredith Michaels-Beerbaum her second bronze medal at the World Championships.

FEI World Equestrian Games Aachen 2006

Fazit – Springsport mit Gottschalk-Quoten

Eine Weltmeisterschaft kann nicht spannender und sportlicher sein. Erstklassig waren die Parcours, herausragend die Leistungen der Reiter, sensationell die Qualität der Pferde. Die tragischsten und herrlichsten Überraschungen, die nur der Pferdesport bieten kann, haben der Weltmeisterschaft der Springreiter 2006 ihre spezielle Würze gegeben. Mit 50.000 Zuschauern im Aachener Stadion hatte dieses Weltklasse-Erlebnis eine Weltklasse-Kulisse und mit 3,5 Millionen Fernseh-Zuschauern beim Nationenpreis hat der Reitsport die höchste Quote außerhalb der Olympia-Übertragungen erreicht. „Das sind schon fast Gottschalk-Quoten", freute sich FN-Generalsekretär Dr. Hanfried Haring.

Nach so viel Erfolg werden die Springreiter am Ende der WM mutig und werfen einen Lösungsvorschlag für den lange kritisierten Modus des WM-Finals mit Pferdewechsel in den Raum. „Es müsste nach der Runde der besten 25 einen eigenen Medaillensatz geben – für die besten Pferd und Reiter-Paare nach fünf Runden", schlägt Weltmeister Jos Lansink vor und seine Vize- und Bronze-Kollegen nicken. „Und nach dem Finale mit Pferdewechsel könnte es einen weiteren Medaillensatz geben. Die Dressurreiter verteilen ja auch zweimal ihre Einzelmedaillen." So wären zwei Fliegen mit einer Klappe geschlagen: Die sportliche Fairness mit Medaillensatz Nummer eins und das Spektakuläre mit Medaillensatz Nummer zwei. Meredith Michaels-Beerbaum setzt noch ein Tüpfelchen drauf: „Es würde auch reichen, wenn nur Drei in das Finale mit Pferdewechsel einziehen. Die Pferde müssten eine Runde weniger springen und es müsste kein Finalist ohne Medaille nach Hause."

Conclusion – Show-jumping sport with Gottschalk viewing quotas

A World Championships tournament cannot be more exciting and more sporting. The courses were first class, the riders' performances were excellent, the quality of the horses sensational. The most tragic and wonderful surprises, that only equestrian sport can offer gave the World Show-jumping Championships 2006 their special flavour. This world class experience had a world class setting with 50,000 spectators in the Aachen stadium and attracting 3.5 million TV viewers during the Nations' Cup, the equestrian sport achieved its highest viewing quota ever except for the broadcasts of the Olympic Games. "This almost equals Gottschalk's quotas," the FN General Secretary Dr. Hanfried Haring noted happily.

After so much success the show-jumpers were feeling courageous and put forward a solution for the long-criticised mode of the World Championships Final. "The round of the best 25 should be rewarded with its own medals, after all the horses and riders have already completed five rounds," suggested the World Champion Jos Lansink and his two fellow-medallists nodded in agreement. "And the Final with rotation of horses would be rewarded with a further set of medals. The dressage riders have also got two individual titles." This should enable two birds to be killed with one stone: Sporting fairness would be rewarded with the first medals and the spectacular element with the second medals. Meredith Michaels-Beerbaum went even further: "It would suffice if only three pairs went through to the rotation of horses. It would save the horses having to jump one round and none of the finalists would have to go home without a medal."

Der Goldjunge mit seinen drei Frauen – Weltmeister Jos Lansink mit Silbermedaillengewinnerin Beezie Madden (li.), Meredith Michaels-Beerbaum (Bronze) und der Viertplatzierten Edwina Alexander (re.).
The golden boy with his three ladies – World Champion Jos Lansink with silver medallist Beezie Madden (left), Meredith Michaels-Beerbaum (bronze) and Edwina Alexander who came fourth (right).

Gratulation von ganz oben für ganz oben – Bundeskanzlerin Dr. Angela Merkel und ALRV-Präsident Klaus Pavel gratulieren Weltmeister Jos Lansink.
Congratulations from the right up top for the very top – Federal Chancellor Angela Merkel and ALRV President, Klaus Pavel, congratulate the World Champion, Jos Lansink.

Weltmeister im und unter dem Sattel: Jos Lansink und Cumano – mit nur einem Springfehler in zehn Runden bestes Pferd der WM.
World Champions in and under the saddle: Jos Lansink and Cumano – with only one jumping fault in ten rounds, Cumano was the best show-jumping horse at the WEG.

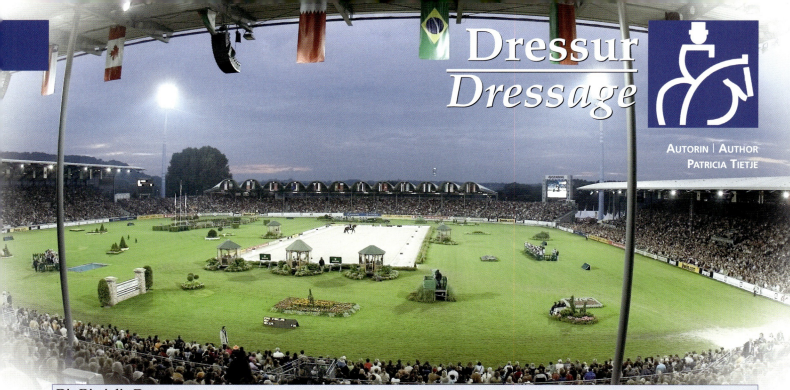

Dressur
Dressage

Autorin | Author
Patricia Tietje

Die Disziplin Dressur

Die Erfolgsbilanz der deutschen Dressurreiter ist beispiellos. In der 40-jährigen Geschichte der alle vier Jahre stattfindenden Dressur-Weltmeisterschaften erreicht das deutsche Team acht Mal die Goldmedaille. Lediglich 1970 in Aachen müssen die Deutschen den starken russischen Reiterinnen und Reitern Mannschafts-Gold überlassen und mit Silber vorlieb nehmen. In diesem Jahr sichert sich Liselott Linsenhoff mit Piaff hinter der Russin Elena Petushkova die Silbermedaille in der Einzelwertung. Schon die Premiere der Weltmeisterschaften 1966 in Bern dokumentiert die deutsche Vormachtstellung auf dem Viereck: Dr. Josef Neckermann geht mit Mariano als erster Dressur-Weltmeister in die Geschichte ein. Das Team mit Neckermann/Antoinette, Dr. Reiner Klimke/Dux und Harry Boldt/Remus gewinnt Mannschafts-Gold. In der Folgezeit reitet zweimal der erfolgreichste deutsche Olympionike, Dr. Reiner Klimke, zu Einzel-Gold: mit Mehmed 1974 in Kopenhagen und mit Ahlerich 1982 in Lausanne. In seine Fußstapfen treten später Nicole Uphoff mit Rembrandt (Weltmeisterin 1990), Isabell Werth mit Gigolo (Weltmeisterin 1994 und 1998) und Nadine Capellmann mit Farbenfroh (Weltmeisterin 2002). Der Austragungsmodus dieser Dressur-Weltmeisterschaft ist nicht mehr derselbe wie beim Championat vor vier Jahren. Der Weltverband FEI beschloss ein neues Reglement, dessen wichtigste Änderung die Vergabe von zwei Einzel-Goldmedaillen ist. Der Weg in die beiden Finals führt zunächst über den Grand Prix. Alle Teilnehmer – ob Einzelreiter oder Teams – starten in dieser Prüfung, die über zwei Tage ausgetragen wird. Der Grand Prix entscheidet wie bislang über die Vergabe der Mannschafts-Medaillen. Die besten 30 Reiter des Grand Prix qualifizieren sich für den Grand Prix Special. Dort beginnen die Teilnehmer wieder mit null Punkten. Anders als in der Vergangenheit werden die einzelnen Prüfungsergebnisse nicht mehr zu einem Gesamtergebnis addiert, sondern jeweils für sich gewertet. Der höchst benotete Reiter dieses Wettbewerbs wird Weltmeister im Grand Prix Special, die beiden nachfolgenden Teilnehmer erhalten Silber und Bronze. Die nächste Medaillenchance bietet die Grand Prix-Kür, für die sich die 15 besten Reiterinnen und Reiter des Grand Prix Specials qualifizieren. In der Kür beginnen sie ebenfalls wieder mit null Punkten und ermitteln den Kür-Weltmeister sowie den Silber- und Bronzemedaillengewinner. Wer überhaupt bei der Weltmeisterschaft starten darf, ist im FEI-Reglement genau festgelegt: Voraussetzung sind zwei Grand Prix-Prüfungen auf internationalen Dressurturnieren (CDI***), in denen der Reiter mit seinem Pferd in der Zeit vom 1. Januar 2005 bis zum 24. Juli 2006 mindestens 65 Prozent erreichte.

The Discipline Dressage

*The record of success of the German dressage riders is without equal. In the 40-year history of the World Dressage Championships, which are held every four years, the German team has won the gold medal eight times. Only in 1970 in Aachen had the Germans to concede the team gold to the strong Russian riders and make do with silver. In that year, Liselott Linsenhoff, on Piaff, secured the silver medal in the individual classification, coming behind the Russian Elena Petushkova. Even at the 1966 premiere of the World Championship in Berne, German supremacy in the dressage arena was evident: Dr. Josef Neckermann with Mariano made history as the first world dressage champion. The team with Neckermann/Antoinette, Dr. Reiner Klimke/Dux and Harry Boldt/Remus won team gold. In the following years, the most successful German Olympic rider, Dr. Reiner Klimke, won twice individual gold: in 1974 with Mehmed in Copenhagen and in 1982 with Ahlerich in Lausanne. Later, Nicole Uphoff with Rembrandt (1990 world champion), Isabell Werth with Gigolo (1994 and 1998 world champion) and Nadine Capellmann with Farbenfroh (2002 world champion) followed in his footsteps. The format of this World Championship has changed compared to four years ago. The FEI has introduced new rules, with the most important change being the award of two individual gold medals. The qualification for both finals is the Grand Prix. All participants – both individuals and team riders – compete in the Grand Prix, which takes place over two days. As previously, the Grand Prix decides the team medals. The 30 best riders from the Grand Prix qualify for the Grand Prix Special. The riders start again with a clean slate. Unlike in the past, the results of the individual tests are not added up to a total result, and the Grand Prix Special and the Grand Prix Kür (Freestyle to Music) are separate competitions. The rider with the highest marks in this competition becomes world champion in the Grand Prix Special, the subsequent two riders receive the silver and bronze medal respectively. The Grand Prix Kür offers another chance for a medal. The 15 best riders from the Special are allowed to compete in the final test, the Grand Prix Kür, where they will start again from scratch. The title of Kür world champion is contested for, and again three medals are awarded. The FEI rules clearly define who is allowed to take part in the World Championship: the requirements are a result of 64% or more at two Grand Prix tests at international dressage competitions (CDI***) between 1st January 2005 and 24th July 2006. .*

Die deutsche Mannschaft | The German Team

Reiter Rider	Alter Age	Pferd | Horse Pfleger | Groom	Alter Age	Zuchtgebiet Breeding Area	Züchter | Breeder Besitzer | Horse Owner
Nadine Cappellmann (Würselen)	41	Elvis VA Sabine Domhöfer	10	Hannover	Christian Pfeil (Bremerhaven) Nadine Cappellmann
Heike Kemmer (Walle)	44	Bonaparte 67 Doreen Suda	13	Hannover	Monika Jacob-Goldeck (Wedemark) Heike Kemmer
Hubertus Schmidt (Borchen-Etteln)	46	Wansuela Suerte Rachel Wilson	13	Hannover	Conrad Hogrefe (Eickeloh) Martina u. Günter Teichert
Isabell Werth (Rheinberg)	37	Satchmo Anna Kleniuk	12	Hannover	Hinrich Luessen, (Kirchlinteln) Madeleine Winter-Schulze (Wedemark)

Equipechef | Chef d'Equipe	Bundestrainer | National Trainer	Tierarzt | Veterinarian	Hufschmied | Farrier
Ferdi-Jörgen Wassermeyer	Holger Schmezer	Dr. Björn Nolting	Dieter Kröhnert

Dressur | Dressage

Dressur Grand Prix

Mit dem Beginn des Mannschafts-Grand Prix konnte noch kein Zuschauer, kein Reiter und Richter ahnen, dass er in den nächsten fünf Tagen Zeuge des größten Dressurfestivals aller Zeiten werden dürfte. Zum zweiten Mal in der Geschichte der Weltmeisterschaft wurde in der Aachener Soers um den Titel gekämpft. Genau an dem Ort, an dem sich die deutsche Equipe vor 36 Jahren der Konkurrenz aus der UDSSR geschlagen geben musste. Genau an dem Ort, an dem die deutsche Mannschaft 2005 den Niederländern Gold im Nationenpreis überlassen musste.

Im Vorfeld der Weltreiterspiele sah es dann auch in diesem Jahr nach einer engen Entscheidung aus. Denn während sich die niederländischen Equipe-Pferde Ollright und Lingh nach Verletzungen und längeren Pausen pünktlich zum Championat wieder in guter Form präsentierten, kam in die deutsche Besetzungsliste Bewegung. Zunächst musste Klaus Husenbeth seinen Piccolino nach einer Zerrung in der Hinterhand im Training von der Liste streichen lassen. Für ihn rückte Vize-Europameister Hubertus Schmidt mit seiner Stute Wansuela Suerte nach. Zusammen mit Heike Kemmer und Isabell Werth zog der Borchener bei Mann-

Grand Prix Dressage

When the Team Grand Prix began on Tuesday, none of the spectators, riders or judges could possibly have known that they were going to be witness to the biggest dressage festival of all time. For the second time in the history of the World Championships, the Aachen Soers was the venue for top equestrian sport. At the exact same location where the German equipe were beaten by their fellow-competitors from the USSR 36 years ago. At the exact same location, where the German team had to accept defeat when the Dutch riders claimed gold in 2005 in the Nations' Cup.

In the run-up to the FEI World Equestrian Games it certainly seemed like it was going to be a close competition again this year. Whereas the Dutch equipe horses Ollright und Lingh had found their way back to top form in time for the Championships, after injuries and longer breaks from competition sport, there were suddenly last-minute changes to the German line-up. First of all Klaus Husenbeth had to withdraw Piccolino after he pulled a muscle in his hindleg during training. The Vice-European Champion Hubertus Schmidt with his mare Wansuela Suerte took Husenbeth's vacant place. Together with Heike Kemmer and Isabell Werth, the rider from Borchen moved into the training camp held at Nadine Capellmann's stables, as the final member in the team. Then the next piece of bad news was announced: Warum nicht, Isabell Werth's nominated World Championships horse, injured his fetlock joint and also had to be withdrawn. However, the most successful rider of all time, who comes from Rheinberg/GER, luckily had two horses in the running, since Satchmo had also been nominated, which meant she didn't have to miss out on the FEI World Equestrian Games, she merely had to saddle her other horse. Isabell Werth had made no secret about the fact that the Sao Paulo son had been her favourite candidate anyway. And in spite of all the prophecies of doom, she prove that she had been right.

Hubertus Schmidt rückte mit seiner Wansuela Suerte für den verletzten Piccolino und Klaus Husenbeth nach.
Hubertus Schmidt with Wansuela Suerte takes the vacant place of Klaus Husenbeth and his injured Piccolino.

schaftskollegin Nadine Capellmann in das Trainingslager – aus dem die nächste Hiobsbotschaft verkündet wurde: Warum nicht, Isabell Werths nominiertes Pferd für die WM, verletzte sich am Fesselkopf und fiel ebenfalls aus. Die Rheinbergerin und erfolgreichste Reiterin aller Zeiten hatte mit Satchmo allerdings noch ein zweites Eisen im Feuer und musste so nicht auf die Teilnahme bei den Weltreiterspielen verzichten, sondern schlicht umsatteln. Dass der kleine Sao Paulo-Sohn eh ihr heimlicher Favorit war, daraus machte Isabell Werth keinen Hehl. Und sie sollte allen Unkenrufen zum Trotz Recht behalten.

Doch bis zu ihrem Start hieß es warten. Den Anfang in der Mannschaftswertung des Grand Prix, für den 89 Reiter aus 27 Nationen gemeldet waren, machten am ersten Tag Hubertus Schmidt und Heike Kemmer. Als nachgerückter Reservereiter wollte Hubertus Schmidt seine Nominierung natürlich durch einen besonders guten Ritt rechtfertigen. Doch Wansuela Suerte zeigte sich von der Atmosphäre im Hauptstadion, das bis dahin den Springreitern in Aachen vorbehalten war, sichtlich beeindruckt. Die Grußaufstellungen, die zuletzt bei den Turnieren kein Problem mehr darstellten, waren unruhig und auch im Schritt ließ sich die 13-jährige Fuchsstute nicht los. 69,20 Prozent hieß die Beurteilung für Schmidt und das Auftaktergebnis für Deutschland. „Ich bin schon etwas enttäuscht", urteilte der Reitmeister nach seinem Ritt. „In den vergangenen Jahren war ich häufig die Stütze im Team, jetzt muss ich hoffen, dass mich die Damen mit durchziehen." Das taten sie. Heike Kemmer absolvierte mit ihrem Bonaparte die Runde ihres Lebens. Was die Stute einschüchterte, spornte den Fuchswallach nur noch an. „Er liebt diesen weiten Blick, wenn alles großräumig angelegt ist. Dazu der Applaus und die Stimmung im Publikum – da wächst Bonni über sich hinaus", freute sich Kemmer über ihre 75,79 Prozent. Einerwechsel wie an

Yet, she had a long wait before finally being able to compete. Hubertus Schmidt and Heike Kemmer rode for Germany on the first day of the team classification of the Grand Prix, which was entered by 89 riders from 27 nations. Originally only the reserve rider, Hubertus Schmidt wanted to justify his nomination with a particularly good ride. However, Wansuela Suerte let herself be visibly distracted by the atmosphere in the main stadium in Aachen that had hitherto been reserved for the show-jumpers. The 13-year-old chestnut mare was fidgety after the entry, which had no longer been a problem at recent competitions and didn't relax in walk either. The overall outcome for Schmidt and the opening result for Germany was 69.20 percent. "I am a little disappointed," concluded the professional rider after his dressage performance. "I was often the pillar of the team over the past years, now I am just hoping that the ladies manage to pull me through." And this they did. Heike Kemmer delivered the show of her life with Bonaparte. Everything that had overawed Schmidt's mare, proved to further motivate the chestnut gelding. "He loves to have a far-reaching view and a spacious arena. Add the applause and the crowd's mood to this and Bonni really comes into his own," commented Kemmer overjoyed at achieving 75.79 percent. Perfect one-tempi flying changes and centred pirouettes meant that the rider was awarded plenty of eights for the individual movements. A big challenge for the Dutch riders, who had been fortunate enough to draw the 18th, and thus final, starting place under the teams.

Sie trugen mit einem nahezu perfekten Ritt entscheidend zu Mannschaftsgold bei: Heike Kemmer und Bonaparte.
Their almost perfect ride contributed considerably towards the team gold: Heike Kemmer and Bonaparte.

der Schnur gezogen und zentrierte Pirouetten ließen das Punktekonto mit durchgängigen Bewertungen im Achter-Bereich klingeln. Für die Niederländer, denen das Losglück den 18. und damit letzten Startplatz unter den Mannschaften zugespielt hatte, eine hohe Herausforderung.

Für Laurens van Lieren begann sein Aachener Auftritt nicht optimal. Ein Steward hatte ihn am Abreiteplatz zum Wechseln der Schabracke aufgefordert. Angeblich wäre das Sponsorenlogo unzulässig. Tatsächlich handelte es sich bei dem Logo aber um den offiziellen Teamsponsor. Die Aufklärung erfolgte jedoch zu spät, van Lieren hatte durch den Ritt zum Stall und zurück schon 15 Minuten verloren. „Das war für mich sehr schade, da mir so wichtige Zeit fehlte, um Ollright in Ruhe abzureiten. Aber besser, dieses Missverständnis ist bei mir als viertem Teamreiter statt bei einem unserer anderen Reiter passiert", zeigte sich der junge Niederländer versöhnlich. Das Defizit im Warm-up offenbarte sich jedoch deutlich in der Prüfung. Ein explosiv aufgeladener Ollright, der nicht nur die gesamte Schritttour übereilig und nervös absolvierte, konnte mit 68,50 Prozent Mannschaftskollegin Imke Schellekens-Bartels nicht bei dem Aufbau eines soliden Punktekontos unterstützen. Die Tochter von Tineke Bartels, die in Athen noch den hannoverschen Hengst Lancet unter dem Sattel hatte, der in Aachen nun von Emma Hindle vorgestellt wurde, präsentierte mit Sunrise eine Zukunftshoffnung des Oranje-Teams. Trotz kleiner Fehler, wie dem Rückwärtstreten in der Grußaufstellung und einem kurzen Haker in den Einerwechseln, konnte die 29-Jährige mit 71,54 Prozent und dem vorläufigen Platz zwei hinter Heike Kemmer mehr als zufrieden sein.

Durch die Hektik auf dem Abreiteplatz wollte sich Laurens van Lieren Ollright auch im Viereck nicht richtig loslassen.
As a result of the incident on the warm-up area, Laurens van Lieren's Ollright couldn't settle down in the dressage arena either.

The competition in Aachen didn't get off to an ideal start for Laurens van Lieren. A steward on the warm-up area had ordered him to change the numnah under his saddle. Allegedly the sponsor logo was not permissible, whereby in actual fact the logo in question was the emblem of the official team sponsor. However, the clarification of the matter took too long, van Lieren had already lost 15 minutes warm-up time as a result of having to ride to the stables and back again. "It was a real shame, because it meant I lost vital time to prepare Ollright for the ride. But fortunately this misunderstanding happened to me, the fourth team member, as opposed to one of our other riders," said the young Dutch rider placidly. Nevertheless, the consequences of the warm-up deficit were clearly noticeable during the dressage test. Almost ready to explode, Ollright, was hasty and nervous not only during the entire walk sequence, and attaining a score of 68.50 percent he wasn't really able to support his team colleague Imke Schellekens-Bartels in establishing a solid basis. Tineke Bartels' daughter, who competed with the Hanoverian stallion, Lancet, in Athens, ridden here in Aachen by Emma Hindle, presented an aspiring Oranje team horse: Sunrise. Despite small mistakes, such as stepping back after greeting and a small error in the one-tempi changes, the 29-year-old could be more than satisfied with her result – 71.54 percent and second in the preliminary results behind Heike Kemmer.

On the second day the German team's aim was to hold or even further expand their comfortable lead of almost five percent ahead of the Dutch. Elvis VA with the local rider Nadine Capellmann were the ninth pair to enter the dressage arena. The 10-year-old chestnut proved to be clearly more relaxed than at the trials in Munster and the fruits of the efforts of National Coach, Holger Schmezer were noticeable in the piaffes. However, the Dutch judge, Ghislain Fouarge, only awarded the pair 69 percent, which brought the overall score to 72.83 percent and fifth place in the Grand Prix. "I am not totally happy with the result, but there's still another two competitions for me to focus my efforts on," commented the double World Champion of Jerez, who was defending both the team and individual titles. Directly after Nadine Capellmann came the rider the Dutch were pinning all their hopes on: Anky van Grunsven. However, Salinero appeared to be extremely nervous already on the way to the dressage arena and was completely sweated up after even a few rounds. In addition to this the pair experienced unaccustomed communication problems: After the passage, the Salieri son struck off in counter canter, and couldn't be persuaded to correct it, so in the end they rode eleven two-tempi flying changes instead of nine, which was unfortunately not regarded as being a bonus, it actually counted as a mistake. The Olympic gold medallist only scored 75 percent. Not enough to ensure a premature victory in the duel between the German and Dutch teams. Everything was now down to Isabell Werth. Satchmo displayed a relaxed and concentrated per-

Imke Schellekens-Bartels ist mit ihrer Stute Sunrise eine der größten Nachwuchshoffnungen der Niederlande.
Imke Schellekens-Bartels with her mare, Sunrise, is one of the most aspiring young riders of the Netherlands.

FEI World Equestrian Games Aachen 2006

Für den zweiten Tag hieß es nun für das deutsche Team, den komfortablen Vorsprung von fast fünf Prozentpunkten auf die Niederländer zu halten, zu vergrößern oder vielleicht doch noch zu verlieren. Als neuntes Pferd ging Elvis VA mit Lokalmatadorin Nadine Capellmann an den Start. Der gerade zehnjährige Fuchs zeigte sich deutlich gelassener als bei der Sichtung in Münster und besonders in den Piaffen fruchtete die Arbeit mit Bundestrainer Holger Schmezer. Trotzdem sah der niederländische Richter Ghislain Fouarge das Paar nur bei 69 Prozent und das Gesamtergebnis lag damit bei 72,83 Prozent und Platz Fünf im Grand Prix. „Damit bin ich nicht ganz glücklich, aber es gibt ja noch zwei Prüfungen, in denen ich erneut angreifen kann", so die Doppelweltmeisterin von Jerez, die neben dem Mannschafts- auch den Einzeltitel zu verteidigen hatte. Nach Capellmanns Ritt kam die niederländische Hoffnungsträgerin an den Start: Anky van Grunsven. Doch deren Salinero zeigte sich schon auf dem Weg zum Viereck äußerst nervös und nach nur wenigen Runden im Selbigen war der Schwarzbraune schweißnass. Dazu addierten sich

formance – both inside and outside of the stadium. An almost perfect ride was rewarded with the same score that Anky van Grunsven had received and joint third place. "I had to ride accurately, without taking too many risks," said the rider from Rheinberg, beaming. "This one medal is worth almost more than all of my others added together." Because prior to the World Championships nobody would have believed that her problem child, who had often simply refused to cooperate in the past, would play such a decisive role in the German equipe – i.e. claiming their tenth gold. Apart from Isabelle herself of course. And yet her personal willpower, the fighting spirit of the team and a strong feeling of solidarity, uncommon until now among the German riders, made this fantastic result possible.

Subsequently, Edward Gal would have had to have reached a score of 77 percent in order to affect the order of the medals. But with an error in the one-tempi changes, only 6 points for the walk and stepping back in the piaffe – otherwise one of his

Nach ihren beiden Goldmedaillen in Jerez mit Farbenfroh trat Nadine Capellmann diesmal mit Elvis die Titelverteidigung an.
After winning both gold medals in Jerez with Farbenfroh, Nadine Capellmann defended her title this time with Elvis.

DRESSUR | DRESSAGE

ungewohnte Kommunikationsprobleme: Nach der Passage galoppierte der Salieri-Sohn zunächst falsch an, ließ sich nicht zum Durchparieren überreden und dann wurden aus den neun elf Zweierwechsel, was leider nicht als Bonus, sondern als verfehlte Lektion betrachtet wird. 75 Prozent nur für die Olympiasiegerin. Nicht genug, um den Zweikampf zwischen Deutschland und den Niederlanden vorzeitig zu entscheiden. Dies lag nun in den Händen von Isabell Werth. Ihr Satchmo präsentierte sich gelassen und gänzlich konzentriert – sowohl außerhalb wie im Stadion. Eine nahezu fehlerfreie Runde ergab die gleiche Punktzahl wie bei Anky van Grunsven und einen gemeinsamen dritten Platz. „Ich musste zwar präzise, aber nicht auf volles Risiko reiten", strahlte die Rheinbergerin über das ganze Gesicht. „Diese Medaille ist mir beinahe mehr wert, als alle meine anderen." Denn dass sie mit ihrem Sorgenkind, der in der Vergangenheit mehrfach die Arbeit aufgekündigt hatte, entscheidend zum zehnten Mannschaftsgold der Deutschen beitragen würde, hätte vor der WM wohl niemand gedacht. Außer eben sie selbst. Doch ihr persönlicher Wille, der Kampfwille im Team und ein selten zuvor da gewesener Zusammenhalt der deutschen Reiter machte den fantastischen Erfolg möglich.

Im Grand Prix unterliefen dem Erfolgspaar Anky van Grunsven und Salinero ungewohnte Fehler.
The successful pair, Anky van Grunsven and Salinero, made some uncommon mistakes in the Grand Prix.

strengths – his ultimate score of 71.37 percent didn't change anything. So the German equipe won gold with a comfortable lead of 5.7 percent ahead of the Dutch (217.91 points) and the Americans – this also means that all three teams automatically qualify for the Olympic Games 2008 in Hong Kong.

The US team trained by Klaus Balkenhol that was to support Debbie McDonald and her horse Brentina, was announced only a few weeks before the World Championships. However, in the end it wasn't Debbie's chestnut mare, but Steffen Peters and his 16-year-old Floriano with a score of almost 73 percent (sixth place), who contributed to the US equipe taking the bronze medal again. After sustaining an injury during the Grand Prix Brentina namely had to be completely withdrawn from the rest of the competition. The Danish team followed in fourth place and they were pleased with their performance. Since if the equipe trained by Rudolf Zeilinger had have claimed a precious medal, it would have been totally down to the merit of one rider. After his top horse, Blue Hors Don Schufro, had not managed to recover from injury on

Gut gemacht! Gratulation von Hubertus Schmidt für seine Teamkollegin Isabell Werth nach ihrem Ritt, der Deutschland Gold brachte.
Well done! Hubertus Schmidt congratulates his team colleague, Isabell Werth, after her ride which brought Germany gold.

FEI World Equestrian Games Aachen 2006

Ungehemmte Freude auf der Reitertribüne über das zehnte deutsche Mannschaftsgold
Uninhibited joy on the Riders' Stand over the tenth German team gold medal

So strahlen glückliche Sieger. Bundestrainer Holger Schmezer mit seinem Gold-Team und der Königlichen Hoheit, Benedikte von Dänemark.
Elated winners. National Coach, Holger Schmezer, with his gold team and Her Royal Highness Benedikte of Denmark.

Der nachfolgende Edward Gal hätte nun auf 77 Prozent reiten müssen, um an der Medaillenvergabe noch etwas zu ändern. Doch Fehler in den Einerwechseln, die Note Sechs im Schritt und eine Piaffe im Rückwärts – die Piaffe ansonsten eine seiner Stärken – konnten an den 71,37 Prozent nichts ändern. Damit gewann die Deutsche Equipe mit satten 5,7 Prozent Vorsprung Gold vor den Niederlanden (217.91 Punkte) und den Amerikanern – und für alle drei Teams hieß das damit auch die Qualifikation für die Olympischen Spiele 2008 in Hongkong.

Das US-Team von Klaus Balkenhol hatte sich dabei erst wenige Wochen vor der WM um Teamstütze Debbie McDonald und ihre Brentina klar formiert. Doch am Ende war es nicht die Fuchsstute, die auf Grund einer in der Prüfung auftretenden Lahmheit nach dem Grand Prix sogar ganz aus dem weiteren Wettbewerb genommen wurde, sondern Steffen Peters und der 16-jährige Floriano, die mit Platz sechs und knapp 73 Prozent zur erneuten Bronzemedaille der US-Equipe beitrugen. Sie verwiesen die Dänen auf Rang Vier, mit dem das Team aber auch gut leben konnte. Denn hätte die von Rudolf Zeilinger trainierte Mannschaft Edelmetall geholt, wäre es einzig und allein der Verdienst eines einzelnen Reiters gewesen. Andreas Helgstrand, der von dem nicht rechtzeitig wieder genesenen Blue Hors Don Schufro auf die erst neunjährige Matine umsatteln musste, bestätigte die gute Saisonform der Stute, die als jüngstes Pferd zur Weltmeisterschaft in der Dressur antrat. Mit einer sensationellen Piaff-Passage-Tour, die das fachkundige Aachener Publikum zu Standing Ovations veranlasste, und Traversalen mit enormer Schulterfreiheit, fuhr er das beste Ergebnis der beiden Tage ein und durfte sich mit 76,33 Prozent verdient über Rang Eins freuen. „Das ist einfach unglaublich". Zu den Verkaufsgerüchten über sein Pferd zitierte er dessen Besitzer: „Matine ist ein Pferd zum Kaufen und nicht zum Verkaufen." Für seine Teamkollegen verlief der WM-Auftakt nicht ganz so erfreulich. Besonders Lone Jörgensen erwischte mit ihrem Ludewig einen rabenschwarzen Tag. Nach einer zackeligen Schritttour reihten sich im Galopp Fehler an Fehler, sodass die in Baden-Württemberg lebende Dänin mit 62,50 Prozent sogar den Einzug in den Special verpasste, wie auch Nathalie zu Sayn-Wittgenstein und Anders Dahl, der Afrikka, das Pferd seiner Lebensgefährtin Fiona Bigwood vorstellte, die auf Grund ihrer Schwangerschaft auf einen Teamplatz bei den Briten verzichten musste.

time, Andreas Helgstrand, was forced to saddle his young nine-year-old mare, Matine. The youngest horse to compete in the Dressage World Championships, Matine confirmed her present good form: With a sensational piaffe/passage tour, rewarded with standing ovations by the dressage fans in the stadium, and half-passes with enormous elasticity in the shoulders, he walked off with the best result of the two days and quite deservedly took first place with 76.33 percent. "It is simply unbelievable". Regarding the rumours that his horse was up for sale, he quoted the horse's owner: "Matine is a horse that one buys not sells." The opening competition of the World Championships didn't run as smoothly for his team colleagues. Specifically Lone Jörgensen had a terrible day with her Ludewig. After a shaky walk sequence, the canter tour was also riddled with mistakes and after scoring only

Andreas Helgstrand und seine Matine passagierten sich überraschend zum Sieg im Grand Prix.
Andreas Helgstrand and Matine unexpectedly "passaged" their way to victory in the Grand Prix.

FEI World Equestrian Games Aachen 2006

Neben den Dänen blieben auch die Schweden etwas hinter den Erwartungen. Jan Brink und sein Björsells Briar zeigten sich nach der Verletzung des Hengstes im Juli zwar wieder frisch und schön im Vorwärts, aber erreichten auch für ihre Paradelektionen wie Piaffe und Passage nicht die Punkte, die das Paar sonst bei ähnlichen Vorstellungen erhielt. Auch Louise Nathhorst konnte mit ihrem Guiness das Richterquintett nicht überzeugen und fiel auf Rang 36. Freudigste Überraschung war für die Blau-Gelben sicher der Auftritt von Tinne Vilhelmson und ihrem Solos Carex. Nach dem Tod ihres Spitzenpferdes Just Mickey im Frühjahr war die sympathische Schwedin zunächst gar nicht für das Team vorgesehen. Doch die Ausfälle von Patrick Kittel und dann auch Kristian von Krusenstierna verhalfen Vilhelmson nach Aachen, und mit 70,33 Prozent und Platz 14 im Grand Prix durfte die 39-Jährige äußerst zufrieden sein.

Ohne Gram zeigte sich auch Jean Bemelmans. Der spanische Nationalcoach musste vor der WM den Ausfall seiner Spitzenreiterin Beatrice Ferrer-Salat bekannt geben. Ihr 19-jähriger Beauvalais, der bei den Olympischen Spielen in Athen noch zwei Bronzemedaillen eingelaufen hatte, ging lahm und nahm damit wohl auch seinen Abschied aus dem Spitzensport. Ohne die sympathische Reiterin hatten es die Spanier sichtbar schwer, an die Erfolge der Vergangenheit anzuknüpfen und nur denkbar knapp als 29. erreichte Rafael Soto als Einziger überhaupt die nächste Runde – den Special. Trotzdem ließ sich Coach Bemelmans nicht beirren: „Wir sehen das gelassen. Ändern können wir an der momentanen Situation eh nichts", erklärte der am Niederrhein lebende Reitmeister, den in den kommenden Jahren die Zusammenstellung eines neuen Teams beschäftigen wird.

Kaum einer zeigte zentriertere Pirouetten als Jan Brink mit seinem Björsells Briar.
Hardly anyone managed to show more centralised pirouettes than Jan Brink with Björsells Briar.

Rafael Soto war der einzige Spanier, der den Special erreichte. Doch hier war dann für ihn und Invasor Schluss.
Rafael Soto was the only Spanish rider to reach the Spéciale. But that was the end of the line for him and Invasor.

62.50 percent, the Danish rider who lives in Baden-Württemberg/GER didn't even qualify for the Grand Prix Spéciale. Nor did her fellow team members Nathalie zu Sayn-Wittgenstein or Anders Dahl, who rode Afrikka, his partner Fiona Bigwood's horse, who didn't compete for the British team due to being pregnant.

Similar to the Danes, the Swedish team didn't quite live up to the expectations either. Despite the stallion's injury in July, Jan Brink and Björsells Briar gave a fresh and powerful performance, but didn't receive their usual scores for their exemplary movements such as piaffe and passage. Louise Nathhorst wasn't able to convince the five judges with her horse Guiness and fell back to 36th place. Tinne Vilhelmson with Solos Carex provided the most pleasant surprise for the fans of the Swedish team. After the death of her top horse Just Mickey in the spring, the friendly Swedish rider, wasn't originally nominated for the team, but after Patrick Kittel and Kristian von Krusenstierna had to withdraw, Vilhelmson took the vacant place in Aachen. The 39-year-old can be well satisfied with the outcome: she namely achieved a score of 70.33 percent and 14th place in the Grand Prix.

Jean Bemelmans took the bad news well. The Spanish National Coach had had to announce the withdrawal of his top rider Beatrice Ferrer-Salat prior to the World Championships. Her 19-year-old Beauvalais, who won two bronze medals at the Olympic Games in Athens, was lame, which probably means this is the end of his career in competition sport. Without the likeable Ferrer-Salat, it was very difficult for the Spanish team to repeat their

DRESSUR | DRESSAGE

Als Reservereiterin nachgerückt, erritt Tinne Vilhelmson das zweitbeste Ergebnis für die Schweden.
Originally nominated as the reserve rider, Tinne Vilhelmson achieved the second best result for Sweden.

Salieri bestach durch seine ausdrucksstarke Piaff-Passage-Tour, mit der Silvia Iklé über die Tage punkten konnte.
Salieri stood out with his impressive piaffe/passage tour, which brought Silvia Iklé plenty of points over the days.

Ebenfalls mit einem deutschen Coach am Rand konnte die Schweizer Equipe immerhin drei Reiter im Special unterbringen. Auch wenn Silvia Iklé, mit 57 Jahren die älteste Teilnehmerin der Dressurwettbewerbe und Weltranglisten-Sechste, mit Salieri auf Platz 20 nicht zufrieden wirkte und auch nicht sein konnte. Trainer Jürgen Koschel durfte nach Platz Zehn bei den Olympischen Spielen aber immerhin nun mit Rang Acht im Gesamtklassement eine Aufwärtstendenz verzeichnen.

Auf dem Marktplatz in der Aachener Altstadt werden allabendlich die Sieger gefeiert – hier Andreas Helgstrand mit seiner Frau und dem Trainer Rudolf Zeilinger.
The winners were celebrated in the market square of Aachen every evening – here Andreas Helgstrand with his wife and with his trainer, Rudolf Zeilinger.

recent past victories. In fact Rafael Soto only managed to reach the next round, the Spéciale, as an individual rider because a few riders had withdrawn. Nevertheless, the Coach Bemelmans didn't lose his composure: "We don't get worked up about it. We can't change our present situation anyway," explained the Lower Rhine-based riding master, who will concentrate on putting a new team together in the near future.

Also supported by a German trainer, the Swiss equipe did manage to qualify three riders for the Grand Prix Spéciale. Even if Silvia Iklé, at 57 the oldest competitor in the dressage competitions and sixth in the world ranking list, didn't seem happy about coming 20th with Salieri, and she had no reason to be either. The Swiss team came tenth at the Olympic Games, so their Jürgen Koschel was able to record an upwards trend with the team occupying eighth place in the overall team classification.

Favourites, underdogs, winners or losers; the Aachen crowd celebrated all of the riders as if they were heroes. This was a totally new experience for the dressage riders, who are not used to receiving so much attention when they compete. "As far as I am concerned, the World Championships can always be held in Aachen," swarmed winner of the day, Andreas Helgstrand, praising the crowd and the organisers.
Diversity of the Nations – Both a blessing and a curse

FEI World Equestrian Games Aachen 2006

Aber gleich ob Favorit, Außenseiter, Sieger oder Verlierer – das Aachener Publikum feierte jeden einzelnen Reiter wie einen Helden. Für die Dressurreiter, die sonst eher ohne besondere Beachtung ihre Wettkämpfe austragen, eine ganz neue Erfahrung. „Wenn es nach mir geht, könnte Aachen immer die Weltreiterspiele austragen", lobte Tagessieger Andreas Helgstrand Publikum und Veranstalter.

Vielfalt der Nationen – Segen und Fluch

Insgesamt hatten 89 Reiter aus 27 Nationen ihre Startbereitschaft gemeldet. Das kanadische Team war schon vor dem Vet-Check geplatzt, das russische und japanische danach. Trotzdem gab es im Grand Prix interessante Paarungen im Viereck zu bestaunen, die die Globalisierung des Dressursports dokumentierten. Als absolutes Highlight dürfte die für Mexiko startende Bernadette Pujals gewertet werden. Die gebürtige Spanierin, die schon mit Jean Bemelmans, Ellen Bontje und George Theodorescu trainierte, wird mit ihrem 14-jährigen gekörten Hannoveraner Vincent (Weltmeyer x Azur) seit zwei Jahren von Johnny Hilberath betreut. Der rahmige Fuchshengst und seine zierliche Reiterin wussten mit ausdrucksstarken Verstärkungen, perfekten Wechseltouren und drei guten Grundgangarten nicht nur die Zuschauer zu überzeugen. 70 Prozent im Grand Prix hieß das Überraschungsergebnis, wobei die Vorstellung auch mehr verdient hätte. Die in der Nähe von Mexiko City lebende Reiterin schaffte es dann sogar bis in die Kür, die sie mit einem hervorragenden zehnten Platz abschloss. Ein noch nie in der Geschichte des Dressursports da gewesener Erfolg für einen südamerikanischen Reiter. Dass nicht bei allen Teilnehmern die Qualifikation zur WM auch Gleichstand im Leistungsniveau bedeutete, bewies etwa der Ukrainer Andriy Luk Yanov auf seinem Hengst Gopak. Nachdem Chefrichter Stephen Clarke das Paradebeispiel für Disharmonie nach mehrmaligem Kopfschlagen und Verreiten abläutete, versuchte Luk Yanov den Ritt erneut fortzusetzen. Keine 30 Sekunden später und nach vielen Buhrufen des genervten Aachener

Sie war die größte Überraschung der WM: Die Mexikanerin Bernadette Pujals schaffte es souverän mit ihrem Hannoveraner Vincent in die Kür.
She was the biggest head-turner at the World Championships: The Mexican rider, Bernadette Pujals, confidently made her way through to the Freestyle with her Hanoverian stallion Vincent.

Overall 89 riders from 27 nations had entered the tournament. The Canadian team fell apart prior to the vet check, the Russian and the Japanese teams after the horse inspection. Yet, the Grand Prix still offered plenty of interesting pairs to be admired in the dressage arena and they also documented the globalisation of the dressage sport. The Mexican rider, Bernadette Pujals, must be assessed as being an absolute highlight. Born in Spain, previously trained by Jean Bemelmans, Ellen Bontje and George Theodorescu, she and her 14-year-old graded Hanoverian stallion, Vincent (Weltmeyer x Azur), has been coached by Johnny Hilberath for the past two years. The long-lined chestnut stallion and his petite rider convinced both the crowd and the judges with expressive extensions, perfect flying changes and three good paces. 70 percent in the Grand Prix was the surprise result, whereby her performance had deserved an even higher score. The rider, who lives close to Mexico City, even managed to qualify for the Freestyle, in which she also attained an excellent tenth place. The first ever victory in the history of dressage sport for a rider from South America. The rider from the Ukraine Andriy Luk Yanov with his stallion Gopak was proof that although all of the competitors have to qualify for the World Championships, there are still huge differences in the levels of competence. After the head judge, Stephen Clarke, had eliminated the prime example of disharmony after the horse had shaken its head violently several times and the rider had performed the wrong movements,

Bei Kelly Lane und Amoucheur war die Richtung leider nicht klar. Grober Ungehorsam beendete für die Australierin vorzeitig die WM.
Unfortunately Kelly Lane and Amoucheur couldn't find a common basis. Gross disobedience brought the WEG to a premature end for the Australian rider.

DRESSUR | DRESSAGE

Publikums klingelte erneut das Glöckchen. Es blieb die Frage im Raum, wie dieser Reiter die zweifache Bewertung bei unterschiedlichen O-Richtern von über 65 Prozent erhalten hat, um bei der WM an den Start gehen zu können. Andere hatten dagegen auch einfach Pech, wie die von Ulla Salzgeber trainierte Australierin Kelly Lane, deren Amoucheur sich im Stadion überhaupt nicht wohl fühlte und permanent die Flucht suchte. Ein durchgetretenes Rick und schließlich die Aufgabe der Reiterin waren die Folge.

Die Qualität der Grundgangarten

Der Blick für die Zuschauer auf das Open Scoring, also die Bekanntgabe der Noten für jede Lektion, gab nicht nur Aufschluss über die teilweise differenten Richtermeinungen, sondern offenbarte noch ein anderes kleines Geheimnis des Erfolgs oder eben auch Misserfolgs. Es zeigte, wie wichtig auch noch in den höchsten aller Klassen der „gemeine" Schritt bleibt. Diese Lektion, die an sich keine ist, aber über die bloße Darbietung einer Grundgangart sehr schönen Aufschluss über Losgelassenheit, die Reinheit der Gänge und den Gehorsam des Pferdes gibt. Denn all die Paare, die nach ausdrucksstarken Trabtouren und spektakulären Verstärkungen im hohen 70-Prozentbereich lagen, verloren in den 20 Sekunden, die das Überqueren der Diagonalen zumeist benötigt, bis zu sechs Prozent in der Durchschnittsbewertung. Der geneigte Zuschauer konnte im Anschluss dann mit Ruhe verfolgen, wie viel länger es dagegen dauert, diesen Punktverlust in einer sehr guten Galopptour und auf der abschließenden Mittellinie wieder wettzumachen. Den meisten Reitern gelang es gar nicht. Denn der Schritt ist mit dem Koeffizienten Zwei versehen – ist also doppelt so viel wert wie ein spektakulärer Trab oder die schönsten Zweierwechsel. Vielleicht sollte man in der Ausbildung also doch Wert darauf legen, dass diese Grundgangart und all das, was sie uns über unsere Pferde verrät, nicht ganz in Vergessenheit gerät.

Luk Yanov simply attempted to carry on with his ride. Less than 30 seconds later and accompanied by a lot of booing from the irritated Aachen crowd, the bell sounded again. One was left asking oneself, how this rider had possibly managed to obtain over 65% from different official judges at the two necessary trials, in order to be allowed to compete at the FEI World Equestrian Games. In contrast some riders were plainly unlucky, such as the Australian, Kelly Lane, trained by Ulla Salzgeber. Her horse Amoucheur didn't feel at home in the stadium at all and permanently tried to flee. After trampling over the arena fence, the rider eventually retired.

The quality of the paces

The fact that the spectators were able to enjoy open scoring, i.e. the announcement of the scores for each movement, not only offered interesting information on the partially differing opinions of the judges, but also revealed the secret of the riders' success or in some cases failure. It showed how important the "dastardly" walk is, even in the highest classes of top competition sport. This movement, which actually isn't a movement, but in fact just a normal pace, tells the observer a lot about the suppleness, the purity of the gaits and the obedience of the horse. Since all of the pairs, whose scores lay in the 70 percent region and above after showing expressive trot sequences and spectacular extensions, lost up to six percent on average in the 20 seconds that they normally took to cross the diagonal. The spectators that were inclined to do so could then lean back and see how much longer it took to try and make up for these losses with a very good canter tour and with the concluding sequence on the centre line. Most of the riders didn't succeed in doing so, because the walk is multiplied by a coefficient of two – so it is twice as valuable as a spectacular trot or the most perfect two-tempi changes. Perhaps we should therefore make sure, when educating our horses, that this pace and everything it reveals about our horses, doesn't get neglected.

Ein Pferd, das innerlich angespannt und nicht losgelassen ist, zeigt auch selten einen gelassenen und raumgreifenden Schritt.
A horse that is worked up inside and not supple, rarely shows a relaxed and ground-covering walk.

FEI World Equestrian Games Aachen 2006

Dressur Grand Prix Special

Ob durch die neue Regelung oder den günstigeren Wochentag – der Grand Prix Special am Freitag war nahezu ausverkauft mit rund 40.000 Besuchern. Schon vor dem ersten Reiter herrschte im Stadion eine Stimmung, die auch den letzten Pferdefreund mitriss. Sollten die Besucher doch auch an diesem Tag in den Genuss einer Meisterehrung kommen. Denn nach den Weltreiterspielen 1994 in Den Haag wurden in Aachen zum zweiten Mal Medaillen für die Mannschaft, die Sieger des Specials und der Kür vergeben. „Ich war zwar vorher gegen diese Regelung, da ich finde, dass der Weltmeister nicht nach Tagesform, sondern als Ergebnis von drei hochwertigen Prüfungen ermittelt werden soll, aber jetzt profitiere ich natürlich von dem neuen Modus", kommentierte Hubertus Schmidt die neue Situation. Da alle Reiter bei null begannen, war die Medaillenvergabe vollkommen offen. So wollte auch Schmidt mit seiner Wansuela Suerte beweisen, dass ihre Form aus dem Grand Prix noch zu steigern ist. Tatsächlich absolvierte das Championat erprobte Paar eine frische Prüfung mit guten Verstärkungen, einer perfekten Rechtstraversale, schönen Pirouetten und fehlerfreien Wechseln. Doch auch im Special blieb der Borchener unter seinem gewohnten Punkteniveau: 71,04 Prozent und Platz 13 – als punktschlechtester deutscher Reiter in dieser Prüfung war für ihn die WM damit beendet. Sicher den Einzug in das frühere Finale schaffte dagegen Isabell Werth. Sie wurde nicht nur beste Deutsche, sondern beste Reiterin und damit Weltmeisterin im Special. Mit überragenden Verstärkungen und Trab-Traversalen, gleichmäßigen Piaffen und auch Übergängen kam keine Erinnerung an die früheren Probleme in eben dieser Tour auf. Eine Augenoperation soll die Lösung für die Widersetzlichkeiten bei dem kleinen Braunen gewesen sein. „Jetzt findet er sein Vertrauen wieder und ich kann beweisen, warum er für mich immer das beste Pferd war, was ich je geritten bin", strahlte Werth nach ihrer 79,48 Prozent-Runde. „Das war ein Ritt für mein Herz." Wer die Deutsche Vizemeisterin herzzerreißend auf dem Siegerpodest weinen gesehen hatte, glaubte diese Bekundung sofort.

Dressage Grand Prix Spéciale

Whether it was due to the new regulations or the more favourable weekday – the Grand Prix Spéciale on Friday was more or less sold out with a crowd of around 40,000. Even before the first rider had entered the ring there was an amazing atmosphere in the stadium, which swept every single equestrian fan along with it. The visitors were also able to celebrate a Champion on this day too, since here in Aachen for the second time only after the World Equestrian Games in The Hague in 1994, medals were awarded to the best teams, the winners of the Spéciale and the winners of the Freestyle. "I was originally against this regulation, because I feel that the World Champions shouldn't be judged on the day's performance, but should instead by determined on the basis of the result of three high-class competitions, but of course I will now profit from this new modus," was Hubertus Schmidt's comments on the new situation. Since all riders started with a clean sheet again, the competition was completely open. Schmidt wanted to take this opportunity to prove that Wansuela Suerte could improve her form compared to the Grand Prix. And indeed the experienced Championship pair delivered a fresh test with good extensions, perfect half-passes to the right, nice pirouettes and accurate flying changes. Yet, the rider from Borchen still remained under his accustomed score in the Spéciale: 71.04 percent and 13th place – as the German rider with the lowest score in this competition, this meant the World

So traversieren Weltmeister! Satchmo und Isabell Werth auf dem Weg zum Sieg im Special. Ihr Markenzeichen, die geballte Faust, gab es in Aachen endlich wieder häufiger zu sehen.
This is what a World Champion half-pass looks like! Satchmo and Isabell Werth on their way to victory in the Spéciale. In Aachen we finally got the chance to see her hallmark again, the clenched fist.

Dressur | Dressage

Schrecksekunden für alle Beteiligten. Der in der Siegerehrung durchgehende Salinero ließ nicht nur Anky die Luft anhalten.
A hair-raising moment for everyone involved. It wasn't just Anky who held her breath when Salinero bolted during the prize-giving ceremony.

Wie 1994 in Den Haag wurde Isabell Werth so vor Anky van Grunsven Weltmeisterin im Special. Die Niederländerin konnte ihren Salinero zwar deutlich gelassener vorstellen, aber was ihm an Ruhe in der Grußaufstellung fehlte, hätte man sich mehr an Bewegung in der Passage gewünscht. Es fehlte das deutliche Vorwärts und einige Ungleichheiten im Hinterbein ließen die Noten nicht so nach oben schnellen wie in den perfekten Piaffen, Traversalen und einem überraschend guten Schritt. Mit 77,80 Prozent zeigte sich die Ehefrau von Nationaltrainer Sjef Jansen aber zufrieden. „Im Grand Prix habe ich mich über die von mir verursachten Fehler geärgert. Heute bin ich mit mir im Reinen, aber Isabell war halt etwas besser." Van Grunsven zeigte sich auch deshalb erleichtert, weil ihr Salinero in der Siegerehrung zum Grand Prix durchgegangen war und erst von zwei Polizeipferden außerhalb des Stadions gebremst werden konnte. „Als wir ihn heute aus dem Stall geholt haben, hat er noch stark gezittert, sich dann aber mehr und mehr beruhigt und im Viereck hat er sich wieder sicher gefühlt."

Championships had come to an end for him. Isabell Werth in contrast made her way to the final souvereignly. She was not only the best German, but also the best rider altogether in the Spéciale competition. The reward: gold. With excellent extensions and half-passes in trot, consistent piaffes and transitions, there was no sign of the problems that had occurred in this part of the tour in the past. An eye operation is allegedly the solution to the resistance that the small bay had often demonstrated. "His trust has now been restored and I can demonstrate why I always maintain that he is the best horse that I have ever ridden," Werth said with delight after her 79.48 percent ride. "This did wonders for my heart." Everyone who saw the German Vice-Champion sobbing on the winning podium, realises immediately how true this statement was.

Similar to in The Hague in 1994, Isabell Werth became the World Champion in the Spéciale ahead of Anky van Grunsven. The Dutch rider was indeed able to present a clearly more relaxed Salinero, but the calmness that was lacking in the entry and immobility, could perhaps have been redirected into a little more movement in the passage. There was not enough forward motion and a few irregularities in the hindlegs meant that the scores didn't shoot up as high as they did for the perfect piaffes, half-passes and for the surprisingly good walk. The wife of the National Coach, Sjef Jansen, was happy with her score of 77.80 percent. "I was annoyed with myself for the mistakes I caused in the Grand Prix. I am at peace with myself today, Isabell was simply a little bit better than me this time." Van Grunsven was also relieved because Salinero had bolted with her during the prize-winning ceremony of the Grand Prix and didn't stop until outside the stadium where two police horses had to bring him to a halt. "When we fetched him out of the stables today, he was still shaking quite badly, but he gradually calmed down and later in the dressage arena he felt safe again."

Wie bei der WM vor zwölf Jahren konnte Isabell Werth im Special ihre Hauptkonkurrentin Anky van Grunsven dominieren. Andreas Helgstrand strahlt über seine erste Medaille.
Just like twelve years ago, Isabell Werth was able to conquer her biggest rival, Anky van Grunven, in the Spéciale. Andreas Helgstrand beaming with joy after claiming his first medal.

Ergebnisse/ Results Seite/ page 136–138

FEI World Equestrian Games Aachen 2006

Vor heimischen Publikum brillierte Elvis unter Nadine Capellmann besonders in den Passagen.
In front of their home crowd Elvis and Nadine Capellmann particularly excelled in passage.

Andreas Helgstrand secured the bronze medal for himself. The first international individual victory for the 29-year-old, whose wife is expecting her second child only three weeks after the World Championships. The only thing that spoilt the overall picture somewhat was the constant tail swishing of the mare, who only celebrated her international breakthrough a few months previously in Wiesbaden.

Steffen Peters, who was able to maintain the same high level shown in the Grand Prix, came fourth with his 16-year-old Florestan son, Floriano. The pair was even able to hold Nadine Capellmann's Elvis at bay. Albeit with only a minute lead of 0.44 percent. Whereby with the rain pouring down again the judges seemed to have shown a little more reservation when allocating the scores during Nadine Capellmann' ride. Three sixes in the one-tempi changes and sixes in the half-passes – although there were no actual mistakes – cost her important points. The result of Heike Kemmer was also rather sobering. After performing the "ride of her lifetime" in the Grand Prix, she was one of the top candidates for a medal. But Bonni, as Kemmer calls him for short, became a little overwhelmed by the impressive setting and the chestnut gelding didn't move forward like he usually does. Kemmer was not able to balance out the mistakes in the one-tempi changes on the centreline and a short loss of rhythm in the pirouette to the left with the superb extensions and the five 8s she got for the half-passes to the left. The reigning German Champion was nevertheless still in good spirits and looked forward to the Freestyle instead: "I will give it another go," she said optimistically. There was plenty of reason to celebrate anyway due to Isabell winning the gold medal.

Die Bronzemedaille sicherte sich Andreas Helgstrand. Für den 29-Jährigen, dessen Frau nur drei Wochen nach der WM ihr zweites Kind erwartete, der erste internationale Einzelerfolg. Einzig das ständige Schweifschlagen der Stute, die ihren internationalen Durchbruch erst wenige Monate zuvor in Wiesbaden feiern konnte, störte das Gesamtbild.

Auf Rang vier landete Steffen Peters, der seinen Florestan-Nachkommen Floriano auch in der zweiten Prüfung auf dem Niveau aus dem Grand Prix halten konnte und mit dem 16-Jährigen sogar Nadine Capellmanns Elvis in Schach hielt. Wenn auch denkbar knapp mit einem hauchdünnen Vorsprung von 0,44 Prozent. Doch bei dem einsetzenden Regen schienen auch die Richter bei Nadine Capellmann etwas zurückhaltender zu werden. Dreimal die Sechs in den Einerwechseln und Sechsen in den Traversalen – obwohl ohne grobe Fehler – kosteten wichtige Punkte. Etwas ernüchternd auch das Resultat von Heike Kemmer. Nach ihrem „Ritt des Lebens" im Grand Prix war sie eine der heißesten Favoritinnen auf eine Medaille. Doch Bonni, wie ihn Kemmer liebevoll nennt, zeigte sich beeindruckt vom gigantischen Umfeld und zog nicht so nach vorne, wie man es von dem Fuchswallach gewohnt ist. Fehler in den Einerwechseln auf der Mittellinie und ein kurzer Aussetzer vor der Linkspirouette konnte Kemmer auch mit superben Verstärkungen und einer durchgängig mit Acht bewerteten Linkstraversale nicht aufwiegen. Die amtierende Deutsche Meisterin verlor aber nicht ihre gute Laune und freute sich stattdessen auf die Kür: „Da werde ich noch mal angreifen", gab sie sich optimistisch. Grund zum Feiern gab es durch Isabells Goldmedaille ja trotzdem.

Steffen Peters verpasste mit dem 16-jährigen Floriano knapp eine Einzelmedaille und wurde erfolgreichster US-Reiter.
Steffen Peters just missed out on an individual medal with the 16-year-old Floriano and was the most successful rider from the USA.

Dressur | Dressage

Dressur Grand Prix Kür

Um die Ergebnisse aus Den Haag in Aachen auch tatsächlich zu wiederholen, ging der Weltmeistertitel in der Kür an Anky van Grunsven. Mit Salinero gelang ihr am letzten Tag der Dressur-WM vielleicht der erste Ritt, der hundertprozentig ihrem Anspruch entsprach. Mit 86,50 Prozent, viermal Bewertungen über 90 Prozent in der künstlerischen B-Note und damit fünf Prozent Abstand auf den Silbermedaillen-Gewinner Andreas Helgstrand gab es in dieser Sparte weder für die begeisterten 50.000 Zuschauer noch für die fünf Richter Zweifel, wer den Titel verdiente. Obwohl sie zunächst etwas hinter ihrer bekannten Chanson-Musik, arrangiert vom niederländischen Duo Slings und Kerkhof, die auch die Aachener Eröffnungsmusik komponiert hatten, zurückblieb, saß ab dem zweiten Drittel der Prüfung wieder jeder Tritt an der richtigen Stelle. Damit kamen die Besucher der Flutlichtprüfung, für die speziell am Donnerstag Abend noch einmal trainiert wurde, auch in den Genuss, die letzte Aufführung dieser Kür zu sehen, mit der van Grunsven nicht nur Weltcup-, sondern auch Olympiasiegerin geworden war. „Für mich ist das ein Traum, hier in Aachen vor dieser einmaligen Kulisse Weltmeisterin geworden zu sein. Es ist doch besser mit den Downs zu starten und mit den Ups zu enden als andersherum", bilanzierte eine überglückliche Siegerin. Und verriet, dass sie nicht allein im Viereck war. Denn wie bei ihrem Olympia-Sieg in Athen hatte die 37-Jährige einen „Copiloten", der im März 2007 das Licht der Welt erblicken soll. Ebenfalls um einen Platz arbeitete sich Andreas Helgstrand vor. Statt Bronze nun Silber, der Däne konnte sein Glück kaum fassen. So strahlte er auch über das ganze Gesicht, als das euphorische Publikum schon während der Prüfung die exaltierte Passage und Piaffe seiner Schimmelstute mit rhythmischen Klatschen begleitete. Dabei war es für Matine auch erst die zweite Kür nach den

Am letzten Tag gab es die ersehnte Goldmedaille für Anky van Grunsven und Salinero.
Anky van Grunsven won the coveted gold medal with Salinero on the final day.

Dressage Grand Prix Freestyle

Finally, to make sure that the results from The Hague really were repeated in Aachen, Anky van Grunsven took the World Championship title in the Freestyle. On the final day of the Dressage World Championships she achieved her first ride with Salinero that corresponded 100 percent with her own expectations. With a total score of 86.50 percent, four scores over 90 percent for the artistic interpretation and a five percent lead over the silver medallist, Andreas Helgstrand, there was no doubt at all among the enthusiastic 50,000 spectators or the five judges who had deserved to win the title in this category. Although she was a bit behind her well-known melodies, put together by the Dutch duo Slings and Kerkhof, who also composed the music for the Aachen tournament, she managed to get back into perfect synchronisation in the second half of the routine. There was a special training session on Thursday evening for the floodlit competition. Incidentally Aachen was the last opportunity for the spectators to enjoy watching Anky van Grunsven perform this freestyle routine, which she not only won the World Cup with, but which was her Olympic gold freestyle. "For me it is a dream come true, winning the World Championship title here in Aachen in front of this unique setting. It is better to start off with the "downs" and finish off with the "ups", than the other way round," summed up the thrilled winner. And she revealed that she hadn't been alone in the dressage arena. As was the case

Die neunjährige Matine und der erst seit wenigen Jahren im Grand Prix-Sport aktive Andreas Helgstrand übertrafen mit Silber in der Kür alle Erwartungen.
The nine-year-old mare, Matine, and Andreas Helgstrand who has only been riding at Grand Prix level for a few years, exceeded all expectations when they won silver in the Freestyle.

Dänischen Meisterschaften und das erste Mal zu der von Stefan Krawczyk arrangierten Musik mit 70er und 80er Jahre Hits. Technische Höhepunkte, wie aus der doppelten Pirouette in die Einerwechsel und erneut in die doppelte Pirouette – eine Lektionsfolge, mit der auch Debbie McDonalds Brentina sonst punktete – belegten, dass die Stute, die zum Pferdebestand des Legolandbesitzers gehört, nicht nur in der Trabtour auffällt. „Sie ist zwar erst neun, aber gerade diese Lektionen fallen ihr sehr leicht. Ich muss eher etwas an der Basis arbeiten, aber nicht an Piaffe und Passage. Deshalb tut sich Matine im Grand Prix auch nicht schwer", erklärte der ehemalige Springreiter den sensationellen Erfolg seines Pferdes bei dieser WM.

Für Isabell Werth stand dagegen weniger eine Medaille als eine gute Runde unter den gegebenen Bedingungen auf dem Programm. Dass es dennoch für Bronze reichte, freute sie um so mehr. „Wir haben uns bei der Vorbereitung auf den Grand Prix und den Special konzentriert. Auch noch die Kür zu üben, wäre zu viel gewesen. Hier im Flutlicht wollte ich einfach nur, dass er das Vertrauen behält und bei mir bleibt", erklärte Werth die Strategie. Aufgegangen – zwar präsentierte sich Satchmo nicht ganz so exaltiert wie zuvor und hatte den ersten Wechselfehler in den gesamten Tagen zu verzeichnen, aber dass er mit seinen 1,66 Meter trotzdem die für seinen 1,82 Meter großen Stallkollegen Warum nicht zugeschnittene Kür wunderbar ausfüllte, belegten 80,75 Prozent.

Damit wurde es für Lokalmatadorin Nadine Capellmann nur der undankbare vierte Platz. Vom heimischen Publikum allerdings wie die Siegerin gefeiert, ertönten laute Buh-Rufe bei Bekanntgabe des Ergebnisses von 79,90 Prozent. Das Elvis-Medley für den fuchsfarbenen King fanden viele so passend, dass sie die Doppelweltmeisterin von Jerez gerne auf dem Treppchen gesehen hätten. Aber der Zehnjährige hat noch eine längere Sportkarriere vor sich, zu der vielleicht auch die eine oder andere Einzelmedaille gehören wird.

Die nächsten Championate dürfte auch Heike Kemmer im Auge behalten. Mit 13 Jahren gehört ihr Bonni noch lange nicht zum alten Eisen und auch wenn es in Aachen nach einem fünften Platz in der Kür nicht für einen Einzeltitel reichte, haben die Beiden in den nächsten Jahren an der Weltspitze sicher noch ein Wörtchen mitzureden. Zumal der Bon Bonaparte-Sohn in der Kür erneut in höchster Versammlung piaffierte und ein schönes Seitenbild mit sehr guter Anlehnung zeigte.

during her Olympic victory in Athens, the 37-year-old had a "co-pilot", on board, who is going to be born in March 2007.

Andreas Helgstrand also managed to move up a place in the rankings. Silver instead of bronze, the Danish rider could hardly believe his luck. He was already beaming all over his face, as the euphoric crowd started clapping to the rhythm of his grey mare's excellent passages and piaffes during the competition. It was in fact only Matine's second Freestyle test after the Danish Championships and the first time Helgstrand had ridden to the music compiled by Stefan Krawczyk comprising of hits from the 70s and 80s. Technical highlights, such as moving straight into one-tempi flying changes out of a double pirouette and back into a double pirouette – a sequence of movements that Debbie McDonald's Brentina otherwise scores good points with – prove that the mare, who belongs to the owner of Legoland, doesn't just stand out in the movements in trot. "She may only be nine, but she finds these movements particularly easy. I have to concentrate more on the fundamental exercises, rather than on the piaffe or passage. That's why Matine has no problems with the Grand Prix movements," explained the former show-jumper the sensational success of his horse at these World Championships.

Under the circumstances, Isabell Werth's target on the other hand wasn't to win a medal, but to simply perform a good Freestyle. So she was all the more elated at having managed to secure the bronze medal. "In training we concentrated on the Grand Prix and the Spéciale. It would have been too much to practise the freestyle as well. In view of the floodlit conditions, I just wanted to make sure that he retained his confidence and stayed with me," is how Werth explained her strategy. It obviously paid off – admittedly Satchmo didn't stun the crowds as he had done on the previous days and also made his first mistake in the flying changes, but in spite of him being only 1.64 metres high, he still managed to filled out the freestyle routine that had been choreographed for his 1.82 metre high stable mate Apache, and was rewarded with 80.75 percent.

This meant that the local rider Nadine Capellmann, who finished fourth, just missed out on a medal. Her home crowd nevertheless celebrated her as if she had won, and there was loud booing when the result of 79.90 was announced. Many people had found the Elvis medley so fitting for the chestnut King, that they wanted to see the double World Champion of Jerez on the winning podium. But the 10-year-old gelding has still got a long sporting career ahead of him, and will no doubt have plenty of occasions to win an individual medal in the future.

Heike Kemmer will almost certainly be able to compete in the next big Championships too. Her 13-year-old Bonni also still has a few more years of top sport ahead of him, and even though she didn't take the individual title here in Aachen – Kemmer came fifth in the Freestyle – the pair will definitely play a significant role in top dressage over the next few years. Above all the Bon Bonaparte son's piaffe in the Freestyle showed immense collection and the displayed a wonderful profile with correct contact.

Auch wenn es nicht zu einer Einzelmedaille reichte war Heike Kemmer mit ihrem Bonaparte rundum zufrieden.
Even if Heike Kemmer didn't manage to claim an individual medal, she was completely satisfied with her Bonaparte.

DRESSUR | DRESSAGE

Im Mai hatte sich Kyra Kyrklund noch mit Nadine Capellmann ein scharfes Duell um den Sieg beim Aachener CHIO geliefert – diesmal gingen beide leer aus.
In May Kyra Kyrklund and Nadine Capellmann delivered a fierce duel for victory at the CHIO in Aachen – this time both went home empty-handed

Mit neuer Kür und technisch auf Ausnahmeniveau zeigten sich Kyra Kyrklund und ihr Max. Kämpfte die Akkord-Trainerin, die nebenbei elf Schüler in der Dressur und Vielseitigkeit zu betreuen hatte, im Mai noch beim CHIO mit Nadine Capellmann und den Sieg in allen drei Prüfungen, fand sie sich jetzt nicht unter den Medaillenkandidaten wieder. Dabei saß mit der 54-Jährigen ein ausgemachter Profi und Kürspezialist im Sattel: Neben dem Gewinn des Weltcup 1991 in Paris ging Kyra schon bei fünf Olympischen Spielen an den Start und konnte 1990 in Stockholm bei den World-Equestrian-Games Einzelsilber mit nach Hause nehmen. Doch in diesem Jahr sollte es trotz perfekter Raumnutzung, harmonischer und dynamischer Musikabstimmung zu Klängen aus Cabaret und tollen Piaffen mit 77,30 Prozent nur Platz Sieben werden. Vielleicht der Fluch des frühen Starts, denn als vierter Reiter dieser Prüfung zeigten sich die Juroren mit der Punkteausschüttung noch etwas zurückhaltend. Daran lag es bei Emma Hindle und ihrem Hengst Lancet, der bisher nur in den Niederlanden zum Deckeinsatz kam, sicher nicht. Die in Hessen lebende Britin eröffnete zwar die Kür, aber dass sie kein großer Fan dieser Prüfung ist, war dem Paar leider anzumerken. Mit mäßiger Choreographie, bei der teilweise der Eindruck entstand, dass die Linien so nicht auf dem Papier geplant waren und in totaler Disharmonie zur Musik standen, wurden es 69,90 Prozent – für eine Championatskür ein enttäuschendes Ergebnis.

Doch bis zum letzten Starter, Steffen Peters und seinem erneut glänzend vorgestellten Floriano, der nur leichte Abstriche zu den Vortagen hinnehmen musste, hatte das Publikum wunderschöne Präsentationen gesehen, die im hell ausgeleuchteten Stadion den glanzvollen Abschluss nach vier Tagen Spitzensport boten. Bei diesem Championat vertauschten sich vielleicht erstmals ein wenig die Rollen. Denn am Ende wusste man nicht, wer begeisterter von den Weltreiterspielen in Aachen war: Die größte Zuschauermenge, die je bei einem Dressurevent erreicht wurde, oder die Reiter, die noch nie vor solch einer Kulisse antreten durften. Vielleicht auch egal, denn Gewinner waren sie am Ende bei dieser WM alle.

Kyra Kyrklund and her horse Max presented a new Freestyle routine with an extremely high technical level. The busy trainer, who coaches eleven dressage and eventing pupils in between riding, and who duelled out the victories of all of the dressage competitions with Nadine Capellmann at the CHIO, wasn't one of the medal candidates this time round. Although the 54-year-old is an experienced professional and a Freestyle specialist: Besides winning the World Cup in Paris in 1991, Kyra has competed at five Olympic Games and carried home the silver individual medal at the World Equestrian Games in Stockholm in 1990. But this year in spite of a perfect routine layout, an harmonious and dynamic musical interpretation to songs from the musical Cabaret, as well as super piaffes; she was only awarded 77.30 percent (seventh place). Perhaps this was due to the fact that she competed right at the start of the competition when the judges were still somewhat conservative with their scores. This was not the reason in the case of Emma Hindle with her stallion Lancet, who has until now only been at stud in the Netherlands. The British rider who lives in Hessen was the first rider in the Freestyle test, and unfortunately it was noticeable that she is not a fan of this competition. The choreography was mediocre, and sometimes one got the impression that she wasn't following the exact sequence of movements planned on paper, furthermore the movements didn't harmonise with the music. The outcome was 69.90 percent – a disappointing score of a World Championships Freestyle.

However, right up until the last pair, Steffen Peters and his horse Floriano, who once again gave a superb performance, with only a few small deficits compared to the previous days, the crowd was able to enjoy wonderful performances, that brought the four days of top dressage sport to a spectacular close in the brightly illuminated stadium. For the first time probably at these Championships a role changing process had taken place. In the end one could not be certain who was more impressed with the FEI World Equestrian Games in Aachen: The biggest audience that has ever been present at a dressage event, or the riders who have never had the opportunity to compete amid such a setting before. Perhaps it is not so important, because at the end of these World Championships they were all winners.

Die strahlenden Sieger im Kürwettbewerb – der Silbermedaillengewinner Andreas Helgstrand sowie die drittplatzierte Isabell Werth freuen sich mit der Weltmeisterin Anky van Grunsven.
The joyous winners of the Freestyle – the silver and bronze medallists, Andreas Helgstrand and Isabell Werth, shared their happiness with the World Champion, Anky van Grunsven.

Ergebnisse/Results Seite/page 136–138

Vielseitigkeit
Eventing

AUTOREN/AUTHORS
DONATA VON PREUSSEN
UTA HELKENBERG

Die Eröffnungsfeier - Auftakt zu einem noch nicht da gewesenen Triumph der deutschen Vielseitigkeitsreiter (Andreas Dibowski, Ingrid Klimke, Bettina Hoy, Dirk Schrade und Physiotherapeutin Dr. Ina Goesmeier (v.r.n.l.)).
The Opening Ceremony – the starting point for an incomparable triumph for the German eventers: Andreas Dibowski, Ingrid Klimke, Bettina Hoy, Dirk Schrade and physiotherapist Dr. Ina Goesmeier (f.r.t.l.)

Die Disziplin Vielseitigkeit

Wie die Dressur erlebt auch die Vielseitigkeit im Jahr 1966 ihre Weltmeisterschafts-Premiere. Das erste Championat in Burghley (Großbritannien) wird zum Triumph der argentinischen und irischen Reiter. Die deutschen Vielseitigkeitsreiter behaupten sich erstmals 1974 in Burghley auf einem Medaillenplatz, wo das Team hinter den USA und Großbritannien die Bronzemedaille gewinnt. Vier Jahre später in Lexington (USA) greift Helmut Rethemeier auf Ladalco als erster Deutscher nach einer Einzelmedaille: Bronze. 1982 in Luhmühlen vermag sich Rethemeier, diesmal im Sattel von Santiago, sogar noch zu steigern: Silber in Einzel- und Mannschaftswertung. Bei den Championaten 1990 und 1994 platziert sich das deutsche Team jeweils auf dem Bronzerang. Bei den beiden folgenden Weltmeisterschaften (Rom und Jerez de la Frontera) scheidet das deutsche Team aus.

In der Vielseitigkeit dürfen bei Welt- und Europameisterschaft maximal sechs Reiter pro Nation starten, mindestens drei, höchstens vier davon bilden die Mannschaft. Der Wettbewerb besteht aus den drei Teilprüfungen Dressur, Gelände und Springen. In der Dressur wird das Ergebnis des Reiters nach einer festgelegten Formel (auf 100 Prozent fehlende Prozentpunkte mal 1,5) in Minuspunkte umgerechnet. Die Geländeprüfung wird, wie schon bei den Olympischen Spielen von Athen, ohne Rennbahn und Wegestrecken ausgetragen. Nach einem Aufwärmen auf dem Vorbereitungsplatz geht es direkt in die Querfeldeinstrecke, das Herzstück jeder Vielseitigkeit. Vor der abschließenden Springen werden die Pferde den Richtern und der Veterinärkommission in einer Verfassungsprüfung vorgestellt. Nur wer die vorangegangenen Prüfungen unbeschadet überstanden hat und fit ist, erhält das Okay für den weiteren Einsatz. Das Parcoursspringen wird wie eine reguläre Springprüfung gewertet. Ein Abwurf und eine Verweigerung schlagen mit vier Fehlerpunkten zu Buche. Bei Zeitüberschreitung wird je Sekunde ein Strafpunkt berechnet. Neuer Weltmeister der Vielseitigkeit ist derjenige Teilnehmer, der nach drei Teilprüfungen die wenigsten Minuspunkte aufweist. Sieger der Mannschaftswertung ist dasjenige Team mit den wenigsten Strafpunkten, wobei die drei besten Ergebnisse pro Mannschaft gewertet werden.

Die Disziplin Vielseitigkeit

In 1966, the same year as the first dressage World Championships, the inaugural World Championships in eventing were held at Burghley (UK), and they were a resounding success for the riders from Argentina and Ireland. The first time that the German riders were able to mount the winners' rostrum was in 1974 also at Burghley, where the German team won bronze behind the USA and Great Britain. Four years later at Lexington (USA), Helmut Rethemeyer on Ladalco achieved the first individual medal for Germany, a bronze. He went on to better his own record by taking both the individual and team silver at Luhmühlen in 1982, this time riding Santiago. In the 1990 and 1994 Championships the German team won bronze. In the two subsequent World Championships (Rome and Jerez de la Frontera), the German team was eliminated. In eventing at World and European Championship, six riders per nation are allowed to take part; at least three, maximum four of them form a national team for their country. Eventing consists of three stages: dressage, cross-country and show jumping. The first is the dressage test. The final result in percentage is converted into minus points, using a special formula (the difference between 100% and the percentage reached, x 1.5) The cross-country phase has undergone a significant change for the World Championship at Aachen. As was already the case at the Athens Olympic Games, it will no longer include the steeple chase and the roads and tracks. After an individual warm-up, riders tackle the cross-country course, the „heart and soul" of eventing. Before the final stage, the show jumping, the horses are trotted up in front of the judges and the veterinary commission at a final horse inspection, which serves to ensure that only fit and healthy horses continue. The jury has the power to eliminate horses from the competition. The show jumping follows the rules of normal jumping competitions and therefore, a knock-down and a refusal both result in four penalty points (or faults). If the optimum time is exceeded, for each second over the time one penalty point is added. The winner is the rider who has the least penalty points after all three parts of the competition. Winner of the team competition will be the team with the lowest penalty points as an result of the addition of the three best riders.

Die deutsche Mannschaft | The German Team

Reiter / Rider	Alter / Age	Pferd / Horse Pfleger / Groom	Alter / Age	Zuchtgebiet / Breeding Area	Züchter / Breeder Besitzer / Horse Owner
Andreas Dibowski (Egestorf)	40	FRH Little Lemon	15	Hannover	Hanke Meyer (Midlum) Susanna Dibowski, DOKR
		FRH Serve Well Beate Hohnfeldt	12	Hannover	Albert Hohnemann (Wienhauser Beate Hohnfeldt (Amelinghause
Bettina Hoy (Gatcombe/GBR)	44	Ringwood Cockatoo Judith Claire Langley	15	Irland	Hilary Greer (Irland) Frederik u. Mary Davidson (Aust DOKR
Ingrid Klimke (Münster)	38	Sleep Late Carmen Thiemann	15	Großbritannien	DOKR u. FORS
Frank Ostholt (Warendorf)	30	Air Jordan 2 Stephanie Cordugas	11	Hannover	Horst Wesch (Bad Bederkesa) Robert Vietor, DOKR, Frank Osth
Hinrich Romeike (Nübbel)	43	Marius Voigt-Logistic Swantje von Alwörn	12	Holstein	Hans-Werner Ritters (Krumstedt Susanne Romeike (Nübbel)
Dirk Schrade (Warendorf)	28	Sindy 43 Maria Lindén	12	Baden-Württemb.	Tobias Ertle (Sontheim) Carola Liedtke (München)
Equipechef / Chef d'Equipe Hans Melzer		Bundestrainer / National Trainer Chris Bartle		Tierarzt / Veterinarian Dr. Karsten Weitkamp	Hufschmied / Farrier Dieter Kröhnert

VIELSEITIGKEIT | EVENTING

Die sportliche Antwort auf Athen

Nach den unvergessenen Ereignissen bei den Olympischen Spielen von Athen, bei denen die deutschen Vielseitigkeitsreiter die Goldmedaille wegen eines Formfehlers verloren, hatten sich Bettina Hoy, Ingrid Klimke, Andreas Dibowski, Hinrich Romeike und Frank Ostholt fest vorgenommen: „In Aachen geben wir die sportliche Antwort auf Athen." Vor allem „Unglücksrabe" Bettina Hoy war in jedem Interview im Vorfeld darauf angesprochen worden, ob den Deutschen nun in Aachen vor heimischem Publikum die „Revanche" gelingen würde. Auch Bundestrainer Hans Melzer betonte vor der WM immer wieder, dass alles andere als eine Medaille für ihn und seine Mannschaft eine Enttäuschung sei. Dann war es endlich so weit. Bei den Weltreiterspielen in der Aachener Soers waren alle fünf Protagonisten von Athen wieder dabei, und von Prüfungsbeginn an unterstrichen sie ihr Vorhaben mit herausragenden Leistungen.

Erster Akt: Die Verfassungsprüfung

„Es war der Wunsch der Reiter, dass wir so früh wie möglich entscheiden, wer in Aachen für das Team und wer als Einzelreiter startet", sagte Bundestrainer Hans Melzer. Denn anders als bei den Olympischen Spielen bilden bei einer WM nur vier Reiter die Mannschaft. So wurde bereits im Warendorfer Trainingslager zwei Tage vor Abreise bekannt gegeben, dass aus dem Kreis der Athen-Reiter Andreas Dibowski, der sich für den Einsatz von FRH Serve Well entschieden hatte, derjenige sein würde, der nicht für die Mannschaft startet. „Bei fünf wirklich gleich starken Paaren ist die Entscheidung nicht leicht gefallen", sagte Hans Melzer.

80 Reiter stellten bei der ersten Verfassungsprüfung ihre Pferde vor, 79 wurden zur Prüfung zugelassen, so auch Ingrid Klimke mit Sleep Late.
80 riders presented their horses at the first vet inspection, 79 were given the go-ahead to compete, including also Ingrid Klimke with Sleep Late.

The sporting reply to Athens

After the unforgettable incident at the Olympic Games in Athens, when the German eventers were stripped of the gold medal due to a technicality, Bettina Hoy, Ingrid Klimke, Andreas Dibowski, Hinrich Romeike and Frank Ostholt had set themselves a fixed goal: "In Aachen we are going to give the sporting reply to Athens." In interviews prior to the tournament, particularly the "jinxed" Bettina Hoy had continually been asked if the Germans would succeed in taking their "revenge" in front of their home crowd in Aachen. The National Coach, Hans Melzer, also repeatedly stressed before the World Championships that he and his team would be disappointed if they didn't take home a medal. Then the time had finally come. At the FEI World Equestrian Games at the Aachen Soers, all five protagonists from Athens were taking part again and from the start of the competition they underlined their intentions with excellent performances.

First Chapter: The horse inspection

"The riders wanted an early decision on who was going to compete for the team and who would compete as individuals in Aachen", said Hans Melzer, the National Coach. In contrast to the Olympic Games, at the World Championships the team only comprises of four riders. So while we were still in the training camp in Warendorf two days before setting off for the Soers, it was announced that from the Athens squad, Andreas Dibowski, who had chosen to ride FRH Serve Well, would not be competing for the team. "It was a very difficult decision because the five pairs are equally strong," commented Hans Melzer. "FRH Serve Well has not competed in any long competitions this year since the injury he had sustained in training in the spring. This lead to a slight uncertainty concerning his condition compared to the other horses and this was the basis for our decision." All four team riders had previously displayed convincing performance this year. Marius Voigt-Logistic had mastered his 17th S Class competition without an obstacle fault in the cross-country, Sleep Late was second in Badminton. Air Jordan had won the CCI**** in Luhmühlen and Ringwood Cockatoo had claimed victory in the World Cup in Schenefeld. In contrast to France, England and the USA, the Germans were thus able to fall back on their established Athens team. As already announced at the final trials in Schenefeld, the newcomer to the team, Dirk Schrade with Sindy, had been nominated as the second individual rider.

At the first horse inspection 80 riders from 24 nations – the highest number ever – presented their 83 horses to the ground jury in Aachen, which comprised of Brian Ross (USA), Angela Tucker (GBR) and Martin Plewa, Director of the Westphalian Riding & Driving School in Munster. The German horses presented themselves in good form. Although the American veterinarian Jack Snyder, wanted to take a second look at Frank Ostholt's Air Jordan – for whatever reason. Andreas Dibowski presented, as agreed, both FRH Little Lemon and FRH Serve Well, who left an equally excellent impression behind as the three grey horses Ringwood Cockatoo, Sleep Late and Marius Voigt-Logistic. Andrew Hoy and the rider from New Zealand, Heelan Tompkins, had to overcome a few nail-biting moments. Their horses, Master Monarch and the 20-year-old Glengarrick, were sent to the holding box, did however receive the green light from the ground

FEI WORLD EQUESTRIAN GAMES AACHEN 2006

"FRH Serve Well ist wegen ihrer Trainingsverletzung, die sie sich im Frühjahr zugezogen hatte, in diesem Jahr noch keine lange Prüfung gegangen. Insofern gab es ein kleines konditionelles Fragezeichen im Vergleich zu den anderen Pferden und das gab den Ausschlag." Alle vier Mannschaftsreiter hatten in diesem Jahr überzeugende Vorleistungen gezeigt. Marius Voigt-Logistic hatte in diesem Jahr seine 17. S-Prüfung ohne Hindernisfehler im Gelände bewältigt, Sleep Late war Zweiter in Badminton geworden. Air Jordan hatte das CCI**** Luhmühlen gewonnen und Ringwood Cockatoo die Weltcupprüfung in Schenefeld. Im Gegensatz zu Frankreich, England und den USA konnten die Deutschen also auf das bewährte Athen-Team zurückgreifen. Als zweiter deutscher Einzelreiter wurde – wie bereits nach der letzten Sichtung in Schenefeld angekündigt – der Newcomer im Team, Dirk Schrade mit Sindy, nominiert.

80 Reiterinnen und Reiter aus 24 Nationen – so viele wie nie zuvor – stellten ihre 83 Pferde bei der ersten Verfassungsprüfung der Ground Jury vor, der in Aachen Brian Ross (USA), Angela Tucker (GBR) und Martin Plewa, Leiter der westfälischen Reit- und Fahrschule in Münster, angehörten. Die deutschen Pferde präsentierten sich gut in Schuss. Allerdings wollte sich der amerikanische Tierarzt Jack Snyder Frank Ostholts Air Jordan – aus welchen Gründen auch immer – zwei Mal ansehen. Andreas Dibowski stellte, das war so abgesprochen, FRH Little Lemon und FRH Serve Well vor, die ebenso einen hervorragenden Eindruck hinterließen wie die drei Schimmel Ringwood Cockatoo, Sleep Late und Marius Voigt-Logistic. Bange Sekunden hatten Andrew Hoy und die Neuseeländerin Heelan Tompkins zu überstehen. Ihre Pferde, Master Monarch beziehungsweise der 20-jährige Glengarrick, mussten in die Holding Box. Beim zweiten Vortraben erhielten sie das Okay der Ground Jury. Noch vor dem eigentlichen Start kam dagegen das Aus für den 16-jährigen irischen Wallach Drunken Disorderly (Reiter Mark Kyle). Komplette Teams stellten neun Länder, mit nur drei Mannschaftsreitern traten Dänemark, Holland, Belgien, Österreich und Polen an. Einzelreiter kamen aus Kanada, den Niederländischen Antillen, Portugal, Jamaika, Kroatien, Finnland, Weißrussland (Belaurus) und Brasilien.

Dressur: Gelungener Start auf dem Viereck

"Als super sicheres Geländepferd soll Marius für uns die erste Nullrunde abliefern", hatte Hans Melzer die Startreihenfolge der deutschen Reiter begründet, nach der Hinrich Romeike den Auftakt machte, gefolgt von Frank Ostholt, Bettina Hoy und als Schlussreiterin Ingrid Klimke. Und so musste der Zahnarzt aus Nübbel mit seinem Schimmel als erster deutscher Starter ins Viereck in Stadion 2, das bereits am ersten Dressurtag gut besucht war. Es überwogen natürlich die deutschen Fans, die "ihre" Reiter zunächst lautstark begrüßten, dann aber, nachdem sich Hinrich Romeikes Schimmel etwas aufgenervt hatte, den Lautstärkepegel merklich senkten. Dafür gab's dann umso mehr Applaus und Fahnenschwingen nach dem Gruß. Dennoch verließ Hinrich Romeike mit einem enttäuschten Gesicht das Viereck. 52,40 Strafpunkte – so ein Ergebnis hatte es für ihn und seinen Holsteiner noch nie gegeben – standen auf der Anzeigetafel. "Durch

jury after being trotted up the second time. For the 16-year-old Irish gelding, Drunken Disorderly (Rider: Mark Kyle) the competition came to an end before it had actually even started. Nine countries had entered complete teams; Denmark, Holland, Belgium, Austria and Poland had teams comprising of only three riders. There were individual riders from Canada, the Netherlands Antilles, Portugal, Jamaica, Croatia, Finland, Belarus, and Brazil.

Dressage: Successful start in the dressage arena

"Because he is such a reliable cross horse, Marius is to deliver the first clear round for us", is how Hans Melzer justified the starting order of the German riders. Hinrich Romeike made the start, followed by Frank Ostholt, Bettina Hoy and Ingrid Klimke as the final rider. So, the dentist from Nübbel was first to enter the dressage arena in Stadium 2 with his grey horse. This stadium, which is otherwise reserved for the drivers, was well-attended from the first dressage day onwards. The crowd was naturally dominated by German fans, who wanted to give "their" riders a loud welcome, but then, after it became visible that they were making Hinrich Romeike's Marius nervous, the noise level noticeably dropped. To make up for it though there was even greater applause and flag waving after the final greeting. Nevertheless, Hinrich Romeike left the arena disappointed. 52.40 points flashed up on the display – he and his Holstein gelding had never received such a poor result before. "The fact that the fans had cheered so

Nach der Dressur auf dem dritten Platz liegend, nahm Andreas Dibowski mit FRH Serve Well Kurs auf eine Medaille in der Einzelwertung.
Lying in third place after the dressage, Andreas Dibowski and FRH Serve Well were on course for a medal in the individual classification.

VIELSEITIGKEIT | EVENTING

In großer Zahl waren die Fans schon zur Dressur angereist und feierten die deutschen Reiter (hier im Gelände) mit lautem Jubel.
A considerable number of fans already arrived for the dressage and they cheered the German riders on loudly (here at the cross-country).

den Jubel der Fans beim Einreiten war Marius völlig aus dem Konzept geraten", sagte Romeike nach seinem Ritt. Das Anzackeln im Schritt und ein Fehler nach der ersten Galopptraversale ließen den 43-Jährigen auch in der folgenden Galopptour vorsichtig agieren. Auch Frank Ostholts Air Jordan ließ sich von der Kulisse mehr beeindrucken, als es nach außen hin den Anschein hatte. „JoJo war schon vor der Galopptour recht griffig und nervös", erklärte Ostholt einen Schnitzer bei den Galoppwechseln. Sehr viel besser erging es den beiden deutschen Einzelreitern. Dirk Schrade hatte seine baden-württembergische Stute Sindy auf den Punkt vorbereitet und präsentierte sie in schöner Anlehnung. Das wurde von den Richtern, die vor allem bei den ersten Startern recht streng agierten, mit 50,20 Punkten belohnt. Bereits bei den Europameisterschaften im vorangegangenen Jahr im britischen Blenheim hatten FRH Serve Well und Andreas Dibowski eine sehr gute Vorstellung auf dem Viereck abgeliefert, so dass der fast perfekte Auftritt des Paares im Dressurstadion keine ganz große Überraschung war. Bis auf den letzten fliegenden Wechsel gelang ihnen alles, wenngleich Andreas Dibowski nach seinem Ritt selbstkritisch befand: „Erst nach dem starken Trab war die Spannung weg."

Zwei Spitzenvorstellungen wurden den rund 4.000 Zuschauern am Freitagmorgen geboten. Die amtierende Europameisterin Zara

loudly when I entered the arena, had completely knocked Marius of his stride," Romeike explained after his ride. The mistakes in walk and after the first half-pass in canter – Marius had knocked himself – meant that the 43-year-old had ridden the ensuing canter tour, which is normally one of Marius' strong points, with added caution. Frank Ostholt's Air Jordan was more distracted by the setting, than was visible to the outsider. "JoJo was already really uptight and nervous in the canter tour," the second German team rider said explaining a mistake in the flying changes. Things went much better for the two German individual riders. Dirk Schrade had prepared his Baden-Württemberg mare Sindy, a daughter of the thoroughbred stallion, Stan the Man xx, to a tee and showed a wonderful contact during the test. This was rewarded with a score of 50.20 from the judges, who were particularly conservative with the first riders. FRH Serve Well and Andreas Dibowski had already delivered a very good performance in the dressage at the European Championships last year in Blenheim, Great Britain, even if they hadn't received the corresponding score, so it was no real surprise that the pair offered the crowd in the dressage stadium an almost perfect performance. Everything ran smoothly apart from the very last flying change, despite which Andreas Dibowski was very self-critical after his ride: "The tension didn't die down until after the extended trot."

FEI World Equestrian Games Aachen 2006

„Volle Konzentration" im Viereck bewies Ringwood Cockatoo trotz der vielen Fans im Stadion und verhalf seiner Reiterin Bettina Hoy zur Spitzenposition.
Ringwood Cockatoo showed "full concentration" in the dressage arena in spite of the hoards of fans in the stadium, allowing his rider Bettina Hoy to take the lead.

Phillips verließ auf Toy Town mit 41,70 Strafpunkten das Viereck. „Beim Halten habe ich wohl einige Punkte verloren", sagte die Enkelin der britischen Königin, „aber ich bin sehr glücklich." Eine fehlerlose Vorstellung, für die es 36,50 Punkte gab, zeigte einmal mehr Bettina Hoy mit Ringwood Cockatoo. „Natürlich bin ich superzufrieden, allerdings hatte ich gehofft, unter 30 Strafpunkten zu bleiben", sagte die Deutsche Meisterin nach ihrem Ritt. Für das letzte deutsche Paar herrschten am Freitag genau die richtigen Wetterbedin-

On Friday morning the approx. 4,000 spectators experienced two top performances. These were delivered by two ladies who both live in England, Zara Phillips and Bettina Hoy. The reigning European Champion Zara Phillips left the dressage ring on Toy Town with a score of 41.70. "The halt cost me a few points," stated the grand-daughter of the British queen, "but I am very happy." Once again Bettina Hoy gave a faultless performance with Ringwood Cockatoo and received a score of 36.50. "Of course I am delighted, although I had hoped to get a score of less than 30 points," the German Champion said after her ride. It was just the right weather conditions for the last German pair on Friday: no sun and no wind. So Ingrid Klimke's grey gelding Sleep Late was on his best behaviour in the dressage arena and delivered an elastic performance. A slight swerve on the long side and a flying change that was performed too early cost him several points. A score of 39.10 meant second place behind Bettina Hoy with Ringwood Cockatoo (36.50). After the dressage Andreas Dibowski with FRH Serve Well and the US American Kimberly Severson

VIELSEITIGKEIT | EVENTING

gungen: keine Sonne und kein Wind. So zeigte sich Ingrid Klimkes Schimmel Sleep Late mit einer geschmeidigen Vorstellung im Viereck von seiner besten Seite. Nur ein kleiner Schwenker an der langen Seite und ein zu früh gesprungener Wechsel kosteten einige Punkte. 39,10 Strafpunkte bedeuteten Rang zwei hinter Bettina Hoy. Gemeinsam mit je 40,9 Punkten auf Platz drei rangierten nach der Dressur Andreas Dibowski und die US-Amerikanerin Kimberly Severson mit Winsome Andante, Silbermedaillengewinnerin der Olympischen Spiele in Athen und Mitglied des siegreichen US-Teams bei der WM 2002. Auf Rang fünf ordnete sich Zara Phillips vor der Australierin Megan Jones mit Kirby Park King Jester (44,10), Siegerin des CCI**** Adelaide 2005, ein. In der Teamwertung lag Deutschland nach dem ersten Tag mit 122,50 Punkten vor den überraschend starken Australiern (136,10), die sich für zwölf Tage in Bonn-Rodderberg einquartiert und unter Anleitung von Harry Boldt an ihrer Dressur gefeilt hatten, und der Mannschaft aus Großbritannien (138,60).

(USA) with Winsome Andante, silver medallist at the Olympic Games in Aachen and a member of the US Team that was victorious at the FEI World Equestrian Games in Jerez de la Frontera in 2002, were joint third with a score of 40.9. Zara Phillips with Toy Town (41.70) was lying in fifth place followed by the Australian rider Megan Jones with Kirby Park King Jester (44.10), winner of the CCI**** in Adelaide the year before. After the first competition Germany was in the lead with 122.50, ahead of the surprisingly strong Australian team (136.10), who under the supervision of Harry Boldt had moved into Bonn-Rodderberg for 12 days to dedicate time to their dressage training, followed by the team from Great Britain (138.60).

Gelungener Auftakt für Ingrid Klimke: Als letzte deutsche Reiterin platzierte sie sich in der Dressur an zweiter Stelle.
Successful start for Ingrid Klimke: The last German team rider took second place in the dressage.

FEI World Equestrian Games Aachen 2006

Die Querfeldeinstrecke

Im idyllischen Aachener Soerstal wurde erstmals bei einer WM die Geländeprüfung ohne Wegestrecken und Rennbahn ausgetragen, das Aufwärmen fand auf eigens anlegten Vorbereitungsplätzen und einer Galoppierbahn statt. Der Kurs begann mit den Hindernissen 1 (Opening), 2 (Baumstamm) und 3 (Erntewagen), alles bewährte „Klassiker", freundlich und einladend, mit dennoch respektablen Anforderungen, die die Pferde „in Stimmung" bringen sollten. Die erste technische Anforderung folgte mit der Hecken-Kombination 4/5, die auf direktem Weg exakt anzureiten und schräg zu springen oder alternativ ohne Strafpunkte mit einer zeitraubenden Volte zu überwinden war. Bei der Streckenpassage durch das Stadion 2 folgten mit den beiden Remisen (6 und 7) zwei wuchtige Hochweitsprünge auf gebogener Linie, bevor dann nach einer längeren Galoppstrecke über die große Brücke mit dem Coffin „Soerser Canyon" (8a bis 8c) die erste echte WM-Anforderung folgte. Für weniger routinierte Paare wurde auch hier eine Alternative mit vergleichbaren, jedoch geringeren Anforderungen, allerdings auf deutlich längerem Weg angeboten. Nach einem mächtigen Graben mit Hecke (9) folgten zwei auf kleineren Hügeln postierte Hochweitsprünge (10 und 11), mit Windmühlen dekoriert, die ein ausbalanciertes, gut an den Hilfen stehendes Pferd erforderten. Das Gleiche, zusam-

The Cross-country Course

At the World Championships in the idyllic Aachen Soers valley the cross-country course was staged for the first time without roads and tracks and the steeplechase, instead the riders warmed up on specially created warm-up arenas and on a racetrack. The course started with the obstacles 1 (Opening), 2 (Tree Trunk) and 3 (Harvest), all proven "classics", which were designed in a friendly and inviting way but were nevertheless demanding and served the purpose of opening up the horses for the course. The direct way at the hedge combination 4/5 had to be approached accurately with the actual jumps being taken at a slight angle. This was the first technical demand of the course, which of course had an alternative route via a time-consuming circle to avoid unwanted penalties. The next section led via Stadium 2 and consisted of two massive spread obstacles the "Sheds" (No. 6 and 7) situated on a curved line. Thereafter a longer canter sec-

Ein gut funktionierendes Team im Hintergrund – bestehend aus Bundes- und Heimtrainern, Pflegern, Mannschaftstierarzt und Physiotherapeuten, dem Schmied und einer Sportpsychologin – trug mit zum Erfolg der deutschen Reiter bei. Hier wird Bettina Hoy unterstützt von Heimtrainer Dolf-Dietram Keller, ihrem Ehemann Andrew und und der Pferdepflegerin Judith Claire Langley (v.l.n.r.).
A well-functioning team behind the scenes – comprising of the National Coaches, home trainers, grooms, team veterinarian and physiotherapists, the blacksmith and a sport psychologist – contributed to the success of the German riders. In the photo Bettina Hoy with her home trainer Dolf-Dietram Keller, husband Andrew and the groom Claire Langley (f.l.t.r.).

Die Trainer

Das System von Hans Melzer und Christopher Bartle, die Heimtrainer in ihre Arbeit mit einzubeziehen, hat sich bei den Vielseitigkeitsreitern bestens bewährt. Auch in Aachen waren sie vor Ort und bei Dressur und Springen dabei, um bei den letzten Vorbereitungen zu helfen: Heinrich Meyer zu Strohen gab Andreas Dibowski letzte Tipps für seine Vorstellung auf dem Viereck, Dolf-Dietram Keller war für Andrew und Bettina Hoy gekommen, Georg Heyser gab Hinrich Romeike den letzten Schliff, und die Warendorfer Frank Ostholt und Dirk Schrade wurden von Pony-Bundestrainerin Conny Endres betreut. Auch vor dem Parcoursspringen wurden die „Buschis" nicht allein gelassen: Kurt Gravemeier war mit Ingrid Klimke und Frank Ostholt auf dem Abreiteplatz, Elmar Lesch half Andreas Dibowski und aus Schleswig-Holstein war Jörg Naeve für Hinrich Romeike angereist.

The Trainers

Hans Melzer and Christopher Bartle's stategy to involve the home trainers in their work really paid off among the eventers. They were also present in Aachen and were at hand to help the riders during the dressage and jumping competitions: Heinrich Meyer zu Strohen gave Andreas Dibowski a few last tips for his performance in the dressage arena, Dolf-Dietram Keller came to assist Andrew and Bettina Hoy, Georg Heyser gave Hinrich Romeike the last polish, Frank Ostholt and Dirk Schrade from Warendorf were supported by the National Pony Trainer, Conny Endres. The "bush riders" weren't left to their own devices before the show-jumping either: Kurt Gravemeier accompanied Ingrid Klimke and Frank Ostholt to the warm-up arena, Elmar Lesch helped Andreas Dibowski and Jörg Naeve had travelled down from Schleswig-Holstein for Hinrich Romeike.

Erfolgreiches Trainergespann: Hans Melzer und Chris Bartle
Successful trainer duo: Hans Melzer and Chris Bartle

men mit dem notwendigen Mut, Geschicklichkeit und Springvermögen wurde am „Seebad Soers" (12 und 13) abgefragt. Der erste Wasserkomplex umfasste fünf Elemente mit vielseitigen Anforderungen: ein exakt anzureitender Steilsprung (a), gefolgt von einem respektablen Wassereinsprung (b) sowie einem Inselaufsprung (c) und schließlich dem Boot (d): hochweit mit „Ecken" Effekt und dadurch leicht Vorbeiläufer provozierend. Zum Abschluss dieser Passage folgte noch eine technische Abfrage mit „Guckeffekt": der Aachener Klenkes, das Erkennungszeichen der traditionsreichen Aachener Nadelindustrie. Auch hier am ersten Teichhindernis war eine Alternativroute wählbar.

Nach einer längeren Galoppstrecke über die einladende Futterraufe (14) wartete die nächste Herausforderung mit der Normandie-Bank (15 abc), die wiederum energisches Anreiten sowie exaktes Timing auf dem geraden Weg erforderte. Der „Umweg" führte rund um das Fahrhindernis „Oktogon" und kostete sicherlich an die 15 Sekunden Zeitzuschlag. Die sich anschließenden Hindernisse „Bullfinch" (16), „Obsttisch" (17) und „Windbruch" (18) dienten der aktiven Erholung und Motivation für die noch kommenden Herausforderungen. Diese präsentierten sich als eine Doppelhecke (19a) mit Höchstabmessungen, gefolgt von einer exakt auf gebogener Linie zu treffende Ecken (19b) – alternativ bot sich ein gleich gestaltetes Hindernis auf wiederum deutlich einfacher zu bewältigendem Weg an – und dem anschließenden etwas „luftigen" Heckendurchlass (20). Nach einer weiteren Galoppstrecke wartete nach einem klassischen Trakehner (21) eine weitere technische Aufgabe auf Reiter und Pferd: die sogenannte „Sunken Road", die einmal mehr Gehorsam, Reaktionsvermögen, Balance und Kraft erforderte. Der Steg im Wasser (23) – eines der Eifeldorf-Motive – diente als motivierendes Element, bevor die Hindernisfolge 24/25ab auftauchte: die Hügellandschaft „Hillock Landscape" mit einer Heckenkombination (zwei Galoppsprünge) auf dem Gipfel sowie einer am Fuße der Anhöhe platzierten Ecke (26). Der Alternativweg ersparte den Hügelaufstieg, kostete aber auch hier wertvolle Zeit. Durch die Wiesen der Soers, bergan über eine Naturtreppe zum Picknick-Areal mit diversen Tischvariationen (26), führte die Trasse nun zur letzten Hindernisfolge der Strecke, dem malerischen Eifeldorf (27 abc/28), das noch einmal höchste Konzentration, Geschick und präzises Reiten verlangte. Zum Schluss stellten die Einzelsprünge Viehtränke (29), Eulenversteck (30) und Kentucky 2010 (31) noch zweifellos WM-würdige Anforderungen, sollten aber den Teilnehmern einen freudigen Weg ins Ziel einer Geländestrecke weisen, an deren Überwindung sie sich gern erinnern werden.

tion over the great bridge led directly to the first great test of the World Championship course, the "Soers Canyon" (8a – 8c). Here also an alternative route was provided. After a massive ditch and hedge jump (9) two spread fences followed situated on two small hills decorated with windmills, demanded a horse which is balanced and correctly on the aids. The same requirements plus courage, skill and jumping ability, were asked for at the next complex the "Seaside Resort" (12 and 13). This complex contained five elements which indeed required a variety of skills: an upright jump which needed to be approached on a very exact line (a), followed by an impressive fence into the water on a related distance followed by a jump onto an island (c) and followed by the boat (d), a spread obstacle with a corner effect which could tempt horses to a run out. Finally, completing this complex another demanding technical test followed that might cause some horses to spook, the "Klenkes", the well-recognisable emblem of the traditional needle industries of Aachen. Here at this first water combination an alternative route was also possible. After a longer easier gallop over the inviting "Hay rack" (14) the next challenge awaited the riders and horses at the "Normandy Bank" (15 abc) which again required a positive ride towards the obstacle and precision on the straight route. The "detour" led around the driving obstacle "Oktogon" and cost somewhere in the region of 15 seconds extra on the clock. The subsequent obstacles are the "Bullfinch" (16), the "Fruit Table" (17) and the "Fallen Tree" (18) and were supposed to help the horse to recover in order to master the demanding challenges that still lay ahead. The next obstacle was a double hedge (19a) with the maximum permitted dimensions followed by a corner (19b) on a curved line which required precise riding as did the slightly open hedge gap (20). Riders found an alternative to 19a/b as well, designed in a similar way but with an easier approach. After another canter distance the Soerser "wildbach" brook was crossed for the second time over a classical "Trakehner" (21) and there after another technical challenge the "Sunken Road" lay in wait, which demanded once again obedience, ability to react, balance and strength. The "Narrow bridge" (23) in the water – one of the Eifel village motifs - was supposed to serve as a motivation jump before the next series of obstacles (24/25ab): a hilly landscape with a combination of hedges (with a two canter strides distance) on the summit and a corner on the foot of the hill, which had to be accurately approached from a left curve. This would prove another demanding challenge on the direct line. After that the course ran uphill through the meadows of the Soers, first over a natural stairway towards the "Picnic area" with various table variations (26) and then towards the last sequence of obstacles, the "Eifel village" (27 abc/28), which once again required a maximum of concentration, skill and precise riding. At the end the three single obstacles "Water Trough" (29), "Nightowls-Hideaway" (30) and "Kentucky 2010" (31) were without doubt demanding and worthy of the World Championships, but were also intended to provide the riders with a friendly route to the finishing line of the cross country course, which once completed, was supposed to leave a positive impression in the riders' memories.

Viel Lob für Parcourschef Rüdiger Schwarz (re.) gab es unter anderem von Bundestrainer Christopher Bartle (l.).
There was plenty of praise for the course builder, Rüdiger Schwarz (r.) among others from the National Coach, Christopher Bartle (l.).

1 - Opening WEG Aachen 2006

2 - Oaktree

3 - Harvest Wagon

4 + 5 - Road Crossing "Gut Kuckesrath"

6 - Sheds "Hof Heumesser"

7 - Sheds

31 - See You at Kentucky 2010

30 - Night Owl's Hideaway

29 - Cattle Trough

28 - Eifel Village on the Lake

27 - Eifel Village on the Lake (A,B,C)

26 - Picknick Table "Countryside View"

25 - Hillock Landscape (A,B)

24-25 - Hillock Landscape (A,B)

24 - Hillock Landscape

23 - Eifel Village on the Lake

22 - Sunken Meadow AIX-LA Chapelle Mining (A,B,C,D)

21 - Wild

(August 2006)
Subject to change

Landschaftsarchitekten W.Cremer A.Winterscheid   Jülicher Strasse 142   52070 Aachen   Fon 0241/173917   www.la-c-w.de

8 - Soers Canyon (A,B,C)

8 - Soers Canyon (A,B,C)

9 - Ditch and Hedge

10 - Windmills Up and Down

11 - Windmills Up and Down

12 - ABCD - Seaside Resort Soers

12 - ABCD - Seaside Resort Soers

12 - ABCD - Seaside Resort Soers

13 - Needlemakers Mark

14 - Hay Rack

15 - Normandy Bank (A,B,C)

16 - Bullfinch

FEI World Equestrian Games
www.Aachen2006.de

Eventing

- Hindernisse Eventing / Obstacles Eventing
- Catering
- WC Toiletten / Toilets
- P Parken / Parking
- Eingang / Entrance
- 1 - 5 Kasse / Ticket Booth
- Nur für Teilnehmer / Only for competitors
- Sitzplätze / Seating
- Fußweg Strüver Weg - Stadion / Footpath Strüver Weg - Stadium
- Strecke / Track
- Sanitäter / Medical Service
- Die Strecke ist nur an den markierten Punkten zu queren / The track can only be crossed at the marked crossing points

Die markierten Rettungswege sind im Notfall freizuhalten
Please keep of the marked emergency routes in case of an emergency

20 - Hedges and Corners

19 - Hedges and Corners (A,B)

19 - Hedges and Corners (A,B)

18 - Fallen Tree

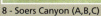
17 - Fruit Table "Hof Sonne"

FEI World Equestrian Games Aachen 2006

Geländeritt: „A lovely day out"

„It was a lovely day out", so beginnen englische Reporter gerne ihren Bericht über den Geländetag einer großen internationalen Vielseitigkeitsprüfung. Auch ein Bericht über den Aachener WM-Geländeritt hat diesen Einstieg verdient. Es begann bereits mit dem Wetter, das entgegen aller Vorhersagen am Samstag schön und trocken war und damit Massen an Zuschauern in die Soers lockte. Über 44.000 Zuschauer säumten die 6.380 Meter lange Geländestrecke und trugen nicht nur die deutschen Teilnehmer auf einer Woge der Begeisterung über die 31 Hindernisse und ihre 45 Sprünge. Die Reiter waren begeistert und erklärten unisono: „So etwas haben wir noch nie erlebt". Bereits nach der Besichtigung hatte Parcourschef Rüdiger Schwarz allenthalben nur

Cross-country: "A lovely day out"

"It was a lovely day out," is how the English reporters like to start their coverage on a cross-country event. And this was a worthy introduction for an article on the World Championships cross-country endurance test in Aachen. Everything started with the weather, in spite of Saturday's forecasts, it was nice and dry, which meant that the spectators poured into the Soers in their masses. Over 44,000 spectators lined the 6,380 metre long cross-country course and they didn't exclusively support the German competitors over the 31 obstacles and its 45 fences with their surge of enthusiasm. The riders were impressed and declared unanimously: "We have never experienced anything like it before". The course builder, Rüdiger Schwarz, had already received

Über 44.000 Zuschauer säumten die 6.380 Meter lange Geländestrecke in der Soers, um die Ritte ihrer Favoriten – hier Bettina Hoy – zu verfolgen.
Over 44,000 spectators lined the 6,380 m long cross-country track at the Soers to follow the rides of their favourites – in this case Bettina Hoy.

Vorbereitung auf den Geländeritt: Bettina und Andrew Hoy beim Abgehen der Geländestrecke.
Getting ready for the cross-country: Bettina and Andrew Hoy walking the course.

VIELSEITIGKEIT | EVENTING

Lob eingeheimst, denn er hatte es verstanden, einen championatswürdigen, aber fairen Kurs zu bauen, dessen Fehlerquellen sich über den ganzen Kurs verteilten. Bundestrainer Christopher Bartle sagte: „Für mich ist Rüdiger Schwarz der zur Zeit beste Aufbauer der Welt", und auch der fünffache britische Mannschaftseuropameister William Fox-Pitt lobte: „Der Kurs ist fantastisch, wahrlich ein Championatskurs."

Die Startnummer eins ist naturgemäß die am wenigsten geliebte. Dieser Startplatz fiel in diesem Jahr den Neuseeländern zu, die als „Pathfinder" Caroline Powell mit dem Schimmel Lenamore, im vergangenen Jahr 14te beim CCI**** Badminton ins Rennen schickten. Probleme in den fliegenden Wechseln hatten sie in der Dressur etliche Punkte gekostet, mit einem Kontostand von 66,30 Strafpunkten startete sie ins Gelände, zu denen sich bereits an der ersten Klippe des Kurses, der Heckenkombination (4/5), weitere 20 für eine Verweigerung gesellten. Besser lief es für die zweite Starterin, die dreifache Mannschaftseuropameisterin und zweifache Badminton-Gewinnerin Mary King aus Großbritannien, die mit Call Again Cavalier bis zum letzten Wasser fehlerfrei blieb. Der erste Starter, der ohne Hindernisfehler innerhalb der erlaubten Zeit ins Ziel kam, war der erste deutsche Teamreiter Hinrich Romeike. Er war zwischendurch angehalten worden, da sich das in einer Wendung reiterlos gewordene Pferd der Australierin Sonja Johnson, Ringwould Jaguar, nicht verladen ließ. „Ich wusste nicht, wie Marius reagieren würde, da uns das noch nie passiert ist", erzählte Romeike später, „aber er hat sofort seinen Rhythmus wiedergefunden."

Insgesamt kamen von den 76 ins Gelände gestarteten Paaren 27 ohne Hindernisfehler nach Hause, elf davon auch ohne Zeitfehler. Unter ihnen der zweite deutsche Teamreiter Frank Ostholt mit Air

Absolvierten den ersten fehlerfreien Ritt durch das Gelände:
Hinrich Romeike und Marius Voigt-Logistic.
Achieved the first clear cross-country round: Hinrich Romeike and Marius Voigt-Logistic.

nothing but praise from everyone after the course inspection, because he had managed to design a fair course that was nevertheless worthy of a World Championships tournament and which included a row of challenging tasks that were well distributed over the track. National Coach Christopher Bartle said: "I personally think Rüdiger Schwarz is the best course builder in the world at the moment." The five-time British team European Champion William Fox-Pitt added further praise: "The course is fantastic, a true Championship track."

*Of course nobody likes being the first to compete. This year the draw picked out the New Zealand rider Caroline Powell as the "pathfinder" with the grey gelding Lenamore, who came 14th last year at the CCI**** in Badminton. She had experienced problems with the flying changes in the dressage, which had cost her valuable points, so she set off on the endurance test with 66.30 penalty points. A further 20 were soon added to the score for a refusal at the first difficult obstacle of the course, the hedge combination (4/5). Things ran more smoothly for the second rider, the three-time team European Champion and two-time Badminton winner, Mary King from Great Britain, who went clear with Call Again Cavalier up until the last water fence. The first competitor to jump clear within the allowed time was the first German team rider, Hinrich Romeike. He had been stopped on the way, because Ringwould Jaguar, who had lost his jockey, the Australian rider Sonja Johnson, in a bend, wasn't very cooperative about getting into the horse box. "I didn't know how Marius would react, because this had never happened to us before," explained Romeike later, "but he found his rhythm again straight away."*

Of the 76 horses that set off on the course altogether, 27 reached the finishing line clear, eleven of them without time faults, including the second German team member Frank Ostholt with Air Jordan. "We showed full concentration from the start to the finish," the rider from Warendorf pointed out. "Air Jordan is always eager to pass through the flags." After these two flawless rounds, the trainers instructed Bettina Hoy to ride home safely, which is why she chose two alternative routes with Ringwood Cockatoo: At the Warsteiner Complex – a hill landscape with a hedge combination (obstacles 24/25) – and at the final water obstacle. She thus reached the finish with 7.20 time faults. Bettina Hoy was nevertheless very content with her ride: "Ringwood Cockatoo was really keen today. But with the team result in mind, it was important not to take any risks."

The fact that the mood in the German camp was somewhat dampened in spite of these fantastic cross-country results was due to the fact that the remaining German eventers had very unfortunate rides, starting with Ingrid Klimke, who set off as the last team rider. Sleep Late simply wasn't the same as usual. Ingrid Klimke had to take a firm hold of the reins, right at the start of the track, after she had the first run-out at the narrow hedge of obstacle 8, the "ABC Soers Canyon" coffin. A further refusal was noted at the entry to the Warsteiner Complex, and after picking up several time faults, she fell back to 39th place in the interim result (96.7 penalty points). "Sleep Late didn't feel right from the very beginning," his understandably deeply disappointed rider explained. "I noticed before obstacle 17 that he had no fuel left in his tank." The cross-country ride took on a surprising turn for Andreas Dibowski as well. Just after the equestrian management

FEI World Equestrian Games Aachen 2006

Ohne Zeit- und Hindernisfehler kamen Frank Ostholt und Air Jordan ins Ziel. Das Paar beendete die WM als beste Deutsche auf dem vierten Platz in der Einzelwertung.
Frank Ostholt and Air Jordan reached the finish without either time or obstacle faults. The pair provided the best German result in the World Eventing Championships, finishing fourth in the individual classification.

Jordan. "Wir waren von Anfang bis Ende sehr konzentriert", erzählte der Warendorfer. "Air Jordan will immer durch die Flaggen durch". Nach diesen beiden makellosen Runden hatte Bettina Hoy von den Trainern die Order erhalten, sicher nach Hause zu kommen. So wählte sie mit Ringwood Cockatoo zwei Mal die Alternative: am Warsteiner Komplex – einer Hügellandschaft mit Heckenkombination (Hindernis 24/25) – und am letzten Wasserhindernis, so dass sie mit 7,20 Zeitfehlern nach Hause kam. Bettina Hoy war mit ihrem Ritt dennoch sehr zufrieden: "Ringwood Cockatoo hatte heute richtig Lust. Aber mit dem Teamresultat im Hinterkopf war es wichtig, nichts zu riskieren."

Dass die Stimmung im deutschen Lager trotz dieser phantastischen Geländeleistungen nicht ungetrübt war, lag am Pech der übrigen deutschen Reiter, angefangen bei Ingrid Klimke, die als letzte Teamreiterin an den Start musste. Nichts war so, wie man es von Sleep Late gewohnt war. Schon zu Beginn der Strecke musste Ingrid Klimke zufassen, an Hindernis 8, dem Coffin "ABC Soers Canyon" gab es am schmalen Heckenaussprung den ersten Vorbeiläufer, die zweite Verweigerung musste am Einsprung des Warsteiner Komplexes notiert werden. Hinzu kamen zwangsläufig etliche Zeitfehler, die sie auf Platz 39 der Zwischenwertung zurückwarfen (96,7 Strafpunkte). "Sleep Late hat sich von Beginn an nicht gut angefühlt", kommentierte seine verständlicherweise zutiefst enttäuschte Reiterin, "und vor Hindernis 17 habe ich gemerkt, dass kein Benzin mehr im Tank war." Auch für Andreas Dibowski lief es im Gelände anders als erwartet. Noch gewohnt souverän meisterten der Pferdewirtschaftsmeister und seine Hannoveraner Stute unter dem Jubel der deutschen Fans die Wasserpassage, doch schon wenige Minuten später kam über den Lautsprecher die Meldung einer Verweigerung. Die Stute war am Aussprung der Hügellandschaft "Hillock Landscape", einer Ecke, vorbeigelaufen. Damit waren alle Hoffnungen des Egestorfers auf eine Einzelmedaille dahingeschmolzen, er fand sich nach dem Geländeritt auf Platz 21 wieder (74,10). Noch gut im Rennen war dagegen Newcomer Dirk Schrade, dessen Sindy wie an der Schnur gezogen die Geländeprüfung bewältigte. Lediglich am ersten Wasserhindernis "Seebad Soers" erlebte das Paar eine Schrecksekunde, als Sindy beim Inselaufsprung kräftig rumpelte. So gab es keine Chance mehr, eine der beiden Bootsecken zu erwischen. Dirk Schrade reagierte blitzschnell und wählte die Alternative. Trotzdem wurden ihm zunächst 20 Strafpunkte für eine Verweigerung angerechnet, die jedoch schon kurze Zeit später von der Anzeigetafel verschwanden. Am Wasseraufsprung war die Prüfung auch für eine der Mitfavoritinnen beendet: Piia Pantsu aus Finnland, Bronzemedaillengewinnerin der WM 2002, musste nach einem Rumpler von Ypäjä Karuso die Prüfung beenden. Nach dem Gelände war Zara Phillips (41,70) an Bettina Hoy (43,70) vorbeigezogen, Frank Ostholt lag auf Rang drei (46,90) vor dem australischen Weltcupsieger Clayton Fredericks mit Ben Along Time (48,80) und Heelan Tompkins mit Glengarrick (49,80). Hinrich Romeike und Dirk Schrade hatten sich auf Rang acht beziehungsweise neun vorgearbeitet. Mit diesen Ergebnissen lag die deutsche Mannschaft mit 143,0 Punkten mit großem Vorsprung vor Großbritannien (175,0), den USA (190,0) und Australien (193,3) auf Platz eins, so dass alle – Reiter, Trainer und natürlich auch die Fans – dem nächsten, entscheidenden Tag voller Hoffnung entgegensahen.

graduate had souvereignly mastered the water obstacle with his Hanoverian mare, cheered on by the German fans, it was announced over the loudspeaker a few minutes later that the mare had refused at the last fence of the hilly landscape "Hillock Landscape", a corner jump. All hopes of an individual medal disintegrated for the rider from Egestorfer, after the cross-country he ranked 21st (74.10). The newcomer, Dirk Schrader, on the other hand was still in with a good chance. His mare Sindy completed the endurance test without any difficulties at all. The pair only experienced a slight hairy moment at the first water obstacle the „Soers Sea Resort " when Sindy clipped the island jump badly, which made it impossible to stay on course for one of the two corners in boat design. Dirk Schrade reacted instantly and chose the alternative route. He was initially penalised with 20 points for a refusal, but these disappeared from the display shortly afterwards. The ride also came to an end for one of the top favourites at the water obstacle: Piia Pantsu from Finland, the bronze medallist of the 2002 World Championships, had to withdraw from the competition after her horse Ypäjä Karuso had difficulties at one of the obstacles. After the cross-country Zara Phillips (41.70) had managed to overtake Bettina Hoy (43.70), Frank Ostholt was lying third (46.90) ahead of the Australian World Cup winner Clayton Fredericks with Ben Along Time (48.80) and Heelan Tompkins with Glengarrick (49.80). Hinrich Romeike and Dirk Schrade had worked their way forward in the ranking to reach eighth and ninth place respectively. In the team result this meant the German squad were clearly in the lead with 143.0 points ahead of Great Britain (175.0), the USA (190.0) and Australia (193.3). So everyone – the riders, trainers and of course the fans – were optimistically looking forward to the deciding competition the next day.

Lagen nach einer gelungenen Geländerunde auf Platz neun: WM-Newcomer Dirk Schrade und Sindy. Infolge eines verlorenen Hufeisens musste der Reiter seine Württemberger Stute allerdings am nächsten Morgen vom Wettbewerb zurückziehen.
Ranked ninth after a successful cross-country round: the World Championships newcomers Dirk Schrade and Sindy. However, after losing a horseshoe, the rider had to withdraw his Württemberg mare from the competition the next morning.

FEI World Equestrian Games Aachen 2006

Ohne Fehler und Tadel im Gelände unterwegs war Weltcupsieger Clayton Fredericks aus Australien.
The World Cup winner, Clayton Fredericks from Australia, without faults or rebuke in the cross-country.

Nach Dressur noch auf Platz drei, verschenkte die US-Amerikanerin Kimberly Severson, Olympia-Silbermedaillengewinnerin 2004, ihre Medaille durch eine Verweigerung am Hindernis 4/5.
In joint third place after the dressage, the US American, Kimberly Severson, Olympic silver medallist in 2004, kissed goodbye to all hopes of a medal after a refusal at the obstacle 4/5.

Ritt sich mit einer Nullrunde im Gelände an die Spitze: Zara Phillips aus Großbritannien.
Rode her way to the top with a clear round in the cross-country: Zara Phillips from Great Britain.

Geländeimpressionen: Ingrid Klimke, Amy Tryon und Andreas Dibowski.
Impressions from the cross-country: Ingrid Klimke, Amy Tryon and Andreas Dibowski.

Der Oldie im Vielseitigkeitssport

Das älteste Pferd der Vielseitigkeits-WM in Aachen wurde mit einem Riesen-Sonderapplaus bedacht: der 20-jährige Glengarrick, der unter der Neuseeländerin Heelan Tompkins mit 53,80 Punkten den siebten Platz belegte. Das ehemalige Rennpferd hatte bereits vor zwei Jahren bei den Olympischen Spielen von Athen das Alterspräsidium übernommen. Vor sechs Jahren hatte Glengarric ebenfalls auf der Liste der neuseeländischen Selektoren gestanden, war dann aber aufgrund seines „hohen" Alters aussortiert worden.

The oldie in the eventing sport

The oldest horse of the Eventing World Championships in Aachen received special applause: the 20-year-old Glengarrick, who took seventh place with a score of 53.80 points under the rider from New Zealand, Heelan Tompkins. The former racehorse already took on the role as the oldest horse two years ago at the Olympic Games in Athens. Six years ago Glengarrick was also on the nomination list of the selectors in New Zealand, but was not chosen because he was too "old"

Der Oldie im Starterfeld: Glengarrick, 20 Jahre alt, landete mit seiner neuseeländischen Reiterin Heelan Tompkins auf Platz sieben.

The oldie among the eventing horses: Glengarrick, 20-years-old, landed in seventh place with his rider from New Zealand, Heelan Tompkins.

Verfassungsprüfung: Pech für Dirk Schrade

Bevor es in den Parcours ging, gab es allerdings eine Hiobsbotschaft für Dirk Schrade. Sindy hatte vor dem ersten Wasser ein Eisen verloren. In der Verfassungsprüfung wurde sie in die Holding-Box geschickt und dann zurückgezogen. Das Gleiche galt für die beiden italienischen Pferde Ecu (Marco Biasia) und Axia (Luisa Palli); alle anderen Pferde passierten ohne Probleme.

Horse inspection: Bad luck for Dirk Schrade

There was bad news for Dirk Schrade prior to the show-jumping competition. Sindy had lost a horseshoe before the first water obstacle in the cross. He was sent to the holding box at the horse inspection and later withdrawn. The same applied for both of the Italian horses Ecu (Marco Biasia) and Axia (Luisa Palli); all other horses passed the vet check without any further problems.

Springen: Go for Gold

An die 30.000 Zuschauer waren gekommen und voller Hoffnung, dass aus den „Olympiasiegern der Herzen" nun endlich „echte" Weltmeister würden. Sieben Springfehler in der Hand – das sollte eigentlich reichen. Spannender wurde es im Kampf um die Einzelmedaillen. Zwei Springfehler lagen zwischen den ersten Fünf, die beiden Erstplazierten Zara Phillips und Bettina Hoy trennten weniger als ein Abwurf. Als erste deutsche Mannschaftsreiterin startete Ingrid Klimke in den 590 Meter langen Parcours. Sleep Late wirkte wieder frisch und munter und kam ohne Springfehler ins Ziel. Ein Springfehler - am Einsprung der Zweifachen - unterlief dagegen Andreas Dibowski und der sonst so springsicheren FRH Serve Well. Er beendete damit die Weltmeisterschaft auf Platz 21. Die Spannung stieg, als Hinrich Romeike und Marius Voigt-Logistic ins Stadion kamen. Wussten doch zumindest alle deutschen Zuschauer, dass der Holsteiner Schimmel gerne einmal für einen – oder gleich mehrere – Fehler gut ist. Bei jedem Sprung ging ein Raunen durch die Zuschauer. „Ich habe an fast jedem Hindernis die Stangen gehört, aber sie sind liegen geblieben", schmunzelte Hinrich Romeike nach seinem Ritt. Unglaublicher Jubel brandete auf und die Erleichterung bei Romeikes Springtrainer Jörg Naeve war groß: „Wir haben immer nur auf

Show-jumping: Go for Gold

Around 30,000 spectators came to watch and were full of expectations that the "would-be Olympic gold medallist" would now finally become "genuine" World Champions. The Germans had a lead of seven jumping faults – which should normally suffice. The battle for the individual medals was more exciting. There were only eight faults difference between the top five, less than a jumping fault separated Zara Phillips and Bettina Hoy. Ingrid Klimke was the first German team member to enter the 590 m long course. Sleep Late made a fresh and lively impression again and reached the finish clear. Andreas Dibowski and the otherwise reliable show-jumper FRH Serve Well picked up four faults at the first fence of the double combination. The final result for him was thus 21st place in the World Championships. The tension rose as Hinrich Romeike and Marius Voigt-Logistic entered the ring. The German fans at least were quite aware that the grey Holstein gelding often knocked one or more fences in the show-jumping. The spectators gasped after every jump. "I heard him knock the poles at nearly every fence, but they stayed in place," grinned Hinrich Romeike after his ride. Immense cheering broke out and the relief on the face of Romeike's jumping trainer, Jörg Naeve, was evident: "We have worked hard for a long time with

FEI World Equestrian Games Aachen 2006

Begeisterten alle mit einer fehlerfreien Runde im Parcours: Hinrich Romeike und Marius Voigt-Logistic beendeten als einziges deutsches Paar die WM mit ihrem Dressurergebnis und wurden Fünfte.
Impressed everyone with a clear round in the show-jumping ring: Hinrich Romeike and Marius Voigt-Logistic were the only German pair to complete the World Championships without adding a single penalty point to his dressage result and ultimately took fifth place.

Aachen in mind," he said happily. Hinrich Romeike and Marius Voigt-Logistic finished the competition in fifth place without adding a single penalty point to his dressage score, something which only four other competitors managed to repeat: The new World Champion Zara Phillips with Toy Town, the bronze medallist Amy Tryon with Poggio II (50.70), the French rider Karim Florent Laghouag with Make My Day (63.70/10th place) and the English rider Daisy Dick with Spring Along (64.30/12th place).

Frank Ostholt had been within arm's reach of the bronze medal at the last European Championships in Blenheim, but time faults had prevented him from leaping up onto the winner's podium. And he missed out again in Aachen by 0.2 penalty points. Air Jordan's jumping fault in the final competition cost the rider from Warendorf the longed-for individual medal. Bettina Hoy was concentrating hard as she entered the ring with Ringwood Cockatoo, who is actually known for his reliable jumping ability. However, the pole fell at the second obstacle, then she collected a further four faults at the last fence of the triple combination plus a time fault. With a total score of 52.70 she thus fell back to sixth place in the individual classification. Understandably, Bettina Hoy was not able to conceal her disappointment at having thrown away the individual medal. Her husband had consoling words for her though: "Bettina fought for the German team. She is my true champion". The stands had in the meantime transformed into a sea of black, red and gold flags, because the German eventers had given the much sought-after "sporting reply to Athens" by winning the first ever World Eventing Championships team gold medal for Germany. It was therefore no surprise whatsoever that at the exact precise moment when Hinrich Romeike, Frank Ostholt, Bettina Hoy and Ingrid Klimke collected their gold medals, the sun began to shine over the Aachen Soers.

Riesenjubel herrschte im deutschen Lager nach dem Ritt von Bettina Hoy und Ringwood Cockatoo: Deutschland ist Weltmeister!
The German fans cheered ecstatically after Bettina Hoy and Ringwood Cockatoo's ride: Germany take the World Championship title!

VIELSEITIGKEIT | EVENTING

„Revanche" für Athen geglückt: Die deutsche Mannschaft ist Weltmeister in der Vielseitigkeit: Frank Ostholt, Ingrid Klimke, Bettina Hoy und Hinrich Romeike (v.l.n.r.).
Successful "revenge" for Athens: The German Eventing Team World Champions: Frank Ostholt, Ingrid Klimke, Bettina Hoy and Hinrich Romeike (f.l.t.r.).

Grenzüberschreitende Freude: Weltmeisterin Bettina Hoy freut sich mit Bronzemedaillengewinner Andrew Hoy.
Transborder joy: World Champion Bettina Hoy shares her joy with the bronze medallist Andrew Hoy.

Aachen hingearbeitet", freute er sich. Hinrich Romeike und Marius Voigt-Logistic beendeten die Prüfung auf Rang fünf mit ihrem Dressurergebnis, was ansonsten nur Bronzemedaillengewinnerin Amy Tryon mit Poggio II (50,70), dem Franzosen Karim Florent Laghouag mit Make My Day (63,70/Platz zehn) und der Engländerin Daisy Dick mit Spring Along (64,30/Platz zwölf) gelang.

Bereits bei den letzten Europameisterschaften in Blenheim war die Bronzemedaille für Frank Ostholt zum Greifen nahe gewesen. Zeitfehler verhinderten damals seinen Sprung auf das Treppchen. Auch in Aachen sollte es nicht sein. Ein Springfehler von Air Jordan kostete den Warendorfer um gerade einmal 0,2 Strafpunkte die ersehnte Einzel-Medaille. Hoch konzentriert begann Bettina Hoy, deren Ringwood Cockatoo eigentlich als sicheres Pferd in der letzten Teildisziplin bekannt ist, den Parcours. Doch bereits am zweiten Sprung fiel die erste Stange, ein weiterer Fehler am Aussprung der Dreifachen sowie ein Zeitfehler ließen sie mit 52,70 Punkten auf Rang sechs der Einzelwertung zurückfallen. Die Enttäuschung über den Verlust der Einzelmedaille konnte Bettina Hoy verständlicherweise nicht ganz verhehlen. Ihr Mann Andrew aber fand tröstende Worte: „Bettina hat für das deutsche Team gekämpft. Für mich ist sie der wahre Champion". Die Tribünen hatten sich inzwischen in ein schwarz-rot-goldenes Fahnenmeer verwandelt, denn die deutschen Vielseitigkeitsreiter hatten die heiß ersehnte „sportliche Antwort auf Athen" gegeben und die erste Mannschaftsgoldmedaille für Deutschland bei einer Weltmeisterschaft überhaupt gewonnen. So war es dann auch nicht verwunderlich, dass in dem Moment als Hinrich Romeike, Frank Ostholt, Bettina Hoy und Ingrid Klimke die Goldmedaillen entgegennahmen, die Sonne über der Aachener Soers in einem ihrer seltenen Momente zu strahlen begann.

Team bronze for Australia

The Australians also had reason for joy, as well as Clayton Fredericks taking individual silver, they claimed team bronze too. The riders from Down Under had one jumping fault less than the Americans in the show-jumping round, although they weren't able to count on the result of their best rider, Sonja Johnson. She took a hard fall after her horse Ringwould Jaguar clipped the Boat Corner of the first water obstacle. The 39-year-old had in fact carried on riding, but in the bend to obstacle 17, her horse had slipped away underneath her and ran off. "So I wasn't able to provide my team with any useful information," she stated. Andrew Hoy had already had a hairy moment during the horse inspection, and this was followed by another one: His Lexington winner, Master Monarch, like many others, ran out at the hedge behind the Normandy Bank, which pushed him back to 22nd place in the end (78.40). Megan Jones, winner of the CCI**** in Adelaide in 2005, experienced the same fate with Kirby Park Irish Jester at the first element of the last water obstacle: Instead of jumping over the "house" of the Eifel village, her grey gelding swerved to the left, so his rider was forced to take the alternative route. This resulted in 20 penalty points for a refusal and time faults, which dashed the Australian's hopes of achieving a good individual ranking. Megan Jones came 16th with a total score of 70.10.

FEI World Equestrian Games Aachen 2006

Mannschaftssilber für England

Die Engländer, die in Gedenken an die eine Woche zuvor bei einem Reitunfall ums Leben gekommene Sherelle Duke eine rot-weiße Schleife am Revers trugen, hatten in diesem Jahr eine neue Taktik gewählt. So waren bereits Anfang des Jahres William Fox-Pitt mit Tamarillo, Zara Phillips mit Toy Town, Mary King mit Call Again Cavalier und Pippa Funnell mit Primmore's Pride, der später wegen Verletzung ausfiel, bereits Anfang des Jahres gesetzt und von der Teilnahme an schweren Prüfungen wie Badminton oder Chatsworth befreit worden. Die Pferde mussten ihre Form lediglich in Springen und Dressur unter Beweis stellen. Die vierte Teamreiterin, Daisy Dick, war im vergangenen Jahr Elfte bei den Europameisterschaften in Blenheim und hatte auch in Badminton eine hervorragende Leistung abgeliefert. Als „Pathfinder" des Teams ging Mary King mit Call Again Cavalier, ein Sohn des von der Familie Johannsen in Tornesch gezogenen Holsteiners Cavalier Royale, einer der besten Galoppierer der Prüfung, auf die Strecke, kassierte aber eine unglückliche Verweigerung am Einsprung des letzten Wassers. Auch William Fox-Pitt, dessen Tamarillo von einem polnischen Distanzpferdevererber und einer Vielseitigkeitsstute abstammt, kam nicht ohne Hindernisstrafpunkte ins Ziel. Tamarillo lief links an der schmalen Hecke hinter der Normandie-Bank vorbei. Gänzlich unbelastet von Zeit- und Hindernisfehlern kamen Daisy Dick und Spring Along ins Geländeziel. Im Parcours erhöhten die Engländer den Druck auf die deutsche Mannschaft, in dem bis auf Mary King, die ohnehin das Streichergebnis lieferte, alle ohne Fehler ins Ziel kamen. „Wir haben versucht den Deutschen das Leben schwer zu machen, aber wir haben es nicht ganz geschafft", sagte William Fox-Pitt im Anschluss an die Prüfung, die er mit 69,0 Punkten als 15ter beendete. Daisy Dick wurde 12te (64,30) und Mary King belegte Rang 24 (81,10).

Team silver for England

The English riders, who were wearing a red and white bow in memory of Sherelle Duke who died in a fatal riding accident the week before, were following a new strategy this year. The team consisting of William Fox-Pitt with Tamarillo, Zara Phillips with Toy Town, Mary King with Call Again Cavalier and Pippa Funnell with Primmore's Pride, who was later withdrawn due to injury had already been nominated at the beginning of the year and didn't have to compete in difficult tournaments such as Badminton or Chatsworth. The horses simply had to prove their form in jumping and dressage. The fourth team rider, Daisy Dick, was eleventh at the European Championships in Blenheim last year and had also given an excellent performance in Badminton as well. Mary King with Call Again Cavalier, a Cavalier Royal son bred by Family Johannsen in Tornesch, with one of the best canters in the field, was sent out as the "pathfinder", but the pair had a rather unfortunate refusal at the first fence of the last water obstacle. William Fox-Pitt, whose Tamarillo descends from a Polish endurance horse stallion out of an eventing mare, didn't reach home without picking up obstacle faults either. Tamarillo ran out to the left at the narrow hedge behind the Normandy Bank. Daisy Dick and Spring Along crossed the finishing line without collecting any penalty points. The English team increased the pressure on the German riders in the show-jumping ring, since they all went clear apart from Mary King, who provided the scratch result. "We tried to make life difficult for the Germans, but we didn't quite manage to pull it off," William Fox-Pitt, who came 15th overall with 69.0 penalty points, commented after the competition. Daisy Dick came 12th (64.30) and Mary King finished 24th (81.10).

WM-Silber gab es für das britische Team: William Fox-Pitt, Mary King, Daisy Dick, Zara Phillips und Teamchef Yogi Breisner (v.r.n.l.).

The British team claimed silver: William Fox-Pitt, Mary King, Daisy Dick, Zara Phillips and Team Manager, Yogi Breisner (f.r.t.l.).

Mannschaftsbronze Australien

Neben der Einzelsilbermedaille von Clayton Fredericks konnten sich die Australier über Mannschaftsbronze freuen. Die Reiter aus Down Under hatten im Springparcours einen Springfehler weniger als die Amerikaner gemacht. Dabei mussten sie auf das Ergebnis ihrer ersten Reiterin Sonja Johnson verzichten. Diese war nach einem Rumpler von Ringwould Jaguar an der Bootsecke des ersten Wassers heftig zu Boden gegangen. Zwar ritt die 39-Jährige weiter, in einer Wendung zu Sprung 17 rutschte ihr Pferd und lief weg. „Ich konnte meinem Team also nicht mit Informationen helfen", sagte sie. Eine Schrecksekunde durchlebte Andrew Hoy bereits in der Verfassungsprüfung, im Gelände gab es dann die zweite: Sein Lexington-Sieger Master Monarch lief, wie etliche andere Pferde auch, am Heckensprung hinter der Normandie-Bank vorbei, so dass es für ihn am Ende Rang 22 (78,40) hieß. Megan Jones, Siegerin des CCI**** Adeleide 2005, erwischte es mit Kirby Park Irish Jester am ersten Element des letzten Wasser: Statt das „Haus" des Eifeldorfes zu überwinden, wich der Schimmel nach links aus, so dass die Reiterin den alternativen Weg einschlagen musste. Dafür gab es 20 Strafpunkte für eine Verweigerung und Zeitfehler, die die Hoffnungen der Australierin auf eine gute Einzelplatzierung zunichte machten. Megan Jones wurde mit 70,10 Strafpunkten 16te.

Einzelgold: Zara Phillips (GBR)

Bereits in der Dressur hatte Zara Phillips, deren Mutter Prinzessin Anne (im englischen Teamoutfit) und Bruder Peter helfend im Hintergrund blieben, mit ihrer harmonischen Vorstellung auf Toy Town den Grundstein zu ihrem späteren Erfolg gelegt. Auf dem Vorbereitungsplatz hatte sie den letzten Schliff von ihrer Stiefmutter Sandy Phillips erhalten, die in Aachen als Mitglied des britischen Dressurteams immerhin den Einzug in den Grand Prix Special schaffte. Im Gelände gab es für Zara Phillips, wie sie selbst zugeben musste, am ersten Wasserkomplex einen „haarigen" Moment als sie nach dem Einsprung ins kühle Nass kurz die Zügel verlor. Reiterin und Pferd managten clever diese Situation und hatten dann alles wieder unter Kontrolle. „Am letzten Wasser hatte ich die Order, die Alternative zu reiten. Ich fühlte mich aber so sicher, dass ich den direkten Weg gegangen bin", erzählte die amtierende Europameisterin. Im Parcours machte Zara Phillips es noch einmal spannend. „Nach dem Ritt von Bettina war der Jubel so groß, dass ich die Uhr nicht gehört habe", begrün-

Bronzemedaillengewinner Australien: Andrew Hoy, Clayton Fredericks, Sonja Johnson und Megan Jones (v.l.n.r.).
The Australian bronze team medallists: Andrew Hoy, Clayton Fredericks, Sonja Johnson and Megan Jones (f.l.t.r.).

Individual gold: Zara Phillips (GBR)

Zara Phillips, whose mother Princess Anne (clad in the English team outfit) and brother Peter were constantly in the background to assist, had already laid the foundation for her subsequent success by offering an harmonious performance during the dressage test with her horse Toy Town. Her step-mother Sandy Phillips, who represented the British dressage team in Aachen and even managed to qualify for the Grand Prix Spéciale, gave her a few final tips on the warm-up arena. As she admitted herself, Zara Phillips, had a „sticky" moment at the first water complex, when she lost her reins after landing in the water. Both horse and rider managed the situation cleverly and soon had everything under control again. "I had received the instruction to take the alternative route at the last water obstacle, but I felt so confident that I took the direct route," the reigning European Champion explained. Zara Phillips heightened the excitement in the jumping competition. "After Bettina rode the crowd were cheering that loud, that I didn't hear the bell," is how she explained her one second delay in setting off. She picked up four faults for knocking a fence and one for exceeding the allowed time, but this was enough to take the victory and the World Championships title. "It was simply fantastic being able to ride in this huge stadium," she said radiantly later. "My horse loves this atmosphere, so I placed all my trust in him in the show-jumping ring." The 25-year-old rider has had Toy Town since he was a five-year-old. She schooled him herself and became Vice European Champion of the Young Riders with him back in 2002.

Blaues Blut unter sich: Haya Bint al Hussein, Prinzessin von Jordanien gratuliert Weltmeisterin Zara Phillips.
Blue blood among themselves: Priness Haya of Jordan congratulates the World Champion, Zara Phillips.

FEI World Equestrian Games Aachen 2006

dete sie ihren – um eine Sekunde – verspäteten Start. Vier Fehlerpunkte für einen Abwurf und ein Fehlerpunkt für Zeitüberschreitung bedeuteten dann aber den Sieg und den Weltmeistertitel. "Es war einfach phantastisch auf diesem großen Platz zu reiten", strahlte sie hinterher. "Mein Pferd liebt diese Atmosphäre, deshalb hatte ich im Parcours großes Vertrauen in ihn." Die 25-Jährige hat Toy Town 5-jährig bekommen und selbst ausgebildet und war mit ihm bereits 2002 Vize-Europameisterin der Jungen Reiter.

Einzelsilber: Clayton Fredericks (AUS)

Der seit langer Zeit in England lebende Clayton Fredericks war vor den Weltreiterspielen so etwas wie ein Geheimfavorit unter den Vielseitigkeitsreitern, hatte er doch mit Ben Along Time, ebenfalls ein Nachkomme des Holsteiners Cavalier Royale, im vergangenen Jahr das Weltcupfinale in Malmö und in diesem Jahr das CCI*** Saumur gewonnen. Bereits im Viereck gelang den beiden eine akkurate Vorstellung, im Gelände kamen lediglich 4,4 Punkte für Zeitüberschreitung hinzu und im Parcours gab es eine sicher herausgerittene Nullrunde. "Ich habe nicht an Medaillen gedacht, sondern mich auf jede einzelne Disziplin konzentriert. In diesem Sport muss man einen klaren Kopf behalten", erzählte Clayton Fredericks. Eigentlich sollte auch seine Frau Lucinda, eine gebürtige Engländerin, nach ihrer hervorragenden Leistung beim CCI**** Luhmühlen in Aachen reiten. Doch es gab ein Problem: Ihr neuer australischer Pass war nicht rechtzeitig eingegangen.

Einzelbronze: Amy Tryon (USA)

Amy Tryon und Poggio II vertraten schon bei den Weltreiterspielen in Jerez de la Frontera und bei den Olympischen Spielen in Athen die amerikanischen Farben. Die hauptamtliche Feuerwehrfrau aus Redmont (Washington) hat ihren 14-jährigen Vollblüter über ein lokales Anzeigenblatt gefunden, in dem er als Handpferd für Bergtouren annonciert gewesen war. Nach der Dressur hatte das Paar noch auf dem 24. Platz gelegen, zu ihren 50,70 Punkten mussten im Verlauf der Prüfung keine weiteren hinzuaddiert werden. "Der Geländekurs ritt sich genauso, wie wir es nach dem Abgehen erwartet hatten", erklärte die Amerikanerin, die als Erste für ihr Team auf die Strecke gegangen war. Das hatte letztendlich im Springen um 0,8 Punkte die Bronzemedaille verpasst. Auch das vermeintlich stärkste Paar des US-Teams, die dreifache Siegerin im CCI**** Lexington und Olympia-Silbermedaillengewinnerin Kimberly Severson und Winsome Andante (71,70/Platz 17) hatten gleich zu Beginn des Kurses eine Verweigerung hinnehmen müssen, danach ging die Reise in Bilderbuchmanier weiter.

Individual silver: Clayton Fredericks (AUS)

Clayton Fredericks, who has been living in England for years, was the eventing insider's secret tip for the World Championships, after winning the World Cup Final in Malmö and the CCI*** in Saumur with Ben Along Time, also a son of the Holstein stallion Cavalier. The pair succeeded in giving an accurate performance in the dressage, only 4.4 penalty points for exceeding the time were added to that in the cross-country and they went clear in a well-ridden show-jumping round. "I didn't think about medals, I merely concentrated on each separate discipline. You have to keep a clear head in this sport," Clayton Fredericks remarked. His wife Lucinda, who was actually born in England, was also supposed to ride in Aachen after her excellent performance at the CCI**** in Luhmühlen, but unfortunately her new Australian passport didn't arrive on time.

Die Siegerfaust war berechtigt: Mit einer Nullrunde im Springen ritt Weltcup-Sieger Clayton Fredericks aus Australien mit Ben Along Time zur Silbermedaille.
The clenched fist was justified: With a clear round in the jumping the World Cup winner from Australia, Clayton Fredericks, took the silver medal with Ben Along Time.

Individual bronze: Amy Tryon (USA)

Amy Tryon and Poggio II already represented the American flag at the FEI World Equestrian Games in Jerez de la Frontera and at the Olympic Games in Athens. The full-time fire-fighter from Redmont (Washington) found her 14-year-old thoroughbred through an advert in a local newspaper, where it was advertised as a pack-horse for mountain tours. After the dressage, the pair was in 24th place, no further penalty points were added to their score of 50.70 in the two subsequent competitions. "The cross-country course was exactly how we expected it to be after walking the course," the American rider explained. She was the first team member to set off on the track. An annoying 0.8 penalty points hindered the team from taking the bronze medal. The allegedly strongest pair in the US team, the three-time winner of the CCI**** in Lexington and Olympic silver medallist, Kimberly Severson and Winsome Andante (71.70/17th) also had a refusal early on, but then mastered the rest of the course in exemplary style.

Lob für Poggio II: Feuerwehrfrau Amy Tryon aus Redmont (Washington) holte Bronze.
Praise for Poggio II: Fire-fighter Amy Tryon from Redmont (Washington), World Champion in 2002, took individual bronze.

Die neue Weltmeisterin Zara Phillips mit Silbermedaillengewinner Clayton Fredericks (AUS) und Bronzemedaillengewinnerin Amy Tryon (USA).
The new World Champion Zara Phillips with silver medallist Clayton Fredericks (AUS) and bronze medallist Amy Tryon (USA).

Vielseitigkeit | Eventing

Qualifiziert für Olympia

Neben den Medaillengewinnern Deutschland, Großbritannien und Australien konnten sich die USA und Schweden direkt für die Olympischen Spiele in Hongkong qualifizieren. Bester Schwede war der Medizinstudent Magnus Gällerdal mit seinem Vollblüter Keymaster xx auf Rang acht (53,80). Dem in England lebenden Dag Albert war es mit Who's Blitz gelungen, genau in der vorgeschriebenen Zeit – 11 Minuten und 12 Sekunden – ins Geländeziel zu kommen. Dafür wurde er am Kürabend genauso wie der bei Familie Hoy trainierende Japaner Yoshiaki Oiwa (Fifth Avenue Fame/74,50/Platz 18/) und Heelan Tompkins mit einem Preis ausgezeichnet. Die vermeintlich stärkste Reiterin der Schweden, Linda Algotsson (96,90/ Platz 35) hatte sich auf der aus eigener Zucht stammenden Stute My Fair Lady gleich zu Beginn der Strecke eine Verweigerung an der Heckenkombination (Hindernis 4/5) eingehandelt. Mit drei für Ballys Geronimo ungewöhnlichen Verweigerungen war Viktoria Carlerbäck (129,60/ Platz 43) ins Ziel gekommen.

Enttäuscht: Neuseeland und Frankreich

Zwei starke Vielseitigkeitsnationen, Neuseeland und Frankreich, haben die direkte Qualifikation für Olympia nicht geschafft. Außer dem 20-jährigen Glengarrick kam kein neuseeländisches Pferd ohne Geländefehler nach Hause. Gleich für die erste Mannschaftsreiterin, Caroline Powell mit Lenamore (88,30/Platz 26), musste eine Verweigerung am zweiten Heckensprung des Hindernisses 4/5 notiert werden, an selber Stelle traf es auch Andrew Nicholsons Lord Killinghurst (79,60/Platz 23), der von Anfang an nicht in seinen Rhythmus kam und bis dahin schon an zwei Sprüngen leichte Probleme hatte. Dennoch kamen die beiden Routiniers ohne Zeitfehler ins Ziel. Bis zum letzten Wasser spielte Joe Meyers Snip (170,80/Platz 51) mit den an ihn gestellten Anforderungen. Vor dem ersten Hauselement des „Eifeldorfes" konnte der Schimmel dann einen Fehler seines Reiters nicht mehr ausgleichen, blieb stehen und Joe Meyer fiel herunter.

Bereits bei der ersten Verfassungsprüfung hatte es eine Überraschung gegeben. Der Europameister von 2003, Nicolas Touzaint, präsentierte nicht sein EM-Sieger- und Olympiapferd Galan de Sauvagère, sondern den elfjährigen braunen Wallach Hildago d'Ile (91,0/Platz 28). Er hatte sich nach der ersten Besichtigung des Geländes für das, wie er meinte, bessere Geländepferd entschieden. Doch dem Paar wurde die Hecke nach der Normandie Bank zum Verhängnis. Gar zwei Verweigerungen aus dem Gelände brachte Titelverteidiger, Jean Teulere mit Espoir de la Mare (144,20/Platz 47) mit nach Hause. Jean Teulere war nach einem Reitunfall lange verletzt gewesen und hat erst in diesem Jahr wieder intensiv mit dem Vielseitigkeitssport beginnen können.

Qualified for the Olympic Games

As well as the medal-winners Germany, Great Britain and Australia, the USA and Sweden were also able to directly qualify themselves for the Olympic Games in Hong Kong. The medical student, Magnus Gällerdal, was the best Swede with his thoroughbred Keymaster xx, finishing eighth (53.80). Dag Albert, who is also resident in England, managed to reach home exactly in the allowed time with Who's Blitz. For which he received a prize on the freestyle evening together with Heelan Tompkins and the Japanese rider Yoshiaki Oiwa (Fifth Avenue Fame/ 74.50/18th) who is trained by family Hoy. The reputedly strongest Swedish rider, Linda Algotsson (96.90/35th) also fell victim to the hedge combination (obstacle 4/5) at the beginning of the course, when her home-bred mare My Fair Lady refused. Viktoria Carlerbäck had had three refusals by the time she reached the finishing line, which is very unusual for Ballys Geronimo (129.60/43rd).

Bester Schwede in Aachen war der Medizinstudent Magnus Gällerdal mit Keymaster
The medical student, Magnus Gällerdal, was the best Swede in Aachen with Keymaster.

Disappointed: New Zealand and France

Two strong eventing nations, New Zealand and France, didn't succeed in directly qualifying for the Olympic Games. Apart from the 20-year-old Glengarrick, no other horse in the New Zealand team reached home clear. A refusal at the second hedge fence of obstacle 4/5 had to be noted for the first team rider, Caroline Powell with Lenamore (88.30/26th), exactly the same thing happened to Andrew Nicholson's Lord Killinghurst (79.60/23rd), who didn't find the right rhythm from the start and who had already had two bad fences until then. However, the experienced duo reached the finished without any time faults. Up until the last water obstacle, Joe Meyer's Snip (170.80/51st) mastered the set challenges with ease. Unfortunately, the grey gelding wasn't able to compensate a mistake by his rider in the approach to the first house of the "Eifel Village" and stopped in front of it, which led to Joe Meyer' fall.

There had already been a big surprise at the first horse inspection. The European Champion of 2003, Nicolas Touzaint, didn't present his European Champion and Olympic Games horse, Galan de Sauvagère, but instead the 11-year-old bay gelding, Hildago d'Ile (91.0/28th). After inspecting the course, he had opted for the best cross-country horse of the two. But, the hedge after the Normandy Bank also led to their doom. In fact the defending titleholder, Jean Teulere, had two refusals with Espoir de la Mare (144.20/47th). After a bad fall Jean Teulere had been out with injury for a long time and was only able to start competing intensively again this year.

Enttäuschung: Mannschafts-Olympiasieger Nicolas Touzaint und Titelverteidiger Jean Teulere (r.) gingen in Aachen leer aus.
Disappointed: Team Olympic gold medallist, Nicolas Touzaint, and titleholder, Jean Teulere (r.), left Aachen empty-handed.

Fahren / Driving

Autor/Author
Rudolf Temporini

Goldteam Deutschland: (v.l.n.r.) Christoph Sandmann, Ewald Meier, Michael Freund und Rainer Duen.
Gold for the German team: (f.l.t.r.) Christoph Sandmann, Ewald Meier, Michael Freund and Rainer Duen.

Die Disziplin Fahren

Die Vierspännerfahrer erleben ihre erste Weltmeisterschaft 1972 in Münster. In der Mannschaftswertung fährt das deutsche Team (Franz Lage, Heinz Funda und Georg Bauer) bei der Premiere auf Anhieb in die Medaillenränge: Bronze hinter Großbritannien und der Schweiz. Alle vier Jahre bislang immer auf europäischen Plätzen ausgetragen, werden die Weltmeisterschaften dominiert von den Fahrsportlern aus Ungarn, Schweden, Belgien, Niederlanden und Deutschland. Die erste Mannschafts-Goldmedaille erreichen die Deutschen (Johann Böhler, Michael Freund und Christoph Sandmann) jedoch erst 1992 in Riesenbeck. Zwei Jahre später, bei den Weltreiterspielen in Den Haag (NED), gewinnt mit Michael Freund erstmals ein deutscher Fahrer in der Einzelwertung Gold. Die Mannschaft gewinnt ebenso die Goldmedaille.

Bei Weltmeisterschaften starten drei Fahrer in der Mannschaft, Gastgeber Deutschland darf bei den Weltmeisterschaften in Aachen zusätzlich zwei Einzelfahrer an den Start schicken. Vergleichbar mit dem Championatsmodus der Vielseitigkeitsreiter, absolvieren auch die Vierspännerfahrer die Prüfung als Kombinierte Wertung in drei Teildisziplinen: Dressur, Gelände- und Streckenfahrt (Marathon) sowie Hindernisfahren. Das Dressurergebnis (Punktsumme der fünf Richterurteile) wird in Strafpunkte umgerechnet. Die zweite Prüfung, die Gelände- und Streckenfahrt, führt die Teilnehmer durch drei Phasen. Der Abschnitt A ist eine Wegstrecke von ca. 7000 m in beliebiger Gangart, in Phase D ist auf eine Länge von ca. 1000 m Gangart Schritt vorgeschrieben. Nach Phase D überprüfen Richter und Tierärzte in der Zwangspause Puls, Atmung und Gesamteindruck der Pferde. Bei Zweifeln an Kondition und Belastbarkeit des Gespanns kann ein Start in der Phase E, der Hindernisstrecke, untersagt werden. Diese letzte Phase, das Herzstück der Gelände- und Streckenfahrt, ist rund 9000 Meter lang und führt durch acht Geländehindernisse. Das Geländeergebnis wird ebenso in Strafpunkte umgerechnet, wobei für jede gebrauchte angefangene Sekunde in den Hindernissen der Teilnehmer 0,2 Strafpunkte bekommt. Den Abschluss der kombinierten Wertung bildet das Hindernisfahren im Kegelparcours. Hierbei wird besonders die Geschicklichkeit beim Fahren durch Kegel, durch Stangenhindernisse, über Brücken und in Schlangenlinien überprüft. Auch dieser Teildisziplin ist eine Verfassungsprüfung vorgeschaltet. Die Kombinierte Prüfung ist nach dem Hindernisfahren entschieden. Ein eventuell notwendiges Stechen fließt nicht in das Gesamtergebnis ein. Sieger ist derjenige Fahrer, der in drei Prüfungen die wenigsten Strafpunkte verbucht. Für die Mannschaftswertung werden je Teilprüfung die Ergebnisse der beiden besten Fahrer addiert.

The driving discipline

The four-in-hand drivers experienced their first World Championships in Munster in 1972. In the team classification the German drivers (Franz Lage, Heinz Funda and Georg Bauer) managed to claim a medal at the debut event: Bronze behind Great Britain and Switzerland. Organised every four years and up until now always at European venues, the World Championships are dominated by drivers from Hungary, Sweden, Belgium, the Netherlands and Germany. However, the Germans didn't take their first team gold medal (Johann Böhler, Michael Freund and Christoph Sandmann) until 1992 in Riesenbeck. Two years later at the FEI World Equestrian Games in the Hague (NED), Michael Freund was the first German driver ever to win individual gold. The team also claimed the gold medal.

At the World Championships three drivers compete in the team. As the hosts of the tournament, Germany was additionally allowed to enter two individual drivers in Aachen. Comparable to the championships mode of the eventers, the four-in-hand drivers also have to complete three competitions in the individual disciplines: Dressage, cross-country (Marathon) and obstacle driving. The dressage result (total sum of the scores of the five judges) is converted into penalty points. The second competition, the Marathon consists of three phases. Phase A is roads and tracks, where a distance of approx. 7,000 has to be completed in the gait of one's choice, Phase D, is a distance of approx. 1,000 m which has to be covered in walk. After Phase D, the judges and veterinarians check the horses' pulse, breathing and general impression during the compulsory break. If any doubt arises as to the condition or the fitness of the driving team, they can be prevented from taking part in Phase E, the Marathon. This last phase, the core element of the cross-country, is around 9,000 m long and leads through eight cross-country obstacles. The Marathon result is converted into penalty points, whereby the drivers receive 0.2 penalty points for every commenced second taken to pass through the obstacles. The final competition is the obstacle driving test. This demands particular skill in steering the carriage through cones, pole obstacles, over bridges and through serpentines. A horse inspection is also carried out prior to this rating competition. After the obstacle driving course the combined result can then be determined. If a drive-off is necessary, the results are not integrated into the overall result. The winner is the driver, who has collected the least penalty points after all three competitions. For the team classification the results of the two best drivers in each rating competition are added together.

Die deutsche Mannschaft | The German Team

Reiter / Rider	Alter / Age	Pferd / Horse Pfleger / Groom	Alter / Age	Zuchtgebiet / Breeding Area	Züchter / Breeder Besitzer / Horse O
Rainer Duen (Friesoythe)	35	Campo 3	12	Oldenburg	Jürgen R. Thumann
		Con Air 11	6	Oldenburg	-
		Leo 388	6	Oldenburg	Rainer Duen
		Magun 2	13	Oldenburg	Bernhard Duen
		Mandy 111	16	Oldenburg	Jürgen R. Thumann
		Monaco 106	7	Oldenburg	Rainer Duen
		Mustang 59	13	Oldenburg	Bernhard Duen
		Santo 42	12	Oldenburg	Bernhard Duen
Michael Freund (Dreieich)	51	Dollart 14	12	Oldenburg	Heinrich Graucob
		Eminenz 22	10	Sachsen	Tucker Johnson
		FORS Babalu	15	Russland	FORS e.V.
		FORS Flambo	13	-	FORS e.V.
		Freak FORS	16	-	FORS e.V.
		Impala 40	12	-	Kathrin Koch
		Pit 57	12	-	Frank Freund
		Squire 4	6	-	Jürgen Scheu
Christoph Sandmann (Lähden)	39	Dicky 7	12	Belgien	Christoph Sandman
		Dinard	12	-	Christoph Sandman
		Erwood	14	-	Christoph Sandman
		Gerlof 1	18	Holland	Christoph Sandman
		Haut Marnais	11	-	Christoph Sandman
		Rambo 156	12	-	Adolf Fischer
		Smash	8	-	Adolf Fischer
Ludwig Weinmayr (Fischbachau)	35	Harris Bey	13	Polen	Ludwig Weinmayr
		Landlord 27	15	Oldenburg	Ludwig Weinmayr
		Libero 89	11	Bayern	Ludwig Weinmayr DOKR
		Limerick 87	9	Bayern	Ludwig Weinmayr
		Red-Run	6	Oldenburg	Ludwig Weinmayr
		Ricardo 467	9	Bayern	Helmut Niedermeie
Josef-Nicolaus Zeitler (Starnberg)	33	Felix 1526	7	-	Josef-Nicolaus Zeitl
		Lines 28	13	Baden-Württemb.	Josef-Nicolaus Zeitl
		Mr. Bexter	12	Russland	Josef-Nicolaus Zeitl
		Pobey	18	-	Josef-Nicolaus Zeitl
		Vadopoi	17	Russland	Josef-Nicolaus Zeitl

Equipechef / Chef d'Equipe	Bundestrainer / National Trainer	Tierarzt / Veterinarian	Hufschmied
Ewald Meier	Eckardt Meier	Dr. Marc Köne	Dieter Kröhner

FAHREN | DRIVING

Mannschaftsgold, Einzelbronze und ein wehmütiger Abschied

Nach den bisherigen Saisonergebnissen zählte das deutsche Team im Vorfeld dieser Weltreiterspiele sowohl in der Einzel- als auch in der Mannschaftswertung sicher nicht zu den großen Favoriten. Jeweils sechste Plätze bei den Nationenpreisen in Breda und Aachen waren keine Visitenkarte, die die Fans optimistisch stimmten. Allein die seit Jahren bekannte Turnierstärke von Freund und Sandmann ließ Hoffnung aufkommen. Im Trainingslager in Lähden wurde das Thema Hindernisfahren in den Mittelpunkt gestellt. Bundestrainer Ewald Meier war klar, dass der Erfolg in dieser Teildisziplin der Schlüssel zu einer Mannschaftsmedaille sein würde.

Verfassungsprüfung

Verfassungsprüfung: Vortraben von Rainer Duen.
Horse inspection: Rainer Duen trotting his horse.

Die Verfassungsprüfung – einige Fahrer behaupten, es sei die schwerste Prüfung überhaupt – verlief ohne jegliche Komplikationen. Alle Pferde wurden anstandslos akzeptiert. Die Ergebnisse des Jahres waren so eindeutig, dass die Entscheidung über die Mannschaftsnominierung für den Bundestrainer nicht schwer war: Rainer Duen, Michael Freund und Christoph Sandmann bildeten das Team. Die beiden Bayern Josef Zeitler und Ludwig Weinmayr starteten als Einzelfahrer.

Die Dressurprüfung

Christoph Sandmann war der Erste aus dem deutschen Team, der in das Dressurviereck musste, und er legte dabei den Grundstein für eine tolle Mannschaftsleistung. Praktisch ohne Patzer fuhr der Emsländer seine Dressur mit deutlich sichtbaren Übergängen und gelungenen Hufschlagfiguren. Der Anfang für eine Erfolgsstory war mit 46,59 Strafpunkten und Platz sieben in der Endabrechnung dieser Teilprüfung gemacht. Bei Rainer Duen lief es nicht so gut wie erhofft. Durch mangelnde Losgelassenheit und eine deutlich sichtbare Problematik in der Anlehnung fand er sich auf Rang 24 wieder. 60,29 Strafpunkte waren ein ungewohntes Ergebnis für den Deutschen Vizemeister. Aber mit Michael Freund stand ja die Trumpfkarte des deutschen Fahrsportes noch aus und der "Weltmeister der Herzen", wie er in Aachen des Öfteren tituliert wurde, erfüllte seine Aufgabe mit höchster Präzision. Kaum einer im internationalen Fahrsport stellt seinen Vierzug mit solch korrekten Hufschlagfiguren und gut erkennbaren und auf den Punkt gefahrenen Übergängen vor wie der deutsche Rekordmeister. Sein Gespann hat nicht die brillante Ausstrahlung eines Vierzuges von Dressursieger Chester Weber (USA) oder des späteren Weltmeisters Felix-Marie Brasseur. Aber dennoch, das Richterkollegium honorierte seine Vorstellung mit 41,60 Strafpunkten. Das bedeutete Platz drei für Michael Freund in dieser Teilprüfung.

Christoph Sandmann – Bronze in der Einzelwertung – war eine „Bank" für das deutsche Team.
Christoph Sandmann – who took individual bronze – was the "pillar" of the German team.

Team gold, individual bronze and a sad farewell

In the run up to the FEI World Equestrian Games the German team certainly didn't belong to the top favourites for individual or team gold especially on closer consideration of the results so far this season. Sixth place at both of the Nations' Cups in Breda and Aachen wasn't exactly a performance that could get the fans feeling optimistic. The only thing that raised a little hope was the tournament strength of Freund and Sandmann that had been well established for years. The theme of obstacle driving was the focal point dealt with at the training camp in Lähden. National Coach, Ewald Meier, was quite sure that a successful result in this competition could be the key to the team medal.

The horse inspection

The horse inspection – some drivers maintain that this is the hardest test of all – ran smoothly. All of the horses passed the check without a hitch. The results of the year were so clear-cut that the National Coach didn't have a difficult decision in nominating the team: Rainer Duen, Michael Freund and Christoph Sandmann were the chosen equipe members. The two drivers from Bavaria Josef Zeitler and Ludwig Weinmayr additionally competed in the individual classification.

Dressage

Christoph Sandmann was the first German team member to enter the dressage arena and he lay the foundation for a super team performance. The driver from Emsland showed an almost flawless dressage test characterised by clearly visible transitions and correctly performed school figures. A score of 46.59 penalty points and seventh overall in the dressage competition set the basis for the success story. Things didn't go as well as expected for Rainer Duen. Due to a lack of relaxedness and visible contact difficulties he received a score of 60.29, an extremely unusual

Ergebnisse/ Results Seite/ page 141

FEI World Equestrian Games Aachen 2006

Felix-Marie Brasseur gewann Einzelgold.
Felix-Marie Brasseur won individual gold.

Tucker Johnson – ein Schützling von Michael Freund – Fünfter in der Dressur.
Tucker Johnson – one of Michael Freund's protégés – was fifth in the dressage.

Der haushohe Favorit Ysbrand Chardon lag nur 0,4 Punkte vor Michael Freund. Eine glänzende Ausgangsbasis für den deutschen Mitfavoriten. In der Teamwertung führten die US-Amerikaner durch die überragende Vorstellung von Chester Weber und eine ordentliche Dressur von Tucker Johnson zunächst recht deutlich vor der deutschen Mannschaft. Einzelfahrer Ludwig Weinmayr fuhr sehr gut; seine beste Dressur in den letzten zwei Jahren. Das Gespann war auf den Punkt topfit und der Bayer überzeugte mit selten gezeigter Harmonie und Taktsicherheit seiner vier Braunen. Tränen der Enttäuschung bei der Engländerin Karen Basset, einer von zwei Damen in der von Männern beherrschten Vierspänner-welt. Sie hatte von ihrem Equipechef eine verkehrte Startzeit genannt bekommen, fuhr ganz ohne Vorbereitung in das Viereck und ihre Leistung war entsprechend.

Die Marathonfahrt

Der Geländetag brachte eine Premiere. Nicht der Aachener Wald sollte Austragungsort des Spektakels Marathon werden, sondern das Gelände direkt neben der Aachener Soers. Hier hatte auch der Geländeritt der Vielseitigkeit stattgefunden. Die Sonne schien, der Dauerregen der vergangenen Tage gehörte der Vergangenheit an. Den Teilnehmern bot sich ein Geläuf vom Allerfeinsten. Parcourschef Dr. Wolfgang Arsendorf (Salzhausen) hatte

Parcourschef Dr. Wolfgang Asendorf, Ysbrand Chardon und Michael Freund (v.l.n.r.) in intensiver Diskussion.
Course builder, Dr. Wolfgang Asendorf, Ysbrand Chardon and Michael Freund (f.l.t.r.) in deep discussion.

result for the German Vice-Champion, which put him down to 24th place in the interim results. But the trump card of the German driving sport was still to come, Michael Freund, the "World Champion of the hearts" as he is often referred to in Aachen, fulfilled his task with highest precision. Hardly anyone else in international driving sport is able to present such correct figures and well recognisable transitions that are carried out on the spot as the German record master. His team of horses doesn't have the breath-taking charm of the horses of the dressage winner, Chester Weber (USA), or of Felix-Marie Brasseur, who was to subsequently become World Champion. And yet the judges honoured his performance with a score of 41.60: Third place in the first rating competition for Michael Freund. The absolute favourite Ysbrand Chardon lay only 0.4 points ahead of Michael Freund. A wonderful starting basis for the German co-favourite. The US Americans had a clear lead ahead of the German drivers in the team classification after the outstanding performance of Chester Weber and an orderly dressage test by Tucker Johnson. The individual competitor Ludwig Weinmayr drove very well; his best dressage test in the

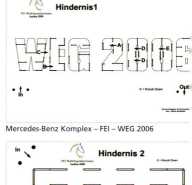

Mercedes-Benz Komplex – FEI – WEG 2006

Warsteiner Komplex – Sunflowers

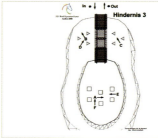

Rolex Komplex – Seaside Resort

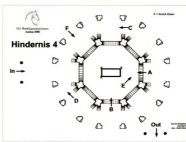

Deutsche Bank Komplex – Aachener Dom/ Oktogon

FAHREN | DRIVING

last two years. The team of horses was top fit and the Bavarian driver convinced the judges, because his four brown horses showed a rarely seen before level of harmony and secure rhythm. Tears of disappointment for the English driver, Karen Basset, one of only two ladies in the four-in-hand world dominated by men: Her Chef d'equipe had told her the wrong starting time, so she had to drive straight into the dressage arena without being able to warm up, and gave a corresponding performance.

The Marathon

The cross-country day featured a premiere; the Marathon didn't take place in the Forest of Aachen as usual, but instead on the area adjacent to the Soers, where the cross-country of the eventers had also taken place. The sun shone, the continuous rain of the past days was a thing of the past. The footing was perfect for the competitors. The course designer, Dr. Wolfgang Arsendorf (Salzhausen), had built very technical, difficult obstacles, but they were fortunately flagged out with many alternatives. For the less experienced drivers there was always the opportunity to take a longer, but safer route.

Rainer Duen meisterte die Geländehindernisse fehlerfrei.
Rainer Duen mastered the cross-country obstacles without picking up any faults.

bwin Komplex – Mikado

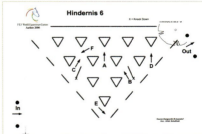
ARAG Komplex – Dreiländereck

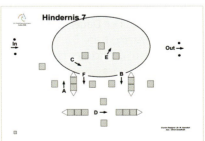
Dubai Equestrian Club Komplex – Arabian Oasis

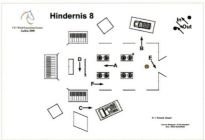
Sparkassen Komplex – Eifel Village

In unmittelbarer Nähe zum Turniergelände wurden die acht Hindernisse der Marathonfahrt extra für die WM angelegt.
The eight Marathon obstacles were built right next to the show grounds especially for the World Championships.

Ergebnisse/ Results Seite/ page 141

FEI WORLD EQUESTRIAN GAMES AACHEN 2006

Ysbrand Chardon war der dominierende Fahrer im Gelände.
Ysbrand Chardon was the superior driver in the Marathon competition.

A demanding walk phase, which was incidentally completely supervised by video cameras, prove to be a headache for some participants and led to the odd penalty point. The team driver Rainer Duen also picked up four penalty points here. Spectacular accidents at obstacle 1, which luckily looked worse than they actually were, startled a few of the spectators. The Irish driver, Barry Capstick, was trapped when the carriage turned over and badly bruised his leg. The accident of the driver from the Netherlands Antilles, Bert Brans, was even more spectacular. His carriage tipped over on the hill. The team of horses bolted, galloped over the warm-up area in the driving stadium, where they fortunately came to a standstill. One of the horses fell and was dragged along by the others for quite a stretch, but by some miracle it only sustained slight injuries. Otherwise there were few unusual occurrences during the Marathon competition, which had attracted approx. 30,000 spectators.

die Hindernisse technisch sehr schwierig, aber mit erfreulich vielen Alternativen ausgeflaggt. Auch für die schwächeren Fahrer gab es jederzeit Möglichkeiten, auf längere, aber sichere Passagen auszuweichen.

Eine anspruchsvolle Schrittstrecke, die übrigens komplett videoüberwacht wurde, bereitete manchem Teilnehmer Kopfzerbrechen und führte zu dem einen oder anderen Strafpunkt. Auch Mannschaftsfahrer Rainer Duen holte sich hier vier Strafpunkte ab.

Spektakuläre Unfälle am Hindernis 1, die aber glücklicherweise glimpflich abliefen, erschreckten den einen oder anderen Zuschauer. Der Ire Barry Capstick wurde von der umstürzenden Kutsche eingeklemmt und erlitt schmerzhafte Prellungen am Bein. Noch spektakulärer war der Unfall von Bert Brans von den niederländischen Antillen. Die Kutsche kippte am Hang um. Das Gespann konnte nicht mehr gestoppt werden, galoppierte über den Abfahrplatz in das Fahrstadion, wo es dann jedoch zum Stehen kam. Ein gestürztes Pferd wurde eine lange Strecke mitgeschleift und wie durch ein Wunder aber nur leicht verletzt. Ansonsten gab es keine besonderen Vorkommnisse an diesem Tag mit rund 30.000 Zuschauern.

Einen knappen Sieg sicherte sich in der Teilprüfung Gelände der holländische Ausnahmekönner Ysbrand Chardon. Die Spitzenfahrer lagen alle eng beisammen. Felix-Marie Brasseur nur 0.43 Punkte hinter Chardon und dann kamen schon der Schweizer Stefan Klay und der schwedische Exweltmeister Thomas Eriksson. Christoph Sandmann hatte als einer der ersten Starter lange die Führung inne; in der Endabrechnung blieb Platz sechs für ihn. Damit ein weiterer Beitrag zum guten Mannschaftsergebnis der Deutschen. Rainer Duen hatte sich die oben erwähnten vier Strafpunkte auf der Schrittstrecke geholt; ansonsten absolvierte er jedoch eine fast fehlerfreie Fahrt und mit 117,07 Punkten zählte sein Ergebnis für die Mannschaft. Michael Freund patzte in den Hindernissen 1 und 2 in ungewohnter Weise. Er fuhr im ersten Hindernis zunächst an Tor D und am Tor E vorbei. Auch gehan-

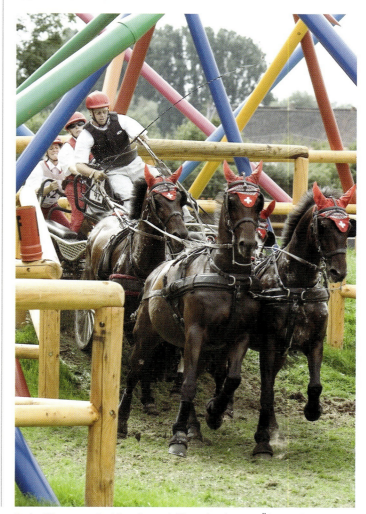

Stefan Klay sorgte im Marathon mit Platz drei für eine Überraschung.
Stefan Klay took a surprising third place in the Marathon.

FAHREN | DRIVING

Auch im anspruchsvollen ersten Hindernis war Christoph Sandmann schnell unterwegs.
Christoph Sandmann also drove through the extremely demanding obstacle number one at top speed.

Das erste Wasserhindernis (hier mit Michael Freund) war ein Publikumsmagnet.
The first water obstacle (in the photo Michael Freund) was a particular crowd-puller.

FEI World Equestrian Games Aachen 2006

Nach langsamen Zeiten in den ersten beiden Hindernissen kam Ludwig Weinmayr immer besser in Fahrt.
After clocking up slow times for the first two obstacles Ludwig Weinmayr got into the swing of things.

dicapt durch die Leine, die sich um seine Peitsche gewickelt hatte, gab es für ihn ganz offensichtlich Orientierungsprobleme. Er verlor in Hindernis 1 rund 30 Sekunden zu dem Besten und damit auch die Chance auf einen Spitzenplatz im Gelände. Aber wenn der Leitwolf schwächelt, springen die Mannschaftskameraden in die Bresche. Die Leistungen von Rainer Duen und insbesondere Christoph Sandmann bescherten dem Team die Führung in der Nationenpreiswertung knapp vor den Niederlanden und Belgien. Christoph Sandmann lag nun in der Einzelwertung auf dem vierten Platz, hauchdünn hinter dem Schweden Thomas Eriksson. Ysbrand Chardon lag knapp vor Felix-Marie Brasseur in Führung. Diese beiden hatten sich vom restlichen Feld abgesetzt. Sandmann und Eriksson hatten in der Zwischenwertung einen beruhigenden Punkte-Abstand zur Verfolgergruppe der Plätze fünf bis zehn. In dieser Gruppe war Michael Freund auf dem neunten Platz vertreten.

Hindernisfahren

Einen technisch anspruchsvollen aber durchaus flüssig zu fahrenden Parcours (siehe Zeichnung S. 83 oben) mit inzwischen gewohnt knappen Zeitrahmen hatte Dr. Asendorf konzipiert.

Josef Zeitler fuhr einen souveränen Kegelparcours.
Josef Zeitler accomplished an exemplary obstacle driving test.

The Dutch outstanding expert, Ysbrand Chardon, enjoyed an albeit narrow victory in the Marathon competition. The top drivers were all very close. Felix-Marie Brasseur only 0.43 points behind Chardon, followed by the Swiss driver, Stefan Klay, and the Swedish ex-World Champion, Thomas Eriksson. One of the first competitors in the cross-country, Christoph Sandmann held the lead for a long time; at the end he was lying in sixth place. A further contribution to the good German team result. As already mentioned, Rainer Duen had collected four penalty points in the walk phase; but otherwise he complete an almost faultless round, his score of 117.07 counted towards the team result. Michael Freund made mistakes at obstacles 1 und 2, which were very unusual for him. In the first obstacle he drove past Gate D and Gate E. Handicapped by the fact that the whip had got tangled up in the reins, he had evident orientation problems. This cost him 30 seconds onto the speed of the best driver at the first obstacle and thus also the chance of obtaining one of the top rankings in the Marathon. But when the leader show signs of weakness, the team colleagues really get down to work. The performances of Rainer Duen and in Christoph Sandmann in particular allowed the team to head the field in the Nations' Cup classification, just ahead of the Dutch and the Belgians. Christoph Sandmann was now lying fourth in the individual classification right on the heels of the Swedish driver, Thomas Eriksson. Ysbrand Chardon lay narrowly in front of Felix-Marie Brasseur. These two had clearly broken away from the rest of their competitors. In the interim results Sandmann and Eriksson had a calming margin of points over the drivers lying behind them in fifth to tenth place. Michael Freund was among them in ninth place.

Obstacles Driving

Dr. Asendorf had designed a technically demanding, but fluent-to-drive course (see picture page 83) which was as usual nowadays tight against the clock.

The drama was clearly defined: In the battle for the medals, Germany had almost 5 points more than Holland and Belgium, who were almost level. In the individual classification Brasseur and Chardon were fighting it out for gold and silver – Eriksson and Sandmann for the bronze medal.

Seppi Zeitler was the first to drive clear in the obstacle driving test. He souvereignly steered his Orlov horses through the cones. His strong performance was rewarded with third place in this rating competition. The Belgian team driver, Geert de Brauwer, collected 15.69 penalty points, which calmed the nerves of German and Dutch fans alike. The first German team member in the course was Rainer Duen. A "safe candidate" over the last few years. However at first his nerves failed him. He drove hesitantly at the beginning, but then the driver from Oldenburg collected himself again. He was, however, too slow, picking up 2.38 penalty points for the team result. Theo Timmermann, the Dutch driver clocked up only 0.41 points. After his team colleague, Kos de Ronde had picked up 4.29 penalty points, everything was down to Michael Freund. The public wanted to welcome him enthusiastically, as they had done on all the previous days, however he signalled to his fans that they should remain quiet. You could have almost heard a needle drop amid the 8,000 silent spectators in the driving stadium. And he managed it – Micha drove clear in the allowed time. The gold medal went to the German team. His

FAHREN | DRIVING

Die Dramaturgie war klar definiert: Bei dem Kampf um die Mannschaftsmedaillen lag Deutschland mit knapp 5 Punkten vor den fast punktgleichen Holländern und Belgiern. Bei der Vergabe der Einzelmedaillen kämpften Brasseur und Chardon um Gold und Silber – Eriksson und Sandmann um die Bronzemedaille.

Die erste Nullfehlerrunde lieferte Seppi Zeitler ab. Souverän steuerte er seine Orlovpferde durch die Pylonen. Mit dieser starken Leistung wurde er Dritter in dieser Teilprüfung. Der belgische Mannschaftsfahrer Geert de Brauwer leistete sich 15,69 Strafpunkte, was die deutschen und holländischen Fans etwas beruhigte. Der erste deutsche Mannschaftsfahrer war Rainer Duen. In den letzten Jahre Jahren eine „sichere Bank". Aber er zeigte zunächst Nerven. Eine unsichere Fahrt zu Anfang, aber dann lief es rund für den Mann aus dem Oldenburgischen. Etwas zu langsam war er dennoch und steuerte so 2.38 Strafpunkte zum Mannschaftsergebnis bei. Bei Theo Timmermann waren es nur 0.41 Punkte für Holland. Als sein Mannschaftskollege Kos de Ronde 4.29 Strafpunkte einfuhr, lag die Bürde der Verantwortung bei Michael Freund. Das Publikum wollte ihn, wie immer in den Tagen von Aachen, mit enthusiastischem Beifall begrüßen. Aber er dirigierte seine Fans souverän zu absoluter Ruhe. Eine Stecknadel hätte man fallen hören können, völlige Stille bei 8.000 Zuschauern im Fahrstadion. Und es gelang – Micha blieb null und in der Zeit. Goldmedaille für das deutsche Team. Mit dieser Runde schob er sich noch auf einen tollen fünften Platz in der Gesamtwertung vor. Aber der Spannungsbogen blieb erhalten. Christoph Sandmann musste ebenfalls unbedingt null fahren, um seine Einzelmedaillenchance zu erhalten und den direkt nach ihm fahrenden Eriksson unter Druck zu setzen. Und das gelang ihm auch. Eine schnelle fehlerfrei Runde und ganze 0.99 Strafpunkte für Zeitüberschreitung des schwedischen Exweltmeisters Eriksson bescherten ihm die Bronzemedaille. Brasseur zeigte eine überragende Leistung im Kegelparcours. Wie auf der Schnur gezogen liefen seine Lusitanos. Es war ein Genuss, ihm zuzusehen. Chardon als letzter Fahrer hatte Pech: ein Vorderpferd trat einen Kegel um.

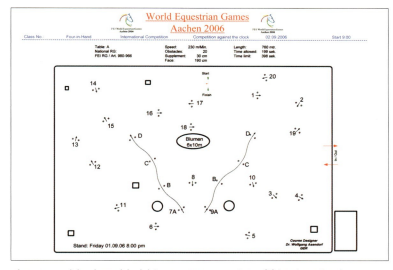

Michael Freund genoss seinen letzten Kegelparcours bei einer Weltmeisterschaft.
Michael Freund enjoyed his last World Championships obstacle course.

clear round had enabled him to move up into fifth place in the overall individual classification. But the excitement still wasn't over. Christoph Sandmann had to drive clear in order to retain his hope of an individual medal and to put Eriksson, who was to drive straight after him, under pressure. He succeeded in doing so. A fast, clear round and the fact that the Swedish driver, ex-World Champion Eriksson collected 0.99 time faults, meant he had won bronze. Brasseur gave an excellent performance in the obstacle driving course. His Lusitanos moved like clockwork. It was a delight to watch. The very last driver, Chardon was very unfortunate: One of the leaders knocked a cone over. That meant gold for Brasseur and silver for Chardon. These magnificent World Championships couldn't have come to a more exciting and dramatic end.

But there was also a sad touch to the conclusion of the tournament, since it was also a day of farewells. The young Stefan Klay (SUI) ended his successful career (hopefully only temporarily), since he no longer has a sponsor. The Swedish driver, Jan Eric Palsson, also said adieu to the crowd in Aachen. After a total of 20 appearances at the Soers and winning many medals at Championships over the last year, he is now planning on spending more time playing golf.

It was also the last appearance for Muschamp Kangoo from the team of the English driver, Karen Bassett. The left leader is retiring at the stately age of 22, after still having competed in all three competitions at the FEI World Equestrian Games. "He is going to keep an eye on my foals out at grass," explained a slightly melancholic Karen Bassett. He was the oldest horse to take part at these World Championships.

The oldest human participant at the Games also came from the driving discipline. At the age of 72, George Bowman (GB) showed a splendid sporting performance and his posture on the bock demanded respect. A lord from head to toe, who furthermore attained a respectable 23rd place in the rankings. He would have been World Champion in 1992 in Riesenbeck, if his groom hadn't dismounted from the carriage in the water unnecessarily. He will most probably no longer be able to fulfil his dream of taking the World Championships title.

"I drove with your father, I have driven with you for many years, and now I am looking forward to your son Marco", the adventurous and future-oriented George Bowman said to Michael Freund, as he learnt that Freund was retiring from the international driving scene.

FEI World Equestrian Games Aachen 2006

Ysbrand Chardon verpasste seinen vierten WM-Titel hauchdünn.
Ysbrand Chardon narrowly missed taking his fourth World Championships title.

Das bedeutete Gold für Brasseur und Silber für Chardon. Spannender und dramatischer hätte der Abschluss dieser tollen Weltmeisterschaft nicht sein können.

Aber es lag auch Wehmut in diesem Abschluss, denn es war auch ein Tag des Abschiednehmens. Der junge Stefan Klay (SUI) beendete (hoffentlich nur vorübergehend) seine erfolgreiche Karriere, da sein Sponsor nicht mehr zur Verfügung steht. Der Schwede Jan Eric Palsson sagte ebenfalls dem Aachener Publikum Adieu. Er wird sich nach insgesamt 20 Auftritten in der Aachener Soers und vielen Medaillen bei Championaten in den letzten Jahrzehnten vermehrt dem Golfspiel zuwenden.

Ein letzter Auftritt auch für Muschamp Kangoo aus dem Gespann der Engländerin Karen Bassett. Das linke Vorderpferd geht mit 22 Jahren nun in Pension, nachdem es bei dieser Weltmeisterschaft noch alle Teilprüfungen mitlief. „Er wird auf der Koppel ein Auge auf meine Fohlen haben", so eine sichtlich wehmütige Karen Bassett. Er war der älteste Vierbeiner, der an dieser WM teilnahm.

This farewell was of course the focus point of the emotions outside of the sporting events. The international driving sport platform is losing a valuable personality, whose victories include among others winning the World Championship title many times, the German Championships 14 times and the World Cup four times. His departure from the sport will leave a big gap, which will be extremely difficult to fill. "Mr. Driving Sport" lived for this discipline, he was an inspirator and a warning factor, he was visionary and sometimes a rather inconvenient lateral thinker, who followed his path unerring and without compromising.

It wouldn't have been possible for Germany to win medals at many of the Championships without him. But even then it wasn't just his sporting merits that counted. He was always the leader, motivator and mentor of the German team. In a small get-together in the drivers' camp after winning team gold, the Chef de Mission, Reinhard Wendt, referred to him as the orientation point of the last years and decades. There is nothing to add to this. There is only one small consolation to this farewell: Michael Freund will always remain active in the driving field – in whatever function.

"Driving always was, always is and always will be my life," the Team World Champion stated. *And coming from him a promise is a promise.*

Belgien (links) und die Niederlande (unten) lieferten sich einen packenden Zweikampf um Silber und Bronze in der Mannschaftswertung.
Belgium (left) and the Netherlands (bottom) battled in out in a thrilling duel for silver and gold in the team classification.

Einzelmedaillengewinner: (v.l.n.r) Ysbrand Chardon – Silber; Felix-Marie Brasseur – Gold; Christoph Sandmann – Bronze.
Individual medallists: (f.l.t.r) Ysbrand Chardon – silver; Felix-Marie Brasseur – gold; Christoph Sandmann – bronze.

FAHREN | DRIVING

Karen Basset verabschiedet in Aachen ihr 22-jähriges Pferd Muschamp Kangaroo.
Karen Basset retired her 22-year-old horse, Muschamp Kangaroo, in Aachen.

Der älteste Teilnehmer bei diesen Weltreiterspielen überhaupt kam ebenfalls aus dem Fahrerlager. Der Brite George Bowman zeigte mit 72 Jahren eine tolle sportliche Leistung und dazu eine Haltung auf dem Bock, die respekteinflößend war. Ein Lord vom Scheitel bis zur Sohle und mit Platz 23 fuhr er ein respektables Ergebnis ein. 1992 in Riesenbeck wäre er übrigens Weltmeister geworden, wenn im Wasser nicht sein Beifahrer unnötigerweise abgestiegen wäre. Den Traum eines WM-Titels wird er sich vermutlich nicht mehr erfüllen können.

„Ich bin mit Deinem Vater gefahren, viele Jahre mit Dir und jetzt freue ich mich auf Deinen Sohn Marco", sagt ein unternehmungslustiger und zukunftsorientierter George Bowman zu Michael Freund, als er von dessen Rücktritt von der internationalen Fahrsportszene erfuhr.

Dieser Abschied stand natürlich im Mittelpunkt der Emotionen, außerhalb des Sportes. Mit dem mehrfachen Weltmeister, 14-maligen Deutschen Meister und vierfachen Weltcupsieger tritt eine Persönlichkeit von der internationalen Fahrsportbühne ab, der eine große, kaum zu schließende Lücke hinterlassen wird. „Mr. Fahrsport" lebte für den Fahrsport, er war Inspirator und Mahner – er war Visionär und manchmal unbequemer Querdenker, der geradlinig und ohne Kompromisse seinen Weg ging.

Bei vielen Championaten wären Medaillen für Deutschland ohne ihn nicht denkbar gewesen. Aber auch hier waren es nicht nur seine sportlichen Meriten, die zählten. Er war immer Leader, Motivator und Vordenker im deutschen Team. Nach dem Gewinn der Mannschaftsgoldmedaille nannte ihn Chef de Mission, Reinhard Wendt, in einer kleinen Runde im Fahrerlager, den Orientierungspunkt der letzten Jahre und Jahrzehnte. Dem ist nichts hinzuzufügen. Etwas Tröstliches bleibt bei diesem Abschied: Michael Freund wird dem Fahrsport erhalten bleiben – in welcher Funktion auch immer.

„Fahrport war, ist und bleibt mein Leben", so der Mannschaftsweltmeister. Und versprochen ist bei ihm versprochen.

Auch mit 72 Jahren Fahrsport auf höchstem Niveau – George Bowman, ein Gentlemen vom Scheitel bis zur Sohle.
Top level driving sport even at the age of 72 – George Bowman, a gentleman from top to toe.

Michael Freund war bei seinem Abschied sichtlich gerührt – Sohn Marco tritt in die Fußstapfen des Vaters.
Michael Freund was visibly moved at his farewell ceremony – son Marco is following in his father's footsteps.

Distanzreiten
Endurance

AUTORIN/AUTHOR
ADELHEID BORCHARDT

Die deutsche Mannschaft / The German Team

Reiter Rider	Alter Age	Pferd / Horse Pfleger / Groom	Alter Age	Zuchtgebiet Breeding Area	Züchter / Breeder Besitzer / Horse
Melanie Arnold (Kirchheim/Teck)	30	Nadira Dominik Schlegel Richard Weismantel, Lioba Wagner Birgit Arnold, Heike Blümel	13	Araber/GER	Manuela Branco/ Adolf Arnold
Sabrina Arnold (Kirchheim/Teck)	26	Madaq Jean-Phillip Frances Thorsten Steuber, Martina Greve Adolf Arnold, Ingrid Löwer	10	Araber/GER	Wolfgang Esch Adolf Arnold
Marianne Hähnel (Falkenstein)	39	Bahida in Nahar Detlef Hähnel Claudia Zerlik, Bernd Theine Sönke Nimphy, Sabine Lotter	13	Araber/GER	Marianne Hähnel/ Marianne Hähnel
Belinda Hitzler (Dillingen)	35	Iris de Soult Stephan Schelldorf Anton Rittel, Regine Müller Stefanie Bonetsmüller	10	Anglo-Araber/FRA	- Belinda Hitzler
Susanne Kaufmann (Hohenstein)	39	Fay el Rat Nina Knapitsch Michaela Martin, Stefanie Matthißen Silke Muyschel-Engel	14	Araber/GER	Firtz Engel Florian Schmidthü… und Susanne Kauf…
Equipechef / Chef d'Equipe Roy Thiele		Bundestrainer / National Trainer Bernhard Dornsiepen jun.		Tierarzt / Veterinarian Martin Grell	Hufschmied / Fa… Nils Muche

Die Disziplin Distanzreiten

Die Distanzreiter traten in Aachen zum elften Mal bei einer Weltmeisterschaft an. Seine Premiere erlebte das Championat 1986 in Rom. Bei dieser ersten Veranstaltung erzielte der Deutsche Bernhard Dornsiepen sen. die Bronzemedaille in der Einzelwertung. Ein solcher Erfolg sollte bislang nicht wieder gelingen: Weder ein Einzelreiter noch eine Mannschaft aus Deutschland konnten sich nach 1986 bei einer WM auf einem Medaillenplatz behaupten, überzeugten aber stets mit guten Leistungen im Mittelfeld. Der Distanzsport wird in starken Maße von Athleten aus der arabischen Welt, den USA und Frankreich geprägt. Die Weltmeisterschaft wird, wie alle bedeutenden internationalen Distanz-Prüfungen (CEI/CEIO), in einem Hundertmeiler entschieden, das heißt Reiter und Pferde haben an einem Tag eine festgelegte Strecke von rund 160 Kilometern Länge zu bewältigen. Da der Kurs über unterschiedliches Geläuf und Steigungen führt, ist die Erfahrung des Reiters notwendig, seine eigenen und die Kräfte des Pferdes genau einzuschätzen und das gewählte Tempo sowie die Gangart den Anforderungen der Strecke anzupassen. Im Wettbewerb sind fünf Zwangspausen (Vet-Gate) vorgeschrieben, in denen Tierärzte die Fitness und den Gesundheitszustand des Pferdes überprüfen. Besonderer Wert wird laut Reglement auf die Pulswerte gelegt. Ist nach einer vorgegebenen Zeit der Puls nicht unter 64 Herzschläge pro Minute gesunken, scheiden Reiter und Pferd aus dem Wettbewerb aus. Eine Besonderheit des Distanzsports ist die nachträgliche Veterinär-Inspektion als Bestandteil der Prüfung: Innerhalb einer halben Stunde nach Erreichen des Ziels werden die Pferde erneut untersucht. Wenn ein Pferd in schlechtem Allgemeinzustand ist oder erhebliche Störungen am Bewegungsapparat wie Lahmheiten, Schwellungen an Sehnen und Bändern erkennbar sind, können Tierärzte und Richter das Pferd aus der Wertung nehmen. Auch im Falle einer tierärztlichen Behandlung des Pferdes innerhalb der ersten zwei Stunden nach Beendigung der Prüfung wird das Pferd disqualifiziert. Die Pferde müssen nach Prüfungsende bis zu 24 Stunden im Stallbereich bleiben. Eine vorzeitige Abreise ist nicht gestattet. Während dieser Zeit nimmt die Veterinärkommission die zehn besten in der Einzelwertung platzierten Pferde in Augenschein, um den „Preis für die beste Kondition" (Best Condition Award) – eine im Distanzsport sehr begehrte Auszeichnung – zu vergeben. Das Mannschaftsergebnis wird durch Addition der Zeiten der drei besten Reiter eines Teams ermittelt, Einzelmedaillen-Gewinner sind die drei schnellsten Reiter.

The Discipline Endurance Ride

For the endurance riders Aachen were the 11th World Championships. The premiere was in Rome in 1986 where Bernhard Dornsiepen Sen. and Drago won the individual Bronze medal for Germany. Since then, the riders from Germany have not been as successful at World Championships but have always been placed well in mid-field. Athletes from arab countries, the USA and France dominate the international endurance scene. The World championship is, like all important international events (CEI/CEIO), a ride over the classic distance of 100 miles (160 km) in one day. The riders will have to cope with varying terrain and gradients. Under these conditions both rider and horse must be well trained and know each other as a team, so that the pace can be adjusted according to the horse's stamina and outside factors such as temperature, humidity and type of track, without over-exerting the horse. There will be five compulsory controls (Vet Gates) in this competition. Here the horses are subjected to a tough veterinary examination regarding pulse, metabolic and locomotor parameters. The horse must be "fit to continue" at all stages of the ride. Before a horse can go into the Vet Gate the pulse rate must have dropped to 64 within 30 minutes of arrival at the Vet Gate. Otherwise the horse is taken out of the competition. A peculiarity of endurance riding is that crossing the finishing line does not mean one has won or finished the ride. A final veterinary inspection is carried out within 30 minutes of arrival and again the horse must still be "fit to continue". Otherwise even at the end of the ride a horse can be eliminated. Horses that require veterinary treatment within two hours of arrival will also be eliminated from the competition. The welfare of the horse is paramount. After the ride, the horses must be kept under supervision for at least 24 hours or until they are given permission to travel by the veterinary commission. An important part of the competition is the Best Condition Award, given on the following day, by the veterinary commission, to the horse that shows the best condition following the ride. The first ten horses to finish the ride, can be nominated for this coveted award. The best three results of the four team riders count towards the team classification, and the individual medals are awarded to the three fastest riders.

DISTANZREITEN | ENDURANCE

Gold, Silber, Bronze: Französische Trikolore in neuen Farben

Sie bleiben das Maß aller Dinge: Die Franzosen haben sich bei den Weltmeisterschaften in Aachen einmal mehr als die Distanzreiter-Nation Nummer eins bewiesen. Bei den fünften Weltreiterspielen gewannen sie das begehrte Mannschaftsgold. Damit aber nicht genug, holten sie auch noch die silberne und bronzene Einzelmedaille. Vor mehr als 20.000 Zuschauern lieferten sich der Spanier Miguel Vila Ubach mit Hungares, Virginie Atger mit Kangoo d`Aurabelle und Elodie de Labourier mit Sangho'Limousian ein spannendes Finish, das der 32-jährige Europameister von 1999 für sich entschied.

Nach neun Stunden und zwölf Minuten im Sattel erreichte Miguel Vila Ubach als erster Reiter das Ziel im Stadion der Aachener Soers. Als beste deutsche Teilnehmerin beendete die 26-jährige Sabrina Arnold aus Kirchheim/Teck den Ritt auf Platz elf. Die deutsche Mannschaftsreiterin legte mit ihrem zehnjährigen Vollblutaraber Madaq die 160 Kilometer lange Strecke in persönlicher Bestzeit zurück (neun Stunden, 48 Minuten, 15 Sekunden/Durchschnittstempo 16,32 Stundenkilometer). Mannschafts-Silber holte sich die Schweiz. Das deutsche Team musste die Bronzemedaille nur knapp den Portugiesen überlassen. Insgesamt waren bei dieser Distanz-WM, die als erste von sieben Disziplinen die Titelkämpfe in Aachen eröffnete, 159 Reiter aus 42 Nationen in einem Massenstart um sechs Uhr in der Früh auf die grenzüberschreitende Strecke durch Deutschland, Belgien und die Niederlande gegangen. Der gesamte Ritt war in sechs Etappen (28, 29, 34, 29, 27 und 13 Kilometern) eingeteilt. Das erste von sechs Teilstücken führte zum sogenannten Vet-Gate im holländischen Vaals, das die Reiter auch nach der zweiten, dritten und vierten Etappe anritten. Die Tierärzte (Veterinäre) haben diesem Teil der Prüfung ihren Namen gegeben. Sie untersuchen dort den Gesundheitszustand der Pferde – Puls, Atmung, Verdauung,

Der neue Mannschafts-Weltmeister ist Frankreich, wie auch schon 2002, 1994 und 1992.
The French Team is the new World Champions, they also took the title in 2002, 1994 and 1992.

Gold, silver, bronze: French tricolour with new colours

They remain the crème de la crème: At the FEI World Equestrian Games in Aachen the French proved once again that they are the top endurance nation. They won the coveted team gold medal at the fifth World Equestrian Games. As if this wasn't enough, they also claimed individual silver and bronze. The Spanish rider Miguel Vila Ubach with Hungares, Virginie Atger with Kangoo d`Aurabelle and Elodie de Labourier with Sangho'Limousian offered the crowd of over 20,000 spectators an exciting finish, it was indeed the 32-year-old Spaniard, the European Champion of 1999, who was ultimately victorious. After nine hours and twelve minutes in the saddle Miguel Vila Ubach was the first rider to cross the line in the Stadium of the Aachen Soers. Sabrina Arnold (26) from Kirchheim/Teck was the best German competitor, completing the ride in eleventh place. The German team rider covered the 160 kilometre distance with her ten-year-old purebred Arabian horse, Madaq, in her personal best time (nine hours, 48 min-

Holten Silber und Bronze: die beiden Französinnen Virginie Atger (rechts) und Elodie de Labourier.
Took silver and bronze: the two riders French Virginie Atger (right) and Elodie de Labourier.

Ergebnisse/ Results Seite/ page 141/142

FEI World Equestrian Games Aachen 2006

Bewegungsapparat. Sie entscheiden, ob ein Pferd auf die nächste Strecke darf oder ob der Ritt hier zu Ende ist. Hat das Pferd den Check bestanden, darf es aber – wie auch der Reiter – erst einmal eine zeitlich vorgegebene Pause von 30 bis 50 Minuten machen. Zeit für Reiter und Pferd, um die Energietanks aufzufüllen. Die fünfte Etappe führte zurück in die Aachener Soers, von wo aus die in der Wertung verbliebenen Paare auf das letzte Teilstück starteten. Nach 160 Kilometern und am Ende des Tages hatten 65 der 159 Paare den Ritt in der Wertung beendet.

Der Ausgang eines 100-Meilers kann sich in der ersten Hälfte entscheiden. Zu hohes Tempo, falscher Ehrgeiz – wenn man den Ritt der Top-Ten-Reiter dieser WM analysiert, sieht man, dass sich die besten Reiter langsam nach vorne gearbeitet haben. Der neue Weltmeister erreichte nach dem Start aller Paare als 47. Teilnehmer das erste Vet-Gate. Dann rückte er langsam vor und verbes-

Distanzreiten ist ein Team-Sport. Sobald Reiter und Pferd das Vet-Gate erreicht haben, kümmert sich ein Tross von Helfern um die zwei- und vierbeinigen Sportler.
Endurance is a team sport. As soon as horse and rider reached the vet gate, a whole troop of helpers ran to assist the two and four-legged athletes.

serte von Etappe zu Etappe seine Platzierung: 33., 21., 16., 8. und schließlich Erster. Auch hatte er die Kräfte seines achtjährigen Araberwallachs Hungares richtig eingeteilt. Ritt Miguel Vila Ubach die vier ersten Etappen in einem Durchschnittstempo zwischen 15,36 und 17,35 Stundenkilometer, so hatte Hungares noch genug im „Tank", um im letzten Viertel Tempo zuzulegen. Der Schimmel lief das vorletzte Stück von 27 Kilometern in 20,26 und die letzten 13 Kilometer in 23,4 Stundenkilometern.

Ähnlich gingen auch die beiden französischen Medaillengewinnerinnen die WM an. Gäbe es eine Medaille für die beste Regenerationszeit, so hätte diese dem Spanier Jaume Punti Dachs und seinem Pferd gebührt. Sein achtjähriger Araber Elvis HB brauchte bei allen sechs Vet-Gates insgesamt nur 16 Minuten und 19 Sekunden, um sich den Tierärzten mit dem geforderten Puls von 64 Schlägen vorzustellen. Den begehrten Konditionspreis für das fitteste Pferd vergaben die Veterinäre am Tag nach dem Ritt allerdings an Hilfrane du Barthas, die elfjährige Araberstute der achtplatzierten Französin Pascale Dietsch.

Mit großen Erwartungen waren die deutschen Distanzreiter zu der WM angereist. Und die Erwartungen waren durchaus realis-

utes, 15 seconds / average speed: 16.32 h/km). New Vice-World Champion is Switzerland. The German team narrowly missed taking the bronze medal, which went to the Portuguese riders.

As the first of seven disciplines, the endurance ride opened up the FEI World Equestrian Games in Aachen. In a mass start at six o'clock in the morning a total of 159 riders from 42 nations set off on the route, which led through Germany and its neighbouring countries Belgium and the Netherlands. The overall ride was divided up into six legs (28, 29, 34, 29, 27 and 13 kilometres respectively). The first of the six sections ended at the so-called vet gate, named after the veterinarians, in Vaals, Holland, which the riders also reached after the second, third and fourth legs. At the gates the veterinarians examine the physical health of the horses – checking their pulse, breathing rates, digestion and gaits. They decide whether a horse is allowed to enter the next leg or whether the ride ends there. If the horse passes the check, it first has to take a compulsory break – together with the rider – of between 30 and 50 minutes. Time for the rider and horse to tank up on energy. The fifth leg brought the riders back to the Aachen Soers, and from here the remaining pairs still left in the race headed off on the final stretch. At the end of the day after travelling 160 kilometres, 65 of the 159 pairs completed the ride and took a place in the rankings.

Er ist der Weltmeister der Distanzreiter: Mit den Worten „Ich kann fliegen" ritt der Spanier Miguel Vila Ubach als erster ins Ziel.
Endurance World Champion: "I can fly" said the Spanish rider, Miguel Vila Ubach, as he crossed the finishing line.

DISTANZREITEN | ENDURANCE

Bei Arnolds ist Distanzreiten ein Familiensport. Die Eltern trossen. Die Schwestern Melanie (30) und Sabrina Arnold reiten.
Endurance is a family sport for the Arnolds. The parents are the grooms. The sisters Melanie (30) and Sabrina Arnold are the riders

Die 26-jährige Sabrina Arnold war mit dem elften Platz beste deutsche Teilnehmerin bei der WM.
Sabrina Arnold (26) was the best German at the World Championships, taking eleventh place in the individual competition.

2002 bei der WM in Spanien noch Platz sechs mit der Mannschaft, jetzt Team-Vierte: Die 39-jährige Servicetechnikerin Susanne Kaufmann und ihre Vollblutaraber-Stute Fay el Rat.
Sixth with the team in Spain at the World Equestrian Games 2002, fourth in Aachen in the team classification: The 39-year-old service technician, Susanne Kaufmann, with her thoroughbred mare Fay el Rat.

Whether a pair is going to drop out during a 100-mile ride is often determined in the first half of the distance – setting the pace too high and false ambition can both lead to the ride coming to a premature end. If one analyses the rides of the top ten competitors of this World Championships, one notices that the best riders all slowly worked their way to the front. After all of the riders set off together, the new World Champion was only reached the first vet gate in 47th place. He then gradually started moving forward improving his position from leg to leg: 33rd, 21st, 16th and 8th before finally taking the lead. He found the right pace for his eight-year-old Arabian gelding Hungares. Whereas Miguel Vila Ubach rode the first four legs at an average speed of between 15.36 and 17.35 h/km, Hungares had enough fuel left in his "tank" to be able to increase the speed over the last quarter of the ride. The grey horse travelled the 27 kilometres of the last but one leg at a speed of 20.26 h/km and covered the last 13 kilometres in 23.4 h/km. The two French World Championship medallists followed a similar strategy. If a medal had been awarded for the best regeneration time, this would have certainly gone to the Spanish rider, Jaume Punti Dachs and his horse. His eight-year-old Arabian horse Elvis HB only took a total of 16 minutes and 19 seconds at all six vet gates to attain the mandatory pulse rate of 64 beats/minute before being presented to the veterinarians. However, the vets awarded the coveted best condition prize for the fittest horse, which is traditionally presented the day after the ride, to Hilfrane du Barthas, the 11-year-old Arabian mare of the French rider, Pascale Dietsch, who ranked eighth in the competition.

Ergebnisse/Results Seite/page 141/142

FEI World Equestrian Games Aachen 2006

Mannschafts-Vierte Belinda Hitzler (links):
Die 35-jährige Betriebswirtin gehörte auch 2002 zum WM-Team.
Team fourth Belinda Hitzler (left): The 35-year-old business graduate was also a member of the team at the WEG 2002.

tisch. „Ich denke, wir waren noch nie so gut vorbereitet," sagte Bernhard Dornsiepen jun. (Balve), der erste Bundestrainer in der Geschichte der deutschen Distanzreiter. Am Ende trennten die Deutschen nur 13 Minuten von der Bronzemedaille und den Portugiesen, deren Reitzeiten der drei schnellsten Reiter sich auf 30 Stunden und 38 Minuten summierten. Sabrina Arnolds Teamkameradinnen Belinda Hitzler (Dillingen) und Susanne Kaufmann

The German endurance riders had great expectations for the World Championships. And these expectations were by all means realistic. "I don't think we have ever been as well prepared," said Bernhard Dornsiepen Jun. (Balve), the first National Coach in the history of German endurance riders. In the end only 13 minutes separated the German team from the bronze medal and the Portuguese riders – the accumulated riding time of their three fastest riders was 30 hours and 38 minutes. Sabrina Arnold's, team colleagues Belinda Hitzler (Dillingen) and Susanne Kaufmann (Hohenstein) cantered to the finish lining head-to-head. This meant 25th place for Belinda Hitzler and her ten-year-old French-bred Anglo-Arab Iris de Soult (10:31:31), and 26th place for Susanne Kaufmann with the 14-year-old purebred Arabian mare Fay el Rat. Both riders already belonged to the World Championship team in 2002. After coming sixth with the team in Jerez, ranking fourth in the team classification in Aachen is a new highlight in the riders' careers. "We are very happy with the result. We have shown a clear improvement by taking fourth place. We beat strong competition in this ride from Australia and New

DISTANZREITEN | ENDURANCE

Nach neun Stunden und 48 Minuten Ziel erreicht und persönliche Bestzeit: Sabrina Arnold hatte allen Grund zum Jubeln. Begeistert von seinem Schützling nimmt Bundestrainer Bernhard Dornsiepen jun. sie in den Arm.
Reached the finish in her personal best time of nine hours and 48 minutes: Sabrina Arnold had reason to rejoice. Thrilled with his protégé, National Coach, Bernhard Dornsiepen jun., threw his arms around her.

(Hohenstein) erreichten Kopf an Kopf im Galopp das Ziel. Für Belinda Hitzler und ihren zehnjährigen, in Frankreich gezogenen Anglo-Araber Iris de Soult hieß das Platz 25 (10:31:31), für Susanne Kaufmann mit der 14-jährigen Vollblutaraberstute Fay el Rat Platz 26. Beide Reiterinnen gehörten schon 2002 zum WM-Team. Schlossen sie in Jerez noch mit dem sechsten Platz für die Mannschaft ab, so steht nach Aachen Team-Platz vier in den Erfolgsbiografien der Reiterinnen. „Wir sind sehr zufrieden mit dem Ergebnis. Mit dem vierten Platz haben wir uns deutlich verbessert. Wir haben die starken Australier und Neuseeländer auf der Strecke geschlagen. Dass sich Melanie Arnolds Pferd Nadira unterwegs verletzte und damit unser stärkstes Paar nach 91 Kilometern ausfiel, war natürlich für uns alle traurig, denn es hat uns die Bronze- vielleicht sogar die Silbermedaille gekostet. Beide waren topfit und wären sicher als schnellstes deutsches Paar ins Ziel gekommen. Ich ziehe aus deutscher Sicht für die WM ein positives Fazit", sagte der Bundestrainer am Tag nach dem Wettkampf. Überschattet wurden die Ereignisse einige Tage später durch den Tod eines Distanzpferdes, das zu Beginn des Rittes einen schweren Kreuzverschlag erlitt. Eine Krankheit, die – wie die Veranstalter und Tierärzte betonten – nicht im Zusammenhang mit dem WM-Ritt stand.

Zealand. Of course we were all very sad that Melanie Arnold's horse Nadira injured itself en route and that our strongest pair had to retire after 91 kilometres, because it cost us the bronze medal and perhaps even the silver medal. Both were top fit and would most certainly have been the first German pair to cross the finishing line otherwise. I can draw a positive balance on the World Championships from a German point of view," the National Coach said the day after the competition. The event was overshadowed a few days later as a result of the death of one of the endurance horses, which had suffered a severe case of myopathy (tying-up) at the beginning of the ride. A disease, which – as the organisers and veterinarians stress – was not connected with the World Championships ride.

Bei einem Distanzritt sind viele Pferdestärken auf der Strecke unterwegs: Vom Auto, das das erste Pferd ankündigt, bis hin zu den Trossfahrzeugen mit den Teams der Reiter.
A lot of horse power is mobilised during an endurance ride: From the car that announces the first horse to the baggage vehicles transporting the teams of the riders.

Ergebnisse/ Results Seite/ page 141/142

FEI World Equestrian Games Aachen 2006

Tierärzte überwachen die Fitness und den Gesundheitszustand der Pferde im Verlauf des Rittes. In den Vet-Gates kontrollieren sie Puls, Atmung, Verdauung, Bewegungsapparat.
Veterinarians inspect the horses' fitness and general state of health during the ride. At the vet gates they check the horses' pulse, breathing, metabolic rate and action.

Interview mit Bundestrainer Bernhard Dornsiepen jun.

Erst 38 Jahre alt und schon eine historische Person: Bernhard Dornsiepen jun. ist der erste Bundestrainer in der Geschichte des deutschen Distanzsportes. Die Weltmeisterschaften im eigenen Land bescherten dieser Ausdauerdisziplin zu Pferde ihren ersten Nationaltrainer. Der Name Dornsiepen hat einen sehr guten Ruf in der Szene – national wie international. Das beginnt mit dem Vater Bernhard Dornsiepen sen., der 1986 bei der ersten WM die bisher einzige Einzelmedaille (Bronze) gewann. Und das endet mit den Erfolgen des noch immer aktiv reitenden Bundestrainers, der seine Schützlinge während der WM-Sichtung auf Ritten schon mal vom Pferd aus als „Konkurrent" beobachtet hat: Vom 13. Platz bei seinem ersten (1990) von drei WM-Auftritten bis hin zum sechsten Platz bei der EM 2003 – der Hufschmied aus dem Sauerland ist aus der internationalen Distanzreiterszene nicht mehr wegzudenken.

„Aachen mitgerechnet, haben die Franzosen bei sieben von elf Weltmeisterschaften Mannschaftsmedaillen geholt. Was ist das Erfolgsgeheimnis der Franzosen?"

Bernhard Dornsiepen jun.: „Es beginnt mit der Zucht. So wie in Deutschland die Warmblutpferdezucht mit dem Sport in den klassischen Disziplinen Dressur, Springen, Vielseitigkeit verzahnt ist, so haben die Franzosen eine eigene Zucht für Distanzpferde. Dort gibt es auch jährlich die Weltmeisterschaften der jungen Distanzpferde. Sie züchten also gezielt die für diese Leistung richtigen Pferde. Das ist die eine Seite. Die andere ist das strategisch und taktisch kluge Reiten, das mit der Vorbereitung beginnt. Die Equipe trainiert gemeinsam. Pferde und Reiter sind aufeinander abgestimmt. Die Paare bleiben vom Start an zusammen und profitieren so von der Ruhe und Stärke, die die Gruppe gibt. Sie gehen ihr eigenes Tempo. Sie lassen sich von den anderen nicht mitreißen und reiten konsequent nach Vorgaben. Auf diese Art rollen sie das Feld dann von hinten auf. Das ist ihnen nicht zum ersten Mal gelungen."

„Wie beurteilen Sie die Entwicklung im internationalen Distanzsport seit der letzten WM 2002?"

Bernhard Dornsiepen jun.: „Der Distanzsport ist schneller und professioneller geworden. Die Leistungsdichte hat zugenommen. Konnte man vor wenigen Jahren noch mit einer Stunde Abstand auf den ersten Reiter unter die Top Ten kommen, so kommt man jetzt nicht mal mehr unter die besten 20. Die Qualifikationsvorgaben des Weltreiterverbandes FEI sind schärfer und damit die Sicherheit für Reiter und Pferde größer geworden. Das Pferd muss einen 100-Meiler und der Reiter drei lange Ritte innerhalb der letzten 24 Monate vor dem Championat nachweisen, um dort starten zu dürfen. Und zu guter Letzt entscheiden die Tierärzte, die bei uns Richterfunktion haben, sehr streng. Das zeigt sich auch in der hohen Zahl von 94 Pferden, die während des Wettkampfes vorsorglich aus dem Ritt genommen wurden."

„Sie sind selbst schon für Deutschland Championate geritten. Welche Erfahrungen haben Sie als aktiver Reiter in die Vorbereitungen der deutschen Teilnehmer einfließen lassen? Was hat sich im Gegensatz zu den früheren Championaten geändert?"

Bernhard Dornsiepen jun.: „Ich versuche mein Amt als Bundestrainer so auszufüllen, wie ich mir als Reiter immer einen Bundestrainer gewünscht habe. Zum einen wollte ich immer eine sportfachlich hauptverantwortliche Person, die als aktiver Distanzreiter aus dem Leistungssport kommt. Zum anderen war mir wichtig, dass diese Person sich durchgehend um die Reiter und Pferde kümmert und diese das ganze Jahr sieht. Das war durch den neuen Sichtungsweg sehr gut möglich. Erstmals mussten sich potentielle WM-Paare nicht mehr über anstrengende, kraftraubende Wettkämpfe für das Championat empfehlen. Wir haben drei Lehrgänge gemacht und zwei Ritte, auf denen die Reiter nach bestimmten Vorgaben, zum Beispiel in Gruppen, geritten sind. Dadurch habe ich Reiter und Pferde alle drei bis vier Wochen gesehen – im direkten Vergleich. Durch das neue Amt des Bundestrainers kam es zu mehr Kapazitäten und einer klaren Kompetenzaufteilung in der Mannschaftsführung, die alle Anforderungen so eines WM-Projektes abdeckte. Als Bundestrainer habe ich mich ganz auf die sportfachliche Vorbereitung, auf Rittstrategie und -taktik konzentriert. Roy Thiele als erfahrener Equipechef kümmerte sich vor Ort intensiv um alle organisatorischen Anforderungen."

DISTANZREITEN | ENDURANCE

Interview with national coach Bernhard Dornsiepen Jun.

Only 38 years old and already an historic figure: Bernhard Dornsiepen Jun. is the first National Coach in the history of the German endurance sport. The World Championships in one's own country was reason enough to appoint the first National Coach for the endurance discipline. The name Dornsiepen has a very good reputation in the scene – at both national and international level, beginning with the father Bernhard Dornsiepen Sen., who won the only individual medal to date (bronze) in 1986 at the first World Championships. And ending with the victories of the National Coach, who is still an active rider, and who during the WEG trials sometimes observed his protégés on horseback taking on the role of a "co-competitor": Having taken part in three World Championships, he came 13th on his first ride (1990) and even managed to secure sixth place at the European Championship in 2003 – the German blacksmith from the Sauerland has become an integral part of the international endurance scene.

"Including Aachen, the French have claimed team medals at seven of the eleven World Championships. What is the secret of the French riders' success?"

Bernhard Dornsiepen Jun.: "It all starts with the breeding. In a similar way that warmblood breeding in Germany is linked with the sport in the classic disciplines of dressage, show-jumping and eventing, the French have their own breeding lines for endurance horses. They even organise annual World Championships for young endurance horses. They breed horses specifically for this purpose. This is one side of it. The other aspect is that when they ride they follow a strategically planned and tactically clever concept, which starts from the very preparation onwards. The team trains together. Horse and rider are completely aligned. The pairs stay together from the very start, thus profiting from the calmness and strength that the group feeling emanates. They hold their own pace. They don't let themselves be influenced by the others and consequently stick to their orders. In this way they gradually overtake the field from the back. This isn't the first time they have succeeded in doing so.

"How do you assess the development of the endurance sport since the last FEI World Equestrian Games in 2002?"

Bernhard Dornsiepen Jun.: "The endurance sport has become faster and more professional. The performance quality has increased. Whereas if you were lagging an hour behind the first rider a few years ago, it was still possible to come under the top ten, today you would no longer come under the best 20 under such circumstances. The qualifying regulations of the International Equestrian Federation, the FEI, have become much stricter so that greater safety is ensured for the horses and riders. In order to be able to compete it is necessary to prove that the horse has taken part in a 100-mile race and that the rider has completed three long rides within the last 24 months before the Championships. And last, but not least the veterinarians, who take on the function of a judge in our discipline, are very strict. This can be seen from the high amount of horses who were eliminated from the ride for precautionary reasons: 94 horses."

"You took part in Championships for Germany yourself. What personal experiences as an active rider have you passed on to the German participants in the run-up to the event? What is different today compared to earlier Championships?"

Bernhard Dornsiepen Jun.: "I remember what I would have required of a National Coach as a rider, and try to fulfil this role today. On the one hand I always wanted a person who was responsible for the sporting aspect, who had been actively participant in endurance competition sport. On the other hand I found it important that this person should take care of the riders and horses continuously and be present throughout the year. This has been made possible as a result of the new trials process. For the first time potential World Championship pairs didn't have to undergo strenuous, exhausting trials to qualify for the Championships. We held three training courses and two rides, which the riders participated in following specific criteria, for instance riding in groups. This allowed me to assess the riders and horses every three to four weeks – in direct comparison. As a result of the newly created National Coach's position, the team management that has to cover all of the requirements involved in such a World Championships project enjoyed a greater capacity and a clearer division of the tasks. Whereas in my role as National Coach, I completely concentrated on the sport-related preparations as well as the strategy and tactics to be employed during the ride, Roy Thiele, the experienced Chef d'Equipe, dedicated his attentions to the organisational requirements on location."

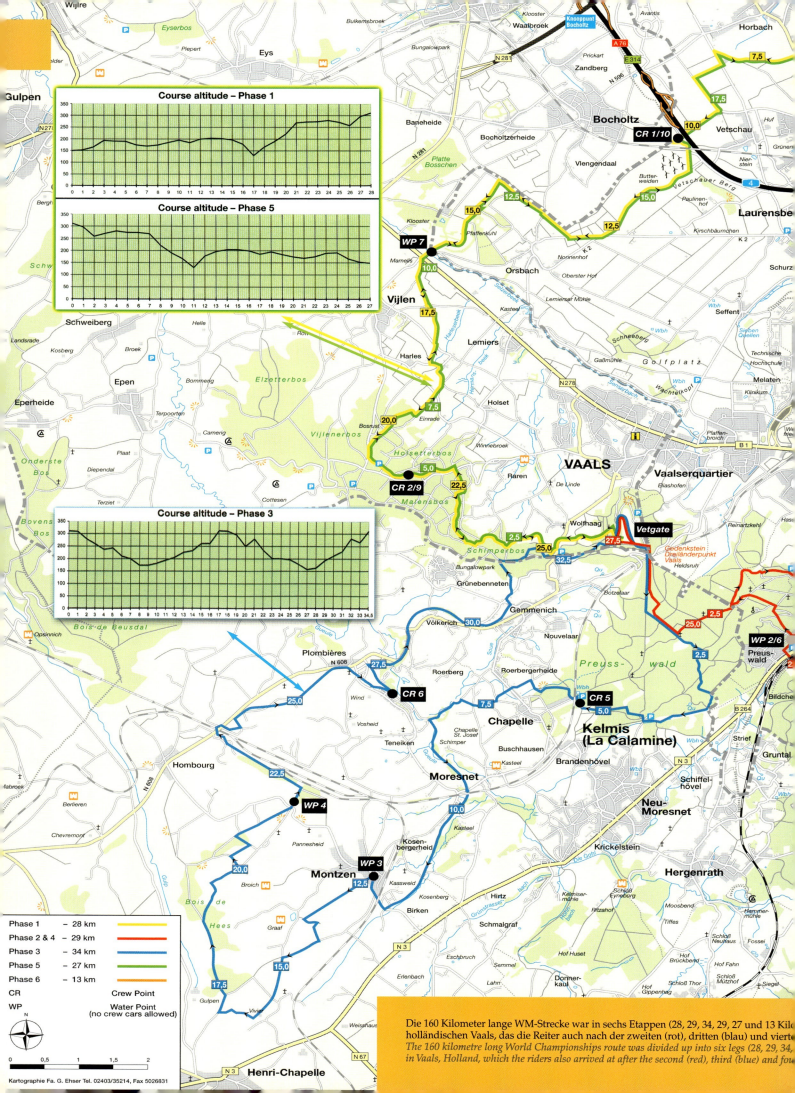

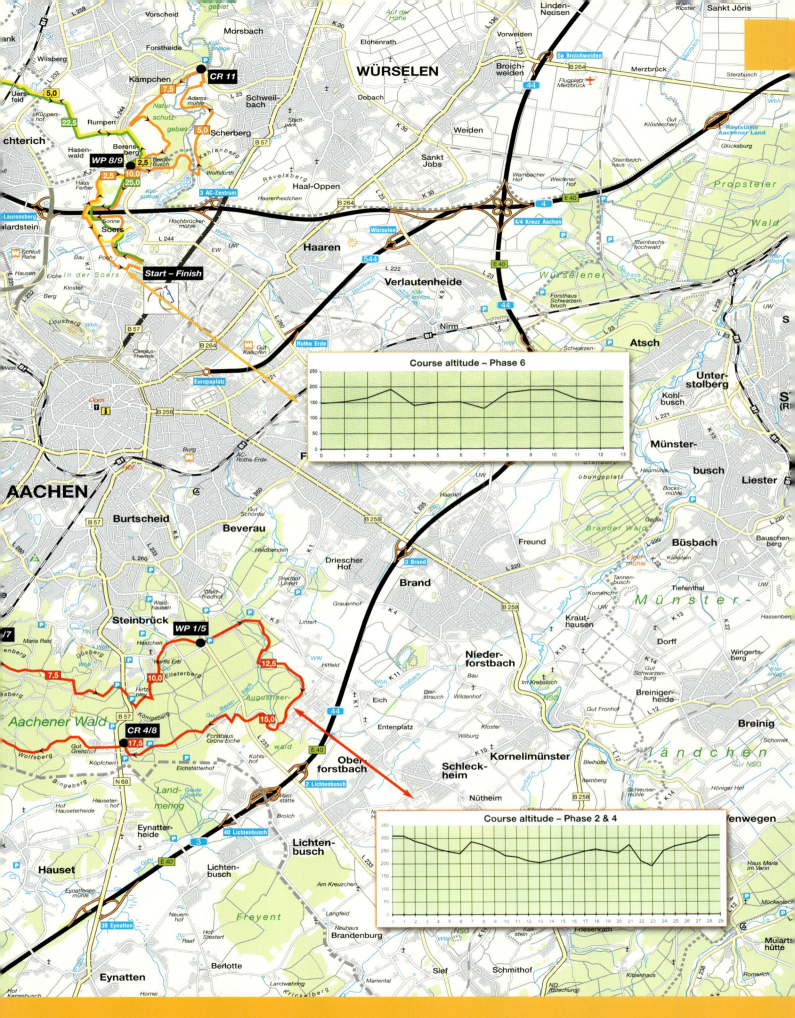

Voltigieren / Vaulting

Die deutschen Voltigierer waren in Aachen mit zwei Goldmedaillen und einer Silbermedaille die erfolgreichste Pferdesportdisziplin.
The German vaulters were the most successful equestrian athletes in Aachen, claiming two gold and one silver medal.

AUTOR/*Author*
DENNIS PEILER

Die Disziplin Voltigieren

Voltigieren bedeutet, turnerisch-gymnastische Übungen auf dem Pferderücken auszuführen. Im Turniersport werden die Figuren alle im Galopp gezeigt. Hierbei ist das harmonische Zusammenspiel von Pferd, Longenführer und Voltigierer für eine optimale Leistungsentfaltung wichtig. Unterschieden wird zwischen Gruppen-, Doppel- und Einzelvoltigieren. Während ein Einzelvoltigierer alleine auf dem Pferd die Bewegungselemente ausführt, sind in der Gruppe bis zu drei Voltigierer zeitgleich auf dem Pferd. Der moderne Voltigiersport ist eine vergleichsweise junge Wettkampfdisziplin zu Pferde: Die ersten Wettbewerbe in Deutschland datieren aus dem Jahr 1953, zehn Jahre später findet die erste Deutsche Meisterschaft statt. Internationale Wettbewerbe werden erstmals 1984 ausgerichtet, unter ihnen auch die ersten Europameisterschaften in Ebreichsdorf (Österreich). Seit 1983 wird das Voltigieren als eigenständige Sportart beim Weltreiterverband FEI geführt. Deutsche Spitzensportler schreiben internationale Voltigiergeschichte. Silke Bernhard und Nadja Zülow gewinnen drei Mal die Weltmeisterschaft, Tanja Benedetto wird zwei Mal Weltmeisterin. Bei den Herren erreicht Christoph Lensing drei Goldmedaillen. Das Gruppenvoltigieren wird viele Jahre von einem Zweikampf zwischen Deutschland und der Schweiz geprägt. Bei Championaten treten die Sportler in drei Wettbewerbsklassen an: Einzelvoltigieren Damen und Herren sowie Gruppenvoltigieren. Bei den Einzelwettbewerben sind pro Nation jeweils drei männliche und weibliche Teilnehmer ab 14 Jahren startberechtigt. Nach oben gibt es keine Altersbeschränkung. Beim Gruppenvoltigieren (jeweils eine Mannschaft pro Nation) bilden sechs Aktive ein Team. Die Altersbeschränkung (18 Jahre) wurde für die Gruppenmitglieder aufgehoben. In Aachen gingen erstmals auch erwachsene Voltigiersportler in der Gruppe an den Start. Bei internationalen Meisterschaften absolvieren die Einzelvoltigierer und Gruppen in der ersten Wertungsprüfung zunächst eine Pflicht mit vorgeschriebenen Übungen auf dem Pferd und eine Kür. In der zweiten Wertung, dem Finale der besten 15 Damen und Herren und der besten zwölf Gruppen, zeigen die Einzelvoltigierer das Technik-Programm und ihre Kür, während die Gruppen nur noch zur Kür antreten. Bewertet werden die Vorstellungen von einer sechsköpfigen Richtergruppe, die Noten von 0 bis 10 gibt. Für die Weltmeisterschaften müssen sich die Einzelvoltigierer auf internationalen Turnieren (CVI**) mit einer Endnote von 6,0 und höher qualifizieren. Die Gruppen, entweder Vereins- oder Nationalmannschaften und die Einzelvoltigierer werden von den nationalen Pferdesportverbänden bestimmt.

The vaulting discipline

*Vaulting involves carrying out acrobatic exercise on the back of a horse. In competition sport the movements are always performed at canter. In this discipline the harmonious interplay between the horse, lunger and vaulters is a prerequisite for an ideal performance. The competitions are divided up into three categories: team, pair and individual vaulting. Whereas an individual vaulter carries out movements on the horse on his own, in the group up to three vaulters are on top of the horse simultaneously. The modern vaulting sport is a comparably young equestrian competition discipline: The first competitions in Germany date back to the year 1953, ten years later the first German Championships were staged. International competitions were first organised in 1984, among them also the first European Championships in Ebreichsdorf (Austria). Vaulting was recognised by the International Equestrian Federation (FEI), as an independent sport in 1983. The German top vaulters have been writing international vaulting history for years. Silke Bernhard and Nadja Zülow won the World Championships three times, Tanja Benedetto was World Champion twice. And in the men's competition Christoph Lensing also claimed three gold medals. Group vaulting was hallmarked by a constant duel between Germany and Switzerland for many years. Championship competitions are divided up into three classes: Ladies individual vaulting, men's individual vaulting and group vaulting. In the individual competitions three female and three male competitors over the age of 14 are allowed to enter per nation. There is no upward age limit. In the group vaulting (one team per nation) a team is made up of six participants. The former age limit (18 years) for the group members has been lifted. In Aachen adult vaulters made up part of the teams for the first time ever. At international championships, in the first rating the individual vaulters and teams have to complete compulsory movements on the horse and a freestyle. In the second rating, the final of the best 15 ladies and men and the best 12 teams, the individual vaulters perform a technical programme and their freestyle routine, whereas the team vaulters only have to complete their freestyle. The performances are evaluated by a panel of six judges, who each award a score between 0 and 10. The individual vaulters have to qualify for the World Championships at international tournaments (CVI**) by reaching a final score of 6.0 and above. The groups, either club or national teams and the individual vaulters are appointed by the national equestrian sport associations.*

Die deutsche Mannschaft / *The German Team*

Reiter / *Rider*	Alter / *Age*	Pferd / *Horse* Longenführer / *Longeur*	Alter / *Age*	Zuchtgebiet / *Breeding Area*	Züchter / *Breeder* Besitzer / *Horse Owner*
Anja Barwig (München)	22	Arador Alexander Hartl	11	Oldenburg	Ilse Ruebken Alexander Hartl
Ines Jückstock (Hamburg)	33	Dallmer's Little Foot Ruth Jückstock	12	Hannover	Bernhard Nordbeck (Iste RV Hoisbüttel
Gero Meyer-Nutteln (Hildesheim)	27	Arador Alexander Hartl	11	Oldenburg	Ilse Ruebken Alexander Hartl
Tim-Randy Sia (Osnabrück)	26	Belmondo Elke Schelp-Lensing	17	Osnabrück	Friedrich Meyer zu West Elke Schelp-Lensing (Ste
Nicola Ströh (Hamburg)	25	Lanson Michael Gnad	8	Hannover	Udo Terfoorth (Balje) Klaus Ströh (Hamburg)
Kai Vorberg (Köln)	24	Picasso Kirsten Graf	15	Rheinland	Mathias Steves (Willich) Reinhold Strang (Leverk

Verein/ (Gruppenmitgl.)	Alter / *Age*	Pferd / *Horse* Longenführer/ Pfleger / *Groom*	Alter / *Age*	Zuchtgebiet / *Breeding*	Züchter / *Breeder* Besitzer / *Owner*
RSV I. SC.36 Neuss-Grimmlinghausen		Cepin Jessica Schmitz Christine Wahlbaum	10	Tschechien	Kirsten Gross	RSV I. SC.36 Neuss-Grimmlinghausen
(Janika Derks)	16				
(Mark Phillip Götting)	18				
(Antje Hill)	19				
(Pauline Riedl)	13				
(Sarah Schäfer)	19				
(Elisabeth Simon)	19				
(Simone Wiegele)	20				
(Ilka Kempkes)					

Equipechef / *Chef d'Equipe*	Bundestrainer / *National Trainer*	Tierarzt / *Veterinarian*
Dr. Andrea Schirmacher	Ulla Ramge	Dr. Arnold Hülsey

VOLTIGIEREN | VAULTING

Deutsche Voltigierer in Aachen weltmeisterlich

Für den Voltigiersport sind in Aachen neue Zeiten angebrochen. 8.000 Zuschauer in den Kürwettkämpfen sorgten für eine Atmosphäre wie bei einem Popkonzert. Ein bis dato in diesen Ausmaßen nicht vergleichbares Medieninteresse umgab die Weltmeisterschaften der Voltigierer und sorgte für eine starke Präsenz der Sportart in Zeitung, Hörfunk und Fernsehen. Mit einer zweistündigen Liveübertragung des Kürfinales der Seniorteams in einem öffentlich rechtlichen TV-Sender erreichte das Voltigieren ein ungeahntes Medieninteresse. Die Liveübertragung der Gruppenküren beinhaltete alles, was eine gute Sportübertragung ausmacht. Eine ausverkaufte Voltigierarena glich vor allem bei den deutschen Startern einem schwarz-rot-goldenen Fahnenmeer. Dies und der ohrenbetäubende Beifall spornten die Sportler zu Höchstleitungen an.

Das Gruppenvoltigieren kann zu recht als Königsdisziplin der Kunstturner auf dem Pferderücken bezeichnet werden. Es lieferte in Aachen eine kaum zu überbietende Dramatik im Wettstreit um das beste Seniorteam der Welt. Deutschland trat als Titelverteidiger an und wollte mit dem RSV Neuss-Grimmlinghausen (Pferd

Champion performance by German vaulters in Aachen

A new age is dawning for the vaulting sport after Aachen. 8,000 spectators at the freestyle competitions provided an atmosphere similar to a pop concert. The World Vaulting Championships were surrounded by huge interest from the media, something the sport has not been familiar with to this extent until now and which in turn also meant that there was considerably more coverage on the sport in the newspapers, radio and television. Vaulting achieved an unexpected level of media attention due to a two-hour live broadcast on the team freestyle final by a public broadcaster. The live transmission of the group freestyles contained everything good sport coverage requires. The vaulting arena that was sold out, resembled a sea of black, red and gold flags, especially when the German participants were competing. This, combined with the deafening applause, motivated the athletes to top performances.

Group vaulting can quite rightly be described as the highlight of the acrobats on horseback. In Aachen a dramatic battle for the title was delivered by the best teams in the world. As the reigning champion, Germany wanted to defend the title that VV In-

8.000 Voltigierbegeisterte machten aus der Voltigierarena einen Hexenkessel.
8,000 vaulting fans turned the vaulting arena into a folks festival.

Ergebnisse/ Results Seite/ page 143/144

FEI World Equestrian Games Aachen 2006

Das Team der USA gewann beide Küren.
The team from the USA won both freestyle rounds.

gelsberg won in 2004. This time they had pinned their hopes on RSV Neuss-Grimmlinghausen (Horse: Cepin, Lunger: Jessica Schmitz). In a thrilling final, the German team just managed to take the gold medal, followed closely in second place by the USA (Grand Gaudino, Dr. Silke Bartel), Austria took bronze (Libretto, Maria Lehrmann).

Whereas in the past the Team Vaulting World Championships were always hallmarked by a duel between Germany and Switzerland, it became clear in the run-up to the WEG, that other nations also had justified claims on the gold medal. From the very start of the World Championships, Germany came under pressure from the Austrians (CVI winners, Stadl Paura), the US Americans (CVI winners, Munich) as well as from the European Champions from Slovakia, from Switzerland and Great Britain. The German team had learnt its lesson from the experiences it made at the European Championships at Brescia (Italy) in 2005, when Ger-

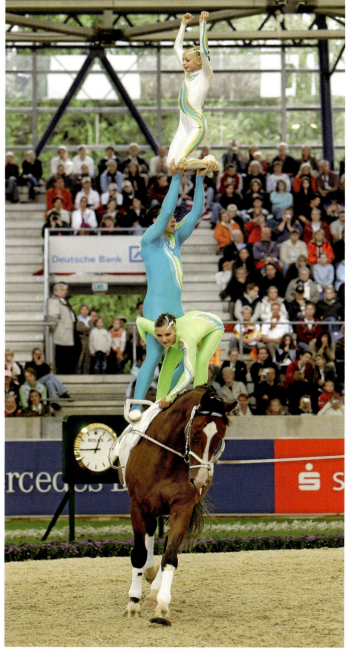

Cepin – Longenführerin Jessica Schmitz) den 2004 durch den VV Ingelsberg gewonnenen WM-Titel verteidigen. In einem Herzschlagfinale sicherte sich das Team Deutschland hauchdünn die Goldmedaille vor den USA (Grand Gaudino – Dr. Silke Bartel) mit Silber und Österreich (Libretto – Maria Lehrmann) mit Bronze.

Waren in der Vergangenheit die Weltmeisterschaften im Gruppenvoltigieren ausschließlich durch einen Zweikampf zwischen Deutschland und der Schweiz geprägt, zeichnete sich bereits im Vorfeld der WM ab, dass auch andere Nationen berechtigte Ansprüche auf Gold anmeldeten. Deutschland wurde bei den Weltmeisterschaften von Beginn an durch die Österreicher (Sieger beim CVI Stadl Paura) und die US-Amerikaner (Sieger beim CVI München) sowie dem Europameister Slowakei, der Schweiz und Großbritannien unter Druck gesetzt. Die Erfahrungen der Europameisterschaften 2005 im italienischen Brescia – Deutschland vergab einen großen Punktevorsprung und holte Silber hinter der Slowakei – lehrte alle Beteiligten, dass ein Vorsprung von einem halben Punkt, der auch die Topteams in Aachen nach der Pflicht voneinander trennte, ohne weiteres in den ausstehenden beiden Küren aufzuholen wäre. Der Verlauf der EM 2005 sollte sich aber aus deutscher Sicht bei den Weltmeisterschaften nicht wiederholen. Den knappen Vorsprung, den die Rheinländer aus der Pflicht

Spektakulär präsentierte sich das österreichische Seniorteam in der Kür.
The Austrian team gave a spectacular freestyle performance.

VOLTIGIEREN | VAULTING

Glückliche Medaillengewinner bei den Teams.
Overjoyed medallists in the team classification.

Der RSV Neuss-Grimmlinghausen sorgte für Gänsehaut-Feeling.
RSV Neuss-Grimmlinghausen mesmerised the crowds.

many only took silver, finishing behind Slovakia despite a clear lead early on in the competition. They were therefore well aware that the lead of half a point separating the top teams in Aachen after the compulsory test was an easy target for other teams to catch up on in the two outstanding freestyle rounds. However, luckily for the German team, the occurrences of the European Championships 2005 didn't repeat themselves. The team from Rhineland managed to defend the marginal lead they had achieved after the compulsory tests, in the two following freestyle rounds, even if other participants dominated these two rounds. The USA vaulted to victory in both freestyle competitions, but was ultimately not able to catch up with Germany in the overall classification. The nail-biting final, meant that the German fans had to keep their fingers tightly crossed that the small lead would suffice to take gold. In the middle of their freestyle programme, that had been almost perfect up until then, the German team horse, Cepin, shied when the music changed. The vaulters couldn't balance out the sudden change in speed in the canter and had to dismount unexpectedly. For a second everyone thought the title had been lost, however the six judges placed the team third in the freestyle, which was enough to take gold.

Ergebnisse/ Results Seite/ page 143/144

FEI World Equestrian Games Aachen 2006

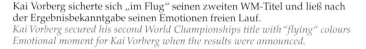

Kai Vorberg sicherte sich „im Flug" seinen zweiten WM-Titel und ließ nach der Ergebnisbekanntgabe seinen Emotionen freien Lauf.
Kai Vorberg secured his second World Championships title with "flying" colours Emotional moment for Kai Vorberg when the results were announced.

Gleich zwei deutsche Einzelvoltigierer standen bei den Herren auf dem Treppchen.
Two German individual vaulters made their way up onto the winning podium.

in die beiden Küren mitnahmen, konnten sie in den Kürprüfungen verteidigen, auch wenn diese durch andere dominiert wurden. Die USA sicherten sich den Sieg in beiden Kürprüfungen, konnten aber den Rückstand von einem halben Punkt aus der Pflicht auf Deutschland am Ende nicht aufholen. Die deutschen Fans mussten allerdings in der Finalkür um die Goldmedaille bangen. In der Mitte der Kür der Deutschen, die bis dahin fast ohne Fehler war, scheute das Gruppenpferd Cepin bei einem Wechsel in der Musik. Die Voltigierer konnten den plötzlichen Tempowechsel in der Galoppade des Pferdes nicht ausgleichen und mussten Cepin unvorhergesehen verlassen. Der Titel schien in diesem Moment verloren gegangen zu sein, doch die sechs Wertungsrichter setzten sie in der Kür auf Platz drei, so dass es am Ende zu Gold reichen sollte.

Weniger spannend machte es der Kölner Kai Vorberg beim Einzelvoltigieren der Herren. Erstmals gelang es einem deutschen Herren, seinen Titel erfolgreich zu verteidigen. Vorberg (Picasso – Kirsten Graf), der die gesamte Saison dominierte, drückte der Herrenkonkurrenz seinen Stempel auf und gewann in Aachen überlegen vor seinem Teamkollegen Gero Meyer-Nutteln (Arador – Alexander Hartl).
Der Hildesheimer holte sich nach den Weltmeisterschaften 2000 in Mannheim und 2002 im spanischen Jerez erneut die Silbermedaille. Über Bronze konnte sich der Slowake Ladislav Majdlen (Catalin III – Marian Pavlak) freuen. Das Ergebnis spiegelte nur bedingt die Dramatik wider, durch die der Herrenwettbewerb geprägt war. Zu Beginn zeichnete sich wie bei den letzten Welt-

Kai Vorberg, Cologne didn't make things as exciting in the men's individual competition. It was the first time that a German was able to defend his title successfully in the men's individual classification. Vorberg (Picasso, Kirsten Graf), who had dominated the whole season, excelled amongst his fellow-competitors and won sovereignly ahead of his team colleague Gero Meyer-Nutteln (Arador, Alexander Hartl).

The vaulter from Hildesheim took a silver medal at the World Championships for the second time, following his silver ranking 2000 in Mannheim and in Jerez, Spain in 2002. The Slovakian Ladislav Majdlen was overjoyed at taking the bronze medal (Catalin III, Marian Pavlak). The result only slightly reflects the dramatic circumstances that hallmarked the men's competition. Similar to the situation at the last World Championships, at the start of the competition all signs indicated that it would end in a duel for gold between double World Champion Matthias Lang (Farceur Breceen, Marina Joosten Dupon) and Kai Vorberg. The French vaulter won the compulsory test ahead of Vorberg, but the rest of the men's competition was a roller coaster of emotions for him. Around half of the horses in the first freestyle weren't prepared for the awe-inspiring conditions. As a result a lot of the horse fled forwards, as if the aim was to complete the circles in the fastest time possible. This made it very difficult for the vaulters concerned to show their freestyle elements correctly and resulted in most of them receiving bad scores. Matthias Lang experienced the same fate. He only just succeeded in reaching the final of the best 15.

VOLTIGIEREN | VAULTING

meisterschaften ein Zweikampf um Gold zwischen Doppelweltmeister Matthias Lang (Farceur Breceen – Marina Joosten Dupon) und Kai Vorberg ab. Der Franzose gewann die Pflicht vor Vorberg, sollte aber im weiteren Verlauf der WM eine Berg- und Talfahrt erleben. Rund die Hälfte der Pferde in der ersten Kür schien den äußeren Bedingungen nicht gewachsen. Folglich ergriffen die Pferde die Flucht nach vorne und galoppierten um die „schnellsten Rundenzeiten". Die betroffenen Voltigierer waren in den Möglichkeiten, ihre Kürelemente zu zeigen, deutlich eingeschränkt und kassierten schlechte Wertnoten. Matthias Lang ereilte das gleiche Schicksal. Er erreichte nur mit Mühe das Finale der besten 15.

Mit dem Tschechen Petr Eim (Catalin IV – Pavlina Neprasova) war ein weiterer Mitfavorit auf Edelmetall betroffen. Auch er war das Opfer eines nervösen Pferdes und verpasste sogar den Finaleinzug. Die Pferde der deutschen Teilnehmer hielten dem Druck stand. Belmondo, das Pferd von Tim-Randy Sia (Elke Schelp-Lensing) erhielt gleich in mehreren Wertungsprüfungen Bestnoten. Sia landete am Ende auf dem fünften Platz in der WM-Wertung. Vorberg und Meyer-Nutteln, der eigentlich nach der WM in Jerez seinen Rücktritt erklärt hatte, dominierten das Technikprogramm und konnten sich im Hinblick auf die Gesamtwertung von der Konkurrenz absetzen. Während „Wolfgang-Amadeus" Vorberg mit seinem Mozart-Programm seine Führung in der Finalkür weiter ausbauen konnte, benötigte Meyer-Nutteln seinen Punktevorsprung als Puffer, um den Silberrang in der Kür (siebter Platz) zu verteidigen.

Gero Meyer wurde zum dritten Mal Vize-Weltmeister.
Gero Meyer became Vice-World Champion for the third time.

The Czech vaulter Petr Eim (Catalin IV, Pavlina Neprasova), also one of the favourites, fell victim to a nervous horse too and didn't even manage to make it into the final. The horses of the German competitors stood up to the pressure well. Belmondo, Tim-Randy Sia's horse (Elke Schelp-Lensing) was awarded best scores in several of the rating competitions. Sia finished the World Championships in fifth place. Vorberg and Meyer-Nutteln, who had actually announced his retirement after the World Equestrian Games in Jerez, dominated the technical programme and was able to break away from his competitors in the overall classification. Whereas "Wolfgang-Amadeus" Vorberg was able to further extend his lead in the final freestyle with his Mozart routine, Meyer-Nutteln had to use his lead as a buffer in the freestyle (seventh place) to defend his silver ranking.

The results of the German ladies at the FEI World Equestrian Games took on a surprising turn. Finishing fourth, fifth and sixth, it was the first time that not a single medal was claimed by a German contestant. Up until now the German individual vaulters always returned from the World Championships with the gold medal in the pocket. In fact they often even won all three medals. The new World Champion is Megan Benjamin from the USA (Leonardo, Lasse Kristensen). The silver and bronze medals went to Katharina Faltin (Pitucelli, Julia Nöbauer) and Sissi Jarz (Escudo Fox, Julia Nöbauer) both from Austria. The medallist's victories did not come unexpectedly since these ladies had already drawn attention to themselves by picking up the victory as well as top placings at the international vaulting competition

Ladislav Majdlen sorgte mit Bronze für eine Überaschung.
Ladislav Majdlen surprised everyone by taking the bronze medal.

Der Deutsche Tim-Randy Sia erreichte Rang fünf. Sein Pferd Belmondo zählte zu den besten Voltigierpferden bei den Weltmeisterschaften.
The German rider Tim-Randy Sia achieved fifth place. Belmondo was one of the best vaulting horses at the Championship.

FEI World Equestrian Games Aachen 2006

Megan Benjamin und Longenführer Lasse Kristensen genossen die Ehrenrunde.
Megan Benjamin and lunger Lasse Kristensen enjoyed the lap of honour.

Die US-Amerikanerin Megan Benjamin sicherte sich als erste Nicht-Deutsche WM-Gold.
The US American Megan Benjamin was the first non-German female vaulter to win World Championship gold.

Etwas überraschend war das Abschneiden der deutschen Damen bei den Weltmeisterschaften in Aachen. Denn mit den Plätzen vier bis sechs gelang es erstmals keiner deutschen Teilnehmerin Edelmetall zu gewinnen.
Bislang kehrten die deutschen Einzelvoltigiererinnen immer mit Gold von Weltmeisterschaften zurück. Nicht selten ging an sie der gesamte Medaillensatz. Die neue Weltmeisterin ist die US-Amerikanerin Megan Benjamin (Leonardo – Lasse Kristensen).

Die Silber- und Bronzemedaille holten sich mit Katharina Faltin (Pitucelli – Julia Nöbauer) und Sissi Jarz (Escudo Fox – Julia Nöbauer) zwei Österreicherinnen. Unerwartet war der Erfolg der Medaillenträgerinnen nicht, denn bereits beim internationalen Voltigierturnier in München machten diese Damen mit Siegen und vorderen Platzierungen auf sich aufmerksam. So gewann Sissi Jarz das CVI** vor Megan Benjamin auf Platz zwei. Gut begannen die Weltmeisterschaften für Ines Jückstock (Dallmers Little Foot – Ruth Jückstock). Die 33-jährige Hamburgerin startete mit einem zweiten Platz in der Pflicht in den Wettkampf und war somit beste deutsche Starterin. Auch im Technikprogramm, der dritten Teilprüfung, war sie auf Tuchfühlung zu den Treppchenplätzen. In den Kürprüfungen gelang es der erfahrenen Einzelvoltigiererin aber nicht, mit den kürstarken Österreicherinnen und der US-Amerikanerin mitzuhalten. Am Ende landete sie in der WM-Wertung auf dem fünften Platz.

Ines Jückstock nahm an ihrer fünften WM teil.
Ines Jückstock took part in her fifth World Championships tournament.

in Munich. Namely, Sissi Jarz won the CVI** ahead of Megan Benjamin in second place. The World Championships got off to a good start for Ines Jückstock (Dallmers Little Foot, Ruth Jückstock). The 33-year-old vaulter from Hamburg was second after the compulsory test as the best German after the first rating. After the technical programme, the third rating competition, a medal was within reach. However, in the final competition the experienced individual vaulter was not able to match the per-

Nicola Ströh verpasste nur knapp Edelmetall.
Nicola Ströh narrowly missed out on a medal.

VOLTIGIEREN | VAULTING

Europameisterin Anja Barwig musste sich in Aachen mit Platz sechs begnügen.
European Champion, Anja Barwig, had to make do with sixth place in Aachen.

Mit Nicola Ströh (Lanson – Michael Gnad) und Anja Barwig (Arador – Alexander Hartl) hatten die Deutschen zwei weitere „heiße Eisen im Feuer". Denn Nicola Ströh trat in Aachen als Weltmeisterin an und wollte ihren Titel erfolgreich verteidigen. Anja Barwig gewann 2005 im italienischen Brescia die Goldmedaille bei den Europameisterschaften. Nach ihrer Knieverletzung, die sich Nicola Ströh bei der Bundessichtung in Barlo Bocholt zugezogen hatte, und einer mehrmonatigen Wettkampfpause, war die WM der zweite große Start nach den Deutschen Meisterschaften in Freudenberg. Während es der Hamburgerin gelang, in der WM-Finalkür die drittbeste Wertung zu erhalten, machte sich die fehlende Wettkampfpraxis im ersten Kürdurchgang bemerkbar. Hier konnte sie ihr volles Leistungspotenzial nicht entfalten. Am Ende wurde sie Vierte in der Gesamtwertung. Anja Barwig,

formances of the Austrians and Americans, who are extremely strong freestyle vaulters. In the end she took fifth place in the World Championships. Germany had also invested great hope in Nicola Ströh (Lanson, Michael Gnad) and Anja Barwig (Arador, Alexander Hartl), after all Nicola Ströh was defending her World Championship title in Aachen. Anja Barwig won the gold medal at the European Championships in Brescia, Italy in 2005. After the knee injury she sustained at the national trials in Barlo Bocholt and having to refrain from competing for several months, Nicola Ströh had only competed at one big competition this year prior the World Championships: the German Championships in Freudenberg. Whereas the vaulter from Hamburg managed to achieve the third best score in the WEG freestyle final, in the first freestyle round the lack of competition experience had been noticeable. She was simply not able to demonstrate her best performance and finished fourth overall. Anja Barwig, who had completed the trials with Magic Dream, had already swapped over to her reserve horse, Arador, for the German Championships in the hope of achieving a better score for the horse at the World Championships. At the European Championships she managed to creep up on her fellow-competitors from behind and won the gold medal. Something, which she didn't manage to repeat in Aachen. In spite of showing good performances, she had to make do with sixth place in the combined result after the four separate competitions.

Mit Sissi Jarz und Katharina Faltin erreichten zwei Österreicherinnen Medaillen.
Two Austrian vaulters claimed individual medals: Sissi Jarz and Katharina Faltin.

FEI World Equestrian Games Aachen 2006

die den Sichtungsweg mit Magic Dream bestritten hatte, wechselte bereits zu den Deutschen Meisterschaften auf das Ersatzpferd Arador mit der Hoffnung, bei den Weltmeisterschaften bessere Bewertungen für das Pferd zu erhalten. Noch bei den Europameisterschaften konnte sie das „Feld von hinten aufrollen" und letztendlich die Goldmedaille erringen. Dieses sollte ihr in Aachen nicht gelingen. Trotz guter Leistungen musste sie sich nach vier Teilprüfungen mit dem sechsten Platz begnügen.

„Kiss-and-Cry" ... und sonstige Neuerungen

Der Voltigierer absolviert sein Wettkampfprogramm wie gewohnt. Zum Abschluss seines Programms erfolgt der Gruß und er läuft im lockeren Dauerlauf von Applaus begleitet in Richtung Stadionausgang. Bis dahin verläuft alles wie gewohnt, doch am Ausgang wird dem Longenführer von Pferdepflegern das Pferd abgenommen und höfliche Stewards bitten ihn und seinen Voltigierer, in einem vorgegebenen Bereich Aufstellung zu nehmen – Die „Kiss-and-Cry-Zone". Hier warten die Starter unter Beobachtung einer Kamera, die ihre Emotionen direkt an den Zuschauer vor den Fernsehbildschirmen weiterleiten soll, auf ihre Wertung. Es sind neue Zeiten für den Voltigiersport angebrochen, denn die „Kiss-and-Cry-Zone" wurde auf Wunsch der Medien installiert. Schließlich wurde das Voltigieren erstmals zwei Stunden live im Fernsehen übertragen.

Gewöhnungsbedürftig sind auch die sechs Wertungsrichter, die zum ersten Mal bei einer WM rund um den Zirkel Platz nehmen und ihr Urteil über Voltigierer und Pferd abgeben. Letzteres rückt bei dieser Weltmeisterschaft vermehrt in den Vordergrund, denn die Pferdenote macht 20 Prozent der Gesamtwertung aus. Nicht selten entscheidet die Pferdenote über eine schlechtere Rangie-

"Kiss and Cry" ... and other innovations

The vaulters complete their competition programme as usual. After their performance they greet and, accompanied by the applause of the crowd, they run towards the stadium exit in a relaxed jog. Up until then everything runs the same as usual, but then at the exit, the grooms take the horse from the lunger, who together with the vaulters is politely asked to take up their positions in the assigned area – the "Kiss and Cry" zone. Here the competitors await their scores, under the keen observation of a camera that is waiting to pass on their emotions directly to the TV screens. A new era has started for vaulting sport, because the "Kiss and Cry" zone was installed at the request of the media. After all this was the first time that vaulting had been broadcast live on television for two hours.

The six judges who were seated around the circle for the first time at a World Championships and who gave their assessment on the vaulters and their horses takes some getting use to. In fact the horse played a larger role at these World Championships than ever before, since the score for the horse represented 20 percent of the overall score. The horse's score was thus often the reason for vaulters ultimately receiving a lower ranking, although they had perhaps received a better score for the compulsory, technical or freestyle programmes. However, the implentation of this new system seems to be undergoing teething problems, since the scores sometimes showed indiscrepancies of between two and three points for the same horse.

„Es müsste alle zwei Jahre Weltreiterspiele geben"

Es waren die ersten Weltreiterspiele für Ulla Ramge als verantwortliche Bundestrainerin für das Voltigieren. Ihre Vorgängerin Helma Schwarzmann gab nach den Weltreiterspielen im spanischen Jerez 2002 das Amt nach elf Jahren an die Warendorferin ab. Insgesamt 64 Medaillen bei Welt- und Europameisterschaften pflastern den Weg von Helma Schwarzmann. Ulla Ramge hat die Aufgabe übernommen, den erfolgreichen Weg deutscher Voltigierer bei Championaten fortzusetzen. Seit den Europameisterschaften 2003 errangen deutsche Voltigierer unter ihrer Führung bislang 15 Medaillen bei einer WM oder EM. Von den letzten Weltmeisterschaften im österreichischen Stadl Paura kehrten die Deutschen mit drei Goldmedaillen zurück.

„Aachen waren Ihre zweiten Weltmeisterschaften, aber Ihre ersten Weltreiterspiele als Bundestrainerin. Wie haben Sie diese erlebt?"
Ulla Ramge: Die WM in Aachen war überwältigend. Meiner Meinung nach müsste es alle zwei Jahre Weltreiterspiele geben. Es war ein Fest des Pferdesports, wo jede Disziplin Achtung vor den Leistungen der anderen hatte. Solche Weltmeisterschaften werden wir so schnell nicht wieder erleben.
„Wie beurteilen Sie die Leistungen der deutschen Voltigierer?"
Ulla Ramge: Insgesamt bin ich sehr zufrieden. Im Teamwettbewerb und bei den Herren hatten wir annähernd 100 Prozent Erfolg. Bei den Damen ist es leider nicht so gut gelaufen.
„Erstmals haben deutsche Damen bei einer WM keinen Titel beziehungsweise keine Medaille gewonnen. Was sind die Ursachen für das Abschneiden der deutschen Damen?"
Ulla Ramge: Dass die anderen Nationen aufgeholt haben, wussten wir bereits vorher. Bei den Herren haben wir das Favoritensterben bei Matthias Lang und bei den Damen bei Nicola Ströh erlebt. Unsere Damen haben keine großen Fehler gemacht, aber man durfte sich hier auch keine kleinen Fehler erlauben, um eine Medaille zu gewinnen.
„Es gab viele Neuerungen bei der WM. Zum ersten Mal waren bei Weltreiterspielen altersoffene Sechserteams am Start, Vokalmusik war erlaubt und vor allem die Pferdenote ging mit 20 Prozent in die Note ein. Drei Richter haben sich ausschließlich mit der Pferdebeurteilung befasst, drei Richter kümmerten sich um die Bewertung der Bewegungselemente. Haben sich die Veränderungen im Reglement positiv oder negativ ausgewirkt?"
Ulla Ramge: Viele Teams haben von der Öffnung der Altersgrenze Gebrauch gemacht und die Gruppen mit über 18-jährigen Voltigierern verstärkt. Die Leistungen haben sich dadurch deutlich nach oben geschraubt. Der Effekt, dass durch die Einführung der Sechserteams, mehr Nationen Mannschaften stellen, ist nur langsam zu erkennen. Ich hätte gedacht, dass dies sprunghafter ansteigen würde. Theoretisch finde ich die Gewichtung der Pferdenote gut, in der praktischen Umsetzung bei den Richtern sehe ich noch Probleme, da die vorhandenen Beurteilungskriterien nicht einheitlich angewendet werden. Es sind unbedingt weitere Richterschulungen notwendig.

rung des Voltigierers, auch wenn dieser im Vergleich zur Konkurrenz die besseren Pflicht-, Technik- oder Kürnoten erhält. In der Realisierung scheint es allerdings noch Probleme zu geben, denn die Bewertungen unterscheiden sich schon Mal zwei bis drei Punkte bei einem Pferd.

Höher, schneller, weiter – so könnte das Motto bei den Teams lauten. Schließlich werden die Obermänner nicht mehr alleine von körperlich leicht überlegenen Voltigierern gehoben, sondern immer öfter von erwachsenen Männern durch die Luft gewirbelt. Dem Schwierigkeitsgrad, aber auch der Choreographie scheinen keine Grenzen gesetzt zu sein. Nahezu jede Mannschaft macht von der Öffnung der Altersgrenze Gebrauch und setzt über 18-jährige Voltigierer, zumeist erfahrene Einzelvoltigierer ein. Die Vokalmusik peppt die Choreographien auf und Themen rücken immer mehr in den Vordergrund der Technik- und Kürprogramme.

The motto of the teams could be: higher, faster, further. Since the smaller vaulters on the top are often no longer twirled around in the air by vaulters of only slightly heavier build, but in the meantime by adult men. There seem to be no limits to the degree of technical difficulty or the choreography. Nearly every team seems to be taking advantage of the fact that the age limit has been lifted, by integrating vaulters, who are mostly highly experienced individual vaulters and over 18. The non-instrumental pieces of music pepped up the choreographies and the use of themes in the technical and freestyle programmes is becoming increasingly popular.

Anspannung und Erleichterung in der „Kiss-and-Cry-Zone".
Tension and relief in the "Kiss and Cry Zone".

"The World Equestrian Games should be held every two years"

They were the first FEI World Equestrian Games for Ulla Ramge in her role as the National Coach for vaulting. Her predecessor, Helma Schwarzmann, handed over office to the lady from Warendorf after the FEI World Equestrian Games in Jerez in 2002, after holding the position for eleven years. During this era Helma Schwarzmann had helped the German vaulters on their way to winning a total of 64 medals at World and European Championships. Ulla Ramge took over the task of assuring the continued success of the German vaulters at Championship level. Since the European Championships in 2003, the German vaulters have been able claim 15 medals at either World or European Championships. The Germans returned from the last World Championship competition in Stadl Paura, Austria with three gold medals.

"Aachen was your second World Championships tournament, but your first as National Coach. What was this experience like for you?"
Ulla Ramge: The FEI World Equestrian Games in Aachen were overwhelming. In my opinion the World Equestrian Games should be held every two years. It was a festival of equestrian sport, where every discipline showed mutual respect for the efforts of the other disciplines. We won't experience such World Championships again in a hurry.

"How would you assess the performances of the German vaulters?"
Ulla Ramge: Overall I am very satisfied. We showed an almost 100 percent success rate in the team and the men's competitions. Unfortunately the ladies' competition did not run quite as smoothly.

"It is the first time that the German ladies didn't take the title or a medal at the World Championships. What were the reasons for this?"
Ulla Ramge: We we already aware beforehand that the other nations had caught up. We saw our favourites knocked out: in the men's competition Matthias Lang and Nicola Ströh in the ladies' competition. Our ladies didn't make any big mistakes, but if you wanted to win a medal in Aachen, you couldn't afford to even make any small errors.

"There were a lot of changes at the World Championships this year. For the first time ever at these World Equestrian Games we saw teams of six vaulters without age limits, non-instrumental music and the score for the horse accounted for 20 percent of the overall score. Three judges occupied themselves exclusively with the assessment of the horses. Did these changes to the regulations have a positive or a negative effect?"
Ulla Ramge: Many teams took advantage of the age limit being lifted and reinforced their groups with vaulters who were over 18. The performance level increased incredibly as a result. The desired aim that more countries take part in the team competitions as a result of the six-man teams, is only happening very slowly. I would have thought that the number of teams had increased rapidly as a result. Theoretically I find the new weighting of the horse correct, but practically I feel that the judges are having a problem realising this, because the existing judging critera is not being applied in a uniform manner. Further training courses are essential for the judges.

Das deutsche Team (v.l.n.r.):/ *The german team (f.l.t.r.):*
Alexander Ripper, Kay Wienrich, Grischa Ludwig, Andreas Mamerow, Nico Hörmann, Maik Bartmann, Sylvia Rzepka.

Reining

AUTORIN/AUTHOR
RAMONA BILLING

Reining

Die Westernreitdisziplin Reining wurde im Jahr 2000 offiziell als siebte reiterliche Disziplin von der FEI anerkannt. Im Jahr 2002 war die ‚Dressur des Westernreitens' erstmals bei den Weltreiterspielen dabei. In der Reining (von engl. Reins = Zügel) ist eine Aufgabe (Pattern genannt) auswendig im Galopp vorzureiten. Diese setzt sich aus spezifischen Lektionen (Manöver genannt) zusammen, zu denen rasante 360° Wendungen auf der Hinterhand (Spins), schnelle große und langsame kleine Zirkel mit deutlichen Tempounterschieden auf feinste Hilfen (Speed Control), fliegende Wechsel, 180°-Wendungen (Roll Backs) und schließlich der berühmte Sliding Stop zählen. Letzterer ist ein Halten des Pferdes aus vollem Galopp, wobei die Hinterhand meterweit gleitet, während die Vorhand locker mitläuft.

Die Disziplin entstammt der Arbeitsreitweise der amerikanischen Cowboys und hat sich seit etwa den frühen 70er Jahren zu einem weltweit betriebenen Sport entwickelt, der teilweise gewaltige Preisgelder auslobt. Im großen internationalen Sport sind überwiegend Pferde der Rasse American Quarter Horse zu finden, gefolgt von Paints und Appaloosas – also alles Westernrassen.

Zu den Spitzenturnieren zählen in den USA u.a. die NRHA Futurity, bei der der Gewinner allein USD 150.000,– erhält und das NRHA Derby, in Europa u.a. die um USD 100.000,– dotierte World Reining Trophy (Mooslague), die NRHA Breeders Futurity und das NRHA Breeders Derby in Deutschland, das italienische Derby und die italienische Futurity und die Americana Bronze Trophy.

Auf den Weltreiterspielen in Aachen war Reining der zweithöchstdotierte Mannschaftswettbewerb. EUR 65.000,– wurden hier an die Top 5 Mannschaften ausgeschüttet, wovon der Weltmeister USA EUR 19.000,– mit nach Hause nehmen konnte. Deutschland gewann mit seinem vierten Platz noch EUR 10.500,–

Die deutsche Mannschaft | *The German Team*

Reiter / *Rider*	Alter / *Age*	Pferd / *Horse* Pfleger / *Groom*	Alter / *Age*	Zuchtgebiet / *Breeding*	Züchter / *Breeder* Besitzer / *Owner*
Nico Hörmann (Schwanewede)	27	Lil Ruf Cody Andrea Freudendahl	6	Quarter Horse/USA	- Rolf u. Monika Reinsc Oberreichenbach
Grischa Ludwig (Bitz)	32	Coeur D Wright Stuff Lutz Pfalz	6	Quarter Horse/USA	- Roy de Bruin, NL
Alexander Ripper (Fahrenbach)	25	Solanoswarlee Boy Dirk Theen	15	Quarter Horse/GER	- Georg Ripper, Fahrenb
Sylvia Rzepka (Neu Mitterndorf)	30	Golden Mac Jac	7	Quarter Horse/AUS	- Peter Prokes, Wien
Equipechef / *Chef d'Equipe* Andreas Mamerow		**Bundestrainer** / *National Trainer* Kay Wienrich		**Tierarzt** / *Veterinarian* Dr. Matthias Gräber	**Hufschmied** / *Fa* Dirk Meyer

Reining

The western riding sport of reining was officially accepted as the seventh riding discipline by the FEI in the year 2000. In the year 2002 the ‚western style dressage' was integrated in the World Equestrian Games for the first time. Reining (which derives from the word reins) involves a series of movements, known as a pattern, being ridden at canter off by heart. These are made up of specific exercises, the so-called manoeuvres, which include fast 360° turns on the hind (spins), large fast and small slow circles with clear changes of speed using the finest aids (speed control), flying changes, 180° turns (roll backs) and finally the famous sliding stop, where the horse is brought to a stop from the full canter, hereby the hindlegs slide several metres along the floor, whilst the forehand continues to run with the movement.

The roots of the discipline stem back to the ranch work of the American cowboys and in the early seventies it developed into a sport that is practised all over the world, endowed to an extent with huge sums of prize-money. In top international sport predominantly American Quarter Horses are implemented, followed by Paints and Appaloosas – in other words all Western breeds.

The top tournaments include, among others in the USA the NRHA Futurity, where the winner alone receives 150,000 US$ and the NRHA Derby; in Europa the World Reining Trophy (Mooslague) endowed with 100,000 US$, the NRHA Breeders Futurity and the NRHA Breeders Derby in Germany, the Italian Derby and the Italian Futurity as well as die Americana Bronze Trophy.

At the FEI World Equestrian Games in Aachen reining was the team competition with the second highest prize-money. 65,000 Euros were divided up among the top 5 teams, the World Champions, the USA, were allowed to take 19,000 Euros home with them. Germany's fourth place brought them the princely sum of 10,500 Euros.

REINING | REINING

Reining – zweit höchstdotierte Mannschaftswertung der WM

**Team: USA wird wieder Weltmeister, Deutschland verpasst nur knapp die Medaillenränge
Einzel: Alle drei Medaillen an Amerika, Deutschland unter den Top Ten**

Mannschaftswertung: USA verteidigen Titel

Dramatischer hätte diese Reining-WM für Deutschland wohl nicht sein können. Am Tag vor dem Mannschaftswettbewerb kamen zwei Pferde des deutschen Teams nicht durch die Verfassungsprüfung. Alexander Rippers (Fahrenbach) American Quarter Horse Hengst Solanoswarleeboy hatte sich beim Transport nach Aachen verletzt. Ebenso fiel Grischa Ludwigs (Bitz) Pferd Coeur D Wright Stuff aus. So sah es kurzfristig aus, als könnte Deutschland gar keine Mannschaft an den Start schicken. Als Retterin in der Not erwies sich jedoch Jutta Weckmüller (Eschwege). Die hessische Züchterin und Besitzerin von Ersatzpferd BV Smart Innuendo stellte ihre Stute, die eigentlich das Pferd von Ersatzreiter Maik Bartmann (Osthofen) war, kurzfristig Grischa Ludwig zur Verfügung. Damit stand eine vollständige Mannschaft zur Verfügung – allerdings ohne potentielles Streichergebnis. Der Druck auf die deutschen Reiter war damit enorm.

In Aachen sollten sie zu den großen Helden werden. Mit hervorragenden Ritten katapultierten Grischa Ludwig (Bitz), Nico Hörmann (Schwanewede) und Sylvia Rzepka (Mitterndorf) Deutschland allen Widrigkeiten zum Trotz in greifbare Nähe der Medaillen und verfehlten diese schließlich nur um einen halben Punkt! Am Ende blieb es bei der gleichen Platzierung wie vor vier Jahren auf den Weltreiterspielen in Jerez de la Frontera, wo Reining erstmals offizielle WEG Disziplin war: Unter insgesamt 21 teilnehmenden Nationen, von denen 15 Mannschaften nach Aachen schickten, wurden die enorm starken Amerikaner erneut Mannschaftsweltmeister. Silber ging an die Kanadier und Bronze an Italien.

Siegerehrung Mannschaft
Prize-giving ceremony of the teams

Reining – Team competition with second highest prize-money at World Championships

*Team: USA wins the World Champion title again, Germany just misses a medal
Individual: All three medals go to North America, Germany under the top ten*

Team classification: USA defends title

The World Reining Championships couldn't have been more dramatic for Germany. On the day before the team competition two of the German horses didn't pass the horse inspection. Alexander Ripper's (Fahrenbach) American Quarter Horse stallion Solanoswarleeboy had sustained an injury while travelling. Grischa Ludwig's (Bitz) horse Coeur D Wright Stuff also had to be withdrawn. So at first it looked like Germany wouldn't be able to put a team together. However, Jutta Weckmüller (Eschwege) came to the rescue. The Hessen breeder and owner of the reserve horse BV Smart Innuendo allowed Grischa Ludwig to ride her mare, which was actually the horse of the reserve Maik Bartmann (Osthofen). This meant Germany had a complete team again – albeit without a scratch result. The pressure on the German riders was thus enormous, because they were supposed to

'Ob das wohl gut ausgeht...': Mannschaftstierarzt Dr. Matthias Gräber und Bundestrainer Kay Wienrich vor dem ersten deutschen Ritt. Sie hätten sich keine Sorgen zu machen brauchen!
"Will everything go alright?...": Team veterinarian Dr. Matthias Gräber and National Coach Kay Wienrich before the first German ride. They didn't need to worry!

Ergebnisse/ Results Seite/ page 144

FEI World Equestrian Games Aachen 2006

Denkbar knapp verpasst Deutschland Bronze

Grischa Ludwig ging als fünfter Reiter mit BV Smart Innuendo ins ‚Rennen'. Getragen von einer unglaublichen Sympathiewelle durch das Aachener Publikum bewies der Baden-Württemberger, der bereits zweimal Deutscher Meister (FN) war, einmal mehr, dass er zur europäischen Reiningspitze gehört und sich kurzfristig auf fremde Pferde einstellen kann. Sicherlich merkte man, dass Pferd und Reiter noch nicht völlig aufeinander eingespielt waren (Grischa Ludwig saß am Vortag das erste Mal auf dieser Stute). Der Ritt ließ gerade deswegen jedoch nichts zu wünschen übrig: Rasante Spins, schöne Arbeit auf den Zirkeln und zum Abschluss drei feine Stops belohnten die fünf Richter mit 218,5 Punkten – ein Ergebnis, das der deutschen Mannschaft ein solides Polster verschaffte und erst vom 16. Starter, dem US-Amerikaner Dell Hendricks und Starbucks Sidekick übertroffen wurde.

Nach nur einem Tag Aneinandergewöhnens zeigten Grischa Ludwig und die in Hessen gezogene BV Smart Innuendo eine tolle Leistung und kamen unter die Top 20 fürs Einzelfinale.
After just one day of getting used to each other, Grischa Ludwig and the Hessen-bred BV Smart Innuendo gave a great performance, came under the top 20 and qualified for the individual final.

Der amtierende Deutsche Meister Nico Hörmann war der zweite deutsche Reiter und ging mit Lil Ruf Cody, einem 6-jährigen American Quarter Horse Hengst im Besitz von Monika und Rolf Reinschmidt, als 23. Reiter an den Start. Hörmann hatte drei der insgesamt fünf Sichtungen (CRI) in diesem Jahr für sich entschieden und galt als sehr sicherer Kandidat. Ausgerechnet ihm unterlief gleich am Anfang des ersten Spins ein Patzer, als Lil Ruf Cody die Hilfen missverstand und zunächst herausspringen wollte. Nico

be celebrated as big heroes in Aachen. Against the odds Grischa Ludwig (Bitz), Nico Hörmann (Schwanewede) and Sylvia Rzepka (Mitterndorf) showed excellent rides and catapulted Germany within arm's reach of the medals – all that separated them from the bronze medal was half a point! In the end they finished in fourth place as they did four years ago at the FEI World Equestrian Games in Jerez de la Frontera, where reining was an official WEG discipline for the first time ever: In Aachen 21 nations participated in the Championships, 15 of whom sent a team to the Soers. The incredibly strong Americans became the World Champions again. Silver went to Canada and bronze to Italy.

Germany narrowly misses bronze

Grischa Ludwig entered the stadium with BV Smart Innuendo as the fifth rider. Greeted by an incredible applause from the crowd in Aachen, the two-time German Champion (FN) from Baden-Württemberg, proved once again that he is an integral part of the European reining elite and can even get used to riding foreign horses in no time at all. Of course it was noticeable that the horse and rider weren't 100 percent conversant with each other (Grischa Ludwig hadn't ever ridden the mare until the day before). Considering the circumstances their ride couldn't be faulted: Fast spins, good work on the circles and three fine stops at the close were rewarded by the judges with a score of 218.5 – a result that gave the German team a solid start. In fact it remained unbeaten until the 16th rider entered the arena, the US American Dell Hendricks with Starbucks Sidekick.

'Glückwunsch Tim!' Grischa Ludwig gratuliert Tim Mc Quay für seinen Erfolg.
"Congratulations Tim!" Grischa Ludgwig congratulates Tim Mc Quay on his success.

The reigning German Champion, Nico Hörmann, was the second German rider and was 23rd on the starting list with Lil Ruf Cody, a 6-year-old Quarter Horse stallion owned by Monika and Rolf Reinschmidt. Hörmann won three of the five trials (CRI) this year and was considered to be a very safe candidate. He of all people made a mistake in the first spin, when Lil Ruf Cody misunderstood the aids and first of all wanted to jump out. It seemed to knock Nico Hörmann off his stride for an instant, but then he immediately prove that he is a true professional, showing a flawless ride with excellent spins, very good speed control and good stops. The outcome was 217.5 points – imagine what score he could have achieved if it hadn't been for the mistake in the spin!

Now everyone placed their hopes on the third rider. Although she is only 31, Germany had one of the most experienced riders in Europe in the team: Sylvia Rzepka, who was born in Starnberg, has been running a training school in Mitterndorf, south of Vienna for the last five years together with her husband Vern Sapergia. Sylvia Rzepka began her riding career as a youngster and was the most successful cutting rider in Europe for several years (Cutting is one of the cattle disciplines in the western riding sport). Then she changed her focal point to reining and started off a new career in this field. She completely justified the confidence that had been placed in her in Aachen – and not only that: She performed a perfect speedy ride on the 7-year-old

REINING | REINING

Sylvia Rzepka mit Golden Mc Jac im Spin - der im Besitz des Österreichers Peter Prokes stehende Hengst war das erfolgreichste in Europa gezogene Pferd. Alle vor ihm platzierten Pferde sind in den USA gezogen.
Sylvia Rzepka with Golden Mc Jac in the spin – the stallion owned by Peter Prokes (AUS) was the most successful European-bred horse. All of the horses that finished above him in the rankings were bred in USA.

American Quarter Horse stallion, Golden Mc Jac, which is owned by Peter Prokes, Austria, and displayed total harmony between the horse and rider. The pair rode out of the stadium with 219.5 points, although many of the spectators had expected an even higher score. This was the best result achieved by the German team and was furthermore the sixth best score of the day!

Hörmann schien für einen Augenblick ein bisschen aus dem Konzept gebracht, bewies dann jedoch umgehend, dass er ein echter Profi ist und zeigte einen fehlerfreien Ritt mit hervorragenden Spins, sehr schöner Speed Control und guten Stops. 217,5 Punkte waren das Ergebnis – was hätte das für ein Score sein können, ohne den Patzer beim Spin!

Nun lagen alle Hoffnungen auf der dritten Reiterin. Mit Sylvia Rzepka, einer gebürtigen Starnbergerin, die seit fünf Jahren zusammen mit ihrem Mann Vern Sapergia einen Trainingsbetrieb in Mitterndorf südlich von Wien betreibt, hatte Deutschland trotz ihrer erst 31 Jahre eine der routiniertesten Reiterinnen Europas in der Mannschaft. Sylvia Rzepka begann ihre reiterliche Karriere bereits als Jugendliche und war mehrere Jahre lang die erfolgreichste Cutting Reiterin Europas (zum Verständnis: Cutting ist eine der Rinderdisziplinen im Westernreitsport). Dann verlagerte sie ihren Schwerpunkt auf Reining und startete hier eine neue Karriere. Das in sie gesetzte Vertrauen rechtfertigte sie in Aachen vollkommen – und mehr als das: Auf dem 7-jährigen American Quarter Horse Hengst Golden Mc Jac aus dem Besitz des Österreichers Peter Prokes zeigte sie einen tempogeladenen Traumritt in völliger Harmonie zwischen Pferd und Reiter. Die beiden kamen mit einer 219,5 aus der Bahn, und dabei hätten viele noch einen besseren Score erwartet. Dies bedeutete das beste Ergebnis der deutschen Mannschaft und das sechstbeste aller Reiner an diesem Tag!

Die deutsche Mannschaft brachte es damit auf ein Gesamtergebnis von 655,5 Punkten. Spätestens seit Aaron Ralstons (USA) Ritt auf Smart Paul Olena (Score 223,5) und Luke Gagnons (CAN) auf Lil Santana war klar, dass die USA und Kanada wohl Gold und Silber unter sich ausmachen würden. Doch mit den Italienern würde es knapp werden – noch war eine Bronzemedaille in greifbarer Nähe. Marco Ricotta und Peppy Secolo lieferten als erste italienische Starter gleich das Streichergebnis mit einer 207,5. Dann jedoch gelang Christian Perez mit Dualin For Me ein ganz hervorragender Ritt mit perfekten flachen Spins und super Stops, der mit einer 221,5 belohnt wurde, was das viertbeste Ergebnis des Tages sein sollte. Ihm folgte als dritter Reiter Dario Carmignani mit Skeets Dun, der ebenfalls einen sehr guten Ritt zeigte und eine 219,5 für Italien holte. Damit kam alles auf den vierten und letzten Starter an: Adriano Meacci und Docs Tivio Hancock. Die beiden kamen mit einer 215 aus der Bahn, wodurch insgesamt 656 Punkte für Italien zusammen brachte. Damit war die Sache entschieden: der amtierende Europameister Italien gewann zum zweiten Mal Bronze bei der WM, Deutschland musste sich mit Platz 4 begnügen.

The overall score of the German team thus amounted to 655.5 points. After Aaron Ralston's (USA) ride on Smart Paul Olena (score: 223.5) and Luke Gagnon's (CAN) on Lil Santana, at the latest, it was obvious that the USA and Canada would be battling it out for gold and silver among themselves. But it was a close race between Italy and Germany – the bronze medal was still within reach. The first Italian rider Marco Ricotta and Peppy Secolo delivered the scratch result of 207.5 points. However, then Christian Perez gave an excellent performance with Dualin For Me that was highlighted by perfect flat spins and super stops. The pair was rewarded with 221.5 points, the fourth best result of the day. He was followed by the third team member Dario Carmignani with Skeets Dun, who also demonstrated a very good ride and claimed a score of 219.5 for Italy. So everything was down to the fourth and final rider: Adriano Meacci and Docs Tivio Hancock. The two left the arena with 215 points, bringing Italy's overall score to 656 points. Hence the reigning European Champions Italy won bronze at the World Championships for the second time and Germany had to make do with fourth place.

FEI World Equestrian Games Aachen 2006

Ein bisschen war den Deutschen die Enttäuschung natürlich schon anzumerken. Sie hätten mehr verdient. „Es war zum Schluss schon gemein knapp, wie wir verloren haben", äußerte sich Bundestrainer Kay Wienrich hinterher. „Aber unsere Leute haben wirklich Hervorragendes geleistet! Und nicht nur die drei, die dann tatsächlich starteten, sondern auch Maik Bartmann, der das Kunststück fertig brachte, Pferd und Reiter in nicht mal 24 Stunden aufeinander einzuspielen!"

Titelverteidiger und Favorit: USA gewinnt Mannschaftsgold

Ihrer Favoritenrolle voll gerecht wurden die US-Amerikaner. Das Mutterland des Westernreitsports hatte ein Team aus zwei überaus prominenten Reitern (Tim Mc Quay, mit über US$ 2 Millionen gewinnreichster Reiningreiter aller Zeiten, und Million Dollar Rider Dell Hendricks) und zwei vielversprechenden ‚Newcomern' (Matt Mills und Aaron Ralston) nach Deutschland geschickt. Dell Hendricks legte mit Starbucks Sidekicks eine 219 vor, der Aaron Ralston mit Smart Paul Olena den zweitbesten Ritt des Mannschaftswettbewerbs folgen ließ: 223,5 Punkte! Tim Mc Quay legte auf Mister Nicadual mit einer 222,5, dem drittbesten Ergebnis der Mannschafts-WM nach, so dass insgesamt 665 Punkte für die USA zusammenkamen. Matt Mills konnte es mit Easy Otie Whiz als 63. Starter also bequem angehen lassen. Mit einer 217,5 lieferte er zwar das Streichergebnis für die USA war aber auf jeden Fall im Einzelfinale dabei.

Of course the Germans weren't able to hide their disappointment. They had simply deserved more. "It was so close at the end, it was mean losing like that," commented the National Coach, Kay Wienrich, afterwards. "But our riders put up an excellent performance! And not just the three team riders who actually competed, but also Maik Bartmann, who worked wonders getting Grischa and his horse used to each other in less than 24 hours!"

Titleholder and favourite: USA wins team gold

The US Americans lived up to their role as favourites. The homeland of western riding had sent to Germany a team comprising of two by all means famous riders: Tim Mc Quay, the reining rider who has won the most prize-money ever (over 2 million US Dollars) and million-dollar rider Dell Hendrick, as well as two aspiring 'Newcomers'; Matt Mills and Aaron Ralston. Dell Hendricks and Starbucks Sidekicks got the team off to a good start with 219 points, which Aaron Ralston outbid with Smart Paul Olena, they achieved the second best score of the team competition: 223.5 points! Tim Mc Quay was close behind him with Mister Nicadual, they recorded a score of 222.5, the third best result in the World Championships team classification. In total that rounded the USA's score up to 665 points. So the fourth team rider Matt Mills, 63rd on the starting list, was able to take things "easy" with Easy Otie Whiz. The judges verdict of 217.5 meant he was the USA's scratch result, but had nevertheless qualified for the individual final.

Aaron Ralston (USA) machte das amerikanische Medaillengewinner-Team komplett - er holte Bronze in der Einzelwertung.
Aaron Ralston (USA) made the American medal winner team complete – he took bronze in the individual classification.

REINING | REINING

Kanadier knapp hinter USA auf Platz 2

Überraschend eng wurde es ganz zum Schluss zwischen Gold und Silber. Luke Gagnon/ Lil Santana (219), Francois Gautier/ Snow Gun (219,5) und Lance Griffin/ Whiz N Tag Chex (219) zeigten durchweg hervorragende Ritte und brachten Kanada auf einen komfortablen zweiten Platz. Dann setzte Duane Latimer mit Hang Ten Surprize als vorletzter Starter dieser Mannschafts-WM noch einmal alles auf eine Karte. Unter tosendem Beifall zeigte der gewinnreichste Reiter Kanadas und NRHA Million Dollar Rider Spins, Zirkel und Stops der Superklasse und erzielte Top Score des Tages: 225,5! Damit schloss die kanadische Mannschaft mit 664 Punkten dicht zu den USA auf.

Canadians right behind the USA in second place

In the end it was surprisingly close between gold and silver. Luke Gagnon / Lil Santana (219), Francois Gautier / Snow Gun (219.5) and Lance Griffin / Whiz N Tag Chex (219) showed excellent rides across the board and put Canada into a comfortable second place. Then the last but one competitor of the team World Championships, Duane Latimer risked everything with Hang Ten Surprize. Amid ecstatic applause the most successful reiner in Canada and NRHA million-dollar rider performed top-class spins, circles and stops to take the top score of the day: 225.5! Thus with an overall score of 664 points, the Canadian team were close on the heels of the US riders.

Packendes Einzelfinale

**Duane Latimer gewinnt nach Stechen Gold in der Einzelwertung
Alle drei Medaillenränge an Amerika, Deutsche unter Top Ten**

Die Weltreiterspiele 2006 endeten für die Reiner in einem fantastischen Duell zwischen Tim Mc Quay und Duane Latimer. Die beiden erreichten im Einzelfinale mit Traumritten jeweils einen Score von 230. Im darauf folgenden Stechen unterlief dem gewinnreichsten Reiner aller Zeiten, Tim Mc Quay, mit Mister Nicadual ein kleiner Moment der Unaufmerksamkeit („Ich hab wohl einen Moment die Zügel locker gelassen", meinte er in der nachfolgenden Pressekonferenz.). Der Mister Dual Pep Sohn im Besitz von Jerry Kimmel, USA, sprang im ersten großen Zirkel vorn kurz um. Tim Mc Quay korrigierte dies und beendete den Ritt mit einer 226. Million Dollar Rider Duane Latimer setzte mit dem etwas müde wirkenden Hang Ten Surprize (Bes. Howard Mann) nochmals alles auf eine Karte. Das Ergebnis: 228 und damit die Goldmedaille. Silber ging an Tim Mc Quay. Auch die Bronzemedaille blieb auf dem amerikanischen Kontinent: sie ging an den jungen Amerikaner Aaron Ralston auf Smart Paul Olena mit einer 227,5. Die zwölf Jahre alte Stute von Smart Chic Olena, die Aaron als 'just a good old mare, a real family horse' bezeichnet, ist im Besitz seiner Frau Meg Griffith-Ralston.

Starke Kanadier: hier Francois Gautier
Strong competition from Canada: In the photo Francois Gautier

FEI World Equestrian Games Aachen 2006

Exciting individual final

**Duane Latimer wins gold in the individual classification after a rein-off
All three medals went to North America, German under top ten**

The FEI World Equestrian Games 2006 ended for the reiners with a fantastic duel between Tim Mc Quay (USA) and Duane Latimer (CAN). Both had achieved a score of 230 in the individual final after showing magnificent rides. In the following rein-off the most successful reiner of all time, Tim Mc Quay, with Mister Nicadual lost his concentration of a split second: "I slackened the reins for a moment," he explained in the subsequent press conference. On the first big circle the Mister Dual Pep son, owned by Jerry Kimmel, USA, briefly changed the lead with his forelegs. Tim Mc Quay corrected this mistake and ended his ride with a score of 226. Million-dollar rider Duane Latimer (CAN) took full risk with Hang Ten Surprize, who appeared to be a little tired in the meantime (owner: Howard Mann, USA). The result: 228 and thus the gold medal. Silver went to Tim Mc Quay. The bronze medal was also claimed by the American continent: It was awarded to the young American rider, Aaron Ralston on Smart Paul Olena, who had scored 227.5. The 12-year-old mare by Smart Chic Olena, who Aaron describes as being 'just a good old mare, a real family horse', is owned by his wife Meg Griffith-Ralston.

Impressionen vom neuen Einzelweltmeister: Duane Latimer.
Impressions of the new individual World Champion: Duane Latimer.

REINING | REINING

2-Million-Dollar-Rider Tim McQuay musste sich erst im Stechen Duane Latimer geschlagen geben.
2 million-dollar rider Tim McQuay had to admit defeat in the rein-off against Duane Latimer.

Ein großartiges Ergebnis konnten die Deutschen erzielen. Sie waren in den Top Ten und Zweit- und Drittbeste bei den europäischen Reitern. Beste Deutsche und zweitbeste Europäerin war Sylvia Rzepka auf Platz acht. Ihr Hengst Golden Mc Jac stolperte kurz vor dem ersten Stop beim Run In und war dann auch beim ersten Spin kurz aus dem Konzept gebracht. Wäre dies nicht gewesen, wäre der Score von 219,5 noch um einiges höher ausgefallen! Jedenfalls ein großartiger Ritt auf einem hervorragenden Pferd!

The Germans achieved a superb result. They came under the top ten and were second and third best European riders. The best German and second best European rider was Sylvia Rzepka in eighth place. Her stallion, Golden Mc Jac (owner: Peter Prokes, AUT) stumbled shortly before the first stop at the run-in and was slightly knocked off course in the first spin. If this hadn't have happened, her score of 219.5 would have been much higher! Indeed a super rider on an excellent horse!

"Yeah!!!!!!" Sylvia Rzepka jubelt nach gelungenem Ritt.
"Yeah!!!!!!" Sylvia Rzepka cheers after her successful ride.

FEI World Equestrian Games Aachen 2006

Dies gilt in gleicher Weise für Nico Hörmann, der mit Lil Ruf Cody (Bes. Monika und Rolf Reinschmidt) eine 219 erritt und damit Platz neun in der Einzelwertung errang.

The same applies for Nico Hörmann, who scored 219 with Lil Ruf Cody (owners: Monika and Rolf Reinschmidt) and thus 9th place in the individual competition.

Zweitbester Deutscher und drittbester Europäer:
Nico Hörmann mit Lil Ruf Cody.
*Second best German and third best European:
Nico Hörmann with Lil Ruf Cody.*

REINING | REINING

Deutschland war nur mit zwei Reitern in der Einzelwertung vertreten, obwohl sich Grischa Ludwig mit BV Smart Innuendo ebenfalls qualifiziert hatte. Die Entscheidung, die Stute nicht noch mal antreten zu lassen, fiel einen Tag zuvor. BV Smart Innuendo war eigentlich das Pferd von Ersatzreiter Maik Bartmann gewesen und kam nach dem Ausfall zweier Pferde unter Grischa Ludwig zum Einsatz, der eine 218,5 in der Mannschaft erritt. Da die erst 6-jährige Stute unter Maik Bartmann die Deutsche Meisterschaft gehen soll und ein Platz unter den Top Ten wohl nur dann hätte erreicht werden können, wenn man das Pferd ans Limit geritten hätte, entschied man sich zur Schonung des Pferdes gegen einen Start. Grischa Ludwig war sichtlich enttäuscht, äußerte sich dann aber sehr sportlich: „Wir sind ein Team, und als Teil des Teams akzeptiere ich diese Entscheidung."

Germany was only represented by two riders in the individual classification, although Grischa Ludwig had also qualified with BV Smart Innuendo. The day before the final it was decided that the mare shouldn't compete. BV Smart Innuendo was actually the horse of the reserve rider Maik Bartmann, and was ridden by Grischa Ludwig in the team event after two horses didn't pass the vet check. The pair scored 218.5 for the team. But since Maik Bartmann is to compete on the only 6-year-old mare at the German Championships and it would have only been possible to obtain a place under the top ten by pushing the horse to the limit, the decision was taken to withdraw the horse from the individual final. Grischa Ludwig was visibly disappointed, but commented very fairly: "We are a team and as part of the team, I accept this decision."

Beste Amazone und gleichzeitig beste Europäerin war die Belgierin Ann Poels.
Best female reiner and also the best European female was Ann Poels, the Belgian rider.

Die Medaillengewinner:
The medalist:
Duane Latimer, CAN (Gold);
Tim Mc Quay, USA (Silber);
Aron Ralston, USA (Bronze)

Bester italienischer Einzelreiter war Dario Carmignani mit Skeets Dun auf Platz 10.
Dario Carmignani was the best Italian individual rider with Skeets Dun in 10th place.

AUTOREN/ *AUTHORS*
DR. TERESA DOHMS DR. HANFRIED HARING DR. KLAUS MIESNER

Zucht | *Breeding*

Die Dominanz gezielter Zuchtprogramme

Das Motto der Weltmeisterschaft „colours of fascination" traf wahrlich auch auf die Vielfalt der in allen sieben Disziplinen vertretenen Pferde von 53 verschiedenen Zuchtverbänden zu. Von den insgesamt 669 in den Final- bzw. Teamwettbewerben angetretenen Pferden gingen allein 158 aus deutscher Zucht an den Start - somit also fast ein Viertel der gerechneten Pferde. Ohne der Verteilung der Medaillen vorzugreifen zu wollen, wäre dies allein schon eine Goldmedaille für die deutschen Züchter wert gewesen.

Das Königliche Warmblutpferdestammbuch der Niederlande (KWPN) war mit 75 Pferden der am stärksten vertretene Zuchtverband in den Disziplinen Springen, Dressur, Vielseitigkeit, Fahren und Voltigieren, gefolgt vom Verband hannoverscher Warmblutzüchter mit 46, dem Verband der Züchter des Holsteiner Pferdes mit 33 und dem Verband der Züchter des Oldenburger Pferdes mit 32 Pferden. In den beiden Disziplinen Distanzreiten und Reining dominierte jeweils eine Rasse das Geschehen, nämlich der Vollblutaraber bzw. das Quarter Horse.

Die diesjährigen Championate demonstrierten die Dominanz der Produkte aus konsequent geführten Zuchtprogrammen. Etliche gekörte und leistungsgeprüfte Hengste absolvierten hoch erfolgreich die an sie gestellten Aufgaben. Die Deutsche Pferdezucht konnte einmal mehr unter Beweis stellen, dass die Verzahnung von Zucht und Sport (Ausbildungs- und Prüfungssystem) in Deutschland Basis und Garant für Top-Erfolge im Spitzensport sind.

The dominance of targeted breeding programmes

The motto of the World Championships "colours of fascination" especially applied to the diversity of the horses from 53 different breeding associations, which took part in all seven disciplines. Of the 669 horses that competed in the final and team competitions, almost a quarter were German-bred – 158 to be exact. Even without taken a closer look at the distribution of the medals, this alone should have been worth a gold medal for the German breeders.

With 75 horses, the Royal Dutch Warmblood Association (KWPN) was the best represented breeding association in the disciplines show-jumping, dressage, eventing, driving and vaulting, followed by the Hanoverian breeders with 46 horses, the Holstein Breeding Association with 33 horses and the Oldenburg Breeding Association with 32 horses. The two disciplines endurance and reining were each dominated by a single breed respectively, namely the Arabian thoroughbred and the Quarter horse.

This year's Championships demonstrated the dominance of the products of consequently executed breeding programmes. Several graded stallions completed the set tasks with great success. The German horse breeding scene was once again able to prove that the link between the breeding system and sport in Germany (training and testing system), are the basis and the guarantee for major successes in top sport.

Medaillenspiegel aller Disziplinen/ *Medal index* **Zuchtverbände** *Breeding Association*	**Gold** Einzel *Individual*	**Gold** Mannschaft *Team*	**Silber** Einzel *Individual*	**Silber** Mannschaft *Team*	**Bronze** Einzel *Individual*	**Bronze** Mannschaft *Team*	Total	nur olymp. Disziplin *only olymp. discipline*
Hannover (HANN)	2	5	1	3	3	2	16	14
Holstein (HOLST)	1	3				4	8	5
Oldenburg (OLDBG)		5	1			1	7	
Bayern (BAVAR)						2	2	1
Rheinland (RHEIN)	1						1	
Trakehner (TRAK)				1			1	
Westfalen (WESTF)						1	1	1
Gesamt Deutschland	**4**	**13**	**3**	**3**	**3**	**10**	**36**	**21**
Koninklijke Warmbloed Paardenstamboek (KWPN)		3	6	4	2	11	26	6
American Quarter Horse Association (AQHA)	1	4	1	3	1	4	14	
Vollblutaraber (ARAB ox)	1	3	1	3	1	1	10	
Lusitano (LUS)	4			4			8	
Irish Sport Horse (ISH)		1	1	2		2	6	6
Belgish Warmbloed Paard (BWP)		2		2	1		5	3
Englisches Vollblut (TB)	1	1		1	1	1	5	5
Französischer Traber		2				2	4	
Danish Warmblood Association (DWB)	1		1		1		3	2
Lipizzaner (LIPIZ)				3			3	
Russisches Warmblut (RUSS)		1					1	
Tchechisches Warmblut (CHECH WB)		1					1	
Sporthorse Breeding in Great Britain (SHBGB)				1			1	1
Paint Horse (PTH)				1			1	
Friese				1			1	
Swedish Warmblood Association (SWB)						1	1	1
Studbook Zangersheide (ZANG)						1	1	1
Saddle Bred						1	1	

Zucht | Breeding

Springen

Der Trend der letzten Championate, dass die Abstammungen der in den Starterlisten aufgeführten Pferde vornehmlich auf deutsche und französische Blutlinien zurückzuführen sind, setzte sich im Springen weiterhin fort. In Aachen waren insgesamt 115 der gestarteten Pferde einem Zuchtgebiet zuzuordnen. Über 40% stammten aus deutschen Zuchtgebieten, 20 % aus den Niederlanden und fast 14% aus Frankreich. Zahlenmäßig am stärksten vertreten waren das KWPN mit 23, der Holsteiner Verband mit 22 und Sellé Francais mit 16 Pferden. Die meisten Nachkommen stellte der selbst international erfolgreiche Quidam de Revel (SF). Dessen Sohn Guidam (KWPN), der international erfolgreiche Darco (BWP) und die Holsteiner Hengste Cantus sowie Burggraaf stellten jeweils drei direkte Nachkommen. Besonders erfolgreich konnte sich natürlich der Holsteiner Cassini I in Szene setzen, dessen Nachkommen Platz 1 und 6 in der Endabrechnung belegten. Als Mutterväter traten besonders der Holsteiner Lord und der Hannoveraner Grannus-Granit mit jeweils drei Enkeln hervor.

Schaut man in das Endergebnis der besten Einzelreiter findet man unter den TOP-30 über 43% mit deutschen Pferden berittene Reiter (7 Holsteiner, 2 Oldenburger, 2 Westfalen, 1 Hannoveraner und 1 Württemberger). Das KWPN war mit 8 Pferden am stärksten in dieser Gruppe.

Ein besonderes Highlight stellte das Finale mit Pferdewechsel dar, in dem mit dem Hannoveraner Shutterfly, der Westfalenstute Pialotta und dem KWPN-Wallach Authentic drei sehr blutgeprägte, moderne Nachkommen von Halbblutstuten gegen den mit schier endlosem Springvermögen ausgestatteten, sehr kaliberigen Holsteiner Cavalor Cumano (Cassini I-Landgraf) zu kämpfen hatten. Mit 3 Gold- und 1 Bronzemedaille war der Holsteiner Verband der erfolgreichste Zuchtverband im Springen, gefolgt vom KWPN mit 1 Gold- und 3 Silbermedaillen, dem BWP mit 1 Gold- und 2 Silbermedaillen. Der hannoverscher Verband konnte 2, der bayerische Zuchtverband 1 und das Stutbuch Zangersheide auch 1 Bronzemedaille gewinnen.

Show-jumping

The trend of the recent Championships that the horses competing in the show-jumping mainly descend from German and French bloodlines continued. In Aachen 115 of the competing horses belonged to a specific breeding area. Over 40% descended from German breeding areas, 20 % from the Netherlands and almost 14% from France. In terms of numbers, 23 horses to be precise, the KWPN was the breeding association with the strongest representation in the show-jumping ring, followed by the Holstein Breeding Association with 22 horses and Selle Francais with 16 horses. The internationally successful Quidam de Revel (SF) sired the most offspring in the competitions (SF). His son Guidam (KWPN), the internationally successful Darco (BWP) and the Holstein stallions Cantus and Burggraaf each sired three direct offspring. Of course the Holstein stallion Cassini I was particularly able to distinguish himself, since his progeny took first and sixth place in the end result. On the dams' side, the Holstein stallion Lord and the Hanoverian stallion Grannus-Granit both contributed well with three grand-children on the starting lists.

If one looks at the end result of the best individual riders, over 43% of the top 30 riders had saddled German horses (7 Holstein, 2 Oldenburg, 2 Westphalian, 1 Hanoverian and 1 Württemberg). The KWPN was the strongest breed in this group, represented by 8 horses.

The Final with rotation of horses was a special highlight. Three thoroughbred types, the Hanoverian gelding Shutterfly, the Westphalian mare Pialotta and the KWPN gelding Authentic, all modern offspring of half-blood mares, had to take on the very solid Holstein Cavalor Cumano (Cassini I x Landgraf), who is equipped with amazing jumping potential.

Winning 3 gold and 1 bronze medal the Holstein Association was the most successful breeding association in the show-jumping discipline, followed by the KWPN with 1 gold and 3 silver medals and the BWP with 1 gold and 2 silver medals. The Hanoverian Association was able to claim 2 bronze medals, the Bavarian Breeding Association and the Zangersheide studbook also won 1 bronze medal apiece.

Authentic (KWPN) v. Guidam - Katell xx (1995, Wallach)
Züchter/ *Breeder*: G.H. Morsink (NED)
Reiterin/ *Rider*: Beezie Madden (USA)

Cavalor Cumano (Holsteiner) v. Corrado I - Masetto (1993, Hengst)
Züchter/ *Breeder*: Willi Lührs, Neumünster
Reiterin/ *Rider*: Jos Lansink (BEL)

Shutterfly (Hannoveraner) v. Silvio I - Forrest xx (1993, Wallach)
Züchter/ *Breeder*: Uwe Dreesmann, Hesel
Reiterin/ *Rider*: Meredith Michaels-Beerbaum (GER)

FEI World Equestrian Games Aachen 2006

Isovlas Pialotta (Westfalen) v. Pilot - Akitos xx (1991, Stute)
Züchter/ *Breeder*: Josef Korthues, Schöppingen
Reiterin/ *Rider*: Edwina Alexander (AUS)

L'Espoir (ZANN) v. Landwind II - Feinschnitt I (1996, Wallach)
Züchter/ *Breeder*: Catherine Duez (BEL)
Reiterin/ *Rider*: Ludger Beerbaum (GER)

Noltes Küchengirl (Bayern) v. Lord Z - Cambridge Cole (1997, Stute)
Züchterin/ *Breeder*: Eva Schmid, Utting
Reiterin/ *Rider*: Marcus Ehning (GER)

Eurocommerce Berlin (Holsteiner) v. Cassini I - Caretino (1994, Hengst)
Züchter/ *Breeder*: Josef Unkelbach, Köln
Reiterin/ *Rider*: Gerco Schröder (NED)

Al Mutawakel (Württemberger) v. Calando Landgraf - Goldpilz (1996, Wallach)
Züchter/ *Breeder*: August u. Paul Ströbele, Öpfingen
Reiterin/ *Rider*: Mohammed Al Kumaiti (UAE)

Medaillenspiegel Springen/ *Medal index show jumping*

Zuchtverb. Breed.Assoc.	Gold	Silber	Bronze
Mannschaftswettbewerb/ *Team Comp.*			
Holstein	2		1
Hannover		1	
Bayern		1	
KWPN	1	2	
BWP	1	2	
ZANG			1
Einzelwettbewerb/ *Individual Comp.*			
Holstein	1		
Hannover			1
KWPN		1	

Dressur

Schaut man in die Pedigrees der in der Dressur erfolgreichen Pferde, lässt sich zum wiederholten Mal feststellen, dass ohne deutsche Blutlinien fast nichts geht. Eine Vielzahl der 85 gestarteten Pferden mit Pedigree hatten deutsche Eltern oder Großeltern.
Über 47% der gestarteten Pferde stammen aus deutschen Zuchtverbänden. In beiden Einzelwettbewerben waren sogar 70% der TOP 10-platzierten Pferde aus Deutschland. Der mit Abstand zahlenmäßig am stärksten vertretene Zuchtverband war der Verband hannoverscher Warmblutzüchter. Mit 11 Einzel- und Teammedaillen sorgten die Hannoveraner für eine klare Überlegenheit ihres Verbandes gegenüber allen anderen teilnehmenden Zuchtverbänden in dieser Disziplin. Das KWPN, der Oldenburger Verband und der Dänische Warmblutverband waren mit 8, 7 bzw. 6 Pferden weitere recht stark vertretene Zuchtorganisationen, wobei das KWPN 2 Silber- und der Dänische Warmblutzuchtverband 1 Silber- und 1 Bronzemedaille gewinnen konnten.

Mit 3 Nachkommen war der selbst international erfolgreiche Donnerhall (Oldb.) am stärksten vertreten. Jeweils 2 direkte Nachkommen hatten die Hengste Weltmeyer (Hann.), Ehrentusch (Westf.), Quattro B (SF) und der Vollblüter Bek. Mütterlicherseits war der Hannoveraner Lungau allein dreimal als Großvater vertreten, davon zweimal unter den TOP 10-Platzierungen.

Schaut man in die Pedigrees der erfolgreichen Dressurpferde dieser Weltmeisterschaften so stellt man fest, dass mittlerweile auch Nachkommen eigentlich eher springbetonter Väter hoch erfolg-

Dressage

If one takes a look at the pedigree of the horses that were successful in the dressage, one quickly comes to the conclusion again that almost nothing is possible without the German bloodlines. The majority of the 85 registered competing horses had either German parents or grand-parents.
Over 47% of the horses that took part descend from German breeding associations. Indeed in both of the individual competitions, 70% of the horses under the top ten came from Germany. Numerically speaking, the Hanoverian warmblood breeders were by far the most strongly represented breeding association. Taking a total of 11 individual and team medals, the Hanoverian Association was clearly superior in this discipline compared to all other represented breeding associations. The KWPN, the Oldenburg Association and the Danish Warmblood Associations were also strongly represented with 8, 7 and 6 horses respectively, whereby the KWPN was able to claim 2 silver medals and the Danish Warmblood Association 1 silver and 1 bronze medal.

Donnerhall (Oldb.) who himself celebrated international success, displayed the strongest representation with three offspring. The stallions Weltmeyer (Han.), Ehrentusch (Westp.), Quattro B (SF) each had 2 direct offspring at the Championships and the Hanoverian stallion Lungau out of a thoroughbred dam was represented by three grand-children, two of which came under the top ten.

If one takes a closer look at the pedigrees of the dressage horses that were successful at the FEI World Equestrian Games, then

ZUCHT | BREEDING

Satchmo (Hannoveraner) v. Sao Paulo - Legat (1994, Wallach)
Züchter/ *Breeder*: Albert Kampert, Halle
Reiterin/ *Rider*: Isabell Werth (GER)

Bonaparte (Hannoveraner) v. Bon Bonaparte - Consul (Trak) (1993, Wallach)
Züchter/ *Breeder*: Monika Jacob-Goldeck, Wedemark
Reiterin: Heike Kemmer (GER)

Elvis VA (Hannoveraner) v. Espri - Garibaldi II (1996, Wallach)
Züchter/ *Breeder*: Christian Pfeil, Bremerhaven
Reiterin: Nadine Capellmann (GER)

Blue Hors Matine (DWB) v. Blue Hors Silver Moon - Matador (1997, Stute)
Züchter/ *Breeder*: Inger B. Katballe (DEN)
Reiter/ *Rider*: Andreas Helgstrand (DEN)

Group 4 Securicor Lingh (KWPN) v. Flemmingh - Columbus (1993, Hengst)
Züchter/ *Breeder*: HS. Dallinga (NED)
Reiter/ *Rider*: Edward Gal (NED)

Keltec Salinero (Hannoveraner) v. Salieri - Lungau (1994, Wallach)
Züchter/ *Breeder*: Horst Bünger, Essel
Reiterin/ *Rider*: Anky van Grunsven (NED)

Sunrise (Hannoveraner) v. Singular Joter - Werther (1994, Stute)
Züchter/ *Breeder*: Manfred Schäfer, Vechelde
Reiter/ *Rider*: Imke Schellekens-Bartels (NED)

Floriano (Westfale) v. Florestan I - Weinberg (1990, Wallach)
Züchter/ *Breeder*: Norbert Borgmann, Ostbevern
Reiter/ *Rider*: Steffen Peters (USA)

Medaillenspiegel Dressur/ *Medal index dressage*

Zuchtverb. *Breed.Assoc.*	Gold	Silber	Bronze
	Mannschaft/ *Team Comp.* Grand Prix		
Hannover	4	2	1
Westfalen			1
Bayern			1
KWPN		2	
SWB			1
	Einzel/ *Indiv.Comp.* Grand Prix Special		
Hannover	1	1	
DWB			1
	Einzel/ *Indiv.Comp.* Grand Prix Kür		
Hannover	1		1
DWB		1	

reich in der Dressur eingesetzt werden. Die Pedigrees der Hälfte der erfolgreichsten zehn Pferde lassen vermuten, dass diese Pferde auch beim Springen eine ordentliche Figur abgeben müssten. Dies beweisen die beiden hannoverschen Goldmedaillengewinner Satchmo und Keltec Salinero. Der erstgenannte hinterließ während der Körung einen guten Eindruck im Freispringen und der Vollbruder von Salinero war Teilnehmer im Springen bei den Olympischen Spielen in Athen.

Interessant auch die Verteilung der Geschlechter: 27 Hengste, 10 Stuten und 52 Wallache gingen an den Start. Unter den Top 10 platzierten sich allein 3 Stuten und 2 Hengste.

one soon notices that offspring of stallions, who are better known for show-jumping lines, are in the meantime also successful in the dressage. The pedigrees of half of the most successful horses led one to believe that these horses must actually be able to jump nicely too. The two Hanoverian gold medallists Satchmo and Keltec Salinero certainly prove this to be true. The former left behind a good impression at the loose jumping during the grading process and Salinero's full brother took part in the jumping competitions at the Olympic Games in Athens.

The distribution of the sexes is also interesting: 27 stallions, 10 mares and 52 geldings competed. Whereby 3 mares and 2 stallions managed to make it under the top ten placings.

FEI World Equestrian Games Aachen 2006

Vielseitigkeit

Die Austragung der Championate nach der Kurzformel, d.h. ohne Rennbahn und Wegestrecke, war im Vorfeld von der Diskussion über eine völlige Veränderung der Pferdetypen bzw. -rassen begleitet worden. Gerade aus Ländern mit hochstehender Vollblut- jedoch wenig ausgeprägter Warmblutzucht, wie z.B. Australien, Neuseeland, aber auch England, war die Befürchtung zu hören, dass das blutgeprägte Vielseitigkeitspferd verschwinden und durch den Warmblüter wie im Springen und in der Dressur verdrängt würde. Auch die Erfahrungen von Aachen zeigen, dass dies keineswegs der Fall ist. Es wurden jedoch durch die höhere relative Wertigkeit der Teildisziplinen Dressur und Springen nicht nur höhere Ansprüche an die Rittigkeit der Pferde, sondern auch an weitere Spezialeigenschaften wie Springvermögen und -technik einschließlich Vorsichtigkeit sowie an die Grundgangarten gestellt. Zu diesen Eigenschaften kann der Warmblüter beitragen.

Von den 79 gestarteten Pferden waren 26, also ein Drittel, reine Vollblüter, davon 4 unter den Top Ten und auch in den Medaillenteams. Das Irish Sport Horse war mit 12 Pferden als stärkster Zuchtverband vertreten. 4 Iren sind unter den Top Ten und 5 trugen zu Mannschaftsmedaillen bei, durch Ringwood Cockatoo auch in unserem Team.

Sieben Pferde stammen aus deutscher Zucht (3 Hannoveraner, je 1 Holsteiner, Westfale, Baden-Württemberger und Trakehner).

Für Deutschland starteten 2 Hannoveraner (Air Jordan von Amerigo Vespucci xx) und FRH Serve Well von Sherlock Holmes xx), ein Holsteiner (Marius von Condrieu xx), ein Baden-Württemberger (Sindy von Stan the Man xx), ein Ire (Ringwood Cockatoo von Peacock xx) und der Vollblüter Sleep Late (von Kuwait Beach). Der Vollblüter Amerigo Vespucci war übrigens der einzige Hengst mit zwei Nachkommen.

Je 4 Pferde waren dem Stutbuch Selle Francais und Schwedisches Warmblut zuzuordnen, 3 weitere im Anglo-Araber Stutbuch eingetragen.

Als Fazit kann die Aussage getroffen werden, dass der Vollblüter auch bei dem gültigen Austragungsmodus eine große Rolle spielen wird, und zwar sowohl als reiner Blüter als auch in zunehmendem Maße als Reitpferd mit sehr hohem Vollblutanteil. Vielleicht ist die Tatsache, dass die USA als einziges Land ausschließlich auf Vollblüter gesetzt hatten, ein weiterer Hinweis.

Eventing

The fact that the World Championships were carried out without a racetrack and roads and tracks, was accompanied by the discussion in the run-up to the event that this would lead to a complete change in the horse types and breeds that were to be implemented. Fears were voiced, particularly by the countries that have a high percentage of thoroughbred horses and few warmblood breeds, such as Australia, New Zealand and also England, that the thoroughbred-type eventing horse would gradually disappear, only to be replaced by the warmbloods as has had happened in the show-jumping and dressage disciplines. And yet the events in Aachen proved that this is not going to be the case at all. However, it did mean that as a result of the higher relative importance of the dressage and show-jumping competitions more significance was laid on the rideability of the horses, as well as on special characteristics such as jumping potential and technique including a certain degree of carefullness as well as on the basic paces. Of course the warmblood can contribute to these characteristics.

Of the 79 horses that competed, 26 were pure thoroughbreds – in other words a third of them – four of which came under the top ten, also among the team medallists. The Irish Sport Horse with 12 horses showed the strongest representation among the breeding associations. 4 Irish horses were placed under the top ten and 5 contributed to team medals, for instance Ringwood Cockatoo in the German team.

Seven horses were German-bred (3 Hanoverians, one Holstein, one Westphalian, one Baden-Württemberg and one Trakehner).

Two Hanoverians competed for Germany (Air Jordan by Amerigo Vespucci xx) and FRH Serve Well by Sherlock Holmes xx), one Holstein (Marius by Condrieu xx), one Baden-Württemberg (Sindy by Stan the Man xx), one Irish horse (Ringwood Cockatoo by Peacock xx) and the thoroughbred Sleep Late (by Kuwait Beach). The thoroughbred Amerigo Vespucci was incidentally the only stallion that was represented by two offspring.

The Selle Francais and Swedish Warmblood studbooks both had 4 horses in the competition, a further three were registered in the studbook of the Anglo-Arabs.

It can therefore be concluded that the thoroughbred will continue to play a large role in eventing despite the new competition mode, both in the form of pure thoroughbreds and to an increased extent as riding horses with a high portion of thoroughbred blood. Further evidence of this is perhaps the fact that the USA was the only country to exclusively enter thoroughbred horses.

Air Jordan (Hannoveraner) v. Amerigo Vespucci xx - Wittensee (1995, Wallach)
Züchter/ *Breeder*: Horst Wesch, Bad Bederkesa
Reiter/ *Rider*: Frank Ostholt (GER)

Marius Voigt-Logistik (Holsteiner) v. Condrieu xx - Laurin (1994, Wallach)
Züchter/ *Breeder*: Hans Werner Ritters, Krumstedt
Reiter/ *Rider*: Hinrich Romeike (GER)

Ringwood Cockatoo (ISH) v. Peakock xx a.d. Bailey´s Folly (1991, Wallach)
Züchterin/ *Breeder*: Hilary Greer (IRL)
Reiterin/ *Rider*: Bettina Hoy (GER)

Zucht | Breeding

Sleep Late xx (Englisches Vollblut) v. Kuwait Beach xx - Evening Trial xx (1991, Wallach)
Züchter/ *Breeder*: England
Reiterin: Ingrid Klimke (GER)

Sindy (Württemberger) v. Stan the Man xx - Tassilo (Trak) (1994, Stute)
Züchter/ *Breeder*: Tobias Ertle, Sontheim
Reiter/ *Rider*: Dirk Schrade (GER)

Madaillenspiegel Vielseitigkeit/ *Medal index Eventing*

Zuchtverband	Gold	Silber	Bronze
Breed. Assoc.	Mannschaft/ *Team Comp.*		
Hannover	1		
Holstein	1		
ISH	1	2	2
TB (xx)	1	1	1
SHBGB		1	
Unbekannt			1
	Einzel/ *Individual*		
TB (xx)	1		1
ISH		1	

Fahren / Driving

Die Anforderungen im Fahrsport sind so gestaltet, dass wieder mehr Rassen den Kampf um Medaillen aufnehmen können.
Von 235 gestarteten Pferden stammten 43 aus deutschen Zuchtbüchern (15 x Oldenburg, 7 x Holstein, 6 x Hannover, 4 x Deutsches Sportpferd, 3 x Trakehner, 3 x Bayern, 2 x Rheinland, je 1 x Westfalen, Württemberg, Zuchtverband für deutsche Pferde). Dann gab es weitere Warmblüter aus Holland (42!!!), Schweden (10), Polen (9), Tschechien (6), Dänemark (4) Russland (4), Schweiz (2), Ungarn (2), Frankreich (1), Belgien (1), Österreich (1). Und dann kommen Barockpferde: Lipizzaner (21), Kladruber (15), Andalusier (Pura Raza Española, 10), Lusitanos (5), Friesen (2). Abgerundet wird das Bild durch Traber (8), Hackneys (5) und Vollblüter (3).
Auch der Blick auf die Medaillenränge gab in Aachen keine klare Aussage zur Überlegenheit einer Rasse. Zwar sind die Warmblüter in der Überzahl, aber es tauchen auch die Barockrassen auf. Der Zug des Einzelsiegers besteht aus Lusitanos und ebenso fuhren Lipizzaner und ein Friese in die Medaillen.
Diese Buntheit tut dem Fahrsport gut und der Sport tut gut daran, die Anforderungen nicht so zu verändern, dass nur eine Rasse oder Herkunft sie erfüllen kann.

The demands required by the driving sport enable a wider range of breeds to take part in the battle for the medals.
Of the 235 horses that competed, 43 were German-bred (15 x Oldenburg, 7 x Holstein, 6 x Hanover, 4 x German Sports Horses, 3 x Trakehner, 3 x Baverian, 2 x Rheinland, 1 apiece x Westphalian, Württemberg, Breeding Association for German Horses). Followed by further warmbloods from Holland (42!!!), Sweden (10), Poland (9), the Czech Republic (6), Denmark (4) Russia (4), Switzerland (2), Hungary (2), France (1), Belgium (1), Austria (1). Barock horses were also represented in high numbers: Lipizzaners (21), Kladrubers (15), Andalusians (Pura Raza Española, 10), Lusitanos (5), Friesians (2). The overall picture was rounded off by Trotting Horses (8), Hackneys (5) and Thoroughbreds (3).
The medal index didn't give a clear indication as to the superiority of a certain breed. The warmbloods were indeed in the majority, but the Barock horses were also well represented. The individual winner's team comprises of Lusitanos and medals were also won by Lipizzaners and a Friesian.
This variety is good for the driving sport and it is important for the sport as a whole that these demands are not changed in such a way that they can only be fulfilled by one specific breed or pedigree.

Kladruber-Gespann/ *Team of Kladrubers*:
Petr Vozab, CZE

Lipizzaner-Gespann/ *Team of Lipizzaners*:
Dick Lane, GBR

Andalusier-Gespann/ *Team of Andalusians*:
Juan Robles Marchena, ESP

FEI World Equestrian Games Aachen 2006

Campo (Oldenburger) v. Cadiz - Vierzehnender xx (1994, Wallach)
Züchter/ *Breeder*: E. Thumann, Düsseldorf
Con Air (Oldenburger) v. Conterno Grande - Landadel (2000, Hengst)
Züchter/ *Breeder*: Harli Seifert, Löningen
Magnum (Oldenburger) v. Matador - Bombay (1993, Wallach)
Züchter/ *Breeder*: Bernhard Möllmann, Quendorf
Monaco (Oldenburger) v. Matador - Classiker (1999, Wallach)
Züchter/ *Breeder*: Hans Janssen, Saterland
Santo (Oldenburger) v. Simply - Grando (1994, Wallach)
Züchter/ *Breeder*: Franz-Josef Schulte, Löningen
Fahrer/ *Driver*: Rainer Duen (GER)

Madaillenspiegel Fahren/ *Medal index Driving*

Zuchtverband Breed. Association	Gold	Silber	Bronze
Mannschaftswettbewerb/ *Team Competition*			
Oldenburg	5		
Holstein			3
KWPN	2	1	11
BWP	1		
LUS		4	
LIPIZ		3	
RUSS WB	1		
Franz. Trab.	2		
Friese		1	
Unbekannt	4	3	2
Einzel/ *Individual*			
LUS	4		
KWPN		5	2
BWP			1
Franz. Trab.			2

Voltigieren / *Vaulting*

Das spezielle Zuchtziel „Voltigieren" gibt es nicht, kann es aus offensichtlichen Gründen auch nicht geben. Da das Voltigierpferd robust, charakterstark, gutmütig sein muss und über weitere hervorragende Interieureigenschaften verfügen muss und neben seiner Hauptaufgabe auch noch geritten wird, wird es wie selbstverständlich unter den Warmblütern gesucht. Diese kamen großen Teils aus Deutschland (7 Hannoveraner, 3 Oldenburger, 2 Rheinländer, je 1 Holsteiner, Trakehner und Bayer).
Weitere Pferde kamen aus Belgien, der Tschechei, Schweden, Polen und der Slowakei.
Unser Goldteam voltigierte auf einem tschechischen Warmblüter; bei den Männern kam das Goldpferd aus dem Rheinland, Silber aus Oldenburg, bei den Damen gab es den Einlauf Dänemark, Trakehnen, Hannover.

There is not a special breeding target for vaulting horses and this is not possible either due to obvious reasons. As well as being robust, strong in character, good natured and disposing of excellent internal qualities, in addition to carrying out their main task, vaulting horses also have to be rideable. So it goes without saying that warmblood horses are the ideal choice. A large amount of the implemented warmbloods were German-bred (7 Hanoverians, 3 Oldenburg, 2 Rhineland, 1 Holstein, 1 Trakehner and 1 Bavarian).

Further horses originated from Belgium, the Czech Republic, Sweden, Poland and Slovakia.
Our gold winning team vaulted on a Czech warmblood; in the men's competition the gold medallist horse came from the Rhineland, the silver medal was won by a horse from Oldenburg, and the ladies performed on horses from the Danish, Trakehner and Hanoverian breeding associations.

Picasso (Rheinland) v. Pageno - Ricardo (1991, Wallach)
Züchter/ *Breeder*: Matthias Stevens, Willich
Voltigierer/ *Vaulter*: Kai Vorberg (GER)

Cepin (CZECH WB) v. Przedswit X a.d. Jiskra (1996, Wallach)
Züchter/ *Breeder*: Czechische Republik
Voltigierteam/ *Vaulting Team*: RSV Neuss

Madaillenspiegel Voltigieren/ *Medal index Vaulting*

Zuchtverb. Breed.Assoc.	Gold	Silber	Bronze
Mannschaft/ *Team*			
Hannover		1	
Oldenburg			1
CZECH WB	1		
Einzel/ *Individual* Männer/ *Men*			
Rheinland	1		
Oldenburg		1	
Einzel/ *Individual* Damen/ *Women*			
Hannover			1
Trakener		1	
DBW	1		

Zucht | Breeding

Distanzreiten

Für die lange Strecke von 160 Kilometern sind Pferde mit viel arabischem Blut besonders geeignet. Von 65 Pferden, die an den Start gingen, waren 44 Vollblutaraber, 4 Anglo-Araber und je ein Achal-Tekkiner, Shagya-Araber und Appaloosa. Die Medaillenpferde waren mit einer Ausnahme alle Vollblutaraber. 11 Pferde waren unbekannter Abstammung.

Im deutschen Team (4. Platz) starteten 2 Vollblutaraber des Verbandes der Züchter des Arabischen Pferdes sowie ein Anglo-Araber aus französischer Zucht.

Da der Distanzsport die am stärksten wachsende FEI-Disziplin ist, bildet sich hier für die Araberzucht ein hochinteressanter Markt, vorausgesetzt, dass sich der Leistungsgedanke weiter fortsetzt.

Madaq (VZAP) v. Nehros ox - Euben ox (1996, Wallach)
Züchter/ *Breeder*: Wolfgang Esch, Diespeck
Reiterin/ *Rider*: Sabrina Arnold (GER)
Nadira (VZAP) v. Nemir ox - Hegab el Arab ox (1993, Stute)
Züchter/ *Breeder*: Manuela Branco, Kerpen
Reiterin/ *Rider*: Melanie Arnold (GER)

Endurance

Horses of Arabian descent are most suitable for the long distance of 160 kilometres. The 65 horses that took part in the competition included 44 full-bred Arabs, four Anglo-Arabs, one Achal-Tekkiner, one Shagya-Arab and one Appaloosa. With one exception all of the horses that claimed medals were full-bred Arabs. Eleven of the horses were of unknown descent.

The German team (4th place) comprised of two full-bred Arabs of the Arabian Horse Breeding Association as well as a French-bred Anglo-Arab. Since endurance is the FEI discipline which is enjoying the strongest growth, this proves to be a highly interesting market for the Arab breeders, provided that the performance concept is pursued further.

Madaillenspiegel Distanz/ *Medal index Endurance*

Zuchtverband *Breed. Assoc.*	Gold	Silber	Bronze
	Mannschaft/ *Team Comp.*		
Arabisches Vollblut (ox)	3	3	1
Saddle Bred			1
	Einzel/ *Individual Comp.*		
Arabisches Vollblut (ox)	1	1	1

Reining

Die Anforderungen in der Reining, der Westerndressur, sind so speziell auf eben diese Westernrassen zugeschnitten, dass auch nur Pferde dieser Rassen teilnahmen, und zwar haben von 47 Pferden 45 einen Abstammungsnachweis der American Quarter Horse Association und zwei der APHA, der American Paint Horse Association.

Das zeigt uns eindeutig, dass die lange und erfolgreiche Zucht des Quarter Horses hier ebenso dominiert wie die Warmblutzuchtgebiete im Springen und in der Dressur. Zucht auf spezielle Leistung ist auch hier kein Mysterium.

Von diesen 45 Quarter Horses sind allerdings mindestens 31 außerhalb der USA geboren, und zwar 9 in Deutschland, je 5 in Österreich und in Schweden, 3 in Holland, je 2 in Ungarn, Brasilien und Italien sowie je eines in Kanada, Frankreich und Tschechien. Das ist ein deutlicher Beweis dafür, dass Quarter Horses auch außerhalb der USA mit Erfolg gezüchtet werden können, natürlich auf amerikanischer Grundlage.

Reining

The requirements set in the reining discipline, the Western dressage, are so specifically tailored to these Western breeds, that only horses of this pedigree took part. Of the 47 horses, 45 were registered with the American Quarter Horse Association and two with the APHA, the American Paint Horse Association.

This clearly demonstrates that the long and successful breeding programme of the Quarter Horses dominates this discipline in the same way that the warmblood breeding areas dominate the show-jumping and dressage. There is no mystery in breeding towards specific performances here either.

However, at least 31 of the 45 Quarter Horses were born outside of the USA; 9 in Germany, 5 in both Austria and Sweden, 3 in Holland, and 2 apiece in Hungary, Brazil and Italy as well as one each in Canada, France and the Czech Republic. This is clear evidence that Quarter Horses can also be successfully bred outside of the USA, of course following the American principles.

Lil Ruf Cody (AQHA) v. Lil Ruf Peppy - Rufos Peppy (2000, Hengst)
Züchter/ *Breeder*: USA
Reiter/ *Rider*: Nico Hörmann (GER)

Hang Ten Surprize (AQHA) v. Hangten Peppy - Topsail Cody (2000, Hengst)
Züchter/ *Breeder*: USA
Reiter/ *Rider*: Duane Latimer (CAN)

Madaillenspiegel Reining/ *Medal index Reining*

Zuchtverband *Breed. Association*	Gold	Silber	Bronze
	Mannschaft/ *Team*		
American Quarter	4	3	4
Paint Horse (PTH)			1
	Einzel/ *Individual*		
American Quarter	1	1	1

AUTOR/AUTHOR
NIELS KNIPPERTZ

Modernste Wettkampfstätten
Top modern competition sites

Neues Richterhaus in Stadion 2.
New judges' hut in Stadium 2.

Sieben Disziplinen – ein Gelände. Das Turniergelände in der Aachener Soers ist wohl nicht nur das weltweit modernste, es bietet zudem die Möglichkeit, alle Wettkampfstätten zu Fuß zu erreichen. Die drei Stadien liegen eng beieinander und bis zur angrenzenden Geländestrecke sind es nur wenige Meter. „Diese Weltmeisterschaften", so Klaus Pavel, Präsident des ausrichtenden Aachen-Laurensberger Rennvereins e.V. (ALRV), „werden sicherlich auch als Weltmeisterschaften der kurzen Wege in Erinnerung bleiben."

Knapp 18 Millionen Euro wurden in den vergangenen Monaten mit Hilfe von Land und Bund investiert - für die WM, aber vor allem, um Aachen dauerhaft als Standort des weltweit wichtigsten Turniers CHIO Aachen zu sichern. Herzstück des Geländes in der Aachener Soers ist das Stadion 1. Hier finden 40.000 Zuschauer Platz. Nie zuvor haben so viele Menschen Pferdesport-Wettbewerbe live miterlebt, bei den Weltmeisterschaften sorgten sie für eine unvergleichliche Atmosphäre. Spektakulär waren vor allem die Entscheidungen unter Flutlicht. Die Dressur Kür und die Entscheidung im Nationenpreis der Springreiter am späten Abend waren unvergessene Momente dieser Weltmeisterschaften. Von vier Masten, jeder knapp 50 Meter hoch, leuchten knapp 300 neue Philips-Scheinwerfer.

Das Wahrzeichen
The trademark

Das Wahrzeichen der umgebauten Anlage steht am Ein- und Austritt des Stadions: Der neu gebaute Richterturm. Er steht zwischen der ebenfalls neu errichteten Reitertribüne – die nicht nur den Sportlern, sondern auch der Presse und Zuschauern Platz bietet – und der kernsanierten Mercedes-Benz-Tribüne. In die Reitertribüne integriert ist das hochmoderne Medienzentrum. 1500 Journalisten haben die Bilder der WM von

Seven disciplines – one show ground. The show grounds at the Aachen Soers are not only the most modern in the world, but also offer the possibility of all competition sites being reachable on foot. The three stadiums lie close together and the adjacent cross-country courses are only a few metres away. "These World Championships," Klaus Pavel, President of the Aachen-Laurensberger Rennverein e.V. (ALRV), the organisers, commented "will no doubt remain in everyone's memories as the World Championships with the shortest routes."

Over the past months with the help of the state and the government, almost 18 million Euros were invested in the World Championships, but above all to secure Aachen as the location of the worldwide significant CHIO Aachen tournament in the longterm. The core element of the show grounds at the Aachen Soers is Stadium 1, which holds 40,000 spectators. Never before have so many people been able to experience equestrian sport competitions live, the crowd was decisive in providing an incomparable atmosphere at the FEI World Equestrian Games. The floodlit competitions were particularly spectacular. The late evening performances of the Dressage Freestyle and the deciding round of the Show-jumping Nations' Cup were unforgettable moments of these World Championships. Almost 300 new Philips spotlights illuminated the stadium from four masts, each 50 metres high.

The landmark of the reconstructed show grounds is located at the entrance to the ring: The newly erected Judges' Tower. It stands between the also newly constructed Riders' Stand – which doesn't just accommodate the sportsmen and women, who it owes its name too, but also the press and spectators – and the completely renovated Mercedes-Benz Stand. The state-of-the-art media centre is integrated into the Riders' Stand. In Aachen 1,500 journalists conveyed the images of the World Championships all over the world, stories about triumphant and tragic moments were written there.

For the first time in the history of the FEI World Equestrian Games, all of the competition sites were situated so closely together that they could be conveniently reached at a few minutes walking distance. The cross-country course is only a few strides away from Stadium 1. Embedded in the Aachen Soers, with its gradual ascent, it offers the spectators a wonderful overview. Compact courses mean that the obstacles of the four-in-hand drivers and the eventers could be reached by foot in the shortest possible time. Tens of thousands of spectators poured onto the cross-country courses during the World Championships and offered the equestrian athletes a memorable platform. "Unbelievable" is how Bettina Hoy described the atmosphere at the gates of Aachen. And for Captain Mark Phillips – who is really no freshman in the business – it was simply "the best course I have ever seen."

Seitenansicht der kernsanierten Mercedes-Benz-Tribüne.
Side view of the renovated Mercedes-Benz Stand.

WM der kurzen Wege
WEG with the shortest routes

hier aus in alle Welt getragen, die Geschichten von triumphalen und von tragischen Momenten wurden hier geschrieben.

Zum ersten Mal in der Geschichte der Weltreiterspiele liegen alle Sportstätten so nahe beieinander, dass sie für die Zuschauer bequem in wenigen Minuten erreichbar sind. So sind es nur einige Schritte von Stadion 1 bis in die Geländestrecke. Eingebettet in die Aachener Soers bietet sie – sanft ansteigend – den Zuschauern einen prima Überblick. Binnen kürzester Zeit sind auf dem kompakten Kurs die Hindernisse des Kutschenmarathons und der Vielseitigkeit zu Fuß erreichbar. Zehntausende Zuschauer strömten während der WM in das Gelände und bereiteten den Sportlern eine bislang nicht dagewesene Bühne. „Unfassbar" fand Bettina Hoy die Stimmung vor den Toren Aachens. Und für Captain Mark Phillips – wahrlich kein Frischling im Geschäft - war es schlicht „die beste Strecke, die ich je gesehen habe."

Ebenfalls neu ist das Richterhaus im Stadion 2. Nicht nur die Richter, auch Teilnehmer und Presse finden auf den Tribünen Platz. Während der Fahr- und Vielseitigkeits-Wettbewerbe waren es 8.000 Zuschauer in diesem Stadion 2 – nahezu ausverkauft, ein absolut würdiger WM-Rahmen. Ein besonders spektakulärer Anblick bot sich während der WM im Deutsche Bank Stadion: Die temporäre Überdachung. Eine Aluminium-Faltdach-Konstruktion machte aus dem Stadion eine geschlossene Arena mit Platz für wiederum 8.000 Zuschauer. Eine ganz besondere Atmosphäre für die Voltigierer und Westernreiter, die hier ihre Champions kürten. Noch wichtiger als der Service für die Zuschauer ist ein Maximum an Komfort für die Pferde. So wurde der Boden im Stadion 1 komplett erneuert, um dadurch auch unter schwierigsten Bedingungen einen optimalen Untergrund zu bieten. Bei den doch mitunter recht verregneten Titelkämpfen sicherlich eine gute Entscheidung. Denn der Boden war trotz des teilweise heftigen Regens in einem ausgezeichneten Zustand. Mit dem Neubau von drei weiteren Stallungen stehen nun rund 400 feste Boxen zur Verfügung. Darüber hinaus wurde ein Veterinärzentrum errichtet, welches modernsten Anforderungen entspricht.

Hochmodernes Verwaltungs- und Medienzentrum.
The state-of-the-art administration and media centre.

Innenansicht.
An inside view.

The judges' house in Stadium 2 is also new. The stands offer enough room for the judges, competitors and press. 8,000 spectators were accommodated in Stadium 2 during the driving and eventing competitions – almost sold out - this was a totally worthy World Championships setting. The Deutsche Bank Stadium also had something spectacular to offer during the World Championships: Its temporary roof. An aluminium folding-roof construction turned the otherwise open stadium into a closed arena seating 8,000 spectators, which provided a special atmosphere for the vaulters and reiners, who crowned their champions there. Of course offering maximum comfort for the horses plays an even more important role than providing extra services for the spectators. As such the ground in Stadium 1 was completely renewed to secure an ideal subsurface that would stand up to the most challenging conditions possible. This proved to be a very good decision considering the amount of rain that fell during the two weeks of the World Equestrian Games. In spite of the partially heavy rainfall, the footing was still excellent. The construction of three further stable buildings brought the total amount of permanent boxes up to around 400. A veterinarian centre featuring up-to-date modern technology, was also newly erected.

Neuer Richterturm mit Ein- und Ausritt sowie Blick auf Teilnehmer- und Pressetribüne des Hauptstadions im Flutlichtschein.
The new Judges' Tower at the entrance to the ring as well as a floodlit view of the Riders' Stand in the main stadium.

Deutsche Bank Stadion mit neuer temporärer Überdachung.
Deutsche Bank Stadium with its new temporary roof.

Kultur | Culture

AUTORIN/AUTHOR
RENATE FAßBENDER

Ein Banner mit dem Slogan der Stadt Aachen „Immer eine Pferdelänge voraus" begrüßt die Gäste am Hauptbahnhof. Am Verkehrsknotenpunkt Hansemann-Platz hing ein weithin sichtbares Riesenbanner, das die Gäste aus aller Welt zur WM willkommen hieß.
A banner bearing the slogan of the City of Aachen "Always a horse's length ahead" welcomed the guests at the main station. A further huge, well-visible banner hung over the traffic junction at Hansemann Square welcoming the guests from all of over the world to the FEI World Equestrian Games.

Rund 200 künstlerisch gestaltete Pferde der World Horseparade stimmten die Besucher der Stadt auf die Pferdesport-WM 2006 ein.
Around 200 artistically designed horses of the World Horseparade got the city in the right mood for the FEI World Equestrian Games 2006.

Und der Kaiser swingt dazu... Fast war es für Karl den Großen so wie vor 1200 Jahren, als er in Aachen die damals bekannte Welt um sich versammelte. Vor seinem Standbild auf dem Aachener Markt drängten sich während der Reit-WM die fünf Kontinente zum Feiern. Aachen international: Mit Show, Event, Information, Entertainment, Rock und Flamenco, Jazz und Pop. Eingefleischte Aachener schwören Stein und Bein darauf, dass ihrem Kaiser bei so viel Rhythmus und Stimmung die ehernen Füße gezuckt haben.

„Aachen typisch": Eine Stadt im fröhlichen Ausnahmezustand. Die City ein Blumen- und Fahnenmeer, Handel und Gastronomie für 14 Tage im Zeichen wehender Mähnen und fliegender Hufe. Auf vier Bühnen in der Innenstadt jeden Abend große und kleine Kunst vor unzähligen Zuschauern und Zuhörern – Aachen zeigte, was es liebens- und lebenswert macht, Crashkurs für neugierige „Fremde" in seinem seltsamen Idiom inklusive. Typisch Aachen eben.

Aachen hilfsbereit: Mehrsprachige „Botschafterinnen" und „Botschafter" standen an zentralen Punkten der Stadt den Gästen mit Rat und Tat zur Seite, Taxi- und Busfah-

And the Emperor is swinging to the beat... For Charles the Great it was almost like 1,200 years ago, when he used to invite famous personalities from all over the world to join him in Aachen. The five continents were united around his life-sized likeness in front of the Aachen market scenery. Aachen international: With shows, events, information, entertainment, rock and flamenco, jazz and pop. Fully-fledged Aacheners were convinced that their Emperor would be tapping his feet in the light of so much rhythm and atmosphere.

"Typical Aachen": A city experiencing joyous exceptional circumstances. For two weeks the city was transformed into a sea of flowers and flags, the businesses and catering establishments hallmarked by flowing manes and flying hooves. Every evening artistic performances of all magnitudes on four stages in the city centre attended by countless spectators and listeners – Aachen demonstrated what makes it so likeable and so liveable, a crash course for curious "foreigners" with its own unusual idiom all-included. Quite simply typical Aachen.

Aachen fully cooperative: Multi-lingual "messengers" were placed at central points in the city to offer the guests advice and assistance, taxi and bus drivers showed their qualities as friendly tour guides. "Aachen – always a horse's length ahead" was the slogan of the riding metropolis. A big promise, which the city was thoroughly capable of holding.

Vor, auf oder neben Straßen, Plätzen, Geschäften und öffentlichen Gebäuden wehten über 300 WM-Fahnen im Wind.
300 WEG flags flattered in the wind in front of, on or next to the streets, squares and shops.

Über 100 ehrenamtliche Bürgerinnen und Bürger der Stadt standen den Touristen als Aachen-Botschafter mit Rat und Tat zur Seite.
Over 100 volunteers from the city, "messengers" of Aachen, offered the tourists support and advice.

rer zeigten ihre Qualitäten als freundliche Fremdenführer. „Aachen – immer eine Pferdelänge voraus", war der Wahlspruch der Reiter-Metropole. Ein großes Versprechen, das die Stadt gehalten hat.

Aachen in Stimmung: Den „Öchern", wie sich die Einheimischen selbst nennen, sagt man „Pferdeverstand" nach. Von Kind auf mit dem CHIO vertraut, wissen sie alles über Oxer, Steilsprünge und dreifache Kombinationen, Stuten und Hengste, Schimmel, Füchse oder Rappen. Aber das ist nicht alles. Vor den Kopf hat die Natur bei ihnen ein großes Herz gesetzt. Das haben sie während der WM ganz weit geöffnet: Ohne Ansehen von Nation, Rang, Geld oder Geltung haben sie ihre Gäste angesteckt mit einer Welle von guter Laune, die über die Ränge der Stadien hinausging bis in die Straßen und Gassen der Innenstadt. Viele Tausende, die „nur" der Pferde wegen nach Aachen gekommen waren, wissen jetzt, was „Aachen typisch" heißt. Sogar Kaiser Karl, eigentlich durch nichts mehr zu erschüttern, hat seine Untertanen von einer neuen Seite kennengelernt. Sein Fuß zuckt noch immer verdächtig...

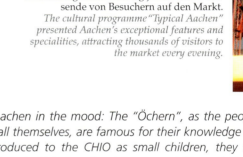

Das Kulturprogramm „Aachen typisch" präsentierte Aachens Besonderheiten und Liebenswürdigkeiten und zog jeden Abend tausende von Besuchern auf den Markt.
The cultural programme "Typical Aachen" presented Aachen's exceptional features and specialities, attracting thousands of visitors to the market every evening.

Der abendliche Höhepunkt auf der Marktbühne: die Champions Ceremony, mit der auch die Stadt die Weltmeister ehrte.
The evening climax on the market stage: The Champion's Ceremony, where the Champions were honoured by the city.

Aachen in the mood: The "Öchern", as the people from the city call themselves, are famous for their knowledge about horses. Introduced to the CHIO as small children, they know everything there is to know about oxers, uprights and triple combinations, mares and stallions, greys, chestnuts or black horses. But that is not all. Mother Nature was even more generous when she handed over the hearts to the people of Aachen. They proved this over the entire duration of the FEI World Equestrian Games: Regardless of nation, rank, financial status or standing, they infected their guests with a surge of good spirits, which spread over the stands of the stadium and through the streets and alleys of the city. Many thousands of visitors, who "only" came to Aachen because of the horses, now know what "typical Aachen" means.

Even Emperor Charles, who is pretty much unshakeable, got to see a new side of his subjects. His foot is still tapping suspiciously...

Malerisch die vier Open-Air-Bühnen in der Innenstadt – hier der Hof.
Picturesque – the four open-air stages in the city centre – here the courtyard.

Vor der Kulisse des historischen Rathauses feierten jeden Abend Menschen aus aller Welt.
Every evening people from all over the world celebrated in front of the magnificent setting of the historical City Hall.

Good Bye

AUTORIN/ *Author*: Patricia Tietje

Als hätte er es schon 2002 gewusst ... Klaus Pavels Siegerpose in Jerez nach Bekanntgabe der Vergabe der Spiele an Aachen. Und er sollte Recht behalten. Die Weltreiterspiele 2006 haben neue Maßstäbe gesetzt!
As if he already knew it then in 2002... Klaus Pavel's victory pose in Jerez after the Games were allocated to Aachen. And he was right too. The FEI World Equestrian Games 2006 set new benchmarks!

Da war sie noch keine Bronzemedaillen-Gewinnerin. Springreiterin Meredith Michaels-Beerbaum mit Jürgen Thumann und Dieter Graf Landsberg-Velen (links).
Not yet bronze medallist here: Show-jumper Meredith Michaels-Beerbaum with Jürgen Thumann and Dieter Graf Landsberg-Velen (left).

Angela Merkel hat bei der Charity-Aktion "Glücksbringer" die Autogrammtafel unterschrieben, die 80.000 Euro fürs Therapeutische Reiten einbrachte.
Angela Merkel signed the autograph board of the "Moments of Luck" charity campaign, which collected 80,000 Euros for therpeutic riding.

Familienzusammenführung! Über den Sieg in der Vielseitigkeit ihrer Tochter Zara freuten sich Captain Mark Phillips, der die amerikanischen Buschreiter betreute, gemeinsam mit seiner geschiedenen Frau Prinzessin Anne.
Family day out! Captain Mark Phillips, who coached the American military riders, shared the happiness over his daughter Zara's eventing victory together with his divorced wife.

Immer nach oben schauen scheint die Anweisung von Trainer Jean Bemelmans an seinen spanischen Schützling zu lauten.
Always keep looking up, is what the trainer Jean Bemelmans seems to be trying to communicate to his Spanish protégé.

Im Gleichschritt Marsch! Eine kleine Armee von Gratulanten wartete bei den Siegerehrungen auf die Übergabe der Medaillen, Ehrenpreise und Blumensträuße.
Altogether now left, right! A small army of congratulators waited at the prize-giving ceremonies for the medals, prizes and flowers to be handed over.

Nach ihrer Silbermedaille bei den Olympischen Spielen in Athen war es etwas ruhiger um Ulla Salzgeber geworden. Trotzdem war sie als Coach der australischen Dressurreiter gefragter Interviewgast.
After her silver medal at the Olympic Games in Athens things have been a lot quieter for Ulla Salzgeber. She was nevertheless still a popular interview guest in her function as coach of the Australian dressage riders.

Zwei Präsidenten unter sich: IOC-Präsident Jacques Rogge mit FEI-Präsidentin HRH Prinzessin Haya Bint al Hussein von Jordanien.
Presidents among themselves: IOC President Jacques Rogge with FEI President Princess HRH Haya Bint al Hussein of Jordanien.

Der Schnäuzer ist geblieben. Und das Lachen auch. Ex-Leichtathletikstar Jürgen Hingsen in charmanter Begleitung
He's still got his moustache. And his laugh too. Ex-athletic star Jürgen Hingsen and his charming escort.

HH Sheik Mohammed bin Rashid Maktoum zeigte sich beeindruckt bei Besuch des Aachener Gelände
HH Sheik Mohammed bin Rashid Maktoum was impressed when she visited the Aachen show ground

Auch Karli passte sich dem Wetter an. An den zwei Wochen in der Soers fielen insgesamt 73 Liter pro Quadratmeter
Karli had to adapt to the weather conditions as well. During the two weeks 73 litres/m² fell at the Soers.

Hoher Besuch bei der Eröffnungsfeier: HH Sheik Nasser bin Hammad al Khalifa, Sohn des Königs von Barein, der sich im Distanzsport engagiert, auf der Ehrengasttribüne.
An important visitor at the Opening Ceremony: HH Sheik Nasser bin Hammad al Khalifa, son of the king of Barein, an engaged supporter of the endurance sport, on the VIP Stand.

Dr. Jürgen Linden, ALRV-Beirat und Oberbürgermeister der Stadt Aachen begrüßte die Zuschauer der Eröffnungsfeier trotz nasskalter Witterung im Kutschenkorso.
Dr. Jürgen Linden, ALRV Advisory Board member and Lord Mayor of the City of Aachen welcomed the spectators at the opening Ceremony from the carriage parade in spite of the wet stormy weather.

Renate Dahmen im Interview über die Arbeit, die sie in die Schaubilder in Aachen investiert hatte.
Renate Dahmen during an interview on the work she had invested into the show performances in Aachen.

Stimmung wie bei der Formel Eins macht Michael Schumachers Ehefrau Corinna auf der Tribüne bei der Reining. Sie besitzt selbst Quarter Horses.
Michael Schumacher's wife, Corinna, helped create a Formula One-like atmosphere on the stands during the reining. She owns Quarter Horses herself.

Bei den Olympischen Spielen in Athen vertrat sie noch die amerikanischen Farben im Dressurteam mit dem Hengst Relevant. Für die Weltreiterspiele kam die mittlerweile wieder in Florida lebende Lisa Wilcox aber trotzdem zurück in ihre jahrelange Zweitheimat. Diesmal allerdings nicht als Teilnehmerin, sondern als Reporterin für Horse TV.
She represented the American flag in the dressage team at the Olympic Games in Athens with the stallion Relevant. Lisa Wilcox has in the meantime moved back to Florida, but she returned to her second home for the FEI World Equestrian Games. Not as a competiior this time though, but instead as a reporter for Horse TV.

Hinter den Kulissen durfte Frank Kempermann auch einmal auf den Siegerpodesten Platz nehmen.
Behind the scenes, Frank Kempermann was also allowed to stand on the winners' podium.

Hoffentlich nicht auf dem Kriegspfad befand sich dieser Betreuer eines Distanzpferdes.
Hopefully this endurance horse groom wasn't on the warpath.

Andi Köpke, DFB-Torwart-Nationaltrainer, ließ sich von Egidius Braun, ehemaliger DFB-Präsident und ehemaliges ALRV-Beiratsmitglied und dem ALRV Präsidenten Klaus Pavel in die Welt des Pferdesports einweisen.
Egidius Braun, former President of the German Football Association and ALRV President, Klaus Pavel, briefed Andi Köpke, National Goalkeeper Coach, on the world of equestrian sport.

Prinzessin Benedikte von Dänemark genoss die Tage in Aachen. Nicht nur, weil ihre Tochter Nathalie zu Sayn-Wittgenstein in der Dressur an den Start ging, sondern auch, weil sich die ambitionierte Züchterin so einen guten Überblick über die aktuellen Blutlinien im Sport verschaffen konnte.
Princess Benedikte of Denmark enjoyed the days in Aachen. Not only because her daughter Nathalie zu Sayn-Wittgenstein competed in the dressage, but also because it gave the ambitious horse breeder a good overview of the current blood lines in the sport.

Familienfreude zum 70. Geburtstag von ALRV-Präsidenten Klaus Pavel.
Family joy on the 70th birthday of Klaus Pavel, president of ALRV.

Eine Stippvisite mit großzügigen Folgen. FEI-Präsidentin Prinzessin Haya besuchte während ihrer Tage in Aachen das Therapeutische Reiten und zeigte sich so beeindruckt von der Arbeit mit den behinderten Kindern, dass sie spontan eine Spende über 100.000 Dollar versprach.
A flying visit with generous consequences. FEI President Princess Haya visited the Therapeutic Riding Centre during her stay in Aachen and was so impressed with the work carried out there with disabled children, that she spontaneously promised them a donation of 100,000 Dollars.

Thomas Bach, Präsident des Deutschen Sportbundes, überreichte dem ehemaligen Innenminister Otto Schilly das Silberne Pferd des ALRV für besondere Verdienste um den Pferdesport.
Thomas Bach, President of the German Olympic Sport Association, handed over the ALRV's Silver Horse to the former Minister of the Interior, Otto Schilly, for his immense services to the equestrian sport.

Das Geld im Reitsport doch eine große Rolle spielt, bewies der Ukrainer Alexander Onischenko. Der Öl-Multi hatte sich in den vergangenen Monaten quer durch die Reiterwelt ein Team zusammengekauft, das seine Landesfarben bei der WM vertreten sollte. Ziel erreicht und darüber hinaus noch hocherfolgreich. Denn die junge und talentierte Mannschaft bestehend aus Björn Nagel, Kathi Offel, Jean Claude van Geenberghe und Gregory Wathelet lehrte den Traditionsteams das Fürchten und hätte Deutschland beinahe noch die Bronzemedaille streitig gemacht.
The fact that money plays a big role in equestrian sport was underlined by the Ukraine oil tycoon, Alexander Onischenko. The oil multi-millionaire had bought himself a team from all over the world a few months prior to the World Championships, which was to ride for his country. He achieved his goal and was moreover highly successful, because the young and talented team comprising of Björn Nagel, Kathi Offel, Jean Claude van Geenberghe und Gregory Wathelet earned the respect of the traditional teams and almost managed to steal the bronze medal away from Germany.

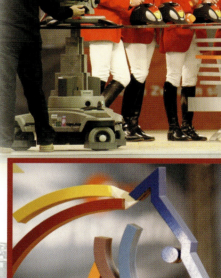

Ob Aktuelles Sportstudio oder Sportschau: Für zwei Wochen bestimmten die Reiter das Medieninteresse. Zweistellige Einschaltquoten und alleine eine Fernseh-Übertragungsdauer von insgesamt 70 Stunden in Deutschland brachten die WM in 157 Länder für Millionen von interessierten Menschen nach Hause in ihre Wohnzimmer.
TV live studios and reports: For two weeks the riders aroused the interest of the media. Double-digit viewing quotas and a total of 70 hours of TV coverage brought the FEI World Equestrian Games into the living rooms of the viewers at home.

Strahlen um die Wette ob des Erfolges des Aachener Events: Turnierorganisator Michael Mronz und WDR-„Equipe"-Chef Heribert Fassbender.
Beaming about the bet on the success of the Aachen event: Tournament organiser, Michael Mronz, and WDR Chef d'Equipe, Heribert Fassbender.

Für die Stewards war es ein ruhiges Turnier. Auf den Abreiteplätzen und dem gesamten Gelände wurde Fair Play gelebt.
It was a quiet tournament for the stewards. Fair play reigned on the warm-up arenas and over the entire show grounds.

Mit dem Goldenen Ring des Aachen-Laurensberger Rennvereins wurde der Ehrenpräsident der Deutschen Reiterlichen Vereinigung, Dieter Graf Landsberg-Velen, ausgezeichnet. Der Träger des Olympischen Ordens wurde damit erneut für seine Verdienste um den Pferdesport geehrt.
Dieter Graf Landsberg-Velen, the Honorary President of the Aachen-Laurensberger Rennverein was awarded the "Golden Ring". The holder of the Olympic Order was thus once again honoured for his extraordinary services to the equestrian sport.

Abschiedstränen für eines der erfolgreichsten deutschen Springpferde: Mannschafts-Olympiasieger Dobel's Cento. "Ich habe Cento elf Jahre lang geritten und große Erfolge mit ihm gefeiert", erklärte sein Reiter Otto Becker. "Ich bin froh, dass ich ihn nun mit seinen 17 Jahren topfit hier verabschieden kann. Das Stadion in der Aachener Soers war für uns beide immer ein besonderer Ort - hier haben wir 2000 den Großen Preis gewonnen und 2004 den Nationenpreis."
Tears of farewell for one of the most successful German show-jumping horses: Team Olympic medallist, Dobel's Cento. "I have ridden Cento for eleven years and we have celebrated big victories together," explained his rider, Otto Becker. "I am delighted that is his being able to retire here, still top fit at the age of 17. The stadium at the Aachener Soers was always a special place for the two of us, we won the Grand Prix here in the year 2000 and the Nations' Cup in 2004."

Neben dem Reiten die zweite Hauptbeschäftigung der Aktiven: Autogramme schreiben!
After riding, the second main occupation of the competitors: Signing autographs!

Neben allen öffentlichen Auftritten blieb für die ehemalige Spring- und Distanzreiterin Prinzessin Haya auch noch die Zeit, sich mal wieder auf die Reitertribüne unter ihre ehemaligen Kollegen zu mischen.
Besides all of her official appearances, Princess Haya, former show-jumper and endurance rider, still found time to chat to her former colleagues on the Riders' Stand.

So schön kann Liebe sein. Und so erfolgreich, wie Bettina Hoy und ihr britischer Ehemann Andrew auf diesem Championat erneut mit ihren Mannschaften bewiesen.
Love can be so nice. And so successful, as Bettina Hoy and her British husband Andrew demonstrated once again with their teams at these Championships.

So stellt man sich nicht unbedingt eine Milliardenerbin vor, aber vielleicht eine engagierte Ehefrau. Ganz leger und nie ums Handanlegen verlegen gab sich Athina Onassis, die ihren Mann zu den Weltreiterspielen begleitete. Dessen Namen hat die passionierte Springreiterin mittlerweile auch angenommen und so hört sie nicht mehr auf Onassis, sondern Miranda de Neto.
This is not exactly the picture one has of a millionairess, it corresponds more with one's image of a dedicated wife. Quite relaxed and always ready to help, Athina Onassis, who accompanied her husband to the World Equestrian Games. The passionate show-jumper has in the meantime taken her husband's name, so she now answers to Miranda de Neto, instead of Onassis.

Ergebnisse / Results — Springen / Jumping

1. Wertungsprüfung für die Einzelwertung – Zeitspringprüfung
1st Rating Competition – Speed and Handiness Competition

Rank	Reiter/ Rider	Nat	Pferd/ Horse	Zeit/ Time	Pen.
1	Beezie MADDEN	USA	AUTHENTIC	77.62 (0)	0.00
2	Eric LAMAZE	CAN	HICKSTEAD 7	78.40 (0)	0.39
3	Gerco SCHRÖDER	NED	EUROCOMMERCE BERLIN	78.47 (0)	0.43
4	McLain WARD	USA	SAPPHIRE	79.35 (0)	0.87
5	Laurent GOFFINET	FRA	FLIPPER D'ELLE HN	79.42 (0)	0.90
6	Sergio ALVAREZ MOYA	ESP	LE REVE DU NABAB	80.09 (0)	1.24
7	Bernardo ALVES	BRA	CANTURO	80.33 (0)	1.36
8	Cassio RIVETTI	BRA	OLONA	80.40 (0)	1.39
9	Marie BURKE	IRL	CHIPPISON	81.04 (0)	1.71
10	Gregory WATHELET	UKR	LORIOT	81.14 (0)	1.76
11	Geir GULLIKSEN	NOR	CATTANI IND	81.30 (0)	1.84
12	Samantha MC INTOSH	BUL	LOXLEY IND	81.65 (0)	2.02
13	Ludo PHILIPPAERTS	BEL	PARCO	81.71 (4)	2.05
14	Edwina ALEXANDER	AUS	ISOVLAS PIALOTTA	82.09 (4)	2.24
15	Jean Claude VAN GEENBERGHE	UKR	OSTA RUGS TRESOR	82.37 (4)	2.38
16	Jürgen KRACKOW	AUT	LOOPING	82.45 (4)	2.42
17	Albert ZOER	NED	OKIDOKI	82.58 (0)	2.48
18	Emilio BICOCCHI	ITA	JECKERSON KAPITOL D'ARGONNE	82.95 (0)	2.67
19	Ludger BEERBAUM	GER	L'ESPOIR	83.01 (0)	2.70
20	Dirk DEMEERSMAN	BEL	CLINTON	83.13 (4)	2.76
21	Royne ZETTERMAN	SWE	ISAAC	83.77 (0)	3.08
22	Jeroen DUBBELDAM	NED	BMC UP AND DOWN	83.82 (0)	3.10
23	Ricardo JURADO	ESP	PROCASA LE MONDE	84.16 (4)	3.27
24	Marcus EHNING	GER	NOLTES KÜCHENGIRL	84.70 (4)	3.54
25	Tina LUND	DEN	CAROLA	84.84 (4)	3.61
26	Carlos LOPEZ	COL	INSTIT	84.86 (0)	3.62
27	Niklaus SCHURTENBERGER	SUI	CANTUS	84.89 (4)	3.64
28	John WHITAKER	GBR	PEPPERMILL	84.98 (4)	3.68
29	Pablo BARRIOS	VEN	SUN GOD	85.43 (4)	3.91
30	Meredith MICHAELS-BEERBAUM	GER	SHUTTERFLY	85.46 (4)	3.92
31	Shane BREEN	IRL	WORLD CRUISE	85.59 (4)	3.99
32	Christian AHLMANN	GER	CÖSTER	85.62 (4)	4.00
33	Piet RAYMAKERS	NED	VAN SCHIJNDEL'S CURTIS	85.71 (0)	4.05
34	Michel ROBERT	FRA	GALET D'AUZAY	85.78 (4)	4.08
35	Luciana DINIZ	POR	DOVER	85.94 (4)	4.16
36	Alvaro MIRANDA	BRA	NIKE	86.09 (4)	4.24
37	Werner MUFF	SUI	PLOT BLUE	87.07 (4)	4.73
38	Max AMAYA	ARG	CHURCH ROAD	87.20 (0)	4.79
39	Rolf-Göran BENGTSSON	SWE	NINJA LA SILLA	87.44 (4)	4.91
40	Jos LANSINK	BEL	CAVALOR CUMANO	87.63 (4)	5.01
41	Jesus GARMENDIA ECHEVERRIA	ESP	MADDOCK	88.29 (8)	5.34
42	Cameron HANLEY	IRL	SIEC HIPPICA KERMAN	88.37 (4)	5.38
43	Hervé GODIGNON	FRA	OBÉLIX	88.42 (4)	5.40
44	Sebastian NUMMINEN	FIN	SAILS AWAY	88.53 (4)	5.46
45	Manuel TORRES	COL	CHAMBACUNERO	88.56 (8)	5.47
46	Michael WHITAKER	GBR	INSUL TECH PORTOFINO	88.67 (4)	5.53
47	Tim GREDLEY	GBR	OMELLI	89.00 (8)	5.69
48	Laura KRAUT	USA	MISS INDEPENDENT	89.57 (4)	5.98
49	Jill HENSELWOOD	CAN	SPECIAL ED	89.95 (4)	6.17
50	Roland ENGLBRECHT	AUT	NIP ARMANI	90.06 (4)	6.22
51	Antonis PETRIS	GRE	GREDO LA DAVIERE	90.22 (8)	6.30
52	Gerfried PUCK	AUT	11TH BLEEKER	90.43 (8)	6.41
53	Mikael FORSTEN	FIN	BMC'S SKYBREAKER	90.49 (4)	6.44
54	Christina LIEBHERR	SUI	L.B. NO MERCY	90.66 (4)	6.52
55	Stefan EDER	AUT	CARTIER PSG	90.69 (4)	6.54
56	Beat MÄNDLI	SUI	INDIGO IX	91.18 (8)	6.78
57	Ricardo KIERKEGAARD	ARG	REY Z	91.23 (8)	6.81
58	James WINGRAVE	HUN	AGROPOINT CALIRA	91.33 (8)	6.86
59	Björn NAGEL	UKR	PILGRIM	91.67 (8)	7.03
60	Taizo SUGITANI	JPN	OBELIX	91.68 (4)	7.03
61	Tony Andre HANSEN	NOR	CAMIRO	92.11 (4)	7.25
62	Judy-Ann MELCHIOR	BEL	GRANDE DAME Z	92.24 (8)	7.31
63	Maria GRETZER	SWE	SPENDER S	92.39 (8)	7.39
64	Katharina OFFEL	UKR	ATLANTA	92.46 (8)	7.42
65	Krzysztof LUDWICZAK	POL	HOF SCHRETSTAKENS QUAMIRO	92.54 (4)	7.46
66	Manuel FERNANDEZ SARO	ESP	QUIN CHIN	92.55 (8)	7.47
67	Marcela LOBO	MEX	JOSKIN	92.82 (4)	7.60
68	Billy TWOMEY	IRL	LUIDAM	92.85 (8)	7.62
69	Nick SKELTON	GBR	RUSSEL	92.89 (8)	7.64
70	Vladimir BELETSKIY	RUS	REZONANZ	93.07 (8)	7.73
71	Giuseppe ROLLI	ITA	JERICHO DE LA VIE	93.44 (4)	7.91
72	Florian ANGOT	FRA	FIRST DE LAUNAY*HN	93.73 (12)	8.06
73	Jose LAROCCA	ARG	SVANTE	94.00 (8)	8.19
74	Jiri PAPOUSEK	CZE	LA MANCHE - T	94.50 (4)	8.44
75	Antonio PORTELA CARNEIRO	POR	ECHO DE LESSAY	94.75 (4)	8.57
76	Abdullah AL SHARBATLY	KSA	HUGO GESMERAY	94.79 (16)	8.59
77	Hanno ELLERMANN	EST	PONCORDE	94.82 (8)	8.60
78	Gennadiy GASHIBOYAZOV	RUS	PAPIRUS	94.99 (12)	8.69
79	Juan Carlos GARCIA	ITA	LORO PIANA ALBIN III	95.66 (4)	9.02
80	Ian MILLER	CAN	IN STYLE	96.36 (12)	9.37
81	Federico FERNANDEZ	MEX	BOHEMIO	96.84 (16)	9.61
82	Ibrahim Hani Kamal BISHARAT	JOR	QWINTO	97.14 (8)	9.76
83	Syed Omar ALMOHDZAR	MAS	LUI	97.26 (8)	9.82
84	H.H. Prince Faisal AL SHALAN	KSA	UTHAGO	98.03 (16)	10.21
85	Gunnar KLETTENBERG	EST	NOVESTA	98.86 (8)	10.62
86	Guillermo OBLIGADO	ARG	CARLSON	100.71 (8)	11.55
87	Rene LOPEZ	COL	ISKY	100.97 (12)	11.68
88	Margie ENGLE	USA	HIDDEN CREEK'S QUERVO GOLD	101.75 (16)	12.07
89	Rod BROWN	AUS	MR BURNS	102.22 (16)	12.30
90	Alberto MICHAN	MEX	CHINOBAMPO LAVITA	102.28 (16)	12.33
91	Jonella LIGRESTI	ITA	QUINTA 27	102.35 (12)	12.37
92	Noora PENTTI	FIN	EVLI CAGLIOSTRO	102.53 (12)	12.46
93	Mohammed AL KUMAITI	UAE	AL MUTAWAKEL	102.60 (12)	12.49
94	Yuko ITAKURA	JPN	PORTVLIET	102.93 (16)	12.66
95	Fabrice LYON	LBA	JASMIN DU PERRON	103.14 (8)	12.76
96	Zsolt PIRIK	HUN	HAVANNA	103.72 (12)	13.05
97	Kamal BAHAMDAN	KSA	CAMPUS	104.00 (12)	13.19
98	Vladimir PANCHENKO	RUS	LANTENO	106.54 (12)	14.46
99	Grant WILSON	NZL	UP AND DOWN CELLEBROEDERSBOS	107.29 (20)	14.84
100	Peter MC MAHON	AUS	KOLORA STUD GENOA	108.01 (4)	15.20
101	Chris PRATT	CAN	RIVENDELL	108.06 (4)	15.22
102	Ariana AZCARRAGA	MEX	SAMBO	109.51 (12)	15.95
103	Karim EL ZOGHBY	EGY	BARAGWAY	110.34 (16)	16.36,3
104	Roger HESSEN	RSA	QUITO	112.44 (16)	17.41
105	Eiken SATO	JPN	CAYAK DH	113.54 (24)	17.96
106	Veronika MACANOVA	CZE	POMPOS	113.99 (8)	18.19
107	Ondrej NAGR	CZE	ATLAS	117.35 (12)	19.87
108	Emmanouela ATHANASSIADES	GRE	RIMINI Z	126.38 (20)	24.38
109	Zdenek ZILA	CZE	PINOT GRIGIO	129.69 (12)	26.04
110	Malin BARYARD-JOHNSSON	SWE	BUTTERFLY FLIP	EL	46.04
110	Barry TAYLOR	RSA	DUXY	EL	46.04
110	H.R.H Prince Abdullah AL-SOUD	KSA	ALLAH JABEK	EL	46.04
110	Mariann HUGYECZ	HUN	SUPERVILLE	EL	46.04
110	Jamie KERMOND	AUS	STYLISH KING	EL	46.04
110	Jose Alfredo HERNANDEZ ORTEGA	ESA	SEMTEX P	EL	46.04
116	Thomas VELIN	DEN	GODSEND DU REVERDY	RET	46.04

Finale Einzelwertung der FEI Weltmeisterschaft Springen – Springprüfung mit Pferdewechsel
Final for the FEI World Individual Jumping – Jumping Competition with Rotation of Horses

Bestes Pferd/ Best Horse : CAVALOR CUMANO

Pferd/ Horse	JOS LANSINK (Gold)	EDWINA ALEXANDER	MEREDITH MICHAELS-BEERBAUM (Bronze)	BEEZIE MADDEN (Silber)	Total points per Horse
CAVALOR CUMANO	0	0	0	0	0
ISOVLAS PIALOTTA	0	0	0	0	0
SHUTTERFLY	0	4	0	0	4
AUTHENTIC	0	0	0	0	0
Total points per Rider	0 Jump Off: 0-45.01	4	0 Jump Off: 4-45.40	0 Jump Off: 4-43.74	

Ergebnisse | Results

Finale für die Mannschaftswertung der FEI Weltmeisterschaft – Springprüfung mit zwei Umläufen
Final Rating for the FEI World Team Jumping Championship – Jumping Competition with Two Rounds

	Nation/ NAT Pferd/ Horse	Reiter/ Rider	Gesamt/ Total Score	1 Day	2 Day R1	3 Day R2
1.	NETHERLANDS		11.01	6.01	1	4
	VAN SCHIJNDEL'S CURTIS	Piet Raymakers		(4.05)	(5)	(18)
	BMC UP AND DOWN	Jeroen Dubbeldam		3.10	1	0
	OKIDOKI	Albert Zoer		2.48	0	4
	EUROCOMMERCE BERLIN	Gerco Schröder		0.43	0	0
2.	UNITED STATES		18.85	6.85	8	4
	HIDDEN CREEK'S QUERVO GOLD	Margie Engle		(12.07)	4	4
	MISS INDEPENDENT	Laura Kraut		5.98	(4)	(8)
	SAPPHIRE	McLain Ward		0.87	4	0
	AUTHENTIC	eezie Madden		0.00	0	0
3.	GERMANY		19.16	10.16	5	4
	L'ESPOIR	Ludger Beerbaum		2.70	0	0
	CÖSTER	Christian Ahlmann		(4.00)	(8)	4
	SHUTTERFLY	Meredith Michaels-Beerbaum		3.92	1	0
	NOLTES KÜCHENGIRL	Marcus Ehning		3.54	4	(EL)
4.	UKRAINE		19.17	11.17	2	6
	PILGRIM	Björn Nagel		7.03	1	5
	OSTA RUGS TRESOR	Jean Claude van Geenberghe		2.38	0	(8)
	LORIOT	Gregory Wathelet		1.76	(8)	0
	ATLANTA	Katharina Offel		(7.42)	1	1
5.	SWITZERLAND		24.89	14.89	5	5
	L.B. NO MERCY	Christina Liebherr		6.52	0	0
	CANTUS	Niklaus Schurtenberger		3.64	1	1
	PLOT BLUE	Werner Muff		4.73	(5)	4
	INDIGO IX	Beat Mändli		(6.78)	4	(4)
6	IRELAND		29.08	11.08	13	5
	WORLD CRUISE	Shane Breen		3.99	0	(12)
	CHIPPISON	Marie Burke		1.71	4	0
	LUIDAM	Billy Twomey		(7.62)	9	5
	SIEC HIPPICA KERMAN	Cameron Hanley		5.38	(9)	0
7.	BELGIUM		30,82	9.82	13	8
8.	SPAIN		30.85	9.85	12	9
9.	GREAT BRITAIN		32.90	14.90	7	11
10.	BRAZIL		56.99	6.99	13	37

FEI Einzelweltmeisterschaft Springen – Ergebnis Runde A+B der 25 Besten
FEI World Individual Jumping Championship – Result Round A+B of the best 25

Rank	Pferd/ Horse	Reiter/ Rider	NAT	1 Day	2 Day R1	3 Day R2	4 Day R1	4 Day R2	Total
1.	AUTHENTIC	Beezie MADDEN	USA	0.00	0	0	4	0	4.00
2.	CAVALOR CUMANO	Jos LANSINK	BEL	5.01	0	0	0	0	5.01
3.	SHUTTERFLY	Meredith MICHAELSBEERBAUM	GER	3.92	1	0	5	0	9.92
4.	ISOVLAS PIALOTTA	Edwina ALEXANDER	AUS	2.24	0	8	0	0	10.24
5.	L'ESPOIR	Ludger BEERBAUM	GER	2.70	0	0	4	4	10.70
6.	EUROCOMMERCE BERLIN	Gerco SCHRÖDER	NED	0.43	0	0	8	4	12.43
7.	SAPPHIRE	McLain WARD	USA	0.87	4	0	8	0	12.87
8.	INSUL TECH PORTOFINO	Michael WHITAKER	GBR	5.53	1	1	6	0	13.53
9.	PARCO	Ludo PHILIPPAERTS	BEL	2.05	4	0	8	0	14.05
10.	CANTUS	Niklaus SCHURTENBERGER	SUI	3.64	1	1	5	4	14.64
11.	BMC UP AND DOWN	Jeroen DUBBELDAM	NED	3.10	1	0	8	4	16.10
12.	CANTURO	Bernardo ALVES	BRA	1.36	0	8	4	4	17.36
13.	L.B. NO MERCY	Christina LIEBHERR	SUI	6.52	0	0	8	4	18.52
14.	ISAAC	Royne ZETTERMAN	SWE	3.08	4	1	9	4	21.08
15.	OSTA RUGS TRESOR	Jean Claude VAN GEENBERGHE	UKR	2.38	0	8	8	4	22.38
16.	PROCASA LE MONDE	Ricardo JURADO	ESP	3.27	0	8	8	4	23.27
17.	LOXLEY	Samantha MC INTOSH	BUL	2.02	5	4	13	0	24.02
18.	LE REVE DU NABAB	Sergio ALVAREZ MOYA	ESP	1.24	4	0	12	8	25.24
19.	NINJA LA SILLA	Rolf-Göran BENGTSSON	SWE	4.91	4	0	9	8	25.91
20.	OKIDOKI	Albert ZOER	NED	2.48	0	4	12	8	26.48
21.	CATTANI	Geir GULLIKSEN	NOR	1.84	4	4	13	4	26.84
22.	ATLANTA	Katharina OFFEL	UKR	7.42	1	1	13	12	34.42
23.	DOVER	Luciana DINIZ	POR	4.16	0	4	8		16.16
24.	CHIPPISON	Marie BURKE	IRL	1.71	4	0	25		30.71
25.	OBÉLIX	Hervé GODIGNON	FRA	5.40	4	1	RE		10.40

Ergebnisse / Results

Dressur / Dressage

FEI Mannschaftsweltmeisterschaft und Qualifikationsprüfung für die Einzelwertung
FEI World Team Dressage Championship and Individual Qualifying Competition

	Reiter/Rider	Nation	Pferd/Horse	Richter/Judges E	H	C	M	B	Total
1.	Andreas Helgstrand	DEN	Blue Hors Matine	78.125 (1)	75.833 (2)	74.375 (3)	77.292 (1)	76.042 (2)	76.333
2.	Heike Kemmer	GER	Bonaparte	76.458 (2)	75.000 (3)	75.625 (1)	74.792 (3)	77.083 (1)	75.792
3.	Isabell Werth	GER	Satchmo	76.042 (4)	76.667 (1)	73.125 (6)	73.542 (4)	75.625 (3)	75.000
3.	Anky van Grunsven	NED	Keltec Salinero	76.042 (3)	72.708 (8)	75.417 (2)	75.833 (2)	75.000 (4)	75.000
5.	Nadine Capellmann	GER	Elvis VA	69.792 (10)	74.792 (4)	73.542 (5)	71.667 (9)	74.375 (5)	72.833
6.	Steffen Peters	USA	Floriano	71.250 (5)	72.917 (7)	72.708 (7)	72.917 (5)	73.750 (6)	72.708
7.	Jan Brink	SWE	Björsells Briar 899	70.625 (7)	73.125 (5)	72.292 (8)	71.875 (7)	72.917 (8)	72.167
8.	Imke Schellekens-Bartels	NED	Sunrise	70.833 (6)	68.542 (19)	73.542 (4)	71.875 (7)	72.917 (7)	71.542
9.	Debbie McDonald	USA	Brentina	69.375 (15)	72.917 (6)	72.083 (9)	72.083 (6)	70.625 (12)	71.417
10.	Edward Gal	NED	Group 4 Securicor Lingh	70.625 (7)	71.042 (15)	71.458 (10)	71.458 (10)	72.292 (9)	71.375
11.	Karen Tebar	FRA	Falada M	69.792 (11)	72.083 (10)	70.833 (15)	70.833 (12)	70.625 (12)	70.833
12.	Kyra Kyrklund *IND	FIN	Max	69.792 (12)	72.292 (9)	70.417 (16)	69.375 (18)	71.250 (11)	70.625
13.	Emma Hindle	GBR	Lancet	68.542 (19)	71.250 (13)	71.250 (12)	69.583 (16)	71.667 (10)	70.458
14.	Tinne Vilhelmson	SWE	Solos Carex	70.208 (9)	71.667 (11)	71.250 (12)	68.125 (25)	70.417 (14)	70.333
15.	Kristy Oatley	AUS	Quando-Quando	68.750 (16)	71.250 (13)	70.417 (17)	70.417 (14)	69.583 (19)	70.083
16.	Bernadette Pujals *IND	MEX	Vincent	69.583 (13)	71.458 (12)	71.042 (14)	68.542 (22)	69.375 (20)	70.000
17.	Günter Seidel	USA	Aragon	69.583 (14)	70.417 (17)	69.792 (19)	68.958 (19)	70.208 (15)	69.792
18.	Hubertus Schmidt	GER	Wansuela Suerte	68.750 (16)	67.500 (25)	71.458 (11)	68.750 (20)	69.583 (18)	69.208
19.	Victoria Max-Theurer	AUT	Falcao	67.500 (21)	70.625 (16)	70.000 (18)	67.500 (30)	70.208 (16)	69.167
20.	Silvia Iklé	SUI	Salieri CH	68.750 (16)	68.125 (23)	68.750 (21)	70.833 (13)	67.292 (26)	68.750
21.	Laurens van Lieren	NED	Hexagon's Ollright	68.333 (20)	67.500 (25)	68.542 (24)	68.125 (26)	70.000 (17)	68.500
22.	Christian Pläge	SUI	Regent	67.500 (21)	69.375 (18)	67.083 (31)	69.792 (15)	68.333 (22)	68.417
23.	Sandy Phillips	GBR	Lara	66.667 (27)	68.333 (22)	67.708 (27)	71.250 (11)	67.500 (24)	68.292
24.	Elena Kalinina *IND	RUS	Royal Black Label	67.083 (25)	67.917 (24)	67.083 (30)	68.750 (20)	67.917 (23)	67.750
25.	Wayne Channon	GBR	Lorenzo CH	66.458 (29)	65.833 (35)	68.542 (23)	68.333 (25)	68.542 (21)	67.542
26.	Laura Bechtolsheimer	GBR	Douglas Dorsey	67.292 (23)	68.542 (21)	67.917 (26)	66.458 (39)	66.667 (29)	67.375
27.	Dominique d'Esmé	FRA	Roi de Cœur GFD	66.250 (30)	65.833 (34)	68.958 (20)	68.333 (24)	66.458 (30)	67.167
28.	Jeroen Devroe	BEL	Paganini	67.083 (26)	65.833 (33)	68.333 (25)	66.667 (38)	66.250 (31)	66.833
29.	Matthew Dowsley	AUS	Cinderella	65.625 (36)	66.042 (31)	68.750 (21)	67.292 (32)	65.625 (37)	66.667
29.	Rafael Soto Andrade	ESP	Invasor	65.208 (41)	65.000 (39)	66.250 (36)	69.583 (17)	67.292 (27)	66.667
31.	Marie-Line Wettstein	SUI	Le Primeur	66.042 (33)	65.417 (36)	67.083 (33)	66.667 (37)	67.500 (24)	66.542
31.	Alexandra Korelova *IND	RUS	Balagur	66.250 (30)	67.292 (28)	66.042 (37)	67.500 (30)	65.625 (37)	66.542
33.	Marcela Krinke Susmelj	SUI	Corinth	67.083 (24)	67.292 (27)	65.625 (39)	65.625 (42)	66.667 (28)	66.458
33.	Anders Dahl	DEN	Afrikka	65.417 (38)	66.250 (30)	67.083 (32)	68.125 (26)	65.417 (40)	66.458
35.	Evi Strasser *IND	CAN	Quantum Tyme	66.042 (34)	64.375 (43)	67.083 (29)	68.333 (23)	66.042 (34)	66.375
36.	Louise Nathorst	SWE	Guinness	65.833 (35)	66.458 (29)	66.458 (35)	66.458 (40)	66.042 (35)	66.250
37.	Ignacio Rambla	ESP	Distinguido 2	66.250 (30)	66.042 (32)	65.625 (39)	67.083 (33)	65.625 (37)	66.125
37.	Hubert Perring	FRA	Diabolo St Maurice	65.208 (40)	65.208 (38)	66.042 (38)	68.125 (26)	66.042 (33)	66.125
39.	Nathalie zu Sayn-Wittgenstein	DEN	Digby	65.625 (36)	68.542 (20)	67.083 (34)	63.125 (56)	66.042 (32)	66.083
40.	Juan Antonio Jimenez	ESP	Guizo	65.417 (39)	64.583 (42)	63.958 (47)	66.667 (36)	64.167 (44)	64.958
41.	Katarzyna Milczarek Jasinska	POL	Lecantos	64.375 (44)	64.375 (43)	65.000 (42)	67.083 (34)	63.333 (50)	64.833
42.	Claudia Montanari	ITA	Don Vittorio	64.792 (43)	64.792 (40)	67.500 (28)	62.708 (60)	63.750 (47)	64.708
43.	Michal Rapcewicz	POL	Randon	64.375 (44)	64.792 (41)	63.958 (49)	64.792 (45)	64.583 (41)	64.500
44.	José Ignacio López Porras	ESP	Nevado Santa Clara	62.917 (50)	63.125 (47)	64.583 (46)	65.833 (41)	65.833 (36)	64.458
45.	Ashley Holzer *IND	CAN	Gambol	62.708 (51)	65.417 (37)	65.000 (42)	64.792 (46)	63.542 (49)	64.292
46.	Leslie Morse	USA	Tip Top 962	66.458 (28)	63.750 (46)	62.708 (54)	63.958 (53)	64.375 (43)	64.250
47.	Anna Merveldt *IND	IRL	Lafitte	63.750 (47)	61.667 (51)	65.625 (39)	64.375 (47)	63.958 (46)	63.875
48.	Anna Paprocka-Campanella	ITA	Andretti H	63.333 (49)	63.125 (47)	64.583 (45)	62.917 (57)	64.583 (42)	63.708
49.	Dr. Cesar Parra *IND	COL	Galant du Serein	63.958 (46)	63.958 (45)	63.333 (50)	64.167 (51)	62.083 (57)	63.500
50.	Constance Menard	FRA	Lianca	63.542 (48)	61.250 (53)	65.208 (42)	65.417 (43)	61.875 (58)	63.458
51.	Mag. Evelyn Haim-Swarovski	AUT	Chopin 43	62.500 (52)	61.667 (50)	63.125 (51)	63.542 (55)	63.125 (51)	62.792
51.	Daniel Pinto	POR	Galopin de la Font	60.417 (63)	60.833 (59)	61.667 (59)	66.875 (35)	64.167 (45)	62.792
53.	Iryna Lis *IND	BLR	Problesk	60.625 (60)	62.292 (49)	62.708 (53)	64.792 (44)	62.917 (53)	62.667
54.	Nina Stadlinger	AUT	Egalité	61.458 (57)	61.250 (53)	62.917 (52)	64.375 (47)	62.500 (55)	62.500
54.	Rachael Sanna	AUS	Chatham Park Jac	64.792 (42)	61.458 (52)	61.875 (58)	61.667 (61)	62.708 (52)	62.500
54.	Lone Jørgensen	DEN	Hardthof's Ludewig G	62.083 (54)	61.042 (55)	63.958 (48)	61.667 (65)	63.750 (47)	62.500
57.	Mieke Lunskens	BEL	Jade	61.875 (55)	61.042 (57)	61.250 (60)	64.167 (50)	62.292 (56)	62.125
58.	Zaneta Skowronska	POL	Romeo	61.667 (56)	61.042 (56)	62.083 (57)	63.750 (54)	60.000 (61)	61.708
59.	Julija Ona Vysniauskas *IND	LTU	Syntax	60.625 (60)	59.583 (64)	62.500 (52)	62.708 (59)	59.167 (67)	60.917
59.	Andre Parada	POR	Landim	60.417 (65)	58.750 (69)	61.250 (60)	64.167 (49)	60.000 (61)	60.917
61.	Eva Rosenthal	ITA	L´Etoile 009	60.417 (64)	60.833 (58)	59.167 (72)	62.292 (62)	60.417 (60)	60.625
62.	Yuriy Kovshov	UKR	Areal	60.208 (68)	59.375 (65)	60.208 (65)	62.917 (58)	60.000 (61)	60.542
63.	Kristian von Krusenstierna	SWE	Wilson	61.042 (59)	58.333 (71)	59.792 (68)	60.000 (75)	62.917 (52)	60.417
64.	Carl Cuypers	BEL	Hofgut Liederbach's Barclay	62.500 (52)	57.708 (75)	59.583 (71)	60.833 (71)	61.250 (59)	60.375
65.	Susan de Klein *IND	AHO	Special	61.250 (58)	60.208 (60)	60.833 (62)	60.208 (74)	58.333 (71)	60.167
66.	Caroline Kottas-Heldenberg	AUT	Exupery	59.792 (70)	56.667 (81)	60.000 (66)	63.958 (52)	59.792 (64)	60.042
67.	Svetlana Yevshchik *IND	BLR	Dombai	60.000 (69)	59.583 (63)	58.958 (74)	62.292 (63)	58.333 (73)	59.833
68.	Igor Maver *IND	SLO	085 Favory Canissa XXII	60.625 (60)	58.333 (70)	60.417 (64)	61.458 (68)	57.917 (74)	59.750

Ergebnisse | Results

	Rider	NAT	Horse	E	H	C	M	B	Total
69.	Francoise Hologne-Joux	BEL	Born	60.208 (66)	57.708 (76)	62.292 (56)	58.958 (77)	59.375 (66)	59.708
70.	Emily Ward *IND	ANT	Vallon	59.167 (71)	59.375 (65)	58.958 (73)	61.458 (69)	59.167 (68)	59.625
71.	Judy Reynolds *IND	IRL	Rathbawn Valet	58.958 (72)	59.167 (67)	60.000 (66)	60.417 (72)	58.750 (69)	59.458
72.	Nuno Vincente	POR	Nostradamus do Top	60.208 (67)	60.000 (61)	60.417 (63)	57.500 (81)	58.750 (69)	59.375
73.	Ioanna Georgopoulou *IND	GRE	Dynastie	58.333 (73)	58.958 (68)	59.583 (70)	61.458 (66)	56.250 (78)	58.917
74.	Kuranojo Saito	JPN	Lotus	57.500 (76)	59.792 (62)	58.125 (76)	61.250 (70)	57.500 (75)	58.833
75.	Yuriko Miyoshi	JPN	Chevalier 66	58.333 (74)	57.917 (74)	57.083 (78)	62.292 (61)	56.875 (77)	58.500
76.	Inna Tzydrenkova	UKR	Odis	57.500 (76)	56.875 (79)	58.125 (76)	59.583 (76)	59.583 (65)	58.333
77.	Natalie Hobday *IND	RSA	Callaho Wenckstern	58.333 (75)	57.917 (72)	58.333 (75)	58.542 (78)	57.292 (76)	58.083
78.	Joelle Kinnen *IND	LUX	Petit Prince 9	56.875 (81)	57.292 (77)	59.792 (69)	56.042 (82)	58.333 (72)	57.667
79.	Zsofia Dallos *IND	HUN	Leonardo	57.292 (79)	57.917 (73)	55.625 (79)	61.458 (67)	55.208 (79)	57.500
80.	Toshihiko Kiso	JPN	Esko 10	57.292 (80)	55.625 (82)	55.417 (80)	60.417 (73)	54.375 (82)	56.625
81.	Robert Acs *IND	HUN	Lagerfeld	57.500 (76)	57.083 (78)	54.792 (82)	58.125 (79)	55.000 (81)	56.500
82.	Jaroslaw Wierzchowski	POL	Wieland	56.667 (82)	56.875 (79)	54.792 (81)	57.917 (80)	55.208 (80)	56.292
83.	Miguel Duarte	POR	Oxalis da Meia Lua	52.292 (83)	55.208 (83)	52.083 (83)	52.917 (83)	52.500 (83)	53.000
84.	Sergey Buikevich *IND	KAZ	Volan						*EL
84.	Andriy Luk'Yanov	UKR	Gopak						*EL
84.	Kelly Layne	AUS	Amoucheur						*EL
	Hiroshi Hoketsu	JPN	Calambo						*DNS
	Tatiana Miloserdova *IND	RUS	Wat a Feeling						*DNS
	Inessa Poturaeva *IND	RUS	Zorro						*DNS

*IND – Einzelreiter/ *Individual Rider*   *EL – ausgeschieden/ *left*   *DNS – nicht gestartet/ *not started*

Richter/ *Judges:* E: Ghislain Fouarage, NED   H: Linda Zang, USA   C: Stephen Clarke, CBR   M: Bernhard Maurel, FRA   B: Dieter Schüle, GER

FEI Mannschaftsweltmeisterschaft und Qualifikationsprüfung für die Einzelwertung
FEI World Team Dressage Championship and Individual Qualifying Competition

Land/ NAT Reiter/ *Rider*	Pferd/ *Horse*	E	H	C	M	B	Total *Score*
1. Deutschland/ GER							**223.625**
Hubertus Schmidt	Wansuela Suerte	68.750	67.500	71.458	68.750	69.583	*69.208
Heike Kemmer	Bonaparte	76.458	75.000	75.625	74.792	77.083	75.792
Nadine Capellmann	Elvis VA	69.792	74.792	73.542	71.667	74.375	72.833
Isabell Werth	Satchmo	76.042	76.667	73.125	73.542	75.625	75.000
2. Niederlande/ NED							**217.917**
Laurens van Lieren	Hexagon's Ollright	68.333	67.500	68.542	68.125	70.000	*68.500
Imke Schellekens-Bartels	Sunrise	70.833	68.542	73.542	71.875	72.917	71.542
Anky van Grunsven	Keltec Salinero	76.042	72.708	75.417	75.833	75.000	75.000
Edward Gal	Group 4 Securior Lingh	70.625	71.042	71.458	71.458	72.292	71.375
3. USA							**213.917**
Leslie Morse	Tip Top 962	66.458	63.750	62.708	63.958	64.375	*64.250
Günter Seidel	Aragon	69.583	70.417	69.792	68.958	70.208	69.792
Steffen Peters	Floriano	71.250	72.917	72.708	72.917	73.750	72.708
Debbie McDonald	Brentina	69.357	72.917	72.083	72.093	70.625	71.417
4. Dänemark/ DEN							**208.874**
Anders Dahl	Afrikka	65.417	66.250	67.083	68.125	65.417	66.458
Nathalie zu Sayn-Wittgenstein	Digby	65.625	68.542	67.083	63.125	66.042	66.083
Lone Jørgensen	Hardthof's Ludewig G	62.083	61.042	63.958	61.667	63.750	*62.500
Andreas Helgstrand	Blue Hors Matine	78.125	75.833	74.375	77.292	76.042	76.333
5. Schweden/ SWE							**208.750**
Kristian von Krusenstierna	Wilson	61.042	58.343	59.792	60.000	62.917	*60.417
Tinne Vilhelmson	Solos Carex	70.208	71.667	71.250	68.125	70.417	70.333
Louise Nathorst	Guinness	65.833	66.458	66.458	66.458	66.042	66.250
Jan Brink	Björsells Briar 899	70.625	73.125	72.292	71.875	72.917	72.167
6. Großbritannien/ GBR							**206.292**
Laura Bechtolsheimer	Douglas Dorsey	67.292	68.542	67.917	66.458	66.667	*67.375
Wayne Channon	Lorenzo CH	66.458	65.833	68.542	68.333	68.542	67.542
Emma Hindle	Lancet	68.542	71.250	71.250	69.583	71.667	70.458
Sandy Phillips	Lara	66.667	68.333	67.708	71.250	67.500	68.292
7. Frankreich/ FRA							**204.125**
8. Schweiz/ SUI							**203.709**
9. Australien/ AUS							**199.250**
10. Spanien/ ESP							**197.750**
11. Österreich/ AUT							**194.459**
12. Polen/ POL							**191.041**
13. Belgien/ BEL							**189.333**
14. Italien/ITA							**189.041**
15. Portugal/ POR							**183.084**
16. Japan/ JPA							**173.958**
Ucraine/ UKRS							

Richter/ *Judges:* E: Ghislain Fouarage, NED   H: Linda Zang, USA   C: Stephen Clarke, CBR   M: Bernhard Maurel, FRA   B: Dieter Schüle, GER

ERGEBNISSE | RESULTS

DRESSUR | DRESSAGE

FEI Einzelweltmeisterschaft Dressur Grand Prix Spezial
FEI World Individual Dressage Grand Prix Special Championship

Rank	Reiter/ Rider	NAT	Pferd/ Horse	- E -	- H -	- C -	- M -	- B -	Total
1.	ISABELL WERTH	GER	SATCHMO	80.600 (1)	79.200 (1)	79.200 (2)	79.400 (1)	79.000 (1)	79.480
2.	ANKY VAN GRUNSVEN	NED	KELTEC SALINERO	76.200 (4)	78.200 (2)	79.600 (1)	78.000 (2)	77.000 (3)	77.800
3.	ANDREAS HELGSTRAND	DEN	BLUE HORS MATINE	76.600 (2)	76.600 (3)	75.800 (3)	75.600 (4)	78.200 (2)	76.560
4.	STEFFEN PETERS	USA	FLORIANO	76.600 (3)	75.600 (4)	73.600 (7)	76.600 (3)	73.600 (6)	75.200
5.	NADINE CAPELLMANN	GER	ELVIS VA	72.800 (8)	75.000 (6)	74.800 (5)	75.200 (6)	76.000 (4)	74.760
6.	SILVIA IKL...	SUI	SALIERI CH	73.200 (6)	73.600 (7)	75.800 (4)	75.400 (5)	70.600 (12)	73.720
7.	HEIKE KEMMER	GER	BONAPARTE	70.800 (14)	73.400 (8)	73.200 (10)	73.800 (7)	74.800 (5)	73.200
8.	JAN BRINK	SWE	BJ÷RSELLS BRIAR 899	71.400 (11)	75.200 (5)	72.200 (12)	73.000 (9)	73.400 (7)	73.040
9.	IMKE SCHELLEKENS-BARTEL	NED	SUNRISE S	73.800 (5)	71.600 (11)	73.200 (9)	73.200 (8)	73.200 (8)	73.000
10.	BERNADETTE PUJALS	MEX	VINCENT	71.200 (13)	73.000 (9)	73.600 (8)	72.800 (10)	71.800 (9)	72.480
11.	EDWARD GAL	NED	GROUP 4 SECURICOR LINGH	71.200 (12)	70.600 (13)	73.600 (6)	72.600 (11)	71.200 (11)	71.840
12.	KYRA KYRKLUND	FIN	MAX	72.600 (9)	72.400 (10)	72.800 (11)	71.200 (15)	69.600 (17)	71.720
13.	HUBERTUS SCHMIDT	GER	WANSUELA SUERTE	72.800 (7)	70.800 (12)	69.600 (16)	72.400 (12)	69.600 (15)	71.040
14.	GUENTER SEIDEL	USA	ARAGON	72.000 (10)	70.400 (14)	69.200 (17)	71.200 (14)	70.000 (14)	70.560
15.	LAURENS VAN LIER	NED	HEXAGON¥S OLLRIGHTEN	68.400 (18)	70.200 (15)	69.600 (15)	72.000 (13)	71.200 (10)	70.280
16.	CHRISTIAN PLƒGE	SUI	REGENT	68.200 (19)	66.600 (24)	70.600 (13)	70.400 (16)	70.200 (13)	69.200
17.	EMMA HINDLE	GBR	LANCET	70.600 (15)	69.600 (16)	70.000 (14)	68.800 (17)	66.600 (25)	69.120
18.	KRISTY OATLEY	AUS	QUANDO-QUANDO	69.800 (16)	69.400 (17)	68.400 (20)	67.800 (19)	69.400 (18)	68.960
19.	RAFAEL SOTO ANDRADE	ESP	INVASOR	69.200 (17)	68.600 (19)	68.600 (18)	68.200 (18)	69.600 (16)	68.840
20.	TINNE VILHELMSON	SWE	SOLOS CAREX	67.200 (21)	68.800 (18)	67.600 (21)	67.600 (20)	68.600 (19)	67.960
21.	LAURA BECHTOLSHEIMER	GBR	DOUGLAS DORSEY	67.800 (20)	67.600 (21)	67.200 (22)	66.800 (22)	68.600 (20)	67.600
22.	JEROEN DEVROE	BEL	PAGANINI	67.000 (22)	68.400 (20)	65.800 (26)	67.000 (21)	65.000 (29)	66.640
23.	MARIE-LINE WETTSTEIN	SUI	LE PRIMEUR	66.600 (23)	67.000 (22)	67.200 (23)	65.400 (26)	66.000 (26)	66.440
23.	WAYNE CHANNON	GBR	LORENZO CH	65.400 (25)	65.600 (28)	67.000 (24)	66.600 (23)	67.600 (21)	66.440
25.	KAREN TEBAR	FRA	FALADA M	66.400 (24)	66.600 (25)	64.800 (28)	64.600 (28)	67.200 (22)	65.920
26.	ELENA KALININA	RUS	ROYAL BLACK LABEL	65.000 (26)	64.600 (30)	68.400 (19)	65.800 (25)	64.200 (31)	65.600
27.	ALEXANDRA KORELOVA	RUS	BALAGUR	64.600 (29)	66.200 (26)	64.200 (30)	66.200 (24)	65.200 (28)	65.280
27.	SANDY PHILLIPS	GBR	LARA	64.800 (27)	66.600 (23)	64.800 (27)	65.200 (27)	65.000 (29)	65.280
29.	VICTORIA MAX-THEURER	AUT	FALCAO	64.400 (30)	65.000 (29)	66.800 (25)	64.000 (30)	66.000 (26)	65.240
29.	MATTHEW DOWSLEY	AUS	CINDERELLA	64.600 (28)	65.800 (27)	64.600 (29)	64.400 (29)	66.800 (23)	65.240
31.	DOMINIQUE D¥ESM...	FRA	ROI DE COEUR GFD	62.000 (31)	64.000 (31)	63.000 (31)	62.800 (31)	66.600 (24)	63.680

Richter/ Judges: E: Linda Zang, USA H: Mary Seefried, AUS C: Dr. Wojciech Markowski, POL M: Dr. Dieter Sch,le, GER B: Bernard Maurel, FRA

FEI Einzelweltmeisterschaft Dressur – Grand Prix Kür
FEI World Individual Dressage – Grand Prix Freestyle Championship

Rank	Reiter/ Rider	NAT	Pferd/ Horse	- E -	- H -	- C -	- M -	- B -	Total
1.	ANKY VAN GRUNSVEN	NED	KELTEC SALINERO	78.000 91.000 (1)	78.500 89.000 (1)	80.500 92.000 (1)	83.500 92.000 (1)	82.500 94.000 (1)	86.100
2.	ANDREAS HELGSTRAND	DEN	BLUE HORS MATINE	73.000 85.000 (2)	76.500 87.000 (2)	80.500 89.000 (3)	76.000 84.000 (4)	79.000 85.000 (2)	81.500
3.	ISABELL WERTH	GER	SATCHMO	72.500 83.000 (5)	73.500 82.000 (5)	79.000 92.000 (2)	77.000 89.000 (2)	75.500 84.000 (4)	80.750
4.	NADINE CAPELLMANN	GER	ELVIS VA	73.000 85.000 (2)	74.000 84.000 (4)	74.500 87.000 (5)	75.500 85.000 (3)	77.000 84.000 (3)	79.900
5.	HEIKE KEMMER	GER	BONAPARTE	72.000 81.000 (6)	76.500 85.000 (3)	76.500 88.000 (4)	71.500 84.000 (8)	72.000 82.000 (7)	78.850
6.	STEFFEN PETERS	USA	FLORIANO	74.000 84.000 (2)	73.500 81.000 (6)	72.500 84.000 (7)	76.000 84.000 (4)	75.000 82.000 (5)	78.600
7.	KYRA KYRKLUND	FIN	MAX	71.000 76.000 (12)	72.000 79.000 (9)	75.500 86.000 (5)	75.000 84.000 (7)	73.500 81.000 (6)	77.300
8.	IMKE SCHELLEKENS-BARTEL	NED	SUNRISE S	71.000 82.000 (6)	71.500 78.000 (10)	70.000 82.000 (11)	76.500 83.000 (6)	72.000 78.000 (10)	76.400
9.	JAN BRINK	SWE	BJÖRSELLS BRIAR 899	68.500 80.000 (11)	71.500 82.000 (7)	72.500 84.000 (7)	71.000 79.000 (9)	71.500 78.000 (11)	75.800
10.	BERNADETTE PUJALS	MEX	VINCENT	72.000 79.000 (8)	70.500 75.000 (12)	72.000 84.000 (9)	72.000 75.000 (11)	71.500 79.000 (9)	75.000
11.	SILVIA IKLÉ	SUI	SALIERI CH	70.000 80.000 (9)	71.000 76.000 (11)	68.500 81.000 (12)	71.500 77.000 (10)	73.500 79.000 (8)	74.750
12.	EDWARD GAL	NED	GROUP 4 SECURICOR LINGH	68.500 75.000 (13)	73.500 80.000 (7)	72.000 82.000 (10)	72.000 75.000 (11)	71.500 78.000 (11)	74.750
13.	GUENTER SEIDEL	USA	ARAGON	69.500 80.000 (10)	67.500 71.000 (14)	67.000 80.000 (13)	68.500 73.000 (14)	70.500 78.000 (13)	72.500
14.	CHRISTIAN PLÄGE	SUI	REGENT	65.500 71.000 (14)	68.500 70.000 (14)	68.500 76.000 (14)	71.000 75.000 (13)	70.500 75.000 (14)	71.100
15.	EMMA HINDLE	GBR	LANCET	66.000 70.000 (15)	70.500 72.000 (13)	69.500 74.000 (15)	69.500 68.500 (15)	70.000 69.000 (15)	69.900

Richter/ Judges: E: Mary Seefried, AUS H: Ghislain Fouarge, NED C: Dr. Dieter Schüle M: Dr. Wojciech Markowski, POL B: Stephen Clarke, GBR

VIELSEITIGKEIT | EVENTING — ERGEBNISSE | RESULTS

FEI Weltmeisterschaft Vielseitigkeit Einzel – Ergebnis nach Springen Finale
FEI World Individual Eventing Championship – Result after Show Jumping Final

Rank Rider NAT.	Horse	Dressage Pen.	Rank	Cross-Country Time	TP	JP	XC	Interim result	Rank	Show Jumping Time	TP	SP	Pen.	Total Pen.
1. Phillips, Zara GBR TEAM	Toy Town	41,70	5.	11:07	0,00	0	0,00	41,70	1	95,74	1,00	4	5,00	46,70
2. Fredericks, Clayton AUS TEAM	Ben Along Time	44,40	7.	11:23	4,40	0	4,40	48,80	4	92,71	0,00	0	0,00	48,80
3. Tryon, Amy USA TEAM	Poggio	50,70	24.	11:07	0,00	0	0,00	50,70	7	89,55	0,00	0	0,00	50,70
4. Ostholt, Frank GER TEAM	Air Jordan 2	46,90	11.	11:01	0,00	0	0,00	46,90	3	91,64	0,00	4	4,00	50,90
5. Romeike, Hinrich GER TEAM	Marius Voigt-Logistik	52,40	27.	11:02	0,00	0	0,00	52,40	8	91,46	0,00	0	0,00	52,40
6. Hoy, Bettina GER TEAM	Ringwood Cockatoo	36,50	1.	11:30	7,20	0	7,20	43,70	2	95,66	1,00	8	9,00	52,70
7. Tompkins, Heelan NZL TEAM	Glengarrick	49,80	20.	11:12	0,00	0	0	49,80	5	86,58	0,00	4	4,00	53,80
8. Hunt, Sharon GBR IND.	Tankers Town	47,40	13.	11:18	2,40	0	2,40	49,80	6	83,26	0,00	4	4,00	53,80
9. Gällerdal, Magnus SWE TEAM	Keymaster 3	47,40	13.	11:45	13,20	0	13,20	60,60	11	95,62	1,00	0	1,00	61,60
10. Laghouag, Karim Florent FRA IND.	Make my Day	63,70	56.	11:09	0,00	0	0,00	63,70	14	89,78	0,00	0	0,00	63,70
11. Townend, Oliver GBR IND.	Flint Curtis	62,00	51.	11:08	0,00	0	0,00	62,00	13	96,57	2,00	0	2,00	64,00
12. Dick, Daisy GBR TEAM	Spring Along	64,30	57.	11:01	0,00	0	0,00	64,30	15	94,06	0,00	0	0,00	64,30
13. Donckers, Karin BEL TEAM	Gazelle de la Brasserie CH	45,20	9.	11:45	13,20	0	13,20	58,40	10	96,28	2,00	4	6,00	64,40
14. Albert, Dag SWE TEAM	Who's Blitz	61,50	48.	11:12	0,00	0	0,00	61,50	12	96,28	2,00	4	6,00	67,50
15. Fox-Pitt, William GBR TEAM	Tamarillo	45,00	8.	11:22	4,00	20	24,00	69,00	17	91,36	0,00	0	0,00	69,00
16. Jones, Megan AUS TEAM	Kirby Park Irish Jester	44,10	6.	11:27	6,00	20	26,00	70,10	19	93,62	0,00	0	0,00	70,10
17. Severson, Kimberley USA TEAM	Winsome Adante	40,90	3.	11:29	6,80	20	26,80	67,70	16	88,12	0,00	4	4,00	71,70
18. Oiwa, Yoshiaki JPN IND.	Fifth Avenue Fame	74,50	73.	11:12	0,00	0	0,00	74,50	23	93,36	0,00	0	0,00	74,50
19 Faudree, Will USA TEAM	Antigua	63,30	53.	11:33	8,40	0	8,40	71,70	20	91,29	0,00	4	4,00	75,70
20 Viricel, Gilles FRA TEAM	Blakring	61,70	49.	11:52	16,00	0	16,00	77,70	26	88,56	0,00	0	0,00	77,70
21. Dibowski, Andreas GER IND.	FRH Serve Well	40,90	3.	11:45	13,20	20	33,20	74,10	21	94,46	0,00	4	4,00	78,10
22. Hoy, Andrew AUS TEAM	Master Monarch	47,60	15.	11:29	6,80	20	26,80	74,40	22	89,60	0,00	4	4,00	78,40
23. Nicholson, Andrew NZL TEAM	Lord Killinghurst	49,60	19.	11:04	0,00	20	20,00	69,60	18	100,37	6,00	4	10,00	79,60
24. King, Mary GBR TEAM	Call Again Cavalier	51,90	26.	11:35	9,20	20	29,20	81,10	29	93,00	0,00	0	0,00	81,10
25. Flarup, Peter Tersgov DEN TEAM	Silver Ray	74,60	74.	11:07	0,00	0	0,00	74,60	24	88,69	0,00	8	8,00	82,60
26. Powell, Caroline NZL TEAM	Lenamore	66,30	58.	11:17	2,00	20	22,00	88,30	35	93,84	0,00	0	0,00	88,30
27. White, Heidi USA TEAM	Northern Spy	50,40	22.	12:29	30,80	0	30,80	81,20	31	91,78	0,00	8	8,00	89,20
28. Touzaint, Nicolas FRA TEAM	Hildago de l'Ile	47,00	12.	12:02	20,00	20	40,00	87,00	33	94,39	0,00	4	4,00	91,00
29. Adde, Jean-Renaud FRA IND.	Haston d'Elpegère	61,70	49.	11:58	18,40	0	18,40	80,10	27	97,23	3,00	8	11,00	91,10
30. Dutton, Phillip AUS IND.	Connaught	51,70	25.	11:43	12,40	20	32,40	84,10	31	91,91	0,00	8	8,00	92,10
31. Ambros, Harald AUT TEAM	Miss Ferrari	58,30	40.	11:48	14,40	20	34,40	92,70	36	93,97	0,00	0	0,00	92,70
32. Beek, Jan van NED TEAM	La Cru -KWPN	58,20	38.	12:09	22,80	0	22,80	81,00	28	96,78	2,00	12	14,00	95,00
33. Magni, Fabio ITA TEAM	Southern King V	58,50	41.	12:47	38,00	0	38,00	96,50	38	92,16	0,00	0	0,00	96,50
34. Klimke, Ingrid GER TEAM	Sleep Late	39,10	2.	11:56	17,60	40	57,60	96,70	39	91,39	0,00	0	0,00	96,70
35. Algotsson, Linda SWE TEAM	My Fair Lady 59	48,90	17.	11:57	18,00	20	38,00	86,90	32	96,12	2,00	8	10,00	96,90
36. Siegl, Harald AUT TEAM	Nebelwerfer	60,90	46.	12:18	26,40	0	26,40	87,30	34	96,21	2,00	8	10,00	97,30
37. Griffin, Niall IRL TEAM	Lorgaine	57,40	36.	11:58	18,40	0	18,40	75,80	25	97,35	3,00	20	23,00	98,80
38. Wardell, Sarah IRL TEAM	Kincluny	58,50	41.	11:53	16,40	20	36,40	94,90	37	95,21	1,00	8	9,00	103,90
39. Grönberg, Tobias SWE IND.	Amaretto	66,50	59.	12:30	31,20	20	51,20	117,70	42	94,08	0,00	8	8,00	125,70
40. Paro, Carlos Eduardo BRA IND.	Political Mandate	72,80	72.	12:15	25,20	20	45,20	118,00	44	99,04	5,00	4	9,00	127,00
41. Megchelenbrink, Chantal NED TEAM	Jacker Cracker	67,20	61.	13:17	50,00	0	50,00	117,20	40	100,42	6,00	4	10,00	127,20
42. O'Connor, Karen USA IND.	Upstage	59,80	44.	12:02	20,00	40	60,00	119,80	45	94,65	0,00	8	8,00	127,80
43. Calerbäck, Viktoria SWE TEAM	Ballys Geronimo	54,80	34.	12:29	30,80	40	70,80	125,60	49	98,08	4,00	0	4,00	129,60
44. Bordone, Susanna ITA TEAM	Carrera	48,90	17.	13:14	48,80	20	68,80	117,70	43	99,77	5,00	8	13,00	130,70
45. Byyny, Jan USA IND.	Task Force	53,30	29.	12:20	27,20	40	67,20	120,50	46	90,36	0,00	12	12,00	132,50
46. Geven, Werner NED TEAM	Esker Riada	69,80	67.	12:37	34,00	20	54,00	123,80	47	86,50	0,00	12	12,00	135,80
47. Teulere, Jean FRA TEAM	Espoir de la Mare	54,60	33.	12:26	29,60	40	69,60	124,20	48	106,44	12,00	8	20,00	144,20
48. Spisak, Pawel POL TEAM	Weriusz	58,20	38.	12:01	19,60	60	79,60	137,80	50	95,00	0,00	8	8,00	145,80
49. Albert, Samantha JAM IND.	Before I Do It	59,80	44.	13:36	57,60	40	97,60	157,40	54	95,81	1,00	0	1,00	158,40
50. Ryan, Michael IRL TEAM	Old Road	63,30	53.	12:09	22,80	60	82,80	146,10	51	95,60	1,00	12	13,00	159,10
51. Meyer, Joe NZL TEAM	Snip 2	50,40	22.	11:58	18,40	85	103,40	153,80	53	100,00	5,00	12	17,00	170,80
52. Bouckaert, Carl BEL TEAM	Rampant Lion	63,30	53.	13:16	49,60	60	109,60	172,90	56	99,46	5,00	0	5,00	177,90
53. Curran, Geoff IRL TEAM	Balladeer Alfred	68,00	65.	12:52	40,00	60	100,00	168,00	55	99,54	5,00	12	17,00	185,00
54. Kazmierczak, Lukasz POL TEAM	Ostler	55,40	35.	12:55	41,20	105	146,20	201,60	57	100,09	6,00	16	22,00	223,60
55. Poita, Viachaslau BLR IND.	Energiya	67,80	64.	15:06	93,60	60	53,60	221,40	58	90,23	0,00	28	28,00	249,40
56. Grave, Carlos POR IND.	Laughton Hills	71,30	70.	15:25	101,20	125	126,20	297,50	59	86,07	0,00	12	12,00	309,50
Biasia, Marco ITA TEAM	Ecu	69,30	66.	13:13	48,40	0	48,40	117,70	41	Not accep. Horse Inspection				
Schrade, Dirk GER IND.	Sindy 43	50,20	21.	11:25	5,20	0	5,20	55,40	9	Withd. b. Horse Inspection				
Palli, Luisa ITA IND.	Axia II	77,20	76.	13:20	51,20	20	71,20	148,40	52	Withd. b. Horse Inspection				
Smith, Donna NZL IND.	Call Me Clifton	45,40	10.	Retired Ph. D										
Pantsu, Piia FIN IND.	Ypäjä Karuso	48,50	16.	Retired Ph. D										
Rose, Shane AUS IND.	All Luck	52,40	27.	Retired Ph. D										
Stibbe, Eddy AHO IND.	Dusky Moon	54,10	31.	Retired Ph. D										
Johnson, Sonja AUS TEAM	Ringwould Jaguar	54,50	32.	Retired Ph. D										
De Luca Oliveira, Alex NZL IND.	Clifton Checkers	61,30	47.	Retired Ph. D										
Kattup, May-Britt DEN TEAM	Victor 87	71,10	69.	Retired Ph. D										
Boiteau, Arnaud FRA TEAM	Expo du Moulin	57,40	36.	Eliminated Ph. D										
Giugni, Alberto ITA IND.	The Nightflight	58,50	41.	Eliminated Ph. D										

Ergebnisse / Results

Vielseitigkeit / Eventing

Rank Rider NAT.	Horse	Dressage Pen.	Rank	Cross-Country Time	TP	JP	XC	Interim result	Rank	Show Jumping Time	TP	SP	Pen.	Total Pen.
Roberts, Ian CAN IND.	Napalm	62,60	52.	Eliminated Ph. D										
Lundin, Johan SWE IND.	Major Tom	66,70	60.	Eliminated Ph. D										
Bertoli, Alice ITA TEAM	Oakengrove Milan	67,20	61.	Eliminated Ph. D										
Rutkowski, Pawel POL TEAM	Fordanser	67,60	63.	Eliminated Ph. D										
Grishin, Andrey RUS IND.	Paul vom Gau	72,60	71.	Eliminated Ph. D										
Tseliapushkina, Alena BLR IND.	Zalim	77,00	75.	Eliminated Ph. D										
Riedl, Harald AUT TEAM	Davigna	77,40	77.	Eliminated Ph. D										
Odelberg -Noyez, Sandra BEL TEAM	Rainman	79,30	78.	Eliminated Ph. D										
Temple, Kelli CAN IND.	Paris McMullen	53,70	30.	Withdrawn before Ph. D										
Puch, Pepo CRO IND.	The Who	69,80	67.	Withdrawn before Ph. D										
Haugaard, Morten DEN TEAM	My Hamlet			Retired Dressage										
Kyle, Mark IRL IND.	Drunken Disorderly			Not accepted 1st Horse In										

79 Teilnehmer / Competitors
Richter:/ Judges: H: Brian Ross (USA), C: Angela Tucker (GBR), B: Martin Plewa (GER)
TP: Zeitfehler/ Time penalties JP: Springfehler/ Jumping penalties XC: Gelände-Hindernisfehler/ Cross-country penalties Pen: Gesamtfehlerpunkte/ Penalties

FEI Mannschaft-Weltmeisterschaft Vielseitigkeit – Endergebnis
FEI World Team Eventing Championship – Final-Result

Nation/ Reiter NAT/ Rider	Pferd Horse	Dressur Dressage		Gelände Cross-Country		Final result after Dressage, Cross-Country, Show Jumping	
1. Germany	Chef d'Equipe: Hans Melzer					**156,00**	
Ostholt, Frank	Air Jordan	46,90	11.	46,90	3.	50,90	4.
Romeike, Hinrich	Marius Voigt-Logistik	52,40	27.	52,40	5.	52,40	5.
Hoy, Bettina	Ringwood Cockatoo	36,50	1.	43,70	2.	52,70	6.
Klimke, Ingrid	Sleep Late	39,10	2.	96,70	39.	96,70	34.
2. Great Britain	Chef d'Equipe: Yogi Breisner					**180,00**	
Toy Town	Phillips, Zara	41,70	5.	41,70	1.	46,70	1.
Spring Along	Dick, Daisy	64,30	57.	64,30	15.	64,30	12.
Tamarillo	Fox-Pitt, William	45,00	8.	69,00	17.	69,00	15.
Call Again Cavalier	King, Mary	51,90	26.	81,10	29.	81,10	24.
3. Australia	Chef d'Equipe: Rob Hanna					**197,30**	
Fredericks, Clayton	Ben Along Time	44,40	7.	48,80	4.	48,80	2.
Jones, Megan	Kirby Park Irish Jester	44,10	6.	70,10	19.	70,10	16.
Hoy, Andrew	Master Monarch	47,60	15.	74,40	22.	78,40	22.
Johnson, Sonja	Ringwould Jaguar	54,50	32.	1000,00		1000,00	
4. USA	Chef d'Equipe: Mark Phillips					**198,10**	
Tryon, Amy	Poggio	50,70	24.	50,70	7.	50,70	3.
Severson, Kimberley	Winsome Adante	40,90	3.	67,70	16.	71,70	17.
Faudree, Will	Antigua	63,30	53.	71,70	20.	75,70	19.
White, Heidi	Northern Spy	50,40	22.	81,20	30.	89,20	27.
5. Sweden	Chef d'Equipe: Jan Jönsson					**218,20**	
Gällerdal, Magnus	Keymaster 3	47,40	13.	49,80	6.	53,80	8.
Albert, Dag	Who's Blitz	61,50	48.	61,50	12.	67,50	14.
Algotsson, Linda	My Fair Lady 59	48,90	17.	86,90	32.	96,90	35.
Calerbäck, Viktoria	Ballys Geronimo	54,80	34.	125,60	49.	129,60	43.
6. New Zealand						**221,70**	
Tompkins, Heelan	Glengarrick	49,80	20.	49,80	5.	53,80	7.
Nicholson, Andrew	Lord Killinghurst	49,60	19.	69,60	18.	79,60	23.
Powell, Caroline	Lenamore	66,30	58.	88,30	35.	88,30	26.
Meyer, Joe	Snip 2	50,40	22.	153,80	53.	170,80	51.
7. France						**312,90**	
Viricel, Gilles	Blakring	61,70	49.	77,70	26.	77,70	20.
Touzaint, Nicolas	Hildagi de l'Ile	47,00	12.	87,00	33.	91,00	28.
Teuerle, Jan	Espoir de la Mare	54,60	33.	124,20	48.	144,20	47.
Boiteau, Arnaud	Expo du Moulin	57,40	36.	10000,00		1000,00	
8. Netherlands						**358,00**	
Beek, Jan van	La Cru	58,20	38.	81,00	28.	95,00	32.
Megchelebrink, Chantal	Jacker Cracker	67,20	61.	117,20	40.	127,20	41.
Geven, Werner	Esker Riada	69,80	67.	123,80	47.	135,80	46.
9. Irland						**361,80**	
10. Austria						**190,00**	
11. Italy						**1227,20**	
12. Belgium						**1242,30**	
13. Poland						**1369,40**	
14. Denmark						**2082,60**	

ERGEBNISSE | RESULTS

FEI Einzelweltmeisterschaft – Viererzug
FEI World Individual – Four-in-Hand Championship

		NAT	Dressage	Rank	Marathon	Rank	Obstacle	Rank	Total	Rank
1.	Felix Marie Brasseur	BEL	41.86	4	104.51	2	0.00	1	146.37	1
2.	Ysbrand Chardon	NED	41.22	2	104.08	1	3.88	15	149.18	2
3.	Christoph Sandmann	GER	46.59	7	107.58	6	0.00	2	154.17	3
4.	Thomas Eriksson	SWE	46.59	7	106.65	4	0.99	9	154.23	4
5.	Michael Freund	GER	41.60	3	121.38	17	0.00	4	162.98	5
6.	József Dobrovitz	HUN	53.89	12	108.71	7	3.00	13	165.60	6
7.	Stefan Klay	SUI	55.42	14	105.83	3	7.47	21	168.72	7
8.	Zoltán Lazar	HUN	53.38	10	106.89	5	9.49	23	169.76	8
9.	Gert Schrijvers	BEL	46.21	6	123.37	19	0.60	8	170.18	9
10.	Benjamin Aillaud	FRA	56.96	16	113.55	11	0.00	4	170.51	10
11.	Daniel Wurgler	SUI	57.60	19	113.34	9	0.53	7	171.47	11
12.	Theo Timmerman	NED	59.39	23	113.34	9	0.41	6	173.14	12
13.	Koos de Ronde	NED	58.62	21	111.11	8	4.29	18	174.02	13
14.	Tucker Johnson	USA	43.26	5	122.15	18	10.09	25	175.50	14
15.	Attila Bardos	HUN	56.96	16	114.42	13	4.14	17	175.52	15
16.	Rainer Duen	GER	60.29	24	116.07	14	2.38	11	178.74	16
17.	Josef-Nikolaus Zeitler	GER	65.41	32	113.67	12	0.00	3	179.08	17
18.	Jan Eric Palsson	SWE	53.50	11	126.42	22	4.02	16	183.94	18
19.	Ludwig Weinmayr	GER	56.32	15	120.88	16	7.89	22	185.09	19
20.	James Henry Fairclough	USA	61.44	25	123.77	21	1.72	10	186.93	20

Gesamt/ Total: 49 Gespanne

FEI Mannschaftsweltmeisterschaft – Viererzug
FEI World Team – Four-in-Hand Championship

		Total Points	A	B	C
1.	GERMANY	311.84	88.19	223.65	0,00
	Rainer Duen		(60.29)	116.07	(2.38)
	Michael Freund		41.60	(121.38)	0,00
	Christoph Sandmann		46.59	107.58	0.00
2.	BELGIUM	316.55	88.07	227.88	0.60
	Felix Marie Brasseur		41.86	104.51	0.00
	Geert de Brauwer		(64.77)	(131.88)	(15.69)
	Gert Schrijvers		46.21	123.37	0.60
3.	NETHERLANDS	319.32	99.84	215.19	4.29
	Ysbrand Chardon		41.22	104.08	3.88
	Koos de Ronde		58.62	111.11	(4.29)
	Theo Timmerman		(59.39)	(113.34)	0.41
4.	HUNGARY	330.01	107.27	215.60	7.14
	Attila Bardos		(56.96)	(114.42)	4.14
	József Dobrovitz		53.89	108.71	3.00
	Zoltán Lazar		53.38	106.89	(9.49)
5.	SWEDEN	338.17	100.09	233.07	5.01
	Thomas Eriksson		46.59	106.65	0.99
	Jan Eric Palsson		53.50	126.42	4.02
	Frederik Persson		(61.44)	(0.80)	(0.00)
6.	SWITZERLAND	340.19	113.02	219.17	8.00
7.	FRANCE	355.75	112.26	240.49	3.00
8.	USA	362.43	104.70	245.92	11.81
9.	GREAT BRITAIN	375.58	115.45	249.18	10.95
10.	PORTUGAL	403.17	122.63	264.66	15.88
11.	AUSTRIA	441.73	128.12	288.88	24.73
12.	SPAIN	455.86	124.29	311.09	20.48
13.	CZECH REPUBLIK	511.47	145.67	326.03	39.77

DISTANZREITEN | ENDURANCE

FEI Mannschaftsweltmeisterschaft Distanzreiten
FEI World Team Endurance Championship

	Team/ Rider	Pferd/ Horse	Riding Time	Total Punkte/Zeit
1	Frankreich/ FRA			28:11:27
	Virginie Atger	Kangoo d'Aurabelle	09:16:13	
	Philippe Benoit	Akim du Boulve	09:24:30	
	Pascal Dietsch	Hifrabe dz Barthas	09:30:44	
2	Schweiz/ SUI			29:57:01
	Urs Wenger	Zialka	09:38:56	
	Anna Lena Wagner	Tessa IV	10:09:02	
	Nora Wagner	Temir	10:09:03	
3	Portugal/ POR			30:38:32
	Joano Raposo	Sultao	09:24:31	
	Ana Margarita Costa	Gozlane de Somali	09:59:31	
	Ana Teresa Barbas	Piperino	11:14:30	
4	Deutschland/ GER			30:51:30
	Sabrina Arnold	Madaq	09:48:15	
	Susanne Kaufmann	Fay el Rat	10:31:37	
	Belinda Hitzler	Iris de Soult	10:31:38	
5	Niederlande/ NED			31:38:11
	Jeanne Linnew.-Ribbers	Riki's Macho Man	10:06:28	
	Jannet van Wijk	Latino	10:37:52	
	Anita Lamsma	Layla Ara Francina	10:53:51	
6	Australien/ AUS			32:50:38
7	Schweden/ SWE			34:40:07
8	Brasilien/ BRA			34:55:06
9	Südafrika/ RSA			38:45:22
10	Spanien/ ESP			18:34:34
11	Bahrain/ BRN			19:33:50
12	Großbritannien/ GBR			21:35:48
13	USA			22:03:53
14	Italien/ ITA			22:33:54
15	Katar/ QAT			23:09:08
16	Namibia/ NAM			23:31:46
17	Kanada/ CAN			24:10:29
18	Russland/ RUS			25:05:28

ERGEBNISSE / RESULTS

DISTANZREITEN / ENDURANCE

FEI Einzelweltmeisterschaft Distanzreiten
FEI World Individual Endurance Championship

	Reiter/ Rider	Land/Team	Durchschnitts-Geschwindigkeit/ Av.Speed	Regenerations-zeit Speed	Gesamt-Zeit/ Total
1	Miguel Vila Ubach	Spanien/ ESP	17,38	00:20:45	09:12:27
2	Virginie Atger	Frankreich/ FRA	17,26	00:24:09	09:16:13
3	Elodie Le Labourier	Frankreich/ FRA	17,26	00:23:47	09:16:14
4	Jaume Punti Dachs	Spaniel/ ESP	17,08	00:16:19	09:22:07
5	Philippe Benoit	Frankreich/ FRA	17,01	00:33:56	09:24:30
6	Joao Raposo	Portugal/ POR	17,01	00:27:49	09:24:31
7	Valerie Ceunick	Belgien/ BEL	16,91	00:40:35	09:27:39
8	Pascale Dietsch	Frankreich/ FRA	16,82	00:31:41	09:30:44
9	Sheikh Duaij bin Salman Al Khalifa	Bahrain/ BRN	16,72	00:22:53	09:34:00
10	Urs Wenger	Schweiz/ SUI	16,58	00:39:19	09:38:56
11	Sabrina Arnold	Deutschland/ GER	16,32	00:31:15	09:48:15
12	Ana Margarita	Portugal/ POR	16,01	00:45:10	09:59:31
13	Florian Legrand	Frankreich/ FRA	16,01	02:16:18	09:59:32
14	Sheikh Nasser bin Hamad Al Khalifa	Bahrain/ BRN	16,00	00:28:08	09:59:50
15	Kathryn Downs	USA	15,83	00:24:21	10:06:27
16	Jeanne Linneweever-Ribbers	Niederlande/ NED	15,83	00:28:12	10:06:28
17	Christine Yeoman	Großbritannien/ GBR	15,80	00:31:15	10:07:35
18	Prince Abdullah bin Fahad Al Saud	Königreich Saudi-Arabien/ KSA	15,77	00:32:32	10:08:34
19	Anna Lena Wagner	Schweiz/ SUI	15,76	00:35:37	10:09:02
20	Nora Wagner	Schweiz/ SUI	15,76	00:35:42	10:09:03
21	Karin Maiga	Schweiz/ SUI	15,76	00:34:16	10:09:04
22	Margaret Mary Sleeper	USA	15,68	00:25:57	10:12:20
23	Kylie Avery	Neuseeland/ NZL	15,65	00:24:53	10:12:22
24	Udo von Schauroth	Namibia/ NAM	15,44	00:34:12	10:21:48
25	Susanne Kaufmann	Deutschland/ GER	15,20	00:34:55	10:31:37
26	Belinda Hitzler	Deutschland/ GER	15,20	00:36:14	10:31:38
27	Rui Pereira	Portugal/ POR	15,18	00:39:19	10:32:22
28	Ahmad Saber Hamcho	Syrien/ SYR	15,18	00:30:26	10:32:23
29	Margaret Wade	Australien/ AUS	15,05	00:19:43	10:37:51
30	Jannet van Wijk	Niederlande/ NED	15,05	00:25:30	10:37:52
31	Jose Maria Viar Canales	Spaniel/ ESP	14,86	00:28:34	10:45:57
32	Jessica Holmberg	Schweden/ SWE	14,82	00:44:58	10:47:49
33	Johanne Hvid	Dänemark/ DEN	14,80	00:39:09	10:48:48
34	Emer Lennon	Irland/ IRL	14.68	00:46:19	10:53:49
35	Anita Lamsma	Niederlande/ NED	14,68	00:30:05	10:53:50
36	Peter Toft	Australien/ AUS	14,64	00:22:45	10:55:39
37	Liv Burdett	Schweden/ SWE	14,43	00:33:51	11:05:26
38	Ruth Sturley	Kanada/ CAN	14,43	00:34:31	11:05:28
39	Gianluca Laliscia	Italien/ ITA	14,40	00:18:27	11:06:30
40	Abdul Aziz Jassim Al Buainain	Katar/ QAT	14,38	00:27:30	11:07:39
41	Ana Teresa Barbas	Portugal/ POR	14,23	01:22:24	11:14:30
42	Brook Sample	Australien/ AUS	14,18	00:52:03	11:17:08
43	Mariana Cesarino Steinbruch	Brasilien/ BRA	13,97	00:42:50	11:27:02
44	Daniela Blasi	Italien/ ITA	13,97	00:47:44	11:27:24
45	Newton Lins Filho	Brasilien/ BRA	13,96	00:24:16	11:27:26
46	Ann Jobson	Großbritannien/ GBR	13,95	01:11:39	11:28:13
47	Penny Toft	Australien/ AUS	13,65	00:38:54	11:43:11
48	Akhmed Makhov	Russland/ RUS	13,48	00:48:15	11:51:57
49	Jennifer Lynn Niehaus	USA	13,38	00:26:53	11:57:26
50	Marguerita Fuller	Österreich/ AUT	13,38	00:36:22	11:57:36
51	Pedro Stefani Marino	Brasililen/ BRA	13,32	00:34:23	12:00:38
52	Valy Schmartz	Luxemburg/ LUX	13,32	00:50:48	12:00:40
53	Atta Mohd Peer Mohammed	Katar/ QAT	13,31	00:49:27	12:01:29
54	Cornelius van Niekerk	Südafrika/ RSA	12,67	00:48:51	12:37:29
55	Jennifer Mary Gilbertson	Australien/ AUS	12,52	02:20:34	12:46:51
56	Ingrid Boström	Schweden/ SWE	12,52	00:42:36	12:46:52
57	Grazina Stugyte	Litauen/ LTU	12,51	00:57:09	12:47:40
58	Feras Boubol	Slowenien/ SVK	12,33	00:41:48	12:58:42
59	Willa Botland	Südafrika/ RSA	12,26	00:30:16	13:02:55
60	Mariaan Liversage	Südafrika/ RSA	12,23	00:37:42	13:04:59
61	Giliese de Villiers	Südafrika/ RSA	12,23	00:32:36	13:05:00
62	Linda Riley	Kanada/ CAN	12,23	00:36:38	13:05:01
63	Yara Ihssan Aslan	Jordanien/ JOR	12,23	00:36:10	13:05:02
64	Armin van Biljon	Namibia/ NAM	12,15	00:45:18	13:09:58
65	Aslan Mambetov	Russland/ RUS	12,10	00:33:01	13:13:31

Von 159 Startern sind 94 disqualifiziert worden!

ERGEBNISSE / RESULTS

FEI Weltmeisterschaft Einzelvoltigieren der Damen – Endergebnisliste
FEI World Female Individual Vaulting Championship – Final Results

Voltigierer/ Vaulter Pferd/ Horse	Nation Longeur/ Longer	1st Round Comp	1st Round Freetest	2nd Round TechTest	2nd Round FreeTest	FINAL	Pl
BENJAMIN, Megan Leonardo	USA KRISTENSEN, Lasse	8,015	8,273	8,673	8,720	8,421	1
FALTIN, Katharina Pitucelli	AUT NÖBAUER, Julia	7,859	8,393	8,390	8,600	8,311	2
JARZ, Sissi Escudo Fox	AUT NÖBAUER, Julia	7,948	8,093	8,567	8,407	8,254	3
STROEH, Nicola Lanson 16	GER GNAD, Michael	7,763	7,967	8,230	8,480	8,110	4
JUECKSTOCK, Ines Dallmers Little Foot	GER JÜCKSTOCK, Ruth	7,967	7,927	8,300	8,187	8,096	5
BARWIG, Anja Arador 2	GER HARTL, Alexander	7,470	8,233	7,880	8,407	7,998	6
GIPPERICH, Jasmin Apollo	AUT HAIDACHER, Klaus	7,685	7,827	7,990	8,240	7,936	7
TOVBORG, Marianne Leonardo	DEN KRISTENSEN, Lasse	7,611	7,613	7,747	8,007	7,745	8
METTLER, Sabrina Carracci S	SUI ZOSSO, Ursula	7,430	7,573	7,703	8,207	7,729	9
LOWE, Tristyn Latinio	AUS BARTEL, Dr. Silke	7,196	7,873	7,317	8,273	7,665	10
10 ECCLES, Joanne W H Bentley	GBR ECCLES, John	6,704	8,180	7,493	8,140	7,630	11
B. DUMONT, Maud Just a Kiss*HN	FRA JOOSTEN DUPON, Marina	7,311	7,820	6,883	8,293	7,577	12
CAVALLARO, Anna Adenauer	ITA VIDONI, Nelson	7,374	7,573	7,400	7,773	7,531	13
BLUNDEN, Samantha Czambul 2	AUS LOTZMAN, Stefan	7,111	7,633	7,627	7,713	7,521	14
GADOLLA, Réka Darius	HUN PASKA, Ildiko	6,941	7,667	7,080	6,740	7,107	15

Richter/ Judges: A: Mrs Schwarzmann, B: Mrs Dolinska, C: Mrs Eriksson, D: Mr Moore, E: Mrs Girard, F: Mrs F.-Prochaska

FEI Weltmeisterschaft Einzelvoltigieren der Herren – Endergebnisliste
FEI World Male Individual Vaulting Championship – Final Results

Vaulter Horse	Nation Longer	1st Round Comp	1st Round Freetest	2nd Round TechTest	2nd Round FreeTest	FINAL	Pl
VORBERG, Kai Picasso 202	GER GRAF, Kirsten	8,096	8,747	8,283	8,967	8,524	1
MEYER, Gero Arador 2	GER HARTL, Alexander	7,822	8,107	8,087	8,627	8,161	2
MAJDLEN, Ladislav Catalin III-73	SVK PAVLAK, Marian	7,644	8,500	7,673	8,780	8,150	3
MARTIN RUIZ, Ararat Grateley Limelight	ESP WEISS, Corinna	7,737	8,287	7,867	8,667	8,140	4
SIA, Tim-Randy Belmondo	GER HSCHELP-LENSING, Elke	7,922	8,553	7,403	8,647	8,132	5
ANDREANI, Nicolas Idefix de Braize	FRA JOOSTEN DUPON, Marina	7,515	8,880	6,790	8,940	8,032	6
CSANDL, Stefan Gigolino	AUT RUF, Birgit	7,778	7,920	7,770	8,500	7,992	7
KLOUDA, Lukas Duke	CZE CINEROVA, Petra	7,378	8,487	7,197	8,687	7,938	8
LOOSER, Patric Key West	SUI KNAUF, Alexandra	7,767	8,373	7,250	8,027	7,855	9
STOECKL, Gregor Apollo	AUT HAIDACHER, Klaus	7,322	8,100	7,110	8,327	7,715	10
WACHA, Lukas Apollo	AUT HAIDACHER, Klaus	7,296	8,207	7,030	8,280	7,704	11
THIEBAUT, Charles Idefix de Braize	FRAU JOOSTEN DUPON, Marina	6,978	8,233	6,870	8,367	7,613	12
LANG, Matthias Farceur Breceen*HN	FRA JOOSTEN DUPON, Marina	8,107	6,907	8,027	7,207	7,562	13
TOTH, Adrian Vilam	SVK MAJDLENOVA, Jana	7,363	7,887	6,707	7,967	7,481	14

Richter/ Judges: A: Mrs Schwarzmann, B: Mrs Dolinska, C: Mrs Eriksson, D: Mr Moore, E: Mrs Girard, F: Mrs F. Prochaska

Ergebnisse / Results

FEI Weltmeisterschaft Gruppenvoltigieren – Endergebnisliste
FEI World Team Vaulting Championship – Final Results

Voltigierer/ Vaulter Pferd/ Horse	Nation Longeur/ Longer	1st Round Comp	2nd Round Freetest	FINAL FreeTest		Pl
RSV Neuss Cepin	GER SCHMITZ, Jessica	7,183	8,814	8,571	8,189	1
F.A.M.E. Grand Gaudino	USA BARTEL, Dr. Silke	6,647	8,900	8,936	8,161	2
RC Wildegg Libretto1	AUT LEHRMANN, Maria	7,169	8,467	8,821	8,152	3
St. Gallen Le Grand	SUI GEBS, Annemarie	6,789	8,238	8,329	7,785	4
Great Britain W H Bentley	GBR ECCLES, John	6,469	8,255	8,331	7,685	5
SOUP Sala Vilam	SVK MAJDLENOVA, Jana	6,691	7,848	8,293	7,611	6
Italy Harley	ITA VIDONI, Nelson	6,446	7,826	7,776	7,349	7
Brazil Rouven 11	BRA MUELLER, Danielle	5,754	7,650	7,924	7,109	8
The Netherlands Muel van het Carelshof	NED DANVERS, Cynthia	5,913	7,226	7,031	6,723	9
Czech Republic Robin Purina	CZE SVANOVA, Andrea	6,222	6,645	7,079	6,649	10
Sweden Rebus	SWE FISKBAEK, Johnny	5,805	6,988	7,093	6,629	11
Interclub Rabka	POL BOROWSKA, Alicja	5,652	7,486	6,260	6,466	12

Richter/ Judges: A: Mrs Schwarzmann, B: Mrs Dolinska, C: Mrs Eriksson, D: Mr Moore, E: Mrs Girard, F: Mrs F.-Prochaska

FEI Mannschaftsweltmeisterschaft Reining
FEI World Team Reining Championship

Rnk.	NAT Pferd/ Horse	Reiter/ Rider	1	2	3	4	5	Total
1.	UNITED STATES OF AMERICA							665.0
	Starbucks Sidekick	Dell HENDRICKS	73.0	72.5	74.0	73.5	71.5	219.0
	Mister Nicadual	Tim MCQUAY	73.5	74.5	74.5	72.5	75.0	222.5
	Easy Otie Whiz	Matt MILLS	72.0	71.5	73.5	72.5	73.0	217.5
	Smart Paul Olena	Aaron RALSTON	74.0	75.0	74.0	74.5	75.5	223.5
2.	CANADA							664.0
	Lil Santana	Luke GAGNON	74.0	73.0	72.0	73.5	72.5	219.0
	Snow Gun	Francois GAUTIER	73.5	72.5	73.0	74.0	73.0	219.5
	Whiz N Tag Chex	Lance GRIFFIN	72.5	72.0	73.0	73.5	73.5	219.0
	Hang Ten Surprize	Duane LATIMER	74.5	75.0	75.5	76.5	75.0	225.5
3.	ITALY							656.0
	Skeets Dun	Dario CARMIGNANI	73.0	73.5	73.0	72.5	73.5	219.5
	Docs Tivio Hancock	Adriano MEACCI	72.5	71.5	72.0	71.0	71.5	215.0
	Dualin For Me	Christian PEREZ	73.5	73.5	74.0	74.0	74.0	221.5
	Peppy Secolo	Marco RICOTTA	68.5	69.0	69.0	69.5	70.5	207.5
4.	GERMANY							655.5
	Lil Ruf Cody	Nico HÖRMANN	72.5	71.5	73.0	72.5	72.5	217.5
	BV Smart Innuendo	Grischa LUDWIG	73.0	72.0	73.5	72.5	73.0	218.5
	Golden Mc Jac	Sylvia RZEPKA	74.5	73.5	73.0	72.5	73.0	219.5
5.	SWITZERLAND							651.5
6.	BELGIUM							650.5
7.	GREAT BRITAIN							643.5
8.	BRASIL							640.0
9.	AUSTRIA							639.5
10.	SWEDEN							638.0
11.	ISRAEL							635.0
12.	FRANCE							624.0
13.	THE NETHERLANDS							615.0
14.	SLOVAKIA							607.5
15.	CZECH REPUBLIC							598.0

Richter/ Judges: 1. Ralf Hesselschwerdt (GER) 2. Allen Mitchells (USA) 3. Patti Carte (CAN) 4. Sylvia Katschker (AUT) 5. Jan Boogaerts (BEL)

FEI Einzelweltmeisterschaft Reining
FEI World Individual Reining Championship

Rank / Rnk	Pferd / HORSE	Reiter / RIDER	NAT	S1	S2	S3	S4	S5	Total
1.	Hang Ten Surprize	Duane LATIMER	CAN	76.5	(74.5)	77.0	(77.0)	76.5	230.0
				76.5	(75.0)	75.5	(77.0)	76.0	228.0
2.	Mister Nicadual	Tim MCQUAY	USA	(78.0)	76.5	76.5	77.0	(75.5)	230.0
				75.0	75.5	75.5	(74.0)	(75.5)	226.0
3.	Smart Paul Olena	Aaron RALSTON	USA	(76.5)	(75.5)	76.0	75.5	76.0	227.5
4.	Easy Otie Whiz	Matt MILLS	USA	75.0	75.0	74.5	(75.5)	(74.0)	224.5
5.	Starbucks Sidekick	Dell HENDRICKS	USA	74.0	(74.5)	(73.0)	73.5	73.5	221.0
6.	Snow Gun	Francois GAUTIER	CAN	(74.5)	(73.0)	73.0	74.0	73.5	220.5
7.	Little Royal BH	Ann POELS	BEL	73.5	74.0	(71.5)	73.0	(74.0)	220.5
8.	Golden Mc Jac	Sylvia RZEPKA	GER	73.5	(73.0)	(74.0)	73.0	73.0	219.5
9.	Lil Ruf Cody	Nico HÖRMANN	GER	73.0	(72.5)	(74.5)	73.0	73.0	219.0
10.	Skeets Dun	Dario CARMIGNANI	ITA	72.5	(71.5)	72.5	(74.5)	73.0	218.0
11.	Just Gotta Shine	Francesca STERNBERG	GBR	72.5	(73.0)	(72.0)	72.5	72.5	217.5
12.	Gallo Pequeno	Evelyne RÖTHLISBERGER	SUI	(70.5)	71.0	73.0	73.5	(73.5)	217.5
13.	Lil Santana	Luke GAGNON	CAN	(73.0)	(72.0)	72.5	72.5	72.0	217.0
14.	Dun It Sugar Quixote	Selina SCHULTHEISS	SUI	(70.5)	72.5	72.5	(72.5)	72.0	217.0
15.	Little Man O'lena	João Felipe LACERDA	BRA	72.0	72.5	(72.5)	72.0	(71.0)	216.5
16.	Custom Wrangler	Bernard FONCK	BEL	(72.0)	71.0	(70.5)	71.5	71.5	214.0
17.	Golden Boy	Jeannette KRÄHENBÜHL	SUI	70.5	70.5	68.5	(67.5)	(70.5)	209.5
18.	Dualin For Me	Christian PEREZ	ITA	(0.0)	0.0	0.0	0.0	(0.0)	0.0
19.	Lil Dry Peppy	Rudolf KRONSTEINER	AUT	(0.0)	0.0	0.0	0.0	(0.0)	EL

Richter/ *Judges:* 1. Ralf Hesselschwerdt (GER) 2. Allen Mitchells (USA) 3. Patti Carte (CAN) 4. Sylvia Katschker (AUT) 5. Jan Boogaerts (BEL)